CORPORATE CHAMPIONS

CORPORATE CHAMPIONS

Excellent Companies of India

B. Karunakar

www.sagepublications.com
Los Angeles • London • New Delhi • Singapore • Washington DC

Copyright © B. Karunakar, 2012

All rights reserved. No part of this book may be reproduced or utilized in any form or by any means, electronic or mechanical, including photocopying, recording or by any information storage or retrieval system, without permission in writing from the publisher.

First published in 2012 by

SAGE Response
B1/I-1 Mohan Cooperative Industrial Area
Mathura Road, New Delhi 110 044, India

SAGE Publications Inc
2455 Teller Road
Thousand Oaks, California 91320, USA

SAGE Publications Ltd
1 Oliver's Yard, 55 City Road
London EC1Y 1SP, United Kingdom

SAGE Publications Asia-Pacific Pte Ltd
33 Pekin Street
#02-01 Far East Square
Singapore 048763

Published by Vivek Mehra for SAGE Publications India Pvt Ltd, typeset in 11/14pt Minion by Star Compugraphics Private Limited, Delhi and printed at Chaman Enterprises, New Delhi.

Library of Congress Cataloging-in-Publication Data Available

ISBN: 978-81-321-0712-5 (PB)

The SAGE Team: Rekha Natarajan, Anupam Choudhury, Anju Saxena, and Deepti Saxena

This book is dedicated to my parents for their loving support, encouragement, and for embodying good values in me.

Thank you for choosing a SAGE product! If you have any comment, observation or feedback, I would like to personally hear from you. Please write to me at contactceo@sagepub.in

—Vivek Mehra, Managing Director and CEO,
SAGE Publications India Pvt Ltd, New Delhi

Bulk Sales

SAGE India offers special discounts for purchase of books in bulk. We also make available special imprints and excerpts from our books on demand.

For orders and enquiries, write to us at

Marketing Department
SAGE Publications India Pvt Ltd
B1/I-1, Mohan Cooperative Industrial Area
Mathura Road, Post Bag 7
New Delhi 110044, India
E-mail us at marketing@sagepub.in

Get to know more about SAGE, be invited to SAGE events, get on our mailing list. Write today to marketing@sagepub.in

This book is also available as an e-book.

*You are today where
your thoughts have brought you;
you will be tomorrow
where your thoughts take you.*

~ James Lane Allen

Contents

List of Tables	xi
List of Figures	xv
Acknowledgments	xix

1	What Is the Book About?	1
2	What Made the Excellent Companies Succeed? Proposed Business Model	15
3	Strategy Theme	27
4	Execution Excellence Theme	100
5	Leadership Theme	121
6	Frequently Asked Questions	167
7	Wrapping It Up	171

Appendix A: Chapter 1—Data	181
Appendix B: Chapter 6—Surveys	203
Appendix C: Chapter 6—Synopses of Two Inspirational Books	205
Appendix D: Profiles of Study Companies	211
Notes and References	366
Index	370
About the Author	379

List of Tables

1.1	List of Study Companies	11
2.1	List of Companies Going Global	16
2.2	List of Companies with Dominant Domestic Market Shares	20
2.3	Study Companies	23
3.1	Turnover of the Different Segments of the Battery Industry	57
3.2	Exide—Market Share	57
3.3	Milestones in Automotives	57
3.4	Hindalco—Product Offerings and Competition	63
3.5	World-class Steelmakers	78
3.6	Coromandel Fertilisers—Divisions and Products	91
3.7	Siemens—Business Segments	99
4.1	Modernization Program	102
4.2	Tata Steel—Improvement Initiatives	104
4.3	BPR Implementation Phases	114
5.1	Tata Group—Performance on Various Parameters	123
5.2	Categories of JRD QV Awards	132
5.3	Aditya Birla Group—Performance on Various Parameters	148
5.4	M&M—Performance on Various Parameters	153
5.5	TVS Group—Performance on Various Parameters	160

7.1	Study Companies in BT 500—India's Most Valuable Companies	172
7.2	Study Companies in Top 100 of the BT Rankings	174
7.3	100 Most Profitable Companies	175
7.4	List of Study Companies	177
A.1	Jim Collins vs. Our Methodology	181
A.2	List of 144 Companies (Listed before 1974)	182
A.3	Cut 3 Analysis Results—Table of 47 Companies	186
A.4	Statistical Significance Test	188
B.1	Sixteen Finalists	203
B.2	Comparison of Methodologies	204
D.1	Financials of Indian Hotels Co. Ltd (₹ million)	213
D.2	Financials of Tata Steel (₹ million)	219
D.3	Financials of Bombay Dyeing & Manufacturing Co Ltd (₹ million)	226
D.4	Financials of Mahindra & Mahindra (₹ million)	234
D.5	Financials of Apollo Tyres (₹ crore)	241
D.6	Financials of Exide Industries (₹ million)	248
D.7	Financials of Hindalco (₹ million)	254
D.8	Financials of Tinplate Company of India Ltd (₹ million)	260
D.9	Financials of Gammon India (₹ million)	262
D.10	Financials of Larsen & Toubro (₹ million)	269
D.11	Financials of Siemens India Ltd (₹ million)	275
D.12	Coromandel Fertilisers—Chronology	281
D.13	Financials of Coromandel Fertilisers (₹ million)	283
D.14	KEC—Joint Ventures, 1995–97	289
D.15	Financials of KEC International Ltd (₹ million)	290
D.16	Financials of Sundaram Fasteners Ltd	298
D.17	Financials of Tata Chemicals Ltd (₹ million)	299

D.18	Operating Divisions of Bajaj Hindusthan	306
D.19	Financials of Bajaj Hindusthan (₹ million)	308
D.20	Major Players in the Bearings Industry	316
D.21	Bearings Industry—Operating Divisions	316
D.22	Bearings Category, Market Share, and Competition	317
D.23	Financials of SKF India (₹ million)	318
D.24	Announced and Under Implementation Power Projects	328
D.25	Peer Comparison of Power Sector Companies	329
D.26	Financials of Tata Power Corp. Ltd (₹ million)	330
D.27	AEC—Chronology	336
D.28	Financials of Ahmedabad Electricity Company (₹ million)	337
D.29	Novartis—Operating Divisions	340
D.30	Novartis—Select Products and Therapeutic Segments	342
D.31	Financials of Novartis India (₹ million)	343
D.32	Mico—Operating Divisions	351
D.33	Financials of Mico Industries Co. Ltd (₹ million)	353
D.34	Pumps Industry in India—Major Players	359
D.35	Financials of Kirloskar Brothers Ltd (₹ crore)	360

List of Figures

1.1	Screening Process for Selecting Excellent Companies in India	7
1.2	Business Model	13
2.1	Business Model	25
3.1	Business Model—Strategy	28
3.2	Indian Hotels—Growth in Total Income (₹ million)	30
3.3	Indian Hotels—Growth in Total Income (Percentage)	31
3.4	Indian Hotels—PAT	32
3.5	Tata Steel— Growth in Total Income (₹ million)	34
3.6	Tata Steel—Growth in Total Income (Percentage)	35
3.7	Tata Steel—PAT	36
3.8	Bombay Dyeing— Growth in Total Income (₹ million)	39
3.9	Bombay Dyeing—Growth in Total Income (Percentage)	40
3.10	Bombay Dyeing—PAT	41
3.11	Value Chain of Textile Production	42
3.12	M&M—Growth in Total Income (₹ million)	45
3.13	M&M—Growth in Total Income (Percentage)	46
3.14	M&M—PAT	47
3.15	Apollo Tyres—Growth in Total Income (₹ million)	48
3.16	Apollo Tyres—Growth in Total Income (Percentage)	49
3.17	Apollo Tyres—PAT	50
3.18	Exide—Export Turnover	53
3.19	Exide Industries—Growth in Total Income (₹ million)	54

3.20	Exide Industries—Growth in Total Income (Percentage)	55
3.21	Exide Industries—PAT	56
3.22	Hindalco—Growth in Total Income (₹ million)	60
3.23	Hindalco—Growth in Total Income (Percentage)	61
3.24	Hindalco—PAT	62
3.25	Gammon India—Growth in Total Income (₹ millions)	65
3.26	Gammon India—Growth in Total Income (Percentage)	66
3.27	Gammon India—PAT	67
3.28	Larsen & Toubro—Growth in Total Income (₹ million)	69
3.29	Larsen & Toubro—Growth in Total Income (Percentage)	70
3.30	Larsen & Toubro—PAT	71
3.31	Siemens— Growth in Total Income (₹ million)	72
3.32	Siemens—Growth in Total Income (Percentage)	73
3.33	Siemens—PAT	74
3.34	Hindalco—PBDIT/Total Income	76
3.35	Hindalco—D/E Ratio	77
3.36	Tata Steel—PBDIT/Total Income	80
3.37	Tata Steel—D/E Ratio	81
3.38	Bombay Dyeing—PBDIT/Total Income	82
3.39	Bombay Dyeing—D/E Ratio	83
3.40	Apollo Tyres—PBDIT/Total Income	86
3.41	Apollo Tyres—D/E Ratio	87
3.42	M&M—PBDIT/Total Income	89
3.43	M&M—D/E Ratio	90
3.44	Coromandel Fertilisers—PBDIT/Total Income	92
3.45	Coromandel Fertilisers—D/E Ratio	93
4.1	Business Model—Execution Excellence	101
4.2	TOP Process	108

5.1	Business Model—Leadership	122
5.2	Tata Business Excellence Model	132
5.3	Tata Code of Conduct	133
5.4	Strategic Planning Process	134
5.5	Market Development Process	135
5.6	Market and Customer Segmentation Process	135
5.7	Information and Performance Management Process	136
5.8	OHS Survey 1	138
5.9	OHS Survey 2	138
5.10	Enterprise Process Model	139
5.11	Overall Approach to Process Management	140
7.1	Business Model	180
A.1	Ahmedabad Electricity (Torrent Power)	189
A.2	Apollo Tyres Ltd	190
A.3	Bajaj Hindusthan Ltd	190
A.4	Bombay Dyeing & Mfg. Co. Ltd	191
A.5	Coromandel Fertilisers Ltd	192
A.6	Exide Industries Ltd	193
A.7	Gammon India Ltd	194
A.8	Hindalco Industries Ltd	194
A.9	Indian Hotels Co Ltd	195
A.10	KEC International Ltd	195
A.11	Kirloskar Brothers Ltd	196
A.12	Larsen & Toubro Ltd	197
A.13	Mahindra & Mahindra Ltd	197
A.14	Motor Industries Co Ltd	198
A.15	Novartis India Ltd	198
A.16	Siemens Ltd	199
A.17	SKF Bearings India Ltd	199
A.18	Sundaram Fasteners Ltd	200
A.19	Surat Electricity Co. Ltd	200
A.20	Tata Chemicals Ltd	201

A.21	Tata Steel	201
A.22	Tata Power Co Ltd	202
A.23	Tinplate Co of India Ltd	202
C.1	Performance of Successful Companies vis-à-vis Others	207
D.1	Sugar Production Value Chain	307
D.2	Novartis—Sales Composition (FY 2002)	339

Acknowledgments

I am deeply indebted to my supervising teacher, Professor Vidyadhar Reddy Aileni, Department of Commerce and Business Management, Osmania University, Hyderabad, India for his valuable guidance and expert advice throughout the research work. Without his constant inspiration and encouragement, it would not have been possible for me to present the thesis followed by the book.

I would also like to acknowledge the guidance that I received from Professor S.N. Sarma. I would like to place on record the help and assistance provided by Professor Jagrook Dawra of IBS in helping me arrive at the final shortlist of companies.

Further, I would like to thank Nrupender Rao, Chairman of the Pennar Group of companies, Dr S. Raghunath, Professor of Corporate Strategy and Policy at IIM Bangalore, and Moid Siddiqui, writer of several management books, for reviewing the manuscript and suggesting important changes.

It gives me pleasure to thank my soul mate and wife, Vedavani, and my son, Aditya Vikram, for their enduring support and understanding, and also for constantly reminding me to stay on track to complete the research work.

Without the blessings of my parents, I strongly believe that I would not have been able to complete my PhD work.

Last but not the least, I thank God for giving me those flashes of insight as I progressed in the research work, which made my whole effort so exhilarating that the work itself has become the reward.

Hyderabad   **B. KARUNAKAR**

What Is the Book About? 1

It is not the strongest who survive nor the most intelligent—but those most responsive to change.

—Charles Darwin

Which are the companies that succeeded in the pre- and post-1991 Liberalization era of the Indian industry and what made these companies succeed?

This book is a humble attempt to answer the above question based on sound research.

While undertaking the quest for this answer, the question arose as to where to begin. It is often said that to understand the present, one must reflect on the past. So the journey began to understand the past.

THE PAST

The first seeds of industrial entrepreneurship through the business families were sown in the 1860s when the first cotton mills came up in Mumbai. Most Indian business families[1] of today trace their history way back to the First World War period. At that point of time, merchants operated largely as communities based on their faith or origins like Parsis, Sindhis, Marwaris, Gujarati Banias,

Jains, etc. Having accumulated wealth during the turbulent period of the war, many of these merchants went on to set up enterprises that flourished under their successors to become mammoth business enterprises. The surviving business family of today is India's proudest institution—symbolizing courage and common sense, energy and enterprise, and aspiration and adventurousness.

It was thanks largely to the endeavors of pioneers like J.N. Tata, G.D. Birla, etc., that India had developed quite a few indigenous industries like steel, textiles, automobiles, power, aviation, sugar, and paper by the time it freed itself from the yoke of the British. Without the contribution of these visionaries, India's independence would have had no meaning.

ECONOMIC FREEDOM IN 1991

The Indian economic reforms that began in 1991 have unleashed progressive forces in the Indian Economy in the past decade. Three things have changed since then: first, foreign firms could now much more freely invest in India, include setting up 100 percent subsidiaries. Second, the change in competition meant that there was a demand for new technology—to introduce new products and more efficient processes. The Indian firm often sought this technology from its foreign partner. And third, the foreign firms' perception of the Indian market had changed dramatically. There was a sudden discovery of a large (and usually grossly overestimated) middle class that was clearly going to be one of the world's top markets in a few years.

The period from 1991 to 1999 can be divided into two phases—the boom from 1991 to 1996 and the slowdown from 1996 to 1999.

The five years' period from 1991 to 1996 saw a boom: the lifting of controls on licensing in particular, but also technology import and foreign investment, led to a big increase in industrial investment. A major liberalization of the capital market freed firms to price their own issues instead of pricing being determined by a government regulator, and this combined with the strong feel good factor of operating in a new era that could only be good for industry. The result was a major increase in domestic and foreign investment, all driven by the private sector. Industrial investment rose dramatically.

The slowdown has been particularly important as a driver of change in industry. Many industrialists reflect that the period from 1991 to 1996 was one where the sudden burst of freedom meant one could simply do more—enter new fields, license new technologies, and expand capacity. In spite of record growth, in sales and profits of many forms, change in what firms did and how they did it was relatively modest. It was only as growth fell and profit margins were squeezed that firms started to seriously restructure. During the economic boom, domestic and foreign private investment was made without significantly altering the structure and operation of existing Indian firms. The ensuing slowdown during 1996–99 revealed the internal weaknesses of Indian industry and started to drive changes.

CHALLENGES DURING THE 1990s

The government had already done a lot in terms of giving protection for four decades, long enough for any company to mature. There were some Indian firms that have built up their technical capabilities that made India proud.

The changes since 1991 have unleashed a new dynamic in Indian industry, a dynamic that forced change in every sector as firms finally were forced by new firms and the availability of imported products to provide consumers with products, prices, and service that began to approach internationally comparable levels.

Before 1991, the investment in R&D, with its heavy emphasis on indigenization, failed to enhance the efficiency and productivity of Indian industry. The pressure brought by the liberalization of 1991–99 spurred fundamental changes in technology and innovation, especially at the micro level. Indian firms have become more efficient, imported more foreign technology, and restructured and increased in-house R&D. There has been an improvement of productivity of capital, machines, and people. Efficient firms have benefited, even thrived in the new environment. Inefficient ones improved, merged, or finally began to disappear.

CONTEXT

Did the business family group survive the forces of liberalization and the competition from the MNCs? It is in this context and background that this book analyzes the companies.

If we examine the statistics of performance of the top 100 companies operating in India during the period 1991–2002, we will notice that a large number of companies had dwindling performance and slipped to lower ranks while during the same period, a few companies not only sustained but also surpassed many others to achieve much higher rank within the list.

Only 27 companies remained among the top 100 while 73 companies, which were among the top 100 companies in market capitalization in the year 1991, were no more in the list and were replaced by other companies in the year 2001. During this period, some companies that were at much lower ranks moved up significantly.

Business Today (BT) carried out a research project in 1997 to check whether India's 50 biggest business groups would still be at the top 50 years hence! The ranking was based on the measure of market capitalization. After all, only seven of the first 50 in 1947 were even in business in 1997. Thirty-two of the country's 50 largest corporations in 1969 are no longer among the Top 50 in 1997. What led to the decline of these companies? While one saw how companies like Reliance became competitive, one was distressed that simple lessons like focus, integration, and professionalism were forgotten. While these lessons were desirable in the old economy, they had become essential in the new economy.

The work of Jim Collins had inspired the research in this book in the Indian context. Collins had written two well-researched books. One is *Built to Last* (1995) and the other is *Good to Great* (2001). These two books identify the factors that made visionary companies and what made some companies make the leap from good to great. The methodology used in the book to distill the excellent companies in the Indian context is modeled on the method elucidated by Jim Collins in his book *Good to Great*.

The other source of inspiration for the research in this book is from the work of Sumantra Ghoshal—*Managing Radical Change* (2000) and *World Class in India* (2001). Most Indian companies went through difficult times since the liberalization process. Many of them went through restructuring programs. In the drive toward productivity, there have been cost-cutting exercises and job reductions. Most of them could not cope with the turbulent changes.

STUDY OBJECTIVES

We started the study in the Indian context with the following question in mind: *Which companies in India fall in the category of "Excellent Companies" as defined by the study?*

We looked for companies that showed exceptional returns. *We looked for companies that had cumulative returns at least three times the market over the years.*

A question arises here: Why three times the market? Three times the market because it exceeds the performance of most widely acknowledged companies. We took companies that were incorporated and listed before 1974 as these companies transcend the onetime wonders, as well as lucky breaks, and would exceed the normal tenure of most CEOs.

DATA AND METHODOLOGY

Data was obtained from CMIE's Prowess database. (CMIE stands for Centre for Monitoring Indian Economy.) The data was obtained for the period 1974–2002. Prowess contains a highly normalized database built on a sound understanding of disclosures of around 7,000 companies in India. These companies belong to various sectors: food and beverages, textiles, chemicals, non-metallic mineral products, metals and metal products, machinery, transport equipment, paper, leather, electricity, services like banks, financial services, publications, etc. The database contains financial statements, ratio analysis, funds flow, product profiles, etc. The database is complemented with powerful analytical software tools to enable extensive querying and research.

We adopted the methodology outlined in Table A.1. Our methodology is modeled on the method used by Jim Collins. We took the "365 days average" market capitalization in 2002 and the past stock market returns since 1974.

We used a sieving process with increasingly tighter screens to identify the excellent companies. The sieving process had three layers of analysis as referred in Figure 1.1.

Our steps were as follows:

Cut 1: From the Universe (All the Companies Listed on the Indian Stock Exchanges) of Companies to Arrive at 144 Companies

Our companies were:

FIGURE 1.1 Screening Process for Selecting Excellent Companies in India

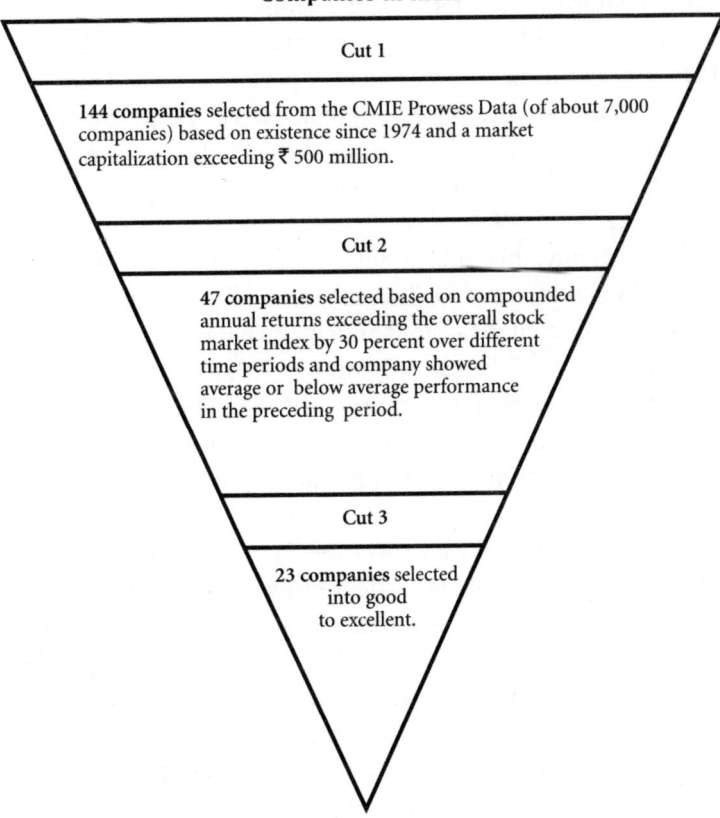

Source Author.

1. publicly traded, listed companies since 1974;
2. have been in existence since 1974;
3. showed positive profits consistently; and
4. had a market capitalization (365 days average) of ₹ 500 million in 2002.

One hundred and forty four companies passed the above four criteria. For the list of companies, please see Table A.2.

We have selected 1974 as the cut-off year, i.e., only those companies make the cut which were established and listed prior to 1974. We decided that *a period of minimum 25 years* should be taken so as to eliminate any element of personal bias and make sure that "onetime wonders" were not considered. Hence many good companies in the Indian scenario, especially the IT power horses (Infosys, Satyam, Wipro, etc.) couldn't make the cut. As a result, even though some of these companies have been performing very well consistently, they still couldn't make it to our list. Also many good public sector units like Indian Oil, Hindustan Petroleum, etc., and several good public sector banks could not make the cut as they went in for IPO and listing only after the 1991 economic reforms.

Market Capitalization as criteria was adopted for short-listing of companies. The prerequisite for consideration is that to make the cut a company must have a market capitalization, which was at least ₹ 500 million in 2002.

The market capitalization was the "365 days average" market capitalization for a company. The returns to the investor for a particular year are the "365 days average closing" stock prices increase/decrease over the previous year. The compounded annual total return to an investor till a particular Z year would mean the cumulative returns from the year 1974 till that particular Z year.

The final list of companies performed three times above the general market.

Overall Share Price Index (OSPI) is calculated by taking the average of the "compound annual total returns" for all the 144 short-listed companies.

Cut 2: From 144 Companies to 47 Companies

We had the following four tests:

> **Test 1.** Compounded annual total return to investors over the period 1996–2002 exceeded the OSPI for the same

period by 30 percent, and the company showed evidence of average or below average performance in 1974–95.

Test 2. Compounded annual total return to investors over the period 1991–2002 exceeded the compound annual average return OSPI for the same period by 30 percent, and the company showed evidence of average or below average performance in 1974–90.

Test 3. Compounded annual total return to investors over the period 1985–2002 exceeded the compound annual average return OSPI for the same period by 30 percent, and the company showed evidence of average or below average performance in 1974–84.

Test 4. Compounded annual total return to investors over the period 1974–2002 exceeded the compound annual average return OSPI for the same period by 30 percent.

All companies satisfying any one of the above criteria were selected. A total of 47 companies passed the test. For the list of companies, please see Table A.3.

Why did the authors take the aforementioned specific time periods? The Indian economy had the following significant years. One is the year of 1985 when liberalization was introduced in a modest way under Rajiv Gandhi's government. While it started off well, the reforms lost momentum. The year 1991 was the real turning point as far as the economic reforms are concerned. The country had to seek IMF loans that were tied up with the liberalization mandate and had to accelerate reforms. The subsequent five years were critical for most companies as they had to adjust to the new economic environment that signified a move away from the license quota system to the free market system.

Given this context, the author adopted the following three years *(i)* 1985, *(ii)* 1991, and *(iii)* 1996 as the key turning years and therefore the rationale and logic for the corresponding three periods.

Cut 3: From 47 Companies to the 23 "Excellent" Companies

The author studied the charts and identified companies based on when the actual stock returns showed a visible upward shift relative to the OSPI × 3 curve.

Criterion 1. The company shows a transition to increased performance, but the rise in performance is not sustained. After the initial rise, it goes flat or declines relative to the market until 2002.

Criterion 2. The company demonstrates a volatile pattern of returns—large upward and downward swings.

Criterion 3. The company falls for brief periods below the **three times** OSPI mark, demonstrating difficult times.

Criterion 4. The company comes near or exceeds **three times** the market average returns.

RESULTS

The research distilled around 23 companies. Companies were studied that made it into the final list. While seven companies made it past the above fourth criteria, the remaining 17 companies made it past the above third criteria had shareholder returns falling for brief periods below the three times OSPI mark, demonstrating difficult times. Significantly the brief period was from 1998–2002. The 23 companies are listed in the Table 1.1.

To explain this further, let us take the example of Coromandel Fertilisers (Figure A.3). We plotted cumulative total stock returns of Coromandel Fertilisers from 1974 till 2002. This line is reflected with the marks of a rhombus. The other line in the graph represents the three times OSPI. Notice that the company's total stock returns graph is consistently above the share price index line. Note that the performance is an upward trend. The rise in performance is sustained and is consistently above the three times OSPI mark.

What Is the Book About? | 11

TABLE 1.1   List of Study Companies

Sr. No.	Excellent companies
1.	Ahmedabad Electricity Company (now Torrent Power)
2.	Apollo Tyres Ltd
3.	Bajaj Hindusthan
4.	Bombay Dyeing & Manufacturing Ltd
5.	Coromandel Fertilisers Ltd
6.	Exide Industries
7.	Gammon India Ltd
8.	Hindalco Industries Ltd
9.	Indian Hotels Co. Ltd
10.	KEC International Ltd
11.	Kirloskar Brothers Ltd
12.	Larsen & Toubro Ltd
13.	Mahindra & Mahindra Ltd
14.	Motor Industries Co. Ltd
15.	Novartis India Ltd
16.	SKF Bearings India Ltd
17.	Siemens Ltd
18.	Sundaram Fasteners Ltd
19.	Surat Electricity Company (now Torrent Power)
20.	Tata Chemicals Ltd
21.	Tata Iron & Steel Co. Ltd
22.	Tata Power Co. Ltd
23.	Tinplate Co. of India Ltd

The performance of the stock market returns of these companies have been plotted along with the OSPI × 3 times, given in Figures A.1–A.23.

The data points have been put to regression with the objective of demonstrating statistically that the trend lines are different. This is shown in Table A.4. Significance test means significant difference between study company and the OSPI × 3.

FINDINGS

The companies' performances were analyzed based on a number of parameters. An effort was made to determine those factors that made them perform and to understand what made these companies tick. We collected secondary data about these organizations from a variety of sources and tried to then understand what separated these companies from the others. A case study method was adopted and an attempt was made to arrive at a business model.

In researching the "Good to Excellent Companies," various journals, newspapers, and magazines like *Business World*, *Business Today*, *Analyst*, *Business Standard*, *Economic Times*, *India Today*, and *Outlook* were referred and the same has been referenced at appropriate places. Further, companies' websites and annual reports were studied to understand the factors that made them consistently successful. The AIMA 2005 publication *Best of the Best—Insight from Leading International and Indian Organizations* (2005) gave additional insights on the Tata Business Excellence Model. In understanding history and leadership, the book by Gita Piramal—*Business Maharajas* (1996)—was researched with respect to the select companies.

It is interesting to note that the companies that have qualified as good to excellent companies have existence of 40 years or more, possibly because of the screening criteria adopted by us in our study that the companies should have been listed from the year 1974. Another interesting feature is that these companies belong to different industries and have stuck to their respective core businesses. The industries range from textiles, hotels, sugar, power, automotives, chemicals, tires, fasteners, aluminum, etc.

Quite a few Tata Group companies find their place, viz., Indian Hotels, Tata Power, Tata Chemicals, Tata Steel, and Tinplate Company. Tata Power stuck to its knitting in power business and remained as a single business company; Tata Chemicals as dominant business; M&M as related diversifier in metal-based companies; Siemens as a related diversifier in electricity companies. Hindalco, Tata Steel, and Apollo Tyres pursued a dominant vertical strategy.

A study of these companies made the research work propose a business model that is based on strategy, execution excellence, and leadership (referred in Figure 1.2) that provides a compelling explanation of their exceptional performance.

FIGURE 1.2   Business Model

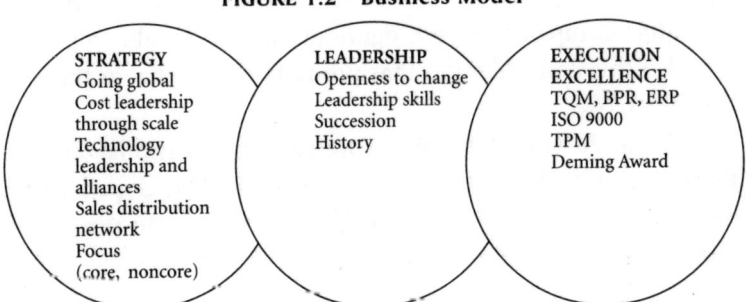

Source   Author.

The Business Model Consists of Three Themes

Strategy

Going global, cost leadership through scale, technology leadership and alliances, sales distribution network, focus (core, noncore).

Execution Excellence

Total Quality Management, Business Process Reengineering, Six Sigma, Enterprise Resource Planning, e-business (process, people, and productivity); responsiveness to change: shop floor, R&D, IT, and Human Resources Management; structure; operating mechanisms.

Leadership

Change management, professionalism, culture, succession planning, internal stability, passion to win, will, vision, and values.

Unlike America, India is a young democracy that has achieved its economic independence in 1991 with the reforms of liberalization, globalization, and privatization. Unlike America, India is not as mature in terms of its economic growth. India earned its right to freedom and self-determination in 1947 while America got it way back in 1776. It is this context and backdrop that make us refer to the Indian companies as "Excellent" instead of "Great." Most of the Indian companies do not figure in the top global companies. It is also this consideration that prompts us to refer to them as "Excellent."

Perhaps, 20 years later, when we carry out a similar kind of analysis at a time that India would have attained developed nation status, it would become more appropriate to refer to those then companies that would have satisfied our current screening criteria as "Great."

What Made the Excellent Companies Succeed? Proposed Business Model 2

Vision without action is merely a dream. Action without vision just passes time. But vision with action can change the world.
—Joel Arthur Barker

It is interesting to note that the companies that have qualified as Good to Excellent companies have existence of 40 years or more, possibly because of the screening criteria adopted by us in our study that the companies should have been listed from the year 1974. Another interesting feature is that these companies belong to different industries and have stuck to their respective core businesses. The industries range from textiles, hotels, sugar, power, automotives, chemicals, tires, fasteners, aluminum, etc. Table 2.1 provides a glimpse of these companies' efforts in going global.

Most of the above companies have gone global, while sticking to a business that they knew best. A few companies like Bombay Dyeing and Indian Hotels went global in 1979, almost 12 years before the 1991 Economic Reforms. Even companies like Tata Power that have served the domestic market since ages, have started going global. Its power systems division has not only emerged as a major player in the EPC transmission business in the country but also won the largest transmission line construction export contract in Bangladesh against stiff competition from Indian and international transmission line EPC companies.

Exception to the companies going global are companies in the power generation and distribution, like Ahmedabad Electricity, etc. (now part of the Torrent Power), Tata Power, where there is so

TABLE 2.1 List of Companies Going Global

No.	Year	Years old (as of 2006)	Company	Business	Global
1.	1945	61	Mahindra & Mahindra Ltd	Automotives	In 1994, the company started distribution of tractors in the USA with the formation of Mahindra USA Inc.
2.	1902	104	Indian Hotels Co. Ltd	Hotels	In 1979, IHCL operations in Colombo, Sri Lanka; management contracts for hotels in Dubai and Mauritius. Today, it is the largest hotel chain in South Asia. It has 51 hotels in India and 12 hotels abroad across 8 countries. Recently, in 2006, it acquired 100% stake in Boston Ritz-Carlton, USA.
3.	1879	126	Bombay Dyeing & Mfg Co. Ltd	Textiles	One of the largest exporters of textiles, with more than 50% of its production going to global markets. In 1979, set up a company in Indonesia and started sales in the Far East.
4.	1945	61	KEC International Ltd	Power transmission EPC	The company has a client base spread over 20 countries and over 75% of its projects are executed overseas with a strong presence in Middle East, Africa, and Pacific Rim countries during the last 50 years. During 1995–97, it set up JVs in Vietnam, Malaysia, Brazil, and Saudi Arabia.
5.	1962	44	Hindalco	Aluminum	In February 2007, Hindalco acquired Novelis, world's leading producer of aluminum-rolled products for an all-cash transaction worth $ 5.95 billion. Novelis operates through 36 manufacturing locations in 11 countries and has around 12,500 employees. The combination will establish a global integrated aluminum producer with low-cost alumina and aluminum production facilities combined with high-end aluminum-rolled products capabilities.

6.	1927	Tata Chemicals (1939)	Chemicals		
7.	1919	Tata Power Corp. Ltd	Power generation and distribution	87	Power Systems Division of the company has emerged as a major player in the EPC Transmission business in the country. The division has won the largest transmission line construction export contract in Bangladesh against stiff competition from Indian and international transmission line EPC companies.
8.	1966	Sundaram Fasteners	Auto components	40	In 1992, SFL entered into an agreement with General Motors that led to the creation of EOU for manufacture of radiator caps, oil filler caps, and petrol filler caps. SFL has been focusing on new markets and customers for its growth in exports while stepping up supplies to its existing customers. The company has been making supplies to Daimler Benz, AG, Germany (through Kamax); Cummins Engine Company Inc., USA; and General Motors Corporation, USA that contributed to its growth and profits.
9.	1964	SKF Bearings India	Bearings	42	India has been exporting low-value small bearings in small quantities. The country is not competitive when it comes to large-sized bearings in the export market due to the following reasons: (*i*) international market is highly quality conscious and in the past the quality of bearings manufactured in India was not of international standard except for a few big manufacturers, (*ii*) relatively small size of operation of

(Table 2.1 continued)

(Table 2.1 continued)

No.	Year	Years old (as of 2006)	Company	Business	Global
					existing players which makes it difficult to adhere to timely delivery schedules, (*iii*) high cost of production, and (*iv*) ensured domestic market for the existing players. SKF and Tata Timken have started exports to neighboring countries and are planning to export to developed countries as well.
10.	1972	34	Apollo Tyres	Tyres	In 1991, Apollo Tyres undertook exports of LCV and farm tyres in addition to truck tyres. In 1994, it emerged as the largest exporter of tyres.
11.	1922	84	Tinplate Company of India Ltd	Tin manufacturing	It is today the largest indigenous producer of tin-coated and tin-free steel sheets in India, enjoying 35–40% market share and undoubtedly the industry leader for 85 years. The company exports about 20–25% of its production directly to end-users (can-makers) and its products are well accepted in the markets of SE Asia, Middle East and some developed countries in Europe.
12	1960	46	Exide Industries	Automotive and industrial batteries	Exide Industries Limited is the largest battery exporter from India. Batteries manufactured by Exide are exported across the world to Armenia, Australia, Bahrain, Bangladesh, Belgium, China, Chile, Columbia, Cyprus, Ethiopia, France, Germany, Greece, Ivory Coast, Italy, Kenya, Kuwait, Lebanon, Mauritius, Myanmar, Netherlands, Oman,

13.	1907	99	Tata Steel	Flat products, long products, tubes, bearings	Paraguay, Peru, Qatar, Russia, Rwanda, Saudi Arabia, Sierra Leone, Singapore, South Africa, Spain, Sri Lanka, the UAE, United Kingdom, Uruguay, Vietnam, Yemen, Zambia, and Zimbabwe. In February 2007, Tata Steel acquired Corus Steel for $12.1 billion in a bidding process against the rival CSN, Brazilian steelmaker. Corus makes nearly four times more steel than Tata Steel. Together the combine becomes the fifth largest producer in the world and the second in Europe. The combine will be the second largest tin-plate maker in the world.

Source Company websites and author's research.

much of unmet demand in the country and also Bajaj Hindusthan that is in an agro-based industry like sugar. Table 2.2 provides a glimpse of these companies' efforts in going global.

TABLE 2.2 List of Companies with Dominant Domestic Market Shares

No.	Year	Years Old (as of 2006)	Company	Business	Dominant domestic market shares
1.	1931	75	Bajaj Hindusthan	Sugar	
2.	1913	93	Ahmedabad Electricity Co. Ltd (Torrent Power Group)	Power generation and distribution	
3.	1902	104	Indian Hotels	Hotels	15%
4.	1962	44	Hindalco	Aluminum	70%
5.	1879	126	Bombay Dyeing	Textiles	75% in DMT
6.	1972	34	Apollo Tyres	Tyres	25%
7.	1945	61	M&M	Automotives	26% in tractors 53% in MUVs
8.	1945	61	KEC International	Power transmission EPC	30%
9.	1907	99	Tata Steel	Steel	15%
10.	1964	42	SKF Bearings	Bearings	30%

Source Company websites.

Quite a few Tata Group companies find their place, viz., Indian Hotels, Tata Power, Tata Chemicals, Tata Steel, and Tinplate Company.

Among the MNCs, Siemens, pharma majors like Novartis and German Remedies (now part of Zydus Cadila), SKF India, and Motor Industries find their place in the list of excellent companies.

LITERATURE REVIEW

Pursuing the review of literature to understand what strategic drivers led Indian companies to succeed in the Indian context, some interesting findings were made.

G.S. Shergill and Revti Raman[1] highlighted the extent and nature of diversification of 67 Indian companies during 1979–89. They classified the companies into four strategic categories as three points in time: 1979, 1984, and 1989. The study showed that there is a trend upward toward higher diversification but it is very gradual. Industry-wise analysis showed that *single business* is popular in hotel, power supply, and shipping; *dominant business* in chemicals; *related business* in metals; and *unrelated business* in cement, paper, and jute industries.

In 1989, Tata Power finds a mention in the single business companies; Tata Chemicals as dominant business; M&M as related diversifier in metal-based companies; Siemens as a related diversifier in electricity companies. Under the dominant business category, Hindalco, Tata Steel, and Apollo Tyres were found in dominant vertical strategy.

A.M. Shah[2] identified critical success factors and key strategies to be pursued by companies. Based on questionnaire data collected from 125 CEOs, the study spelt out 11 *critical success factors/areas* for companies operating in the Indian market. These were (*i*) product quality, (*ii*) relative product cost, (*iii*) good people, (*iv*) innovativeness, (*v*) advanced technology, (*vi*) strategic alliances, (*vii*) market knowledge, (*viii*) flexibility, (*ix*) business reputation, (*x*) distribution networks, and (*xi*) information systems. While improvement in all these critical areas is necessary for strengthening the competitiveness of organizations, a relatively greater emphasis on one or the other depends upon the strategies pursued by an organization at a particular period of time. This chapter identifies the five *key strategies* for competing successfully in the Indian market. The strategy "good quality and low price" was ranked first in importance followed by "product innovation," "cost leadership and differentiation," "niche marketing" (Apollo Tyres focused on heavy vehicle tyre segment only), and "superior quality and premium price." The two generic strategies identified by Porter (1985) are cost leadership and differentiation.[3] While cost leadership is usually aimed at attracting a broad market base so that the small per unit profit margins are offset by large number of unit sales, a perfect differentiation strategy enables the firm command a premium price. Though Porter advocates that companies should concentrate on one strategy or the other to avoid a situation where they fall between the two stools and follow neither strategy successfully, 84 percent of the 125 CEO respondents mentioned that a combination of two strategies is needed for succeeding in the Indian markets.

Sundaram Fasteners finds a mention in the critical success factor of product quality, where quality has immensely contributed to the success. Sundaram Fasteners took advantage of an offer to make radiator caps for General Motors (GM) and redefined its production and quality norms on GM's terms. Ever since the first consignment was dispatched to GM in March 1993, the company has become very important for GM to meet its customer needs. The company is not only GM's sole global supplier of metal radiator caps, it has also bagged the American auto giant's Best of the Best Award for 1997 for the second year in a row. The company is also the domestic leader in hi-tensile fasteners, with a 52 percent market share.

M&M finds a mention in the critical success factor of strategic alliances. Its tie-ups with Peugeot for light utility vehicles and AVL for tractors provides it with access to technology.

Rajnish Karki[4] mentions that for Indian organizations in the coming decade, corporate strategy should be built around (*i*) the root of "being honest" and "being world-class" and (*ii*) one of the three viable branches or types of strategic direction—"India focused," "India diversified," and "global focused."

THE BUSINESS MODEL CONSISTS OF THREE THEMES

To arrive at the various themes of strategy, execution excellence, and leadership the following companies were studied in a case study mode to understand what they did right (Table 2.3).

TABLE 2.3 Study Companies

Strategy	Execution excellence	Leadership
Going global	Indian Hotels, Tata Steel, Bombay Dyeing, M&M, Apollo Tyres, Exide Industries, Sundaram Fasteners, L&T, Gammon, Siemens	Tata Steel, Tinplate, Tata Chemicals, Indian Hotels, Bombay Dyeing, M&M, Apollo Tyres, Sundaram Fasteners, Kirloskar Brothers	Tata Steel, Tata Chemicals, Indian Hotels, Bombay Dyeing, Hindalco, Coromandel Fertilisers, M&M, Apollo Tyres, Kirloskar Brothers, Sundaram Fasteners, Exide Industries, Larsen & Toubro, Gammon, Siemens
Cost leadership and economies of scale	Hindalco, Tata Steel, Bombay Dyeing, Apollo Tyres, M&M, Coromandel Fertilisers		
Sales distribution network	Tata Steel, Bombay Dyeing, M&M, Apollo Tyres, Exide Industries, and Siemens		

A close study of the short-listed companies makes us propose **a business model based on Strategy, Execution Excellence, and Leadership** (as shown in Figure 2.1) that provides a compelling explanation of their exceptional performance. It may be noted that the companies used a combination of different elements in strategy, execution excellence, and leadership as dominant themes in attaining their superior performance. Companies that did not pursue global sales aimed at dominant domestic market shares in India. While companies like Indian Hotels, Apollo Tyres, etc., pursued global sales at an early stage, other companies like Hindalco, Tata Steel, etc., pursued dominant domestic market shares before going global. Further, companies like Bajaj Hindusthan, a sugar company, still continue to pursue dominant domestic market shares.

Strategy

Going global, cost leadership through scale, technology leadership and alliances, sales distribution network, focus in core business.

The research work of the study companies shows that there is an assertion of strategic intent in terms of going global or at least pursuing global scale. Attendant to this choice is the pursuit of economies of scale giving the company a cost advantage. The generic choice for business group is between cost leadership and product focus as it strives to attain the distinctive competitive edge that scores over the competition.

In cost leadership strategy, the key idea is to **establish world-class plants, keep cost of funds low, ensure high rates of capacity utilization and control costs**. Two key ingredients that go into the making of a global cost leader are *Scale* and *Vertical Integration*. The company's cost position as against its rivals, supported by backward linkages to operations aim to provide the lowest prices in the marketplace. Following these choices, there is a pursuit of factors like economies of scale, technological leadership, sales distribution network, and core competency-driven focus.

What Made the Excellent Companies Succeed? | 25

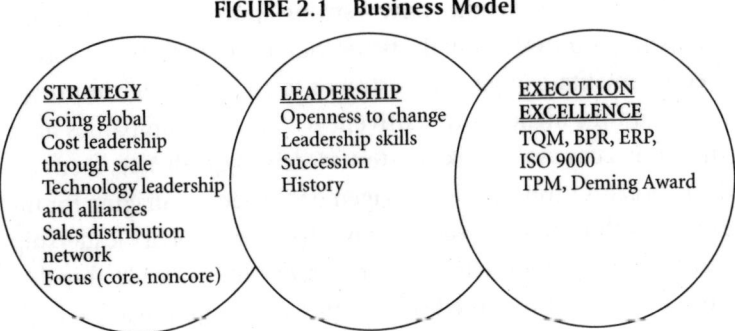

FIGURE 2.1   Business Model

Execution Excellence

Total Quality Management, Business Process Re-enginnering (BPR), Six Sigma, ERP, E-business (process, people, and productivity); IT, R&D, responsiveness to change: shop floor, and HRM; structure; operating mechanisms.

Process improvement is one area where improvements will directly impact customer satisfaction. The key traits required in an organization to achieve excellence are: (i) having customer insights, (ii) focusing business strategies on customer value, (iii) quality commitment, (iv) upgrading knowledge and processes, and (v) management by facts and feedback.

The quest for operational efficiencies is normally made by companies in a bid not only to contain costs but also to optimize product quality. Various management techniques like benchmarking, TQM, JIT inventory management, BPR, SCM, or customer and employee surveys are deployed by companies to sharpen operations.

Leadership

Change management, professionalism, culture, succession planning, internal stability, passion to win, will, vision, and values.

Typically, the companies have a strong approach toward robust systems and processes, with the belief that more efficient and robust processes facilitate quicker adjustment to change, faster improvement, and thus higher competitiveness. Also, the companies have well-defined core values like customer-driven excellence, focus on future, organization agility, management by fact, managing for innovation, valuing employees and partners, and visionary leadership among others. The companies identify leadership as "leadership that delivers." In order that the leadership is not limited to a few individuals, and lest it should be viewed as a one-time performance, a "Leadership System" is typically developed to guide the leadership. Leadership at these companies is built on a strong ethical foundation defined in their Code of Conduct and guided by their core values. This constitutes the rigid base that does not move.

Strategy Theme 3

> *Competition is the greatest teacher for improving products, reducing cost and improving quality. Competition may hurt us in the short term but this is the route to sustained growth.*
>
> —Rahul Bajaj, CMD of Bajaj Auto Ltd, 1991

GOING GLOBAL, COST LEADERSHIP THROUGH SCALE, TECHNOLOGY LEADERSHIP AND ALLIANCES, AND SALES DISTRIBUTION NETWORK

The Indian business houses have traditionally sacrificed strategy at the altar of opportunism. The generic choice for today's business group is between cost leadership and product focus as it strives to attain the distinctive competitive edge that scores over the competition.

Its cost position vis-à-vis rivals, supported by backward linkages to operations, reveal whether or not it is aiming to provide the lowest prices in the marketplace. Alternatively, the business that makes uniqueness its strategic base must invest in and deliver differentiated products that competition cannot match (Figure 3.1).

Following these choices, there is a pursuit of factors like "economies of scale, technological leadership, marketing skills, and core competency-driven focus."[1] *A corollary factor is that going global provides the impetus to economies of scale.*

FIGURE 3.1 Business Model—Strategy

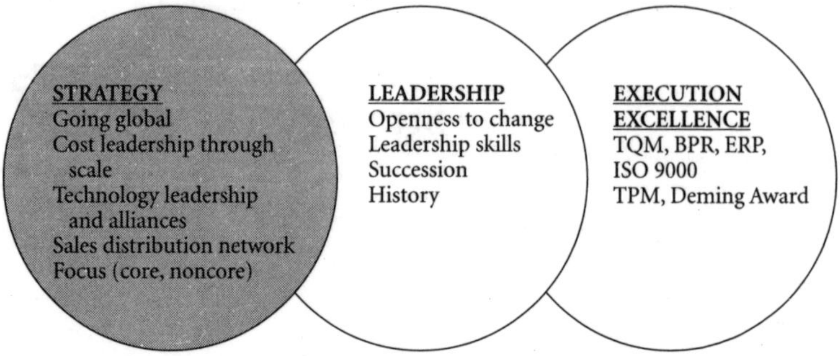

STRATEGY
Going global
Cost leadership through scale
Technology leadership and alliances
Sales distribution network
Focus (core, noncore)

LEADERSHIP
Openness to change
Leadership skills
Succession
History

EXECUTION EXCELLENCE
TQM, BPR, ERP,
ISO 9000
TPM, Deming Award

The extent to which a business house concentrates on its core business is a vital measure. Most important, the determination to persist with its strategic positioning is visible in its efforts to build competitive advantages at every stage of the value chain.

The proof that such a choice is being made improves the prospects of the company. Conversely, the absence of such decisions implies that the businesses in question have no defined distinctiveness and offer little by way of unmatched value to the customer.

Going Global

The research work of the study companies shows that there is an assertion of strategic intent in terms of going global or at least pursuing global scale. Attendant to this choice is the pursuit of economies of scale giving the company a cost advantage.

As cited earlier, most companies went global, while sticking to a business that they knew best. A few companies like Bombay Dyeing and Indian Hotels went global in 1979, much before the 1991 Economic Reforms. **What the reader can expect to read in this section is to understand the trajectory the companies took in going global as a part of their growth strategy.** In this section, the reader would draw lessons on global growth from Indian Hotels, TISCO, Bombay Dyeing, M&M, Apollo Tyres, Exide Industries, Sundaram Fasteners, L&T, Gammon, Siemens, etc.

Indian Hotels

As early as 1979, Indian Hotel Corporation Ltd (IHCL) put up a hotel of international standards in Colombo, Sri Lanka. IHCL has franchises and management contracts for hotels in Dubai and Mauritius. In 2006, IHCL acquired 100 percent stake in Boston Ritz-Carlton, USA, for a consideration of $ 170 million (Figure 3.2).[2] Today, it is the largest hotel chain in South Asia, operating a total of 63 hotels with about 8,020 rooms in India and abroad with 51 hotels in India and 12 across eight countries.

Indian Hotels caters to a wide cross-section of travelers with its luxury, business, and leisure hotels (among them beach resorts, garden retreats, and palace hotels) making it the best hotel chain in the country. IHCL has consistently been conferred a number of awards that highlight its position as one of the world's leading hotel chains. The readers of *Travel & Leisure* named Taj Mahal Hotel, Mumbai, the winner of the 2003 World's Best Business Hotels. The Taj Hotels was voted the Best Hotel group in India in the 2003 Selling Long Haul Travel Awards by Travel Agents, UK.

Indian Hotels owns its hotels either directly or through its subsidiaries or through its associates and partners. It has a 15 percent market share in the Four Star, Five Star, and Five Star Deluxe segments. From the hotels operating in India, it faces competition from the Oberoi group, ITC Welcome group, Leela group, government-owned Indian Tourism Development Corporation (ITDC) hotels, Hotel Corporation of India (HCI) hotels, etc.

IHCL growth strategy has been through product extension and geographical expansion. IHCL has leveraged its brand equity and service excellence to forge alliances with partners and associates to build growth through a de-risking business model.

FIGURE 3.2 Indian Hotels—Growth in Total Income (₹ million)

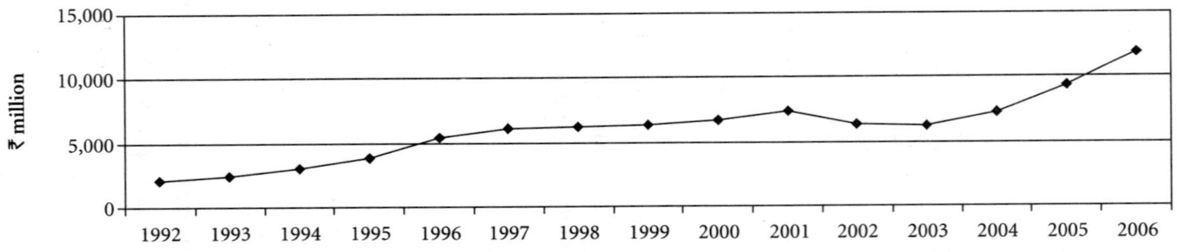

	Mar-1992	Mar-1993	Mar-1994	Mar-1995	Mar-1996	Mar-1997	Mar-1998	Mar-1999	Mar-2000	Mar-2001	Mar-2002	Mar-2003	Mar-2004	Mar-2005	Mar-2006
Total Income	208	243	301	379	547	613	618	636	666	741	633	626	732	929	1190

Source Author.

Indian Hotels' total income grew from ₹ 2,080 million in 1992 to ₹ 11,900 million in 2006 (Figure 3.3). While its profit after tax (PAT) went through ups and downs to go from ₹ 220 million in 1992 to ₹ 1,840 million in 2006 (Figure 3.4).

FIGURE 3.3   Indian Hotels—Growth in Total Income (Percentage)

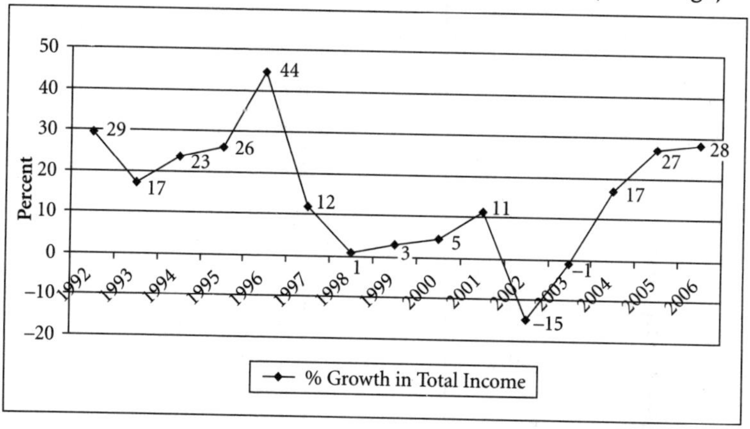

[Line chart showing % Growth in Total Income from 1992 to 2006 with data points: 1992: 29, 1993: 17, 1994: 23, 1995: 26, 1996: 44, 1997: 12, 1998: 1, 1999: 3, 2000: 5, 2001: 11, 2002: −15, 2003: −1, 2004: 17, 2005: 27, 2006: 28]

Source   Author.

TISCO: Globalization—Corus Steel Acquisition

In February 2007, Tata Steel[3] acquired Corus Steel for $ 12.1 billion in a bidding process against the rival CSN, Brazilian Steelmaker. Corus makes nearly four times more steel than Tata Steel. Together the combine becomes the fifth-largest producer in the world and the second in Europe. *The combine will be the second-largest tin-plate maker in the world.*

Globally, the steel industry is witnessing consolidation and changes in the traditional business model. Instead of moving large quantities of iron ore, companies are now moving efficient material which is steel based (de-integrated production). By acquiring Corus, Tata Steel expects to improve Corus's profitability and operational efficiencies by adopting a philosophy of de-integrated production.

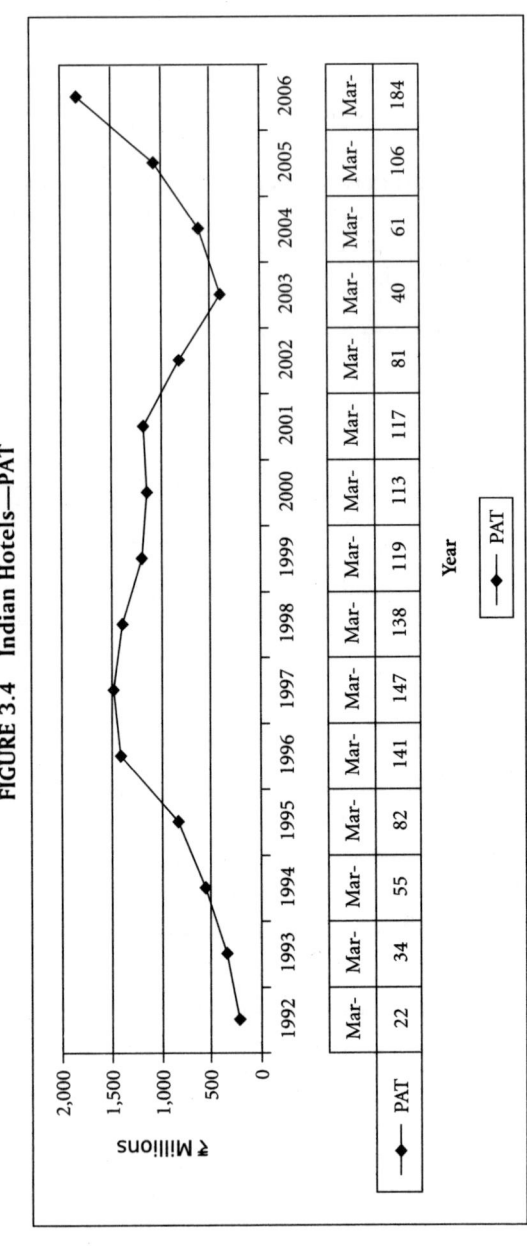

FIGURE 3.4 Indian Hotels—PAT

Source: Author.

The rationale behind the acquisition was the expected long-term synergies in manufacturing, access to global customers, opening India to Corus, or leveraging R&D for Tata Steel's greenfield projects.

The value creation is expected to come from three areas: (*i*) synergies from sharing of manufacturing practices, shared services, and purchasing; (*ii*) sharing complementary strengths—Corus has strong R&D and product development capabilities for value-added products in the automobile, construction, and packaging markets that will complement what Tata Steel is doing in the fast-growing Asian markets; and (*iii*) option for the future to bring low-cost slabs once Tata Steel has completed its greenfield projects.

Currently, the combine is making 25 MT and the aspiration is to increase the total capacity to 100 MT by 2015 (Figure 3.5).

Since 1991, the Indian steel industry had witnessed a lot of changes. In 1991, the government liberalized import and licensing policies considerably. Licensing for manufacture of steel, price controls, and quotas were abolished. With funding from financial institutions, the private sector contribution to total steel production increased to 68 percent in 2002 from 46 percent in 1991 (Figure 3.6). A lot of new industrial groups/companies like Essar, Lloyds, Jindal, Mittal, and Mideast entered the steel industry that was traditionally dominated by the SAIL and Tata Steel.

Most of the steel produced in India is consumed domestically, and the country does not rely too much on the export of steel. It exports 12 percent of its total steel production. The consumption of steel in India is largely driven by infrastructure and construction industry.

During the early 1980s, Tata Steel initiated a modernization program for its steel plants. By the mid-1990s, Tata Steel was Asia's first and India's largest integrated steel producer in the private sector. By 2000, eight divisions of Tata Steel were ISO 14001 certified. By early 2000, Tata Steel had completed four phases of the modernization program.

FIGURE 3.5 Tata Steel—Growth in Total Income (₹ million)

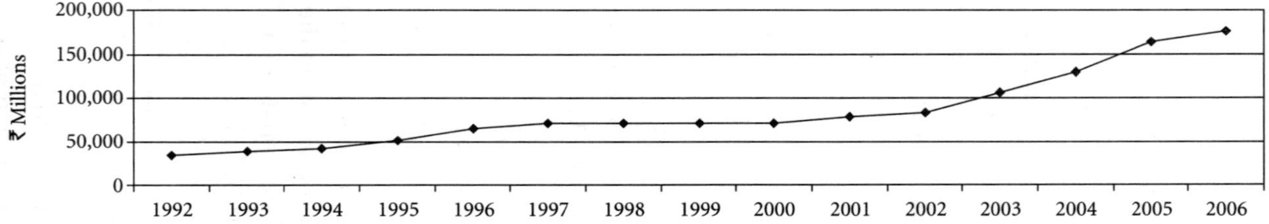

	Mar-1992	Mar-1993	Mar-1994	Mar-1995	Mar-1996	Mar-1997	Mar-1998	Mar-1999	Mar-2000	Mar-2001	Mar-2002	Mar-2003	Mar-2004	Mar-2005	Mar-2006
Total Income	33,140	38,590	41,150	50,210	64,920	71,120	71,340	70,28	70,500	78,700	83,500	105,960	128,720	163,200	175,030

Source Author.

FIGURE 3.6 Tata Steel—Growth in Total Income (Percentage)

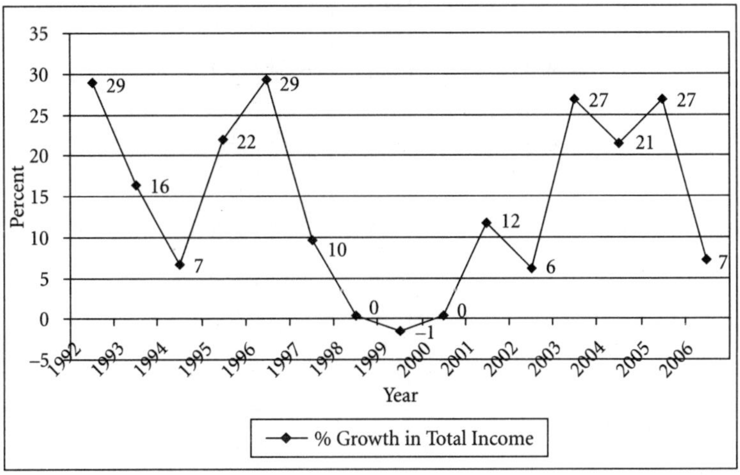

Source Author.

In the late 1990s, the global steel industry was reeling under overcapacity and poor demand mainly triggered by the Southeast Asian currency crisis. The crisis led to problems for developed countries. In order to protect their domestic steel industries, the EU, the US, and Canada started imposing higher tariffs. As a result, Indian steel exports were hit. Moreover, these countries started dumping cheap steel in India leveraging the advantage of the lower import duty structure after liberalization. All these factors led the Indian steel industry to one of its worst years in 2001–02. The bottom lines of all the major steel companies in India were badly hit.

By April 2001, Tata Steel was the world's lowest-cost producer of steel. Tata Steel's operating cost at the "hot metal" liquid stage was $ 75 per ton. The company's cost per ton of finished steel stood at $ 152 for the year ending March 2001. One would notice from Figure 3.7 that the PAT jumped significantly from the year 2003 with profit after tax of ₹ 10,120 million and was the most profitable steel company in India as a result of its successful cost leadership strategy and execution excellence initiatives.

FIGURE 3.7 Tata Steel—PAT

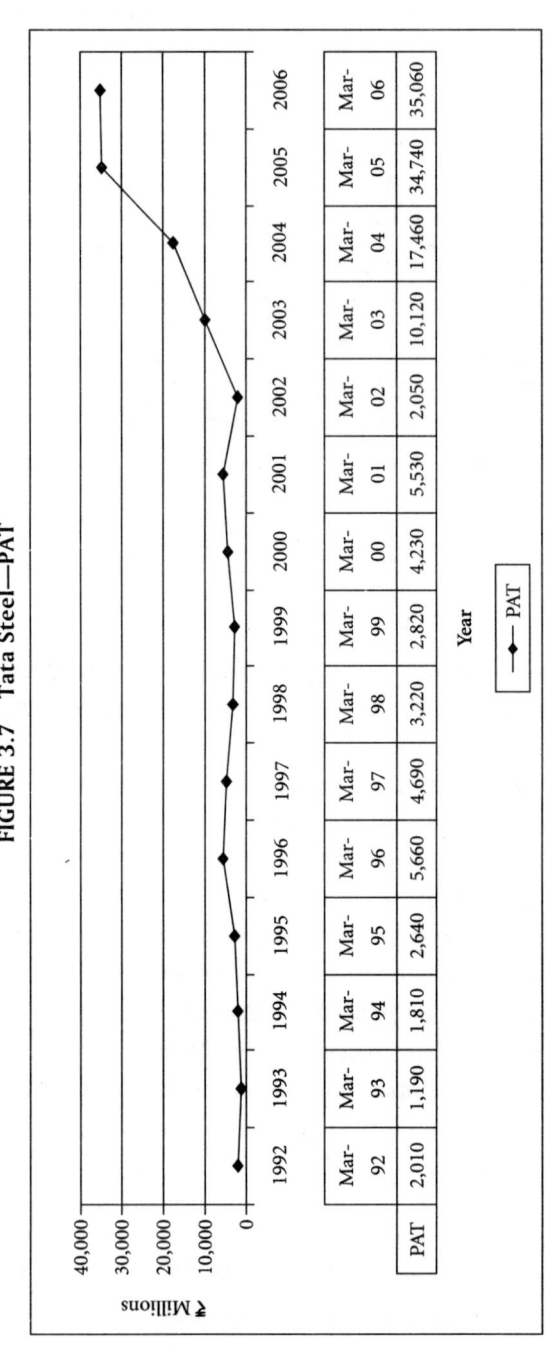

Source Author.

Tata Steel's total income grew from ₹ 33,140 million in 1992 to ₹ 175,030 million in 2006. While its PAT went through ups and downs to go from ₹ 2,010 million in 1992 to ₹ 35,060 million in 2006. Today, Tata Steel produces a wide range of products including hot rolled/cold rolled (HR/CR) coils and sheets, tubes, construction bars, forging quality steel, rods, structural, strips, and bearings. It also manufactures material handling equipment, ferro alloys and other minerals, software for process controls, and provides cargo-handling services.

Bombay Dyeing

Bombay Dyeing is a leading exporter for sheets and is among the top five for towels and linens. More than 50 percent of its production finds its way to countries such as USA, Canada, UK, Germany, Netherlands, Italy, France, Poland, former Czechoslovakia, New Zealand, Switzerland, Sweden, Denmark, Australia, Sri Lanka, Mauritius, Singapore, Hong Kong, China, Malaysia, Indonesia, UAE, South Africa, East Africa, and Argentina. It distributes the products in foreign countries through direct sales force agents as far as institutional needs are concerned. It ships its products through large mail order houses under their brand labels. It also uses the departmental stores.

In 1979, the company started sales in Indonesia through an incorporated company named P.T. Five Star Industries Ltd.[4] The activities of the group span several countries in the Far East.

In the year 1998–99, the company won the SRTEPC and the TEXPROCIL Gold Trophies for its outstanding export performance for poly-cotton blended fabrics and made ups.

Global customers want well-integrated vendors, i.e., fiber to fashion. The company's products already have a presence in major retail chains abroad like Marks & Spencer's, Bed Bath, JC Penny, Federated Stores, and others.

Its main competition is from Abhishek Industries (Trident) and Welspun in the Towels segment and from Handfan in Linens segment.

Bombay Dyeing's total income grew from ₹ 5,450 million in 1992 to ₹ 11,160 million in 2006. While its PAT went through ups and downs to go from ₹ 440 million in 1992 to ₹ 610 million in 2006. (See Figures 3.8–3.10.)

Textile production involves spinning, weaving, dyeing, printing, and finishing. This makes textiles more capital intensive compared to garmenting that involves fewer steps with high level of labor. The focus is on producing large textiles that is capital intensive which is an effective entry barrier. Labor costs approx 7 percent of the company's sales.

The Value Chain in Figure 3.11 shows how the final product is manufactured.

The initial procurement is from farmers and cooperatives. Thus the company's dependence on agricultural sector is quite high. It is also into silk, which makes the company even more dependent. Among the man-made fibers, the company uses polyester, nylon, rayon, acetate, and others. Bombay Dyeing is the largest producer of dimethyl terephthalate (DMT) in the country and has around 75 percent market share.

In case of cotton fiber and animal fiber, it is spun into yarn, while in the case of silk the fiber is drawn into filament.

The fabrics that are woven from yarns or filaments are denim, print cloth, broadcloth, and sheeting. Nonwoven fabrics and industrial products also form a good share of the company's business.

Coming to the final product, apparel and made ups, the company is a leader in home textiles, i.e., towels, sheets, pillow covers, curtains, and drapes. Apart from these products, carpets and rugs make up a major business.

The consumer range includes bed linen, towels, furnishings, fabrics for suits, shirts, dresses, and saris in cotton and polyester brands. The company has a wide range of industrial fabrics that

FIGURE 3.8 Bombay Dyeing—Growth in Total Income (₹ million)

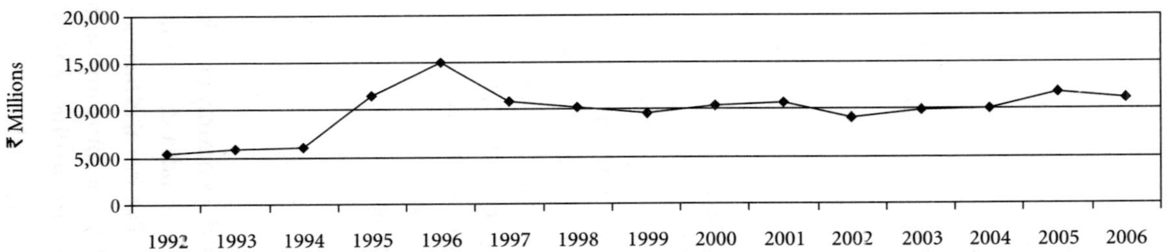

	1992	1993	1994	1995	1996	1997	1998	1999	2000	2001	2002	2003	2004	2005	2006
	Mar-	Mar-	Mar-	Mar-	Mar-	Mar-	Mar-	Mar-	Mar-	Mar-	Mar-	Mar-	Mar-	Mar-	Mar-
Total Income	5,446	5,934	6,042	11,490	14,980	10,860	10,110	9,448	10,380	10,590	8,969	9,847	10,030	11,730	11,160

Source Author.

FIGURE 3.9 Bombay Dyeing— Growth in Total Income (Percentage)

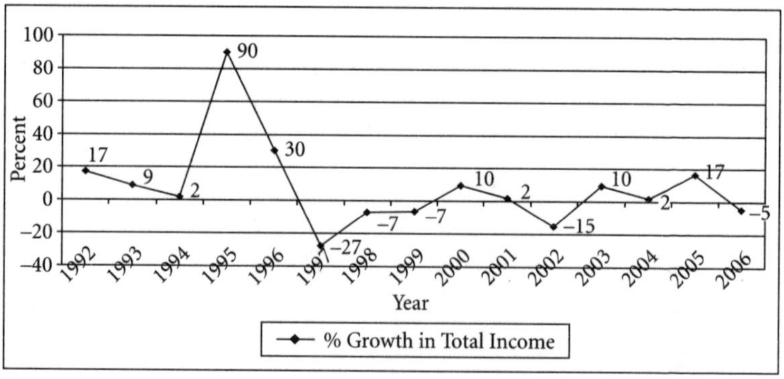

Source Author.

include microdot interlining; fabrics for shoe uppers, adhesives, abrasives, leather cloth, and filters. The target customers for rags, sheeting, and bed sheets are the institutional players that consist of hotels, restaurants, and others in the hospitality industry. It has a strong presence in the retail segment. It is a provider of home needs to so many Indian customers. It also manufactures ready-made garments like school uniforms, etc. A sizable market has been established in ready-mades which include a range of formal and casual wear. Customers still prefer Bombay Dyeing for sheeting and other homemaking sheeting. Even for school uniforms, it is one of the trusted names.

Mahindra & Mahindra

With the opening up of the world economy and the elimination of regulations across the globe, Mahindra & Mahindra (M&M) has been pursuing not just exports but has also been setting up manufacturing bases abroad. In 1994, the company started distribution of tractors in the USA with the formation of Mahindra USA Inc. In 2002, the company went in for a makeover as a carmaker with the launch of Scorpio. Since then, the company has been exploring export opportunities for Scorpio in the Middle East, China, Central

FIGURE 3.10 Bombay Dyeing—PAT

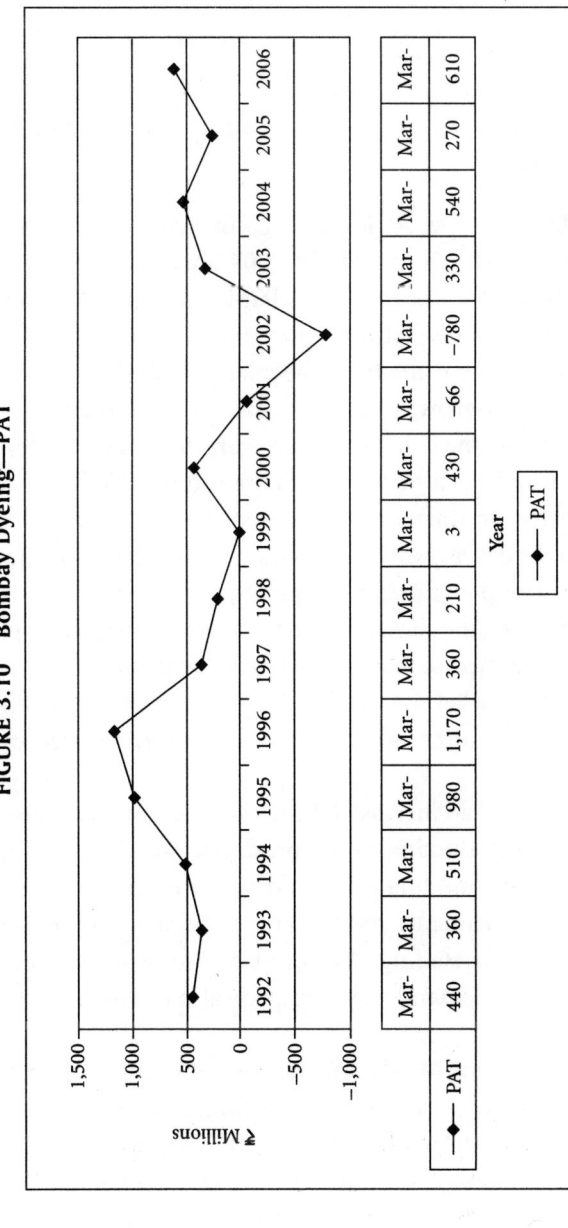

	Mar-1992	Mar-1993	Mar-1994	Mar-1995	Mar-1996	Mar-1997	Mar-1998	Mar-1999	Mar-2000	Mar-2001	Mar-2002	Mar-2003	Mar-2004	Mar-2005	Mar-2006
PAT	440	360	510	980	1,170	360	210	3	430	−66	−780	330	540	270	610

Source Author.

FIGURE 3.11 Value Chain of Textile Production

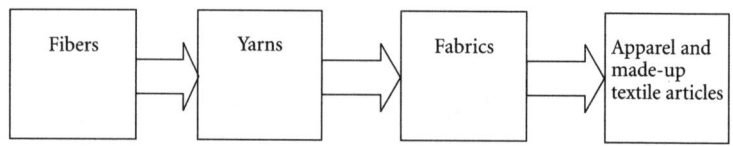

Source Author.

Asia, Eastern Europe, Africa, and Latin America. The company introduced its MUVs in Italy in 2004 and expanded its tractor business in the US and Europe.[5] M&M has formed a JV with the Chinese tractor manufacturer—Jiangling Motor Co.

M&M USA sales came from the sales of low HP tractors, which is hardly a high-growth segment. The low HP tractors—called hobby tractors in the US—are actually targeted at weekend farmers, managers who have a small farm in the country. To really become a global player in tractors, M&M needs to manufacture high HP tractors in the developed markets—something that will require the money the group is at present pumping into its noncore ventures.

Over the years, the company had transformed itself into a globally competitive enterprise that manufactures quality products not just to the Indian market but also to the global markets. Further, the company exited some of its businesses to stay focused on core business.

The company had increased the top line year on year by focusing on growth—introduction of new products/models to meet specific customer needs, building the brand equity of the existing brands through advertisements, strengthening the distribution network, and tie-up with banks/financial companies for wholesale and retail finance to boost demand. The company also expanded into global markets.

Tractor segment: M&M had become the first Indian tractor company to achieve sales of one million units in a year and also India's largest exporter of tractors. It sold 7,600 tractors in 2003–04 in overseas markets. High-potential markets like China, Australia, and Europe also received special attention.

The tractor division had recorded a huge growth in exports in 2003–04, especially to the US. The exports to the US were handled by the 100 percent subsidiary, Mahindra USA (MUSA). MUSA had subsequently started its second assembly plant at Calhoun in Georgia.

MUSA reached the farmers in the US through its website. Since most of the US farmers first checked the product testimonials in chat rooms and community groups before shopping for farm equipments, MUSA made sure that the online word of mouth worked in its favor. MUSA asked farmers who bought its tractors to share their experiences on the web on popular online destinations such as a Yahoo user group. In addition, cable television advertising, radio jingles, and billboards were deployed in Louisiana, Texas, and North Carolina. M&M tractors were also showcased at agricultural fairs. MUSA managers also pitched products at influencers—farmers who were respected as mechanical experts in the local community. Out of MUSA's revenues of $ 150 million in 2004, Indian tractor sales accounted for one-third, while the rest came from Korean and Japanese tractors sold under the MUSA brand.

The company created history in 2004 by becoming the first tractor company in the world to bag the coveted Deming Prize, instituted by Japanese Union of Scientists and Engineers (JUSE) that has become a synonym for quality and excellence.

Automotive segment: The automotive segment targeted markets like South Asia, South Africa, and Latin America that were similar to India. Some 1,600 vehicles were exported in the year 2003–04. Europe and Russia were the new target markets. M&M planned to target Spain and Portugal using Italy as its base.

The company kept a global vision from the outset. It acquired Valtra, the truck maker, and entered into many agreements with global auto majors. Recently, the company signed an MoU with Renault for a Greenfield facility in India to manufacture 0.5 million units per year. Farm equipments and automobiles have been the key for M&M. **Currently M&M is the market leader in farm equipment sector and dominates the automobile sector in the MUV segment.** On the anvil are more distribution and production tie-ups along with product innovations.

M&M's total income grew from ₹ *12,410 million in 1992 to* ₹*95,700 million in 2006. While its PAT went through ups and downs to go from* ₹ *187 million in 1992 to* ₹ *8,570 million in 2006.* (See Figures 3.12–3.14.)

Quality is a driving force of the company with a philosophy of delivering value for money to its customers. The quality theme cuts across products, one's work, and interactions with others.

In 1994, a major restructuring exercise was initiated as a part of a BPR program. *M&M's decision to undertake BPR implementation was largely influenced by its ambition to become a leading tractor manufacturer in the world.* This was accompanied by a decision to focus on enhancing productivity and delivering world-class quality at the least possible cost. The company also undertook total quality management initiative. Various other initiatives such as supplier upgradation, strategic and global sourcing, product development, channel management, and lean manufacturing were also taken up.

The company increases the top line year on year by focusing on growth—introduction of new products/models to meet specific customer needs, building the brand equity of the existing brands through advertisements, strengthening the distribution network, and tie-up with banks/financial companies for wholesale and retail finance to boost demand. The company also expanded into global markets.

The bottom line is improved by controlling costs—lowering cost production facilities at Nagpur plant, shifting production to satellite plants/skid plants geared to meet regional requirements, implementing supply chain management techniques for significant reduction in pipeline stocks, reengineering working capital costs by reducing dealer stocks, adoption of lean manufacturing techniques, etc.

FIGURE 3.12 M&M—Growth in Total Income (₹ million)

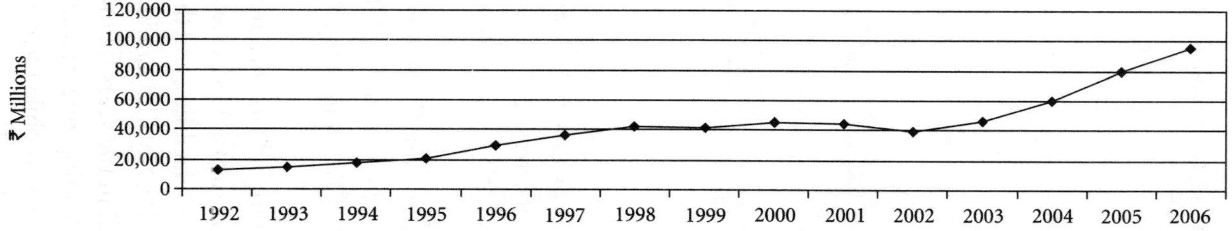

	Mar-92	Mar-93	Mar-94	Mar-95	Mar-96	Mar-97	Mar-98	Mar-99	Mar-00	Mar-01	Mar-02	Mar-03	Mar-04	Mar-05	Mar-06
Total Income	12.410	15,070	17,290	20,790	29,460	36,370	41,880	41,360	45,320	44,260	39,650	45,860	60,300	80,010	95,700

Year

Total Income

Source Author.

FIGURE 3.13   M&M—Growth in Total Income (Percentage)

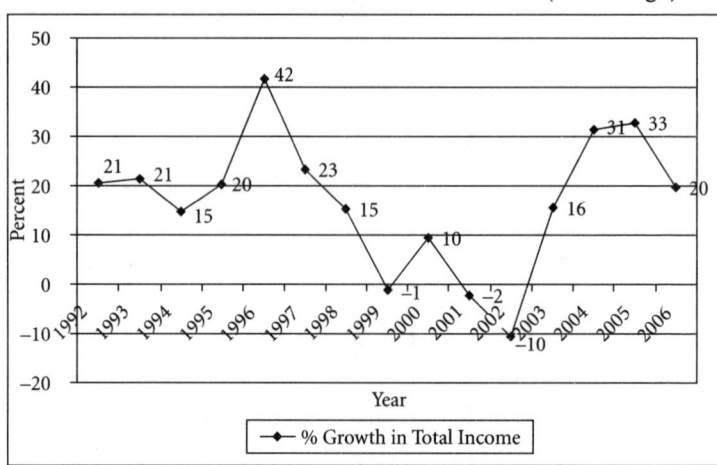

Source   Author.

Apollo Tyres

In 1991, Apollo Tyres[6] undertook exports of LCV and farm tyres in addition to truck tyres. *In 1994, it emerged as the largest exporter of tyres.* It focused on developing markets like Africa, Vietnam, and South America.

Apollo Tyres's total income grew from ₹ 3,800 million in 1992 to ₹ 31,030 million in 2006. While its PAT went through ups and downs to go from ₹ 330 million in 1992 to ₹ 780 million in 2006. (See Figures 3.15–3.17.)

The ₹ 85,000 million Indian tyre industry has attracted substantial foreign interest. Global majors such as Bridgestone and Michelin have invested in Indian production facilities, and the imports from Korean tyre companies are on a rise. Notwithstanding, Apollo Tyres has performed considerably well in the years following 1991.

Apollo Tyres is one of the leading tyre manufacturing companies in India, manufacturing automobile tyres, tubes, and flaps and is well entrenched in the truck and bus tyre replacement that comprises the bulk of the market. **Apollo Tyres is the market leader in the replacement tyre market for heavy vehicle and car**

FIGURE 3.14 M&M—PAT

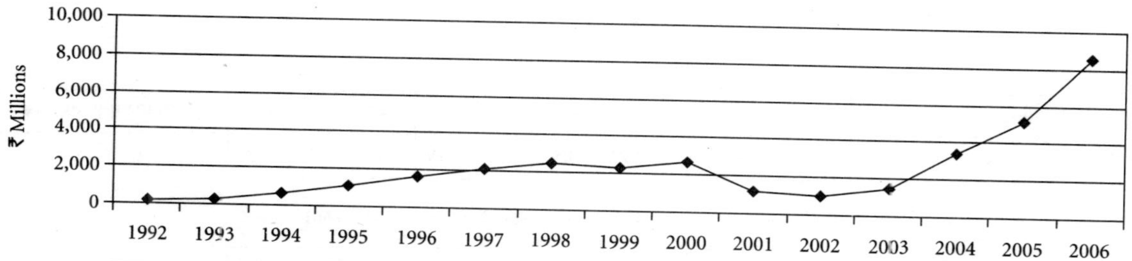

	Mar-1992	Mar-1993	Mar-1994	Mar-1995	Mar-1996	Mar-1997	Mar-1998	Mar-1999	Mar-2000	Mar-2001	Mar-2002	Mar-2003	Mar-2004	Mar-2005	Mar-2006
PAT	187	239	679	1,140	1,620	2,090	2,510	2,260	2,630	1,210	969	1,460	3,410	5,130	8,570

Year

PAT

Source Author.

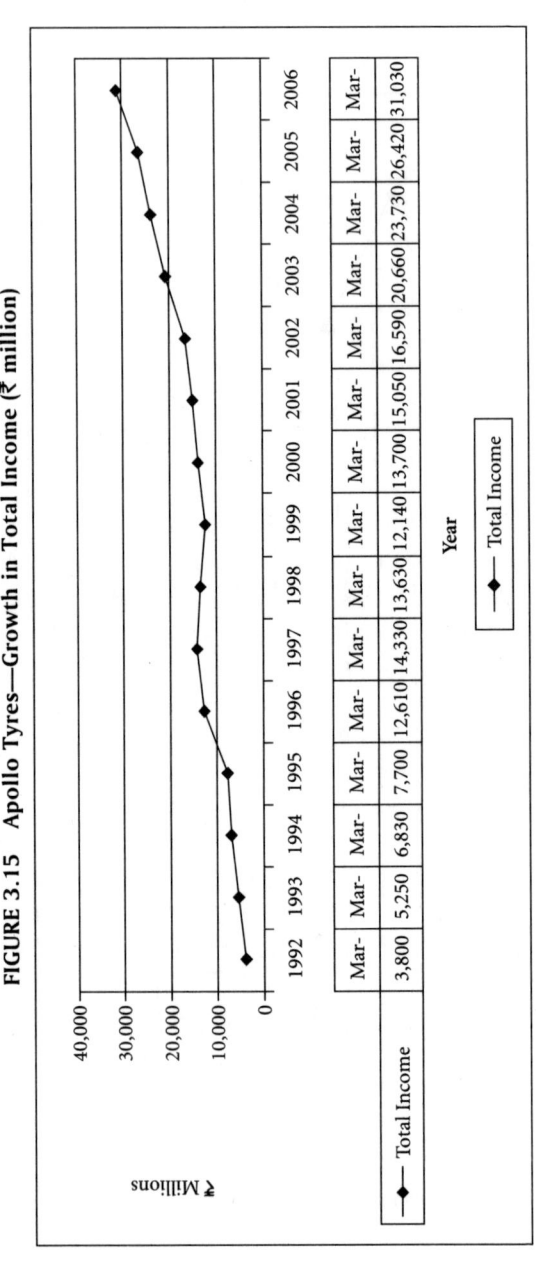

FIGURE 3.15 Apollo Tyres—Growth in Total Income (₹ million)

Source Author.

FIGURE 3.16 Apollo Tyres—Growth in Total Income (Percentage)

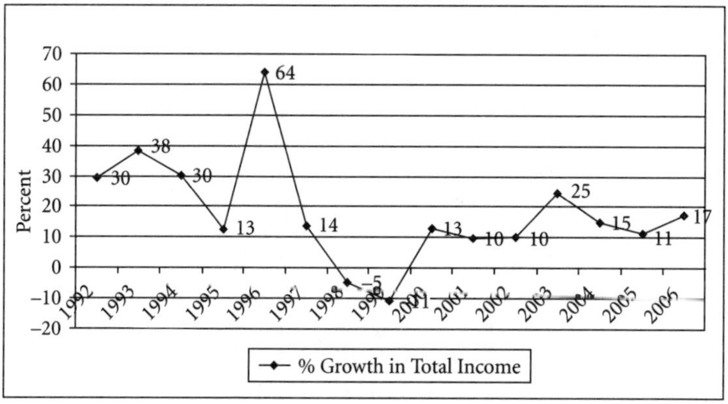

[Chart showing % Growth in Total Income from 1992 to 2006: 30, 38, 30, 13, 64, 14, 13, -5, 10, 10, 25, 15, 11, 17]

Source   Author.

radial segments. Truck and Bus tyres account for 75 percent of the revenues. As the Original Equipment Manufacturer (OEM) market is margin sensitive, the focus is on the lucrative replacement market, especially in the heavy vehicles segment. The size of the truck tyre replacement market is about 0.4 million tyres per month and the company has a 25 percent market share.

The company faces competition from JK, MRF Tyres, Ceat, Goodyear, Dunlop, Bridgestone, etc., and overall it is the fourth-largest player in India. The company has a tie-up with Kotak Mahindra Finance that facilitates sales by providing finance for tyre purchases. The company also has a tie-up with Castrol India that enables the dealers to stock Castrol lubes and improve their earnings.

In 1994, a new plant in Pune was commissioned. The company entered into an agreement with Continental AG, Germany, for setting up a passenger car radial tyre factory. It is the single-largest tube and flaps manufacturing unit and started production in 1996. The entire production was for captive consumption and the outsourcing of tubes came down considerably.

In 1998, a plant to manufacture radials was set up in Vadodara. Premier Tyres, its subsidiary, set up another radials plant at Ropar in Punjab to cater to the tractor and earthmovers segments.

FIGURE 3.17 Apollo Tyres—PAT

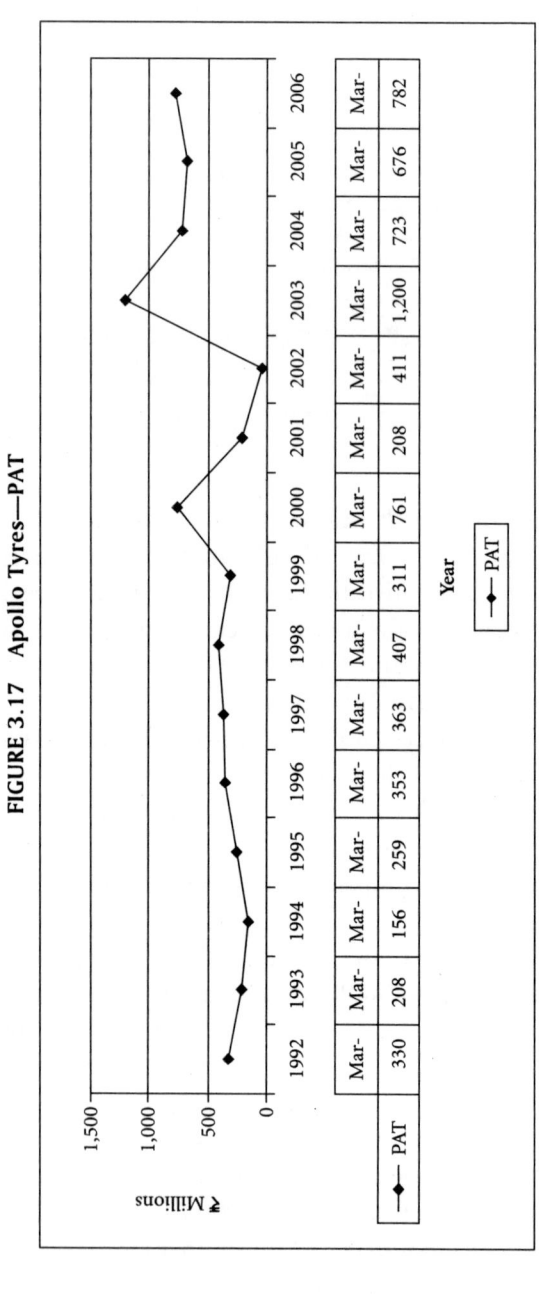

Source Author.

In 2003, Apollo Tyres formed a strategic alliance with Michelin, leader in the global tyre industry. The joint venture, Michelin Apollo Tyres was set up to produce bus and truck radial tyres. This alliance marked the end of the earlier technical collaboration of the company with Continental AG.

There are several interesting facts worth noting on the company:

- It is the first tyre company in the country to get ISO 9001 certification in the year 1997.
- It is consistently rated as "Excellent" in quality audit by the collaborator M/s Continental AG.
- It is ranked 18th in the world tyre industry in terms of sales.
- It is the second-largest company with 15 percent market share operating in the truck and bus segment that accounts for 75 percent of its revenues.
- Overall, it is the fourth-largest tyre player in India after companies like JK, MRF, and Ceat.

Sundaram Fasteners

SFL has been focusing on new markets and customers for its growth in exports while stepping up supplies to its existing customers. The company has been making supplies to Daimler Benz, AG, Germany (through Kamax); Cummins Engine Company Inc., USA; and General Motors Corporation, USA, that contributed to its growth and profits.

Auto giants identify countries to buy a particular component, depending upon the technology and the cost. Quality is an important factor in exports, but not the only criterion; what is important is timely delivery and after-sales service. Though there is a big potential to export fasteners to OEMs abroad, it has not been exploited due to difficulties in setting up service points near each of the OEM manufacturers. Hence, the domestic manufacturers foray abroad is limited to the replacement market.

What is required is a foreign tie-up for marketing and after-sales service. This is evident from the fact that a market leader like SFL has a tie-up with Kamax-Werke Rudolf Kellermann, Germany, for it marketing. SFL, whose production line includes humble items like radiator caps, nuts, and bolts, has acquired Dana Spicer, Europe, the British arm of a global MNC.

Exports of auto components have shot up. The right price quality equation is driving the growth of exports. Auto majors are beginning to discover India as a manufacturing base. The Indian Auto Ancillary Industry exported components worth $ 1 billion in the last fiscal 2004 with major contributions from Bharat Forge and SFL. The exports from the industry is expected to touch $ 10 billion by the year 2010.

Exide Industries

Exide Industries Limited[7] is the largest battery exporter from India (Figure 3.18). Batteries manufactured by Exide are exported across the world to countries like Armenia, Australia, Bahrain, Bangladesh, Belgium, China, Chile, Columbia, Cyprus, Ethiopia, France, Germany, Greece, Ivory Coast, Italy, Kenya, Kuwait, Lebanon, Mauritius, Myanmar, the Netherlands, Oman, Paraguay, Peru, Qatar, Russia, Rwanda, Saudi Arabia, Sierra Leone, Singapore, South Africa, Spain, Sri Lanka, the UAE, the UK, Uruguay, Vietnam, Yemen, Zambia, and Zimbabwe.

India signing of free-trade agreement with Thailand raised the specter of a fresh flood of imports of batteries. This is particularly so as the duty on import of lead in Thailand is much lower than in India, which in turn creates an in-built competitive advantage for producers in that country vis-à-vis domestic industry.

However, India's free-trade agreement with Sri Lanka holds the promise of a counter balance for Exide Industries, in view of its acquisition of a significant shareholding in Associated Battery Manufacturers (Ceylon) Limited in an earlier year. Closer

FIGURE 3.18 Exide—Export Turnover

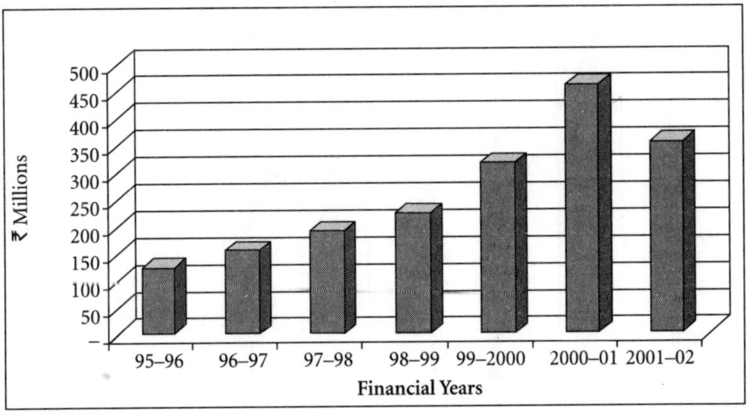

Source Author.

cooperation with this company would result in a mutually beneficial relationship, especially as Sri Lanka enjoys the same duty benefits as are available to producers in Thailand.

Exide Industries's total income grew from ₹ 2,470 million in 1992 to ₹ 17,920 million in 2006. While its PAT went through ups and downs to go from ₹ 140 million in 1992 to ₹ 1,010 million in 2006. (See Figures 3.19–3.21)

The storage battery industry in India is worth ₹ 21,000 million in 2003. The storage battery industry in India constitutes two major segments—industrial and automotive (Table 3.1). Storage batteries are basically used as secondary source of power in four-wheeler vehicles and industrial applications such as telecommunications network and uninterrupted power supply in computer networks and railways. The demand for automotive batteries is dependent on the auto-mobile growth, i.e., OEMs and the replacement market growth. Growth in the industrial batteries segment is driven by infrastructure and technology-related industries.

Exide Industries Limited, India's flagship of the storage battery industry, is also the largest Power Storage Solutions Company in South and Southeast Asia. It manufactures the widest range of storage batteries in the world from 2.5 Ah to 20,000 Ah capacity,

FIGURE 3.19 Exide Industries—Growth in Total Income (₹ million)

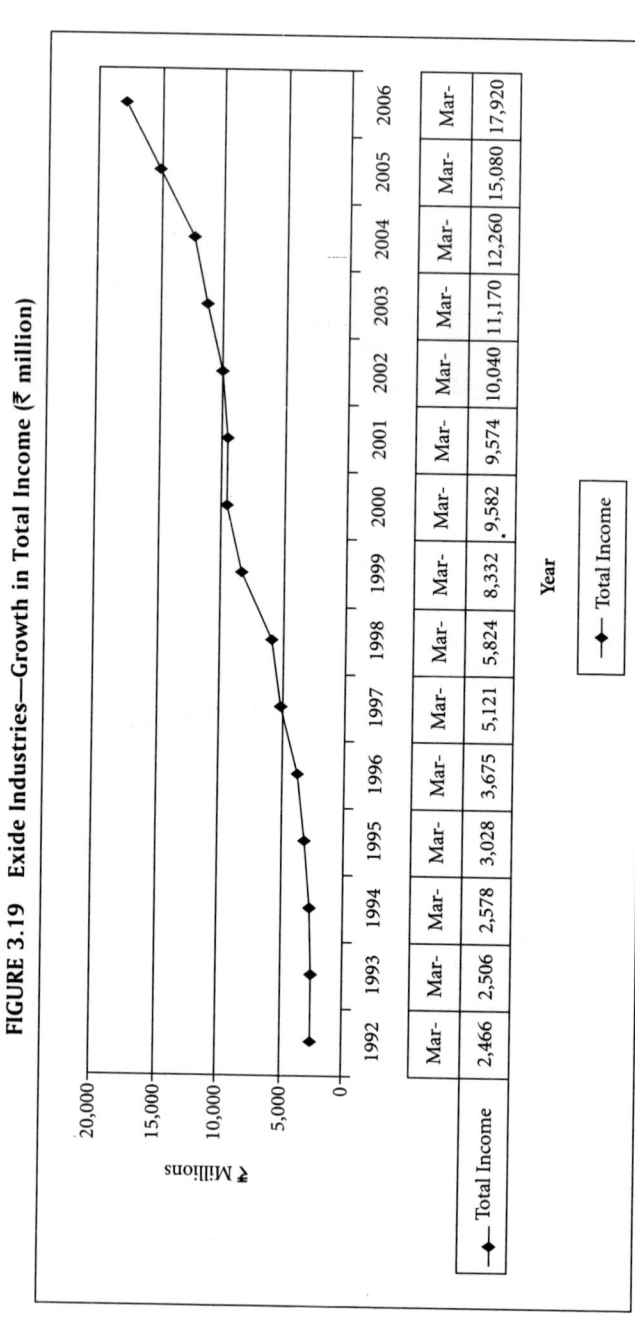

	Mar-1992	Mar-1993	Mar-1994	Mar-1995	Mar-1996	Mar-1997	Mar-1998	Mar-1999	Mar-2000	Mar-2001	Mar-2002	Mar-2003	Mar-2004	Mar-2005	Mar-2006
Total Income	2,466	2,506	2,578	3,028	3,675	5,121	5,824	8,332	9,582	9,574	10,040	11,170	12,260	15,080	17,920

Source: Author.

FIGURE 3.20   Exide Industries—Growth in Total Income (Percentage)

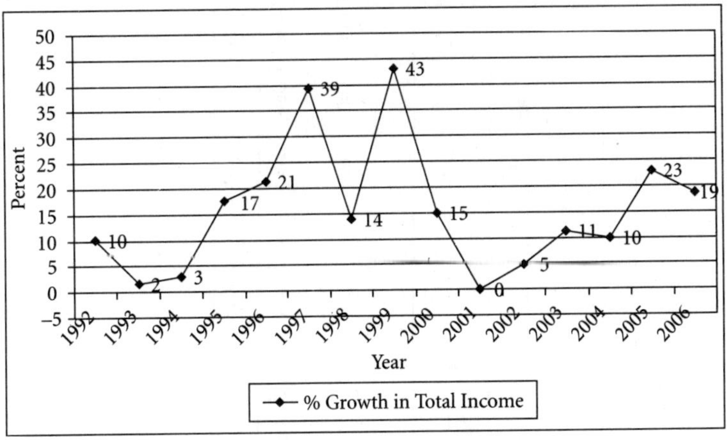

Source   Author.

to cover the broadest spectrum of applications. Table 3.2 gives the market share of its two divisions.

(I) Automotive Industry: The company is the market leader in this segment with a market share of more than 80 percent. Actual production of automotive batteries for four wheelers increased from 3.5 million to 3.9 million units, whereas for two-wheeler batteries the increase was from 3.5 million units to 4 million units. Standard Furukawa, a brand owned by the company, has unveiled the Sonic range of maintenance-free automotive batteries based on the hybrid alloy plate technology. In a strategic move, Exide Industries had acquired the industrial undertakings of Standard Batteries Ltd of the B.M. Khaitan-controlled Williamson Magor Group along with the Standard Furukawa brand for ₹ 1,000 million. Table 3.3 gives Exide's milestones in automotives.

This sector has the two following sub segments:

Original Equipment Segment: In the automotive sector, vehicle production continued to grow in almost all segments with even the tractor segment exceeding the earlier year's level for the first time.

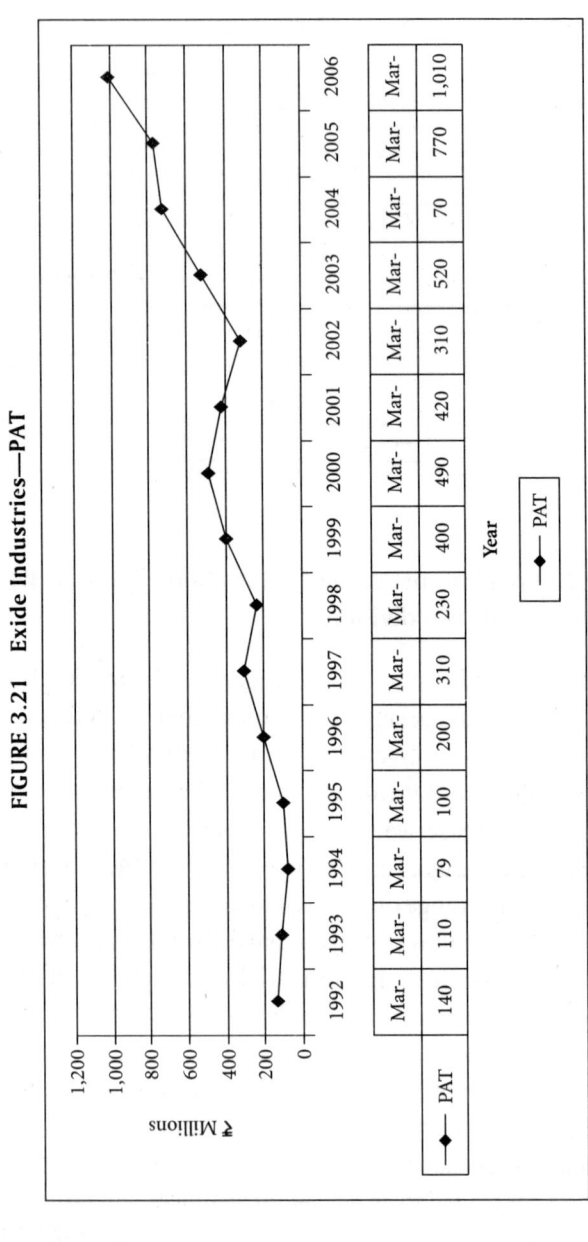

FIGURE 3.21 Exide Industries—PAT

Source: Author.

TABLE 3.1 Turnover of the Different Segments of the Battery Industry

Markets	Segments	Turnover 2003 (₹ Million)
Industrial		**8,600**
	Industrial batteries (Telecom, Railways, Power, UPS)	3,600
	Valve Regulated Lead Acid (VRLA—maintenance free and based on advanced technology)	5,000
Automotive		**12,400**
	OEM	8,000
	Replacement batteries of tractor and commercial vehicles (60–65 percent is dominated by unorganized small scale assemblers.	4,400

Source Author (based on company's website).

TABLE 3.2 Exide—Market Share

Division	Products
Auto battery division	35 percent market share in overall domestic auto battery market; 85 percent market share in automotive OEM
Industrial battery division	50 percent market share in industrial battery market

Source Author (based on business research and company's website).

TABLE 3.3 Milestones in Automotives

1974	First introduced PP batteries
1983	First on Maruti (with the arrival of Japanese cars)
1985–90	First on every single new vehicle launched Mitsubishi Swaraj Mazda, DCM, Toyota, Nissan
1990–98	First on Daewoo Motors, Gm, Hyundai, Telco, Esteem, Zen, Honda, Mercedes Benz
1999	First on Fiat Siena, Accent (Hyundai), Baleno, Wagon R (Maruti), HM Mitsubishi
2001	First on Fiat Palio, Mahindra Scorpio, Versa (Maruti), Hyundai (Sonata)
2002	First on Palio (Fiat), Mitsubishi-Pajero Indigo (TELCO)

Source Author (based on company's website).

A number of new vehicles were introduced where the company's batteries were the preferred choice. "EXIDE" and "SF (Standard Furukawa)," the flagship brands of the company, are also the leading battery brands in the country. The significant feature of this year was India becoming a global hub for small cars, with Hyundai, Maruti, Ford, and Toyota showing their marked preference for the country. This will have long-range implications for the company's products. The two largest motorcycle manufacturers, Hero Honda and Bajaj Auto have both placed the bulk of their business with the company.

Replacement Segment: The replacement segment or the retail market as it is now called revealed another year of buoyant growth for both the Exide and the Standard Furukawa Sonic brands. The significant feature of the year was the continued inroads that the company made in the tractor battery retail market under Project Kisan, where sales during the year crossed the coveted 100,000 units mark. Steady progress was also maintained in the planned penetration of the commercial vehicle market. The two-wheeler battery market continued its year on year growth with sales increasing by over 25 percent. The company has introduced the Batmobile service, by which the consumer can get information and testing of Exide's products at his doorstep. Over 180,000 calls have been attended at an average response time of 28 minutes. The company has also undertaken an extensive exercise in building up a database of its end consumers and these have been used in both loyalty and customer attention programs that are part of the Customer Relationship Management (CRM).

(II) Industrial Sector: Exide is a dominant player in the Industrial Battery segment, with a product range covering capacities from 2.5 Ah to 10,000 Ah and more. The production of batteries for industrial applications touched 600 million Ah. The market for batteries for industrial applications included high-growth areas

for the fast moving range, primarily used in UPS and in digital inverters. The power sector presents new growth avenues, particularly in the fight of the newly introduced and revamped electricity legislation. With the Indian Railways, the company targeted high-tech and high-end products and left the commodity market to the smaller players. With telecom industry, the company continued to maintain its focus while in the mining industry, cap lamp batteries have continued to maintain a steady growth.

Hindalco

In February 2007, Hindalco[8] acquired Novelis, the world's leading producer of aluminum-rolled products for an all-cash transaction worth $ 5.95 billion. Novelis operates through 36 manufacturing locations in 11 countries and has around 12,500 employees. The combination will establish a global integrated aluminum producer with low-cost alumina and aluminum production facilities combined with high-end aluminum-rolled products capabilities.

Hindalco's total income grew from ₹ 9,010 million in 1992 to ₹ 137,590 million in 2006. While its PAT went through ups and downs to go from ₹ 880 million in 1992 to ₹ 16,560 million in 2006 (See Table 3.22 to 3.24). Hindlaco is a flagship company of the Aditya Birla Group. It is structured into two strategic businesses—aluminum and copper—and is an industry leader in both the segments. A nonferrous metals power-house, close to global scale, the company's integrated operations and operating efficiency have positioned Hindalco as India's largest integrated player in aluminum.

Tinplate

Tinplate is today the largest indigenous producer of tin-coated and tin-free steel sheets in India, enjoying 35–40 percent market share and undoubtedly the industry leader for 85 years. The company exports about 20–25 percent of its production directly to end-users

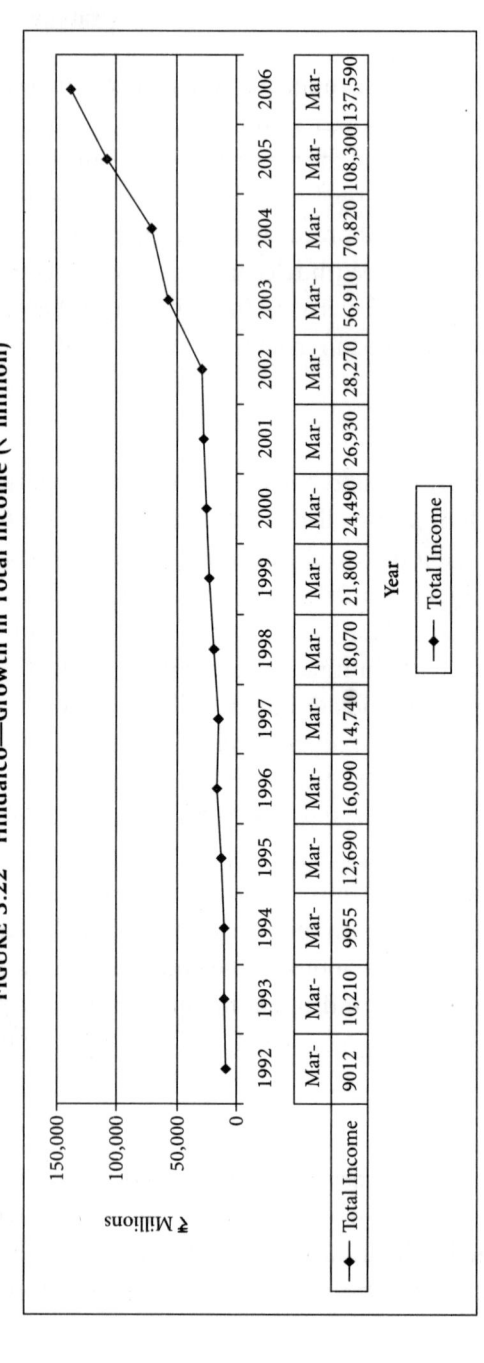

FIGURE 3.22 Hindalco—Growth in Total Income (₹ million)

Source Author.

FIGURE 3.23 Hindalco—Growth in Total Income (Percentage)

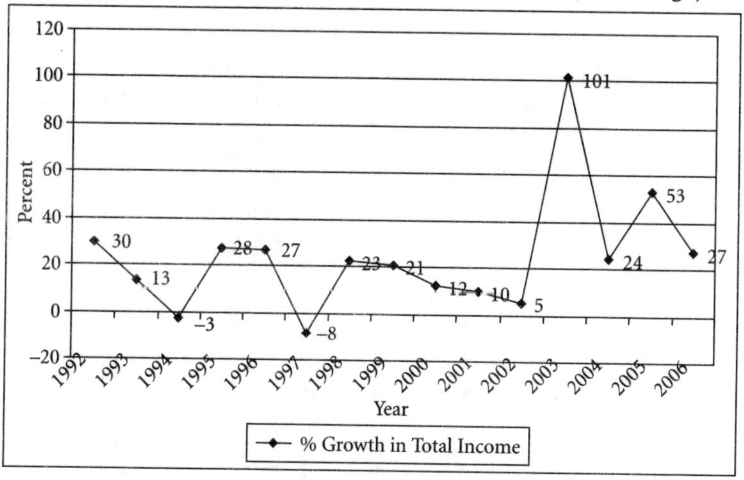

Source Author.

(can-makers) and its products are well accepted in the markets of Southeast Asia, the Middle East, and some developed countries in Europe.

Gammon India

Gammon India Ltd (GIL) has been in the business for nearly eight decades, has created a niche for itself in the civil construction business, and has executed prestigious and renowned projects in the country.

It is primarily engaged in contract execution of infrastructure and civil engineering projects. The company undertakes contracts for designing and construction of concrete bridges, cooling towers, chimneys, power stations, aqueducts, dams, wires, silos, tunnels, industrial and marine structures, including harbors and container freight stations, and general civil engineering works (Table 3.4).

GIL can stake claim for the largest numbers of bridges and flyovers built in India. Some of the major orders executed by GIL include Vidya Sagar Setu, Kolkata (the longest cable-stayed bridge); Gandhi Setu, Patna (the longest river bridge); Sharjah Airport; Alamatti Dam,

FIGURE 3.24 Hindalco—PAT

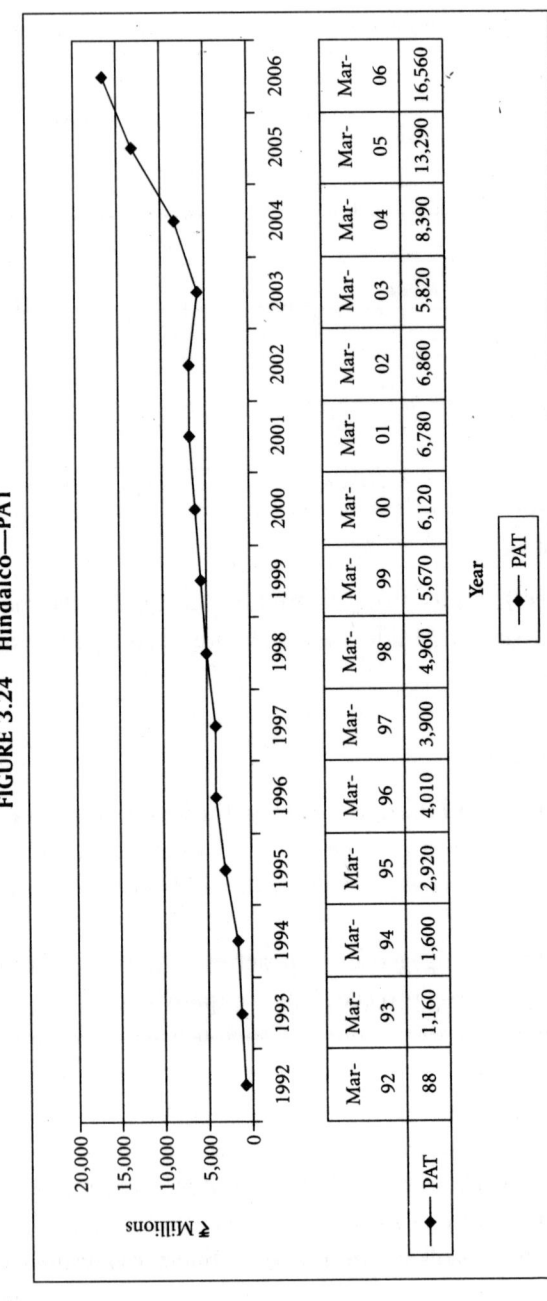

	Mar-92	Mar-93	Mar-94	Mar-95	Mar-96	Mar-97	Mar-98	Mar-99	Mar-00	Mar-01	Mar-02	Mar-03	Mar-04	Mar-05	Mar-06
PAT	88	1,160	1,600	2,920	4,010	3,900	4,960	5,670	6,120	6,780	6,860	5,820	8,390	13,290	16,560

Source Author.

TABLE 3.4 Hindalco—Product Offerings and Competition

Product division	Product offerings	Competition
Primary metals	Aluminum ingots	NALCO
	Aluminum cast slab	BALCO
	Aluminum billet	
	Aluminum alloy wire rod	
Rolled products	Aluminum hot rolled coil	BALCO
	Aluminum plain coil	Pennar Aluminium
	Aluminum stucco embossed coil	Annapurna Foils
	Aluminum paneling sheet	
	Aluminum hot rolled plate	
	Aluminum circle	
Extrusions	Motor body products	MALCO
	Heat sink	BALCO
	Windows section products	Sangam Aluminium
		Century Extrusions
		Sudal Industries
Aluminum Alloy Wheels	Aluminum alloy wheels	
Copper	Copper	Hindustan Copper Ltd

Source Author.

Karnataka; Karbude Konkan Tunnel (the longest railway tunnel); and Kurichu Hydroelectric Project, Bhutan. The company has also been involved in a number of projects abroad, particularly in Nepal, the Middle East, Iraq, and Libya.

Demand for construction is closely linked to the level of economic activity and the impetus given by the government to the infrastructure sector, mainly roads. The general outlook for the construction industry is positive due to the importance given by the Government of India to the infrastructure sector. Construction activities are expected to increase manifold because of the vast potential India offers. The emphasis on large-sized contracts (for economies of scale), superior design specifications, insistence on higher levels of mechanization, increased emphasis on quality works, and an awareness for preventing time and cost overruns will ensure the successful execution of projects. This augurs well for the future of the construction industry and should translate into a higher order book for GIL. Gammon is well positioned to tap the upcoming opportunities in this segment and takes great pride in securing various projects, which are currently being implemented.

A joint study conducted by Construction World and National Institute of Construction Management and Research ranked the company as the number one company amongst India's fastest growing construction companies. Some of GIL's major competitors are Hindustan Construction Corporation, Larsen and Toubro ECC, UP Bridge Corporation, Skanska Cementation India Ltd, AFCONS, Simplex, IVRCL Infrastructure & Projects Ltd, and Nagarjuna Construction Ltd.

Gammon India's total income grew from ₹ 870 million in 1992 to ₹ 16,130 million in 2006. While its PAT went through ups and downs to go from ₹ 28 million in 1992 to ₹ 1,040 million in 2006. (See Figures 3.25–3.27.)

Larsen & Toubro

L&T has an international presence, with a global spread of offices. A thrust on international business over the last few years has seen

FIGURE 3.25 Gammon India—Growth in Total Income (₹ millions)

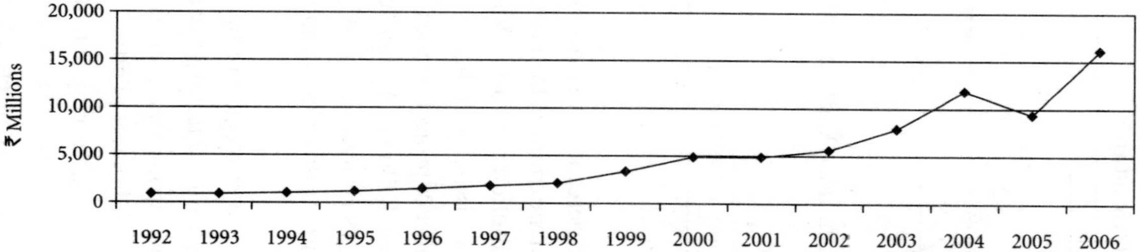

	Mar- 1992	Mar- 1993	Mar- 1994	Mar- 1995	Mar- 1996	Mar- 1997	Mar- 1998	Mar- 1999	Mar- 2000	Mar- 2001	Mar- 2002	Mar- 2003	Mar- 2004	Mar- 2005	Mar- 2006
Total Income	8,668	9,416	1,032	1,232	1,545	1,860	2,183	3,312	4,823	4,846	5,675	7,846	11,880	9,396	16,130

Year

Total Income

Source Author.

FIGURE 3.26 Gammon India—Growth in Total Income (Percentage)

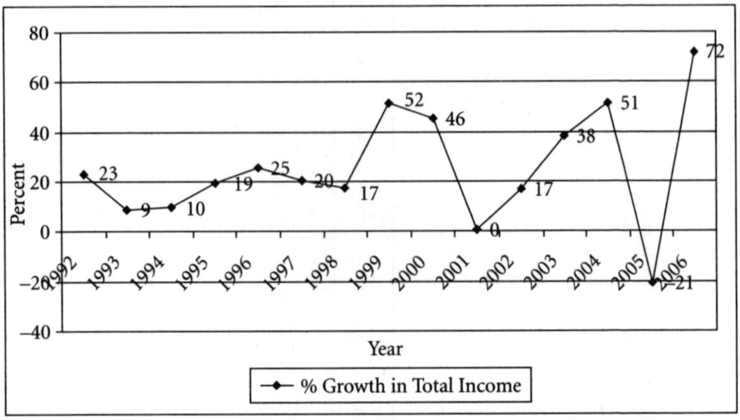

Source Author.

overseas earnings growing to 18 percent of total revenue. With factories and offices located around the country, further supplemented by a wide marketing and distribution network, L&T's image and equity extends to virtually every district of India.

The company bids for a number of projects in the UAE and other countries in the Middle East, Nepal, Bhutan, Bangladesh, Malaysia, Maldives, Sri Lanka, and the CIS countries. It had formed many joint venture companies in Saudi Arabia, Oman, and Malaysia for participating in many tenders.

The company has entered into strategic pre-bid tie-ups with global players possessing the best mix of technology and competitiveness helping it develop new capabilities in areas such as deep sea exploration, airports, ports, and power plants.

L&T had divested from non-engineering activities (cement, food and dairy equipment, tractor manufacturing, and glass). Going forward, the company intends to concentrate on higher end infrastructure building, core sector building, and higher technology manufacturing.

FIGURE 3.27 Gammon India—PAT

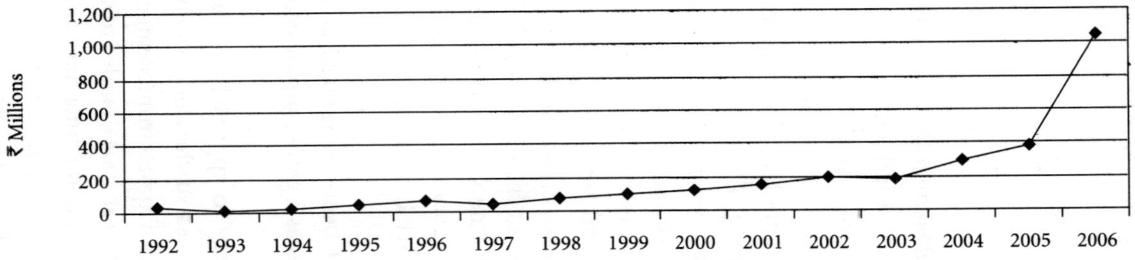

	Mar-1992	Mar-1993	Mar-1994	Mar-1995	Mar-1996	Mar-1997	Mar-1998	Mar-1999	Mar-2000	Mar-2001	Mar-2002	Mar-2003	Mar-2004	Mar-2005	Mar-2006
PAT	28	7	26	44	65	47	71	100	120	150	190	190	290	380	1,040

Source Author.

Larsen & Toubro's total income grew from ₹ 18,020 million in 1992 to ₹ 152,640 million in 2006. While its PAT went through ups and downs to go from ₹ 1,020 million in 1992 to ₹ 10,120 million in 2006. (See Figures 3.28–3.30.)

Siemens Ltd

Siemens Ltd is a subsidiary of Siemens AG, Germany, with a dominant presence in the field of electrical and electronics engineering. It is a leading provider of industry and infrastructure solutions in India. It operates in the core business segments of energy, industry and buildings, information technology, communication, transportation, health care, and lighting. The company has the capability to integrate diverse products, systems, and services into turnkey solutions across the life cycle of a project.

Today, India is no longer seen as an unreliable or low-tech producer by the outside world. This fact can be summarized through Siemen's own export performance. Their technological capabilities and experience have resulted in Siemens India being recognized as quality manufacturers. Siemen's export business has grown substantially with a number of successes, especially in the Middle East, Africa, Bangladesh, Sri Lanka, and other neighboring countries.

The company has in fact been recognized as a competence center in many areas and also as a global supply center for certain products.

The company has a strategy to approach the market through focused clusters and segments as a single window solution provider, helping it to get larger volumes. Exports from Siemens which was at ₹ 1,500 million in the financial year 2004 doubled to ₹ 3,000 million in the financial year 2005. India and China have been recognized by Siemens AG as a strategic pillar in the Asia Pacific Region. Siemens Ltd expects a lot of global scale activities being undertaken from India, with several units being recognized as Global centers of competence, especially in the areas of manufacturing, project management, and R&D.

FIGURE 3.28 Larsen & Toubro—Growth in Total Income (₹ million)

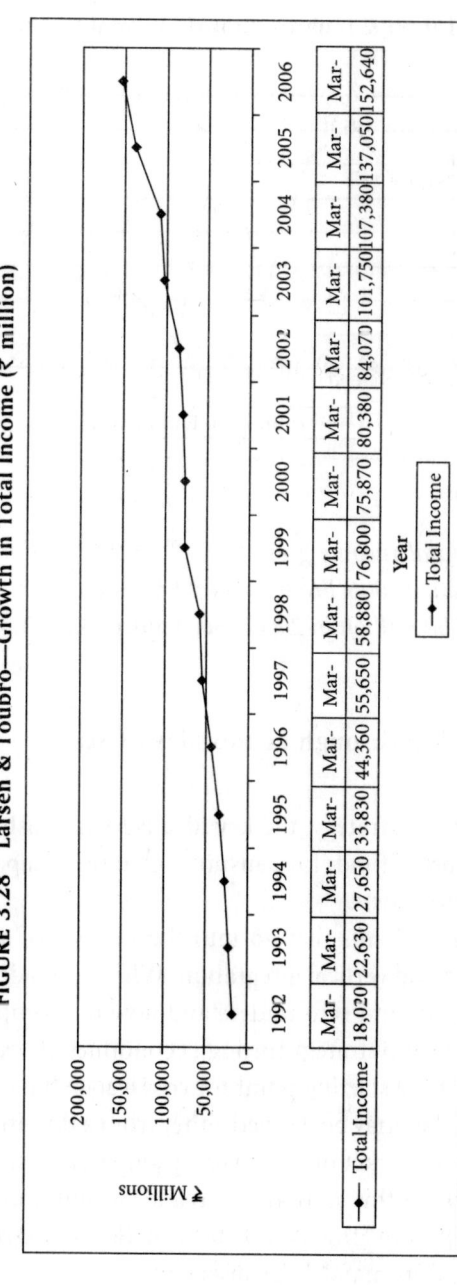

	Mar-1992	Mar-1993	Mar-1994	Mar-1995	Mar-1996	Mar-1997	Mar-1998	Mar-1999	Mar-2000	Mar-2001	Mar-2002	Mar-2003	Mar-2004	Mar-2005	Mar-2006
Total Income	18,020	22,630	27,650	33,830	44,360	55,650	58,880	76,800	75,870	80,380	84,073	101,750	107,380	137,050	152,640

Source Author.

FIGURE 3.29 Larsen & Toubro—Growth in Total Income (Percentage)

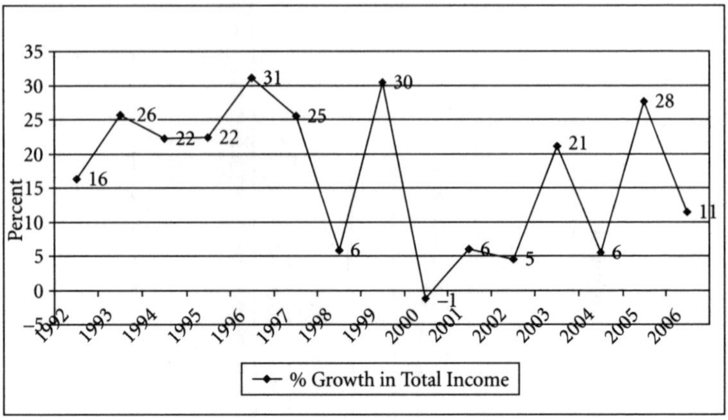

Source Author.

Siemens's total income grew from ₹ 16,950 million in 1992 to ₹ 31,770 million in 2006. From loss of ₹ 1,550 million in 1998, it made profits of ₹ 2,550 million in 2006. (See Figures 3.31–3.33)

Cost Leadership through Economies of Scale

In cost leadership strategy, the key idea is to establish world-class plants, keep cost of funds low, ensure high rates of capacity utilization, and control costs.

Two key ingredients that go into the making of a global cost leader are scale and vertical integration. What the reader can expect to read in this section is to understand how the companies leveraged cost leadership strategy through economies of scale. One may appreciate that the starting point for cost leadership is volumes of demand sales that may be derived either from a dominant position in the domestic market or by pursuing global sales along with the domestic sales. In this section, the reader would draw lessons on cost leadership from Hindalco, Tata Steel, Bombay Dyeing, Apollo Tyres, M&M, Coromandel Fertilisers, etc.

FIGURE 3.30 Larsen & Toubro—PAT

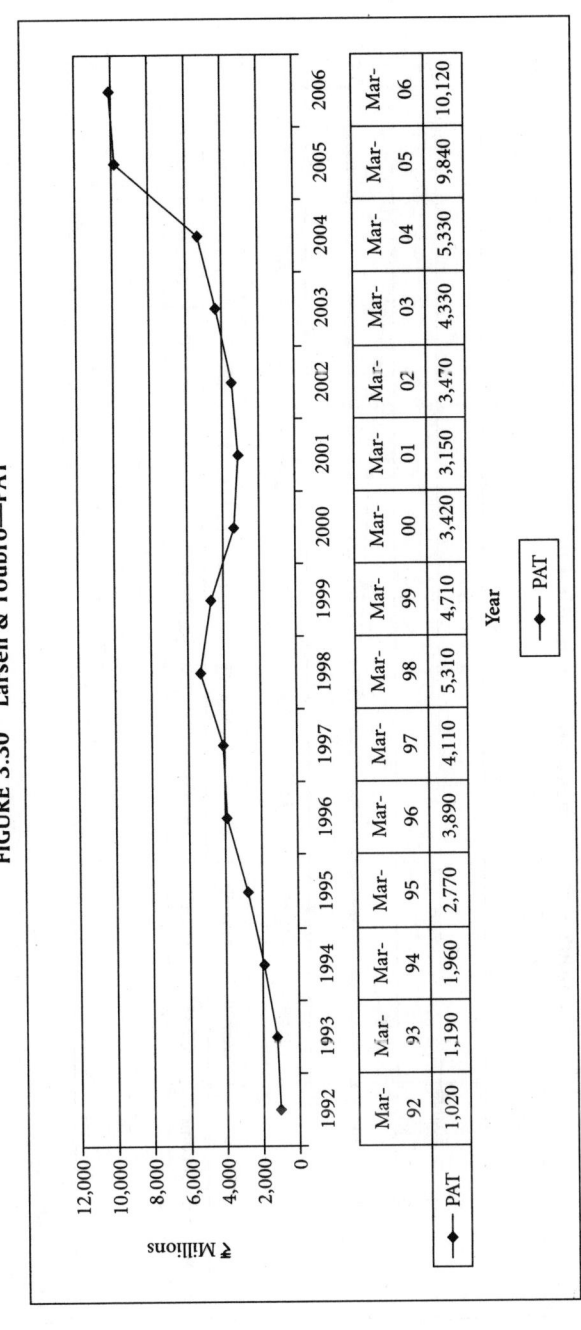

Source Author.

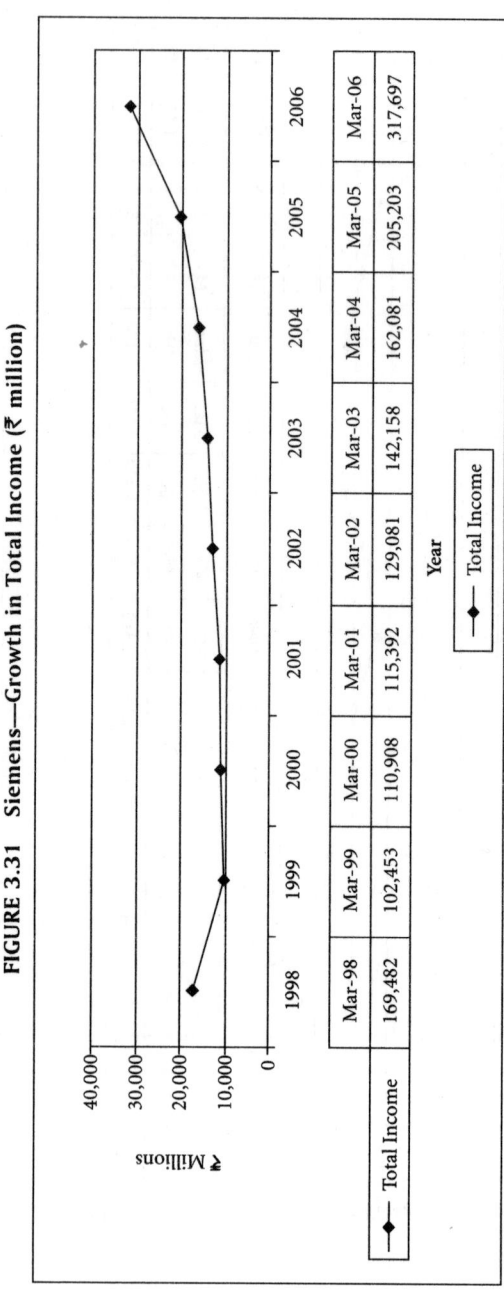

FIGURE 3.31 Siemens—Growth in Total Income (₹ million)

	Mar-98	Mar-99	Mar-00	Mar-01	Mar-02	Mar-03	Mar-04	Mar-05	Mar-06
	169,482	102,453	110,908	115,392	129,081	142,158	162,081	205,203	317,697

Source Author.

FIGURE 3.32 Siemens—Growth in Total Income (Percentage)

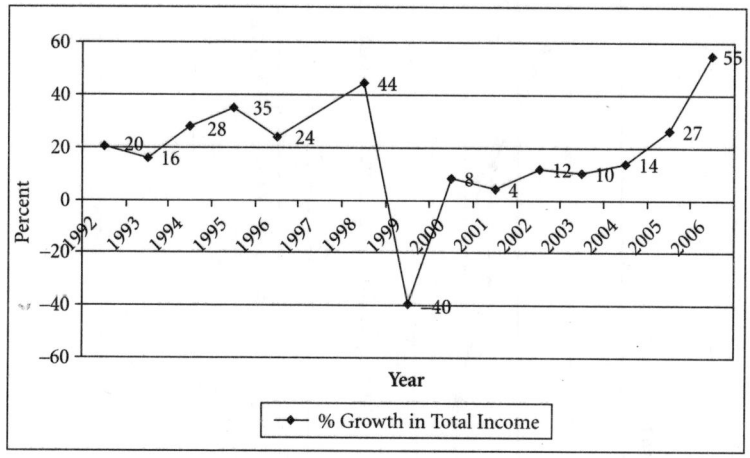

Source Author.

Hindalco

Hindalco is the largest integrated producer of aluminum in the country, with its own bauxite reserves and downstream production facilities. By controlling the two biggest cost factors like power and alumina through its own 500 MW power plant and captive mines, Hindalco had emerged as the lowest cost producer of aluminum in the world even though India accounts for only 3 percent of the world's output of aluminum. Hindalco's cost of manufacturing[9] *is only $ 1,033 per ton compared to Alcan's $ 1,250.*

Since 2000, Hindalco has been driven by rationalization and revitalization. The dominant theme had been consolidation. The logic underpinning consolidation is the push for market leadership, economies of scale, productivity gains, and operational efficiencies, converging to value creation growth. (See Figures 3.34 and 3.35.)

The acquisition of a 74.6 percent equity stake in Indal from Alcan, at an investment of a little over ₹ 10,000 million had been a milestone. Bringing Indal into the Group's fold has helped position the Hindalco–Indal combine in every link of the value chain from metals to downstream products accounting for over 70 percent market share.[10]

FIGURE 3.33 Siemens—PAT

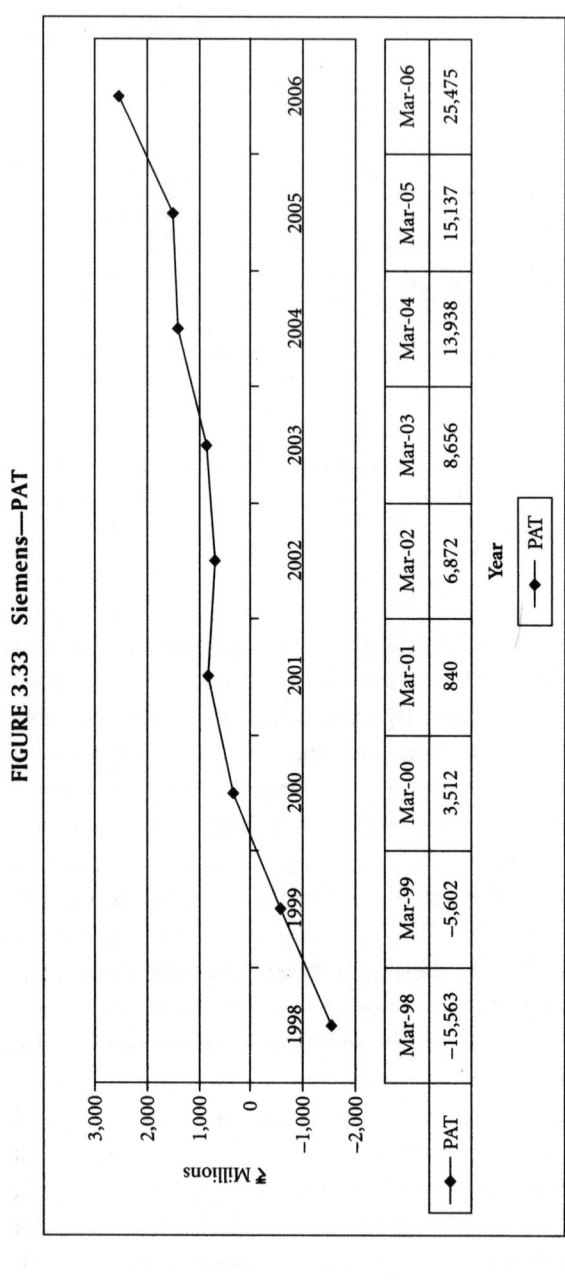

Mar-98	Mar-99	Mar-00	Mar-01	Mar-02	Mar-03	Mar-04	Mar-05	Mar-06
−15,563	−5,602	3,512	840	6,872	8,656	13,938	15,137	25,475

Source Author.

The strategy consideration has been to exit businesses where they are bit players and strengthen the businesses where they have clear competencies, so that they consolidate their position and get to the top of the league. Cells like Strategic cell, project monitoring cell, manufacturing cell through their systems orientation provided necessary help to gain market competitiveness.

Tata Steel

World Steel Dynamics (WSD)[11] identified 12 companies as world-class steelmakers and ranked them based on various factors like operating costs; ownership of low-cost ore and coal; favorable location for procuring raw materials; skilled and productive workforce; price paid for electricity; high quality and niche products; degree of "pricing power" with large steel buyers; dominant in region; balance sheet; borrowed funds and equity on a favorable basis; management is experienced, aggressive, and proactive; low legacy costs; ongoing cost cutting efforts; cost position of nearby competitors; owns downstream steel using businesses; domestic market growth rate; and proportion of domestic sales (Table 3.5 and Figures 3.36 and 3.37).

Jamshed J. Irani discusses the major initiatives undertaken at Tata Steel to respond to the challenge of transforming itself in the wake of India's liberalization measures in 1991and making it an internationally acclaimed company.[12] World Steel Dynamics declared Tata Steel as **number one among its selected 12 world-class steelmakers.** The list consisted of global companies like Nippon Steel, Posco, Usinor, and Nucor.

Tata Steel's achievement of becoming the lowest-cost producer of steel was mostly attributed to its implementation of Total Operational Performance (TOP), a program that focused on improving operational practices and rationalizing procurement costs. TOP was widely regarded, as a program, which would have a maximum positive impact to the bottom line, with minimum investment, required in minimum time. It aimed at achieving large

FIGURE 3.34 Hindalco—PBDIT/Total Income

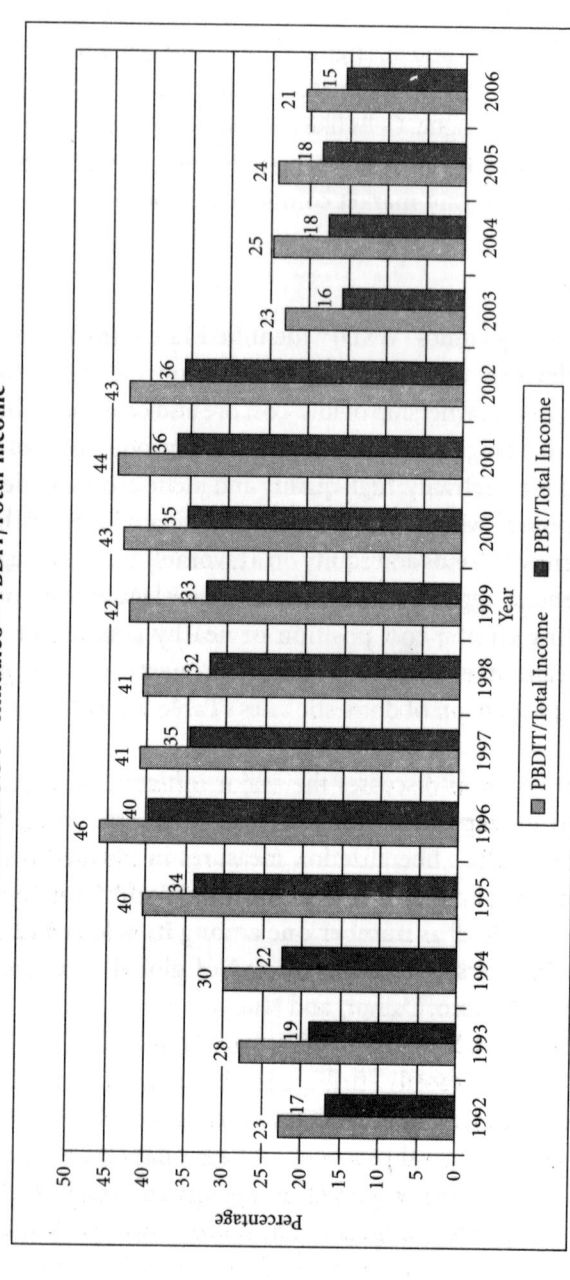

Source Author.

FIGURE 3.35 Hindalco—D/E Ratio

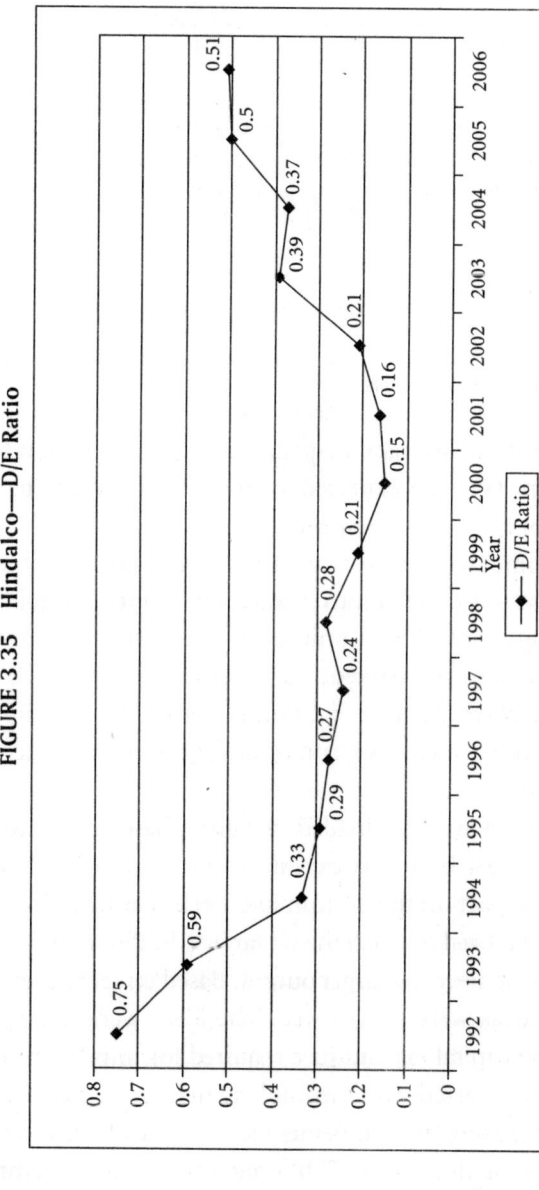

Source Author.

TABLE 3.5 World-class Steelmakers

Company	Ranking	Score
Tata Steel	1	131
Usinor (Russia)	2	129
Posco (Korea)	3	127
CSN (Brazil)	4	123
Baosteel (China)	5	121
China Steel (China)	6	119
Gerdau (Brazil)	7	118
Nucor (US)	8	116
Car-Tech	9	112
Nippon Steel (Japan)	10	111
Severstal (Russia)	10	111
Dofasco (US)	11	109

Source World Steel Dynamics.

improvements in throughput, quality, and cost in the short term. In the long run, TOP was expected to enable the company to achieve high rates of performance improvement.

As the company's scale of operations was quite large, the whole organization was divided into manageable "units" to facilitate the implementation of TOP. A unit team, comprising of a unit leader and two facilitators, worked full time for a period of 12 weeks known as a Wave. Around eight units were addressed simultaneously. The unit leader was responsible for the performance of that particular unit.

The entire Wave was divided into five phases. In Phase I, two weeks long, cost base was examined and the items that had a maximum impact on the bottom line were identified. In Phase II, ideas were explored to reach the set targets. In Phase III, ideas were generated to achieve the target output. Based on techno-economic feasibility, ideas were short-listed. The ideas were then grouped based on the capital expenditure required for implementing each idea. Phase IV started with the implementation of these ideas.

The Waves were first implemented in G blast furnace and then adopted to shop floors. The TOP program helped the company to shift its focus from just producing volumes to costs and quality. It also enabled the company to improve customer satisfaction and loyalty.

Bombay Dyeing

Bombay Dyeing is the largest producer of DMT in the country and has around 75 percent market share (Figures 3.38 and 3.39).[13]

Textile production involves spinning, weaving, dyeing, printing, and finishing. This makes textiles more capital intensive compared to garmenting that involves fewer steps with high level of labor. The focus at Bombay Dyeing is on producing large textiles that is capital intensive which is an effective entry barrier. Labor costs approximately 7 percent of the company's sales.

The company is well integrated from manufacturing to distribution that gives it self-sufficiency and greater control over its operations. The company has a first mover advantage having started operations way back in 1879. Customers still prefer Bombay Dyeing for sheeting and other homemaking sheeting. Even for school uniforms, it is one of the trusted names.

The scales are sufficiently large to attain critical mass. Similarly, its DMT division has a capacity of 165,000 tons a year while the international standard is between 150,000 and 250,000 tons for a single line. Bombay Dyeing's export strategy is to capitalize on the growing volume of sales to world markets by focusing on higher value-added products though most of the exports continue to be commodity products. Fortunately for Bombay Dyeing, it is the leader in the domestic market in home collections and furnishing products with no competitors threatening its well-established position.

The DMT division has been able to retain its edge despite the competitive disadvantage that DMT has against purified terepthalic acid (PTA). Bombay Dyeing's fully depreciated secondhand plant produces DMT at ₹ 20,000 per ton even as the cost of PTS is between ₹ 35,000 and 40,000 per ton. Bombay Dyeing has been able

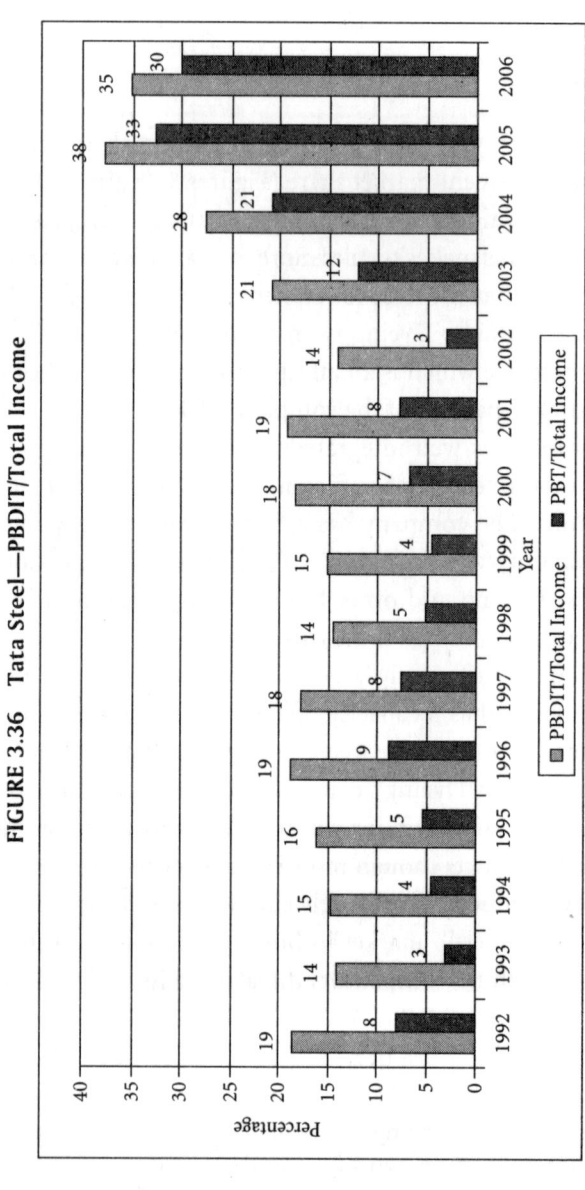

FIGURE 3.36 Tata Steel—PBDIT/Total Income

Source Author.

FIGURE 3.37 Tata Steel—D/E Ratio

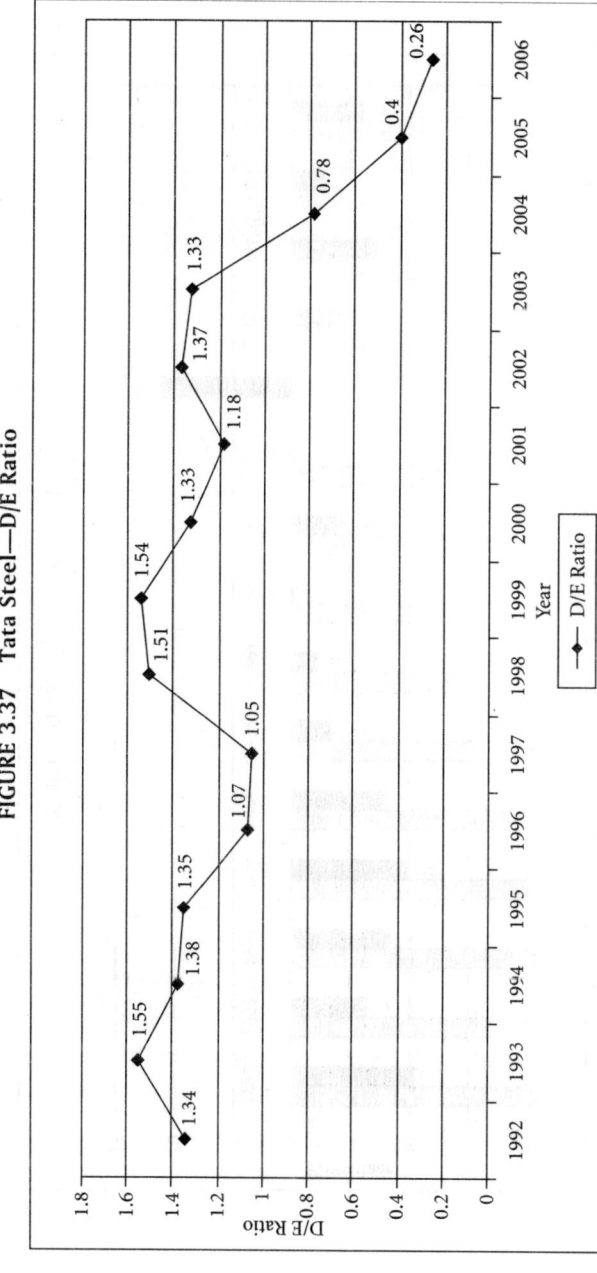

Source Author.

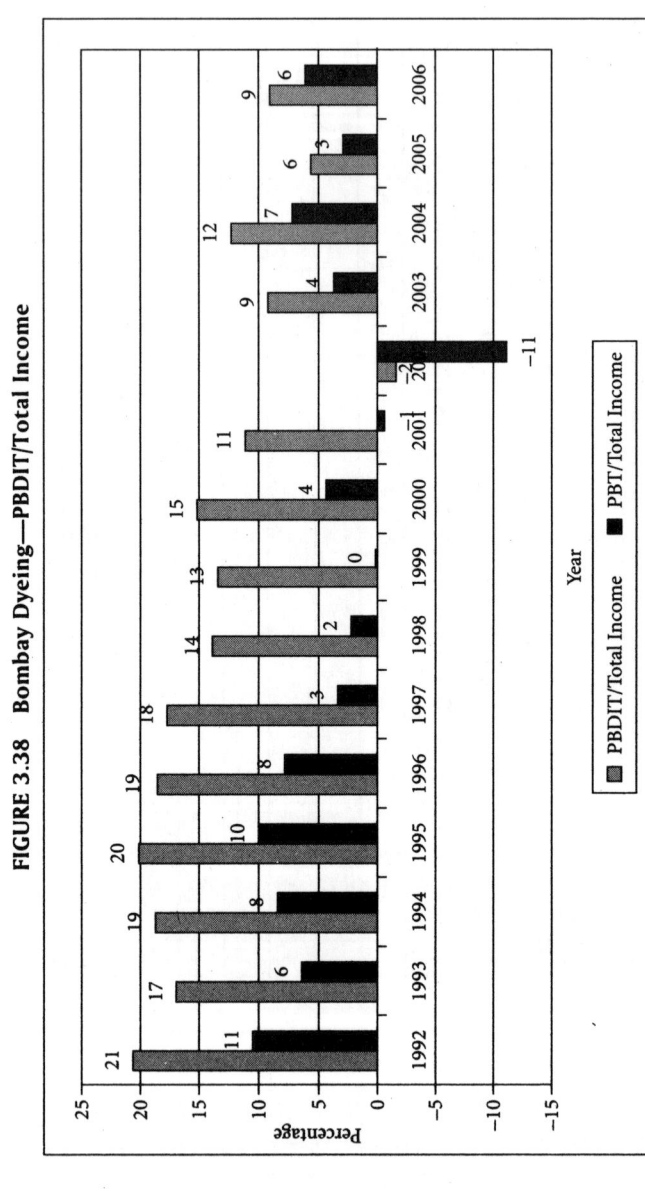

FIGURE 3.38 Bombay Dyeing—PBDIT/Total Income

Source Author.

FIGURE 3.39 Bombay Dyeing—D/E Ratio

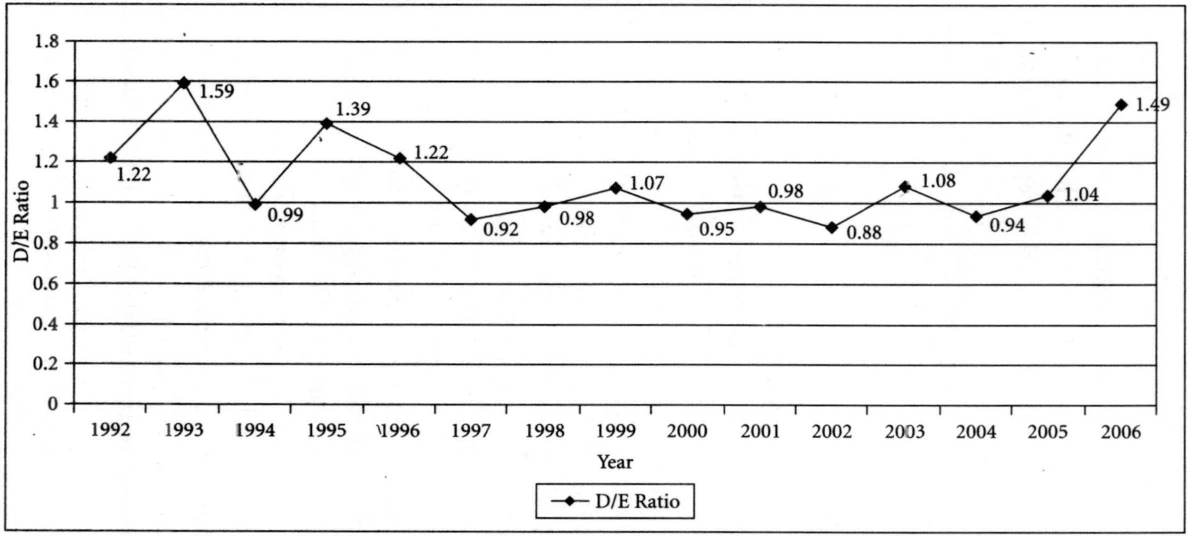

Source Author.

to cut costs by 25 percent in the past eight years by expanding and increasing efficiency. The capacity of DMT plant was increased from 60,000 tons to 160,000 tons by expansion and debottlenecking.

Two factors, however, prevent Bombay Dyeing from being a cost leader—sector and location. The share of the composite mills in the textiles business has been declining steadily. This apart, Bombay Dyeing's location in Mumbai, where the costs of fuel, power, water, and labor are high, explains the squeeze on its margins.

Apollo Tyres

One factor underpins Apollo's success and that is business focus. Apollo Tyres is the market leader in the replacement tyre market for heavy vehicle and car radial segments. As the OEM market is margin sensitive, the focus is on the lucrative replacement market, especially in the heavy vehicles segment. Apollo is a market leader in truck tyres and has the largest distribution network in the tyre industry. It has built its strengths in truck tyres, which accounts for 80 percent of the tyres sold in India.

The company faces competition from JK, MRF Tyres, Ceat, Goodyear, Bridgestone, etc. While other tyre companies like MRF, CEAT, and JK have built product ranges covering all tyre segments, from two-wheelers to eight-wheelers, Apollo chose to stick to the industry's staple product: heavy vehicle tyres. The logic was simple—heavy vehicle tyres account for 80 percent of the market in terms of value and do not require a large advertisement spending. And Apollo linked its fortunes to the replacement market which consumes a huge 75 percent of the country's tyre output. The size of truck tyre replacement market is about 0.4 million tyres per month and the company has a 25 percent market share. Clearly, Apollo's top priority was to shore up its bottom line, even if it meant staying away from the OEM segment.

Even as focus had helped Apollo target its financial and managerial resources better, the group responded swiftly to liberalization. *Between 1992 and 1997, Apollo's sales accelerated from ₹ 5,000 million to ₹ 14,140 million, with its profits increasing from ₹ 230 million to ₹ 420 million* (Figures 3.40 and 3.41). *Just what did Apollo do right?*[14] Realizing that domestic tyre manufacturers would face severe competition from imports as trade barriers came down, Apollo Tyres invested in large capacities to derive economies of scale. Volumes clearly provide economies of scale. It rolled out 2.7 million tyres per year, up from 1.120 million tyres in 1991–92. Equally important was Apollo's decision to move closer to the customer by servicing him directly instead of depending on the dealer.

In 2006, Apollo Tyres acquired a 100 percent stake in Dunlop Tyres for a consideration of $ 66 million.[15]

Three factors threaten to change Apollo's approach to business. First, radial technology is gradually gaining ground in the country. Second, the car tyre segment which is set to grow rapidly. Third, as automobile majors tie-up with tyre manufacturers, and as technology prolongs the life of a tyre, the replacement market that contributes 85 percent of Apollo's sales, is going to gradually diminish in importance. No longer can Apollo bank on improving operational efficiency levels alone. It needs to dwell more on strategic vision that will help the group make the choices that are going to be crucial to its competitiveness tomorrow.

Globally, economies of scale are the biggest entry barriers and there are just half a dozen majors in the business. That is not a hurdle in the Indian market, where capacities are low by global standards. The world's largest manufacturer, Groupe Michelin produces 24 million tyres annually; Apollo produces just 2.7 million tyres. By developing superior processes, Groupe Michelin managed to come up with cheaper and stronger tyres. In such a scenario, Apollo has to reinvent itself.

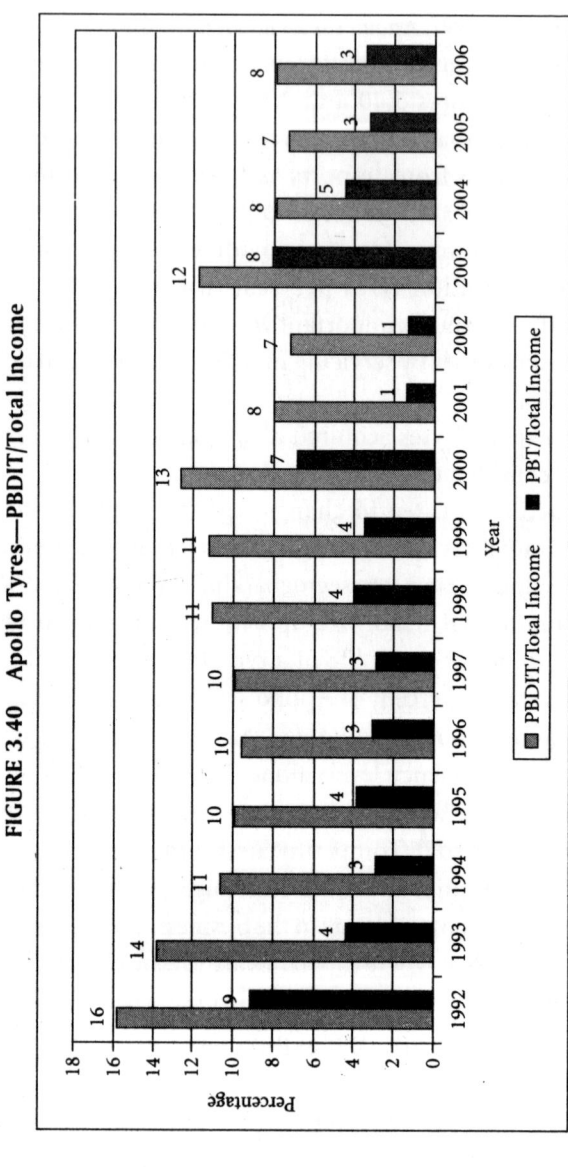

FIGURE 3.40 Apollo Tyres—PBDIT/Total Income

Source Author.

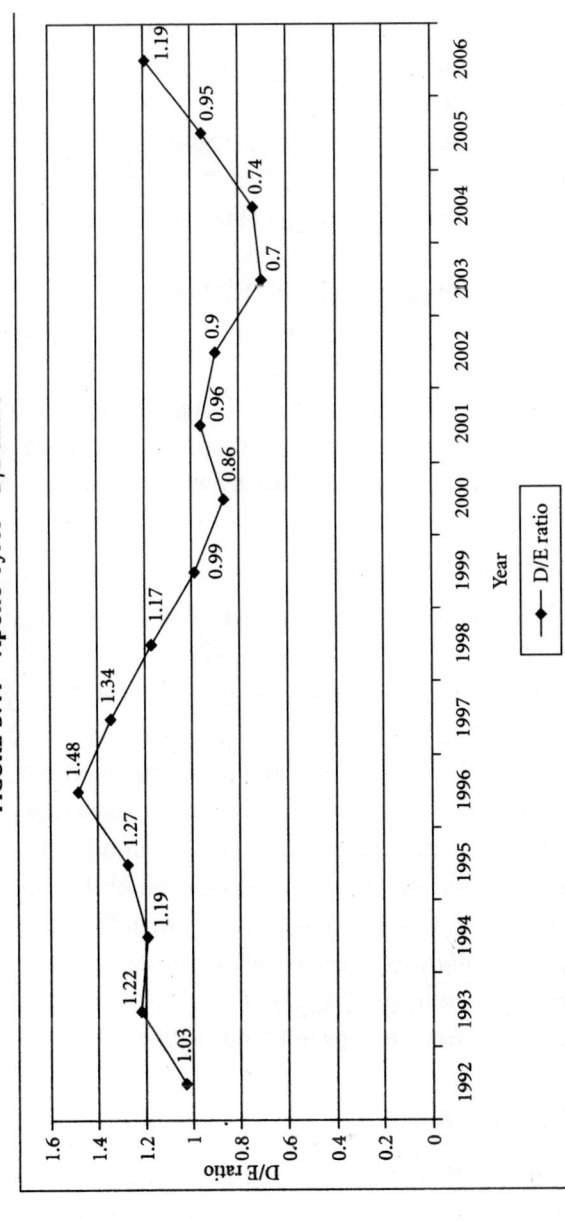

FIGURE 3.41 Apollo Tyres—D/E Ratio

Source Author.

Technology Alliances

O.S. Kanwar, CEO, says that "We try to understand the consumer's buying behavior and provide value. We sell on the strength of our product and consumers respect that."

Taking a leaf out of the books of the South Korean tyre majors, Kumho and Hankook, that simply shopped technology and adopted it, Apollo Tyres formed a strategic alliance in the year 2003 with Michelin,[16] leader in the global tyre industry. A passenger car radial tyre Technical Assistance Agreement has been signed with Michelin Research Asia B.V. in November 2003, enabling the company to have access to world-class technology.

The joint venture, Michelin Apollo Tyres was set up to produce bus and truck radial tyres. This alliance marked the end of the earlier technical collaboration of the company with Continental AG.

Mahindra & Mahindra (M&M)

M&M is a market leader with a market share of 26 percent in tractors and 53 percent in UVs. With the entry of Gypsy of Maruti, Trax of Bajaj Tempo, and Sumo of TELCO, the market share in UVs declined to 31 percent (Figure 3.42 and Figure 3.43). While other auto producers are dependent on the urban market, the M&M product had differentiated itself by pursuing a consumer base that is largely rural. It is least dependent on industrial turnaround as its products are largely sold in rural India. M&M has continuously increased the number of models to seven in its product portfolio.

Technology alliances: Develop what one can and acquire the rest has been the strategy of M&M. Tie-up with Peugeot for LUV and AVL for tractors are steps in that direction.

Coromandel Fertilisers

Coromandel Fertilisers (CFL) manufactures its own requirement of ammonia. To leverage the cost benefits of importing ammonia, it

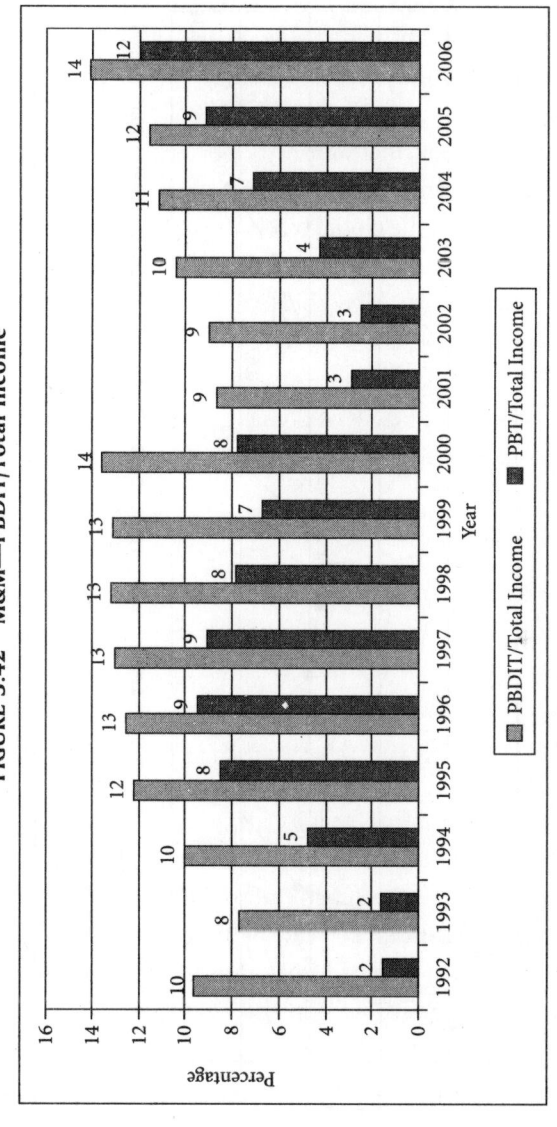

FIGURE 3.42 M&M—PBDIT/Total Income

Source Author.

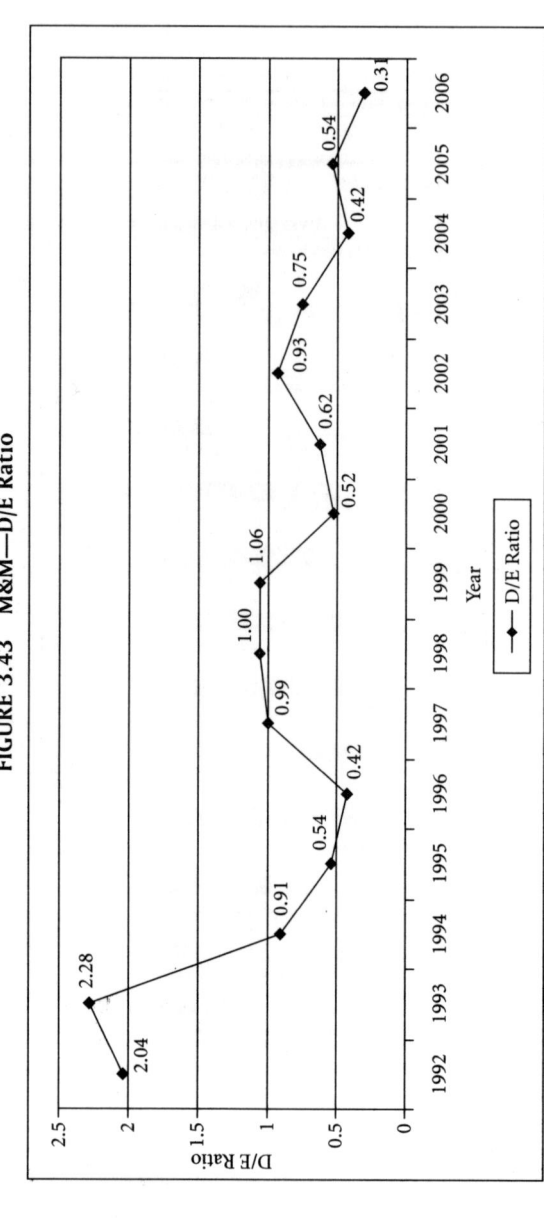

FIGURE 3.43 M&M—D/E Ratio

Source Author.

has built its own berthing facilities so as to cost-effectively transport the imported ammonia from the shipyard to its plant (Table 3.6). Also by innovatively using its by-products, CFL reduces costs.

TABLE 3.6 Coromandel Fertilisers—Divisions and Products

Division	Products
Fertilizers	Phosphatic fertilizers of different grades, trading in potash
Pesticides	Herbicides, fungicides, insecticides

Source Company website.

CFL's total income grew from ₹ 2,820 million in 1992 to ₹ 20,500 million in 2006 (Figures 3.44 and 3.45). *While its PAT went through ups and downs to go from ₹ 94.9 million in 1992 to ₹ 835.5 million in 2006.* The company aims to become one of the leading companies in the field of fertilizers.

The Vision statement clearly spells out its aims and objectives. To be one of the leaders in fertilizer industry, with an all India presence, through:

- High quality products and brand image.
- Modern, cost-effective, and energy-efficient manufacturing facility.
- Sustained growth in profitability.
- *High level of satisfaction to all stakeholders.*

Twin businesses: During the financial year 2003–04 the company transformed itself from a single location fertilizers operation to multi location farm inputs business. Following the merger of the Farm Inputs Division (FIND) of EID Parry (India) Limited with the company effective April 1, 2003, the company's business now comprises both fertilizer and pesticides activities.

Fertilizers division: The company is in the complex phosphatic segment of the fertilizer business, producing and marketing complex fertilizers of different grades. The company also trades in potash, one of the key plant nutrients. These products are sold under the

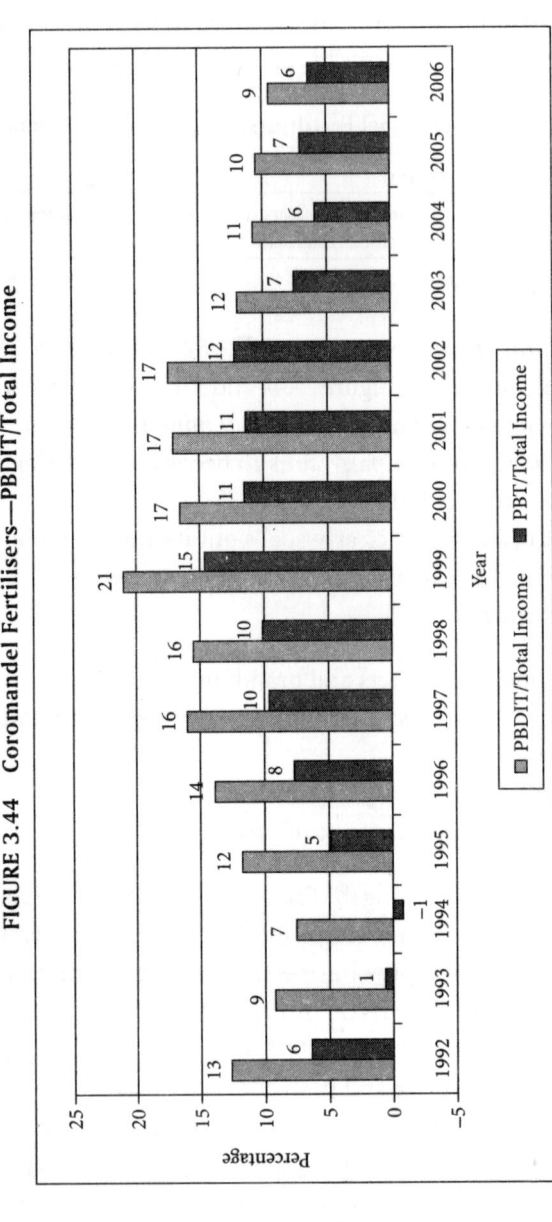

FIGURE 3.44 Coromandel Fertilisers—PBDIT/Total Income

Source: Author.

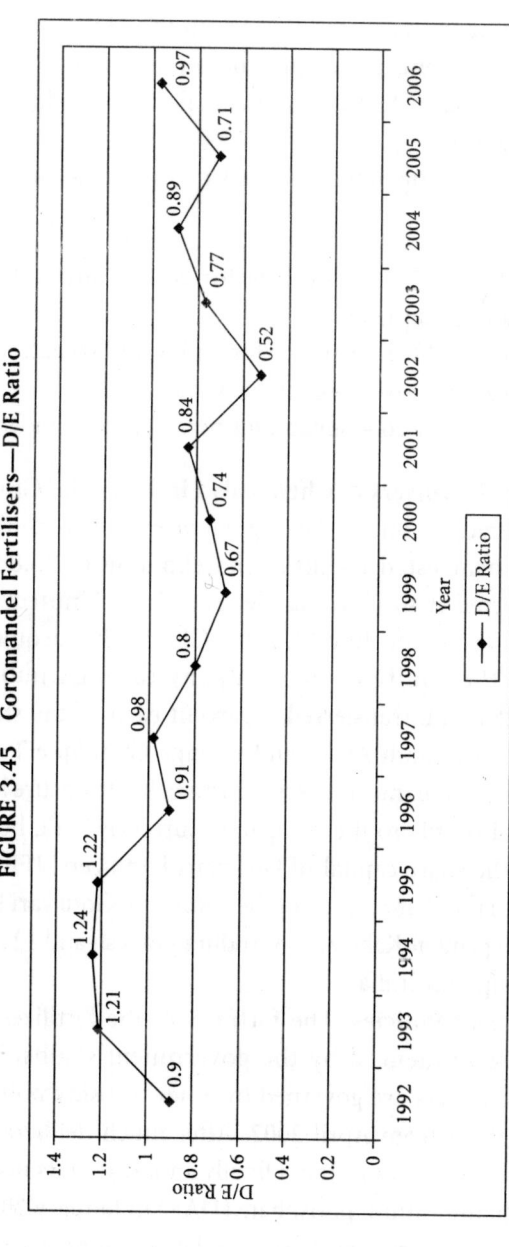

FIGURE 3.45 Coromandel Fertilisers—D/E Ratio

Source: Author.

brand names "Gromor," "Paramfos," and "Parry Super," latter two being brand names acquired along with the FIND business. The company has a strong market presence in Andhra Pradesh, Orissa, Chhattisgarh, Tamil Nadu, Karnataka, parts of Madhya Pradesh, and West Bengal.

The highest selling brand is Gromor. Gromor is sold in the following varieties:

- Gromor 14-35-14—Suitable for cotton, groundnut chilly soybeans, potato, etc.
- Gromor 28-28-0—Suitable for paddy and wheat.
- Gromor 20-20-0-15—Suitable for oil seeds.
- Gromor 10-26-26—Suitable for potato, paddy, and sugarcane.

Godavari Fertilisers & Chemicals Limited: The Government of Andhra Pradesh, one of the original promoters of the Godavari fertilizers, disinvested its entire shareholding of 25.88 percent and transferred it to Coromandel Fertilisers Limited (CFL) of Murugappa group, on July 12, 2003. CFL further acquired 14.93 percent of the equity of the company through public offer. Subsequently, CFL transferred 5 percent each of the share capital to Foskor of South Africa and Groupe Chimique Tunisien of Tunisia and entered into a strategic partnership to ensure long-term raw material supply to the company. Currently, CFL holds 45.07 percent of the share capital of Godavari Fertilizers. IFFCO holds 25 percent of the share capital of the company. Godavari Fertilizers has only one plant at Kakinada in Andhra Pradesh and 12 marketing offices throughout India.

Government Policies: The fortunes of the fertilizer industry in India are influenced by the government's subsidy policy. Complex fertilizers are governed by a new subsidy policy, which came into effect from April 2002. After much deliberations and delay, the Government of India finally announced its new subsidy policy for diammonium phosphate (DAP) in January 2004, which took effect from April 2003 based on the recommendations of the

Tariff Commission. Consequent to this delay, the final rates of subsidy for complex fertilizers for the period from April 2003 were also announced only in January 2004.

Pesticides Division: Pesticides comprising of herbicides, fungicides, and insecticides form an integral part of the agricultural activity. The diversity of crops, farming practices, weather conditions, and crop-growing season are some of the characteristics of this industry.

The pesticide industry performed well during 2003–04 and recorded a growth rate of about 15 percent, reaching a domestic turnover of ₹ 40,000 million. This growth rate has helped industry to reach 2001–02 levels, thus putting behind a disastrous 2002–03. The last two years saw an increased rate of new product introduction, mostly by the MNCs, based upon new chemistry. In the process, the volumes of generics reduced noticeably. This trend requires production flexibility, product diversification, and stronger marketing for other firms to stay competitive.

The export market for off-patented technical from India continues to offer good scope. The industry recorded an export turnover of ₹ 15,000 million.

Sales Distribution Network

What the reader can expect to read in this section is to understand how the companies invested in their sales distribution network as a part of their growth strategy. In this section, the reader would draw lessons growth from Tata Steel, Bombay Dyeing, M&M, Apollo Tyres, Exide Industries, and Siemens.

Tata steel

In April 2000, Tata Steel launched its first branded product in steel—Tata Shaktee GC sheet used for roofing—followed by launch in December 2000 of Tata Tiscon Rebars for construction. In February 2003, Tata Steel[17] launched another brand—Tata Steelium. By September 2003, Tata Steel had three generic (Tata Bearings, Tata Pipes, and Tata Agrico) and three product brands. The branded products accounted for 12 percent of total sales and were expected to rise in the future.

Tata Steel's branding and marketing initiatives were supported by an adequate network of distributors. Tata Steel catered to two distinct customer segments—Business to Business (B2B) and Business to Customers (B2C). The B2B segment consisted of industrial customers such as Maruti, Tata Motors, and Ford who had a technical knowledge of steel and bought products on quality and service value. Eighty percent of its total sales were from 200 large business customers, while around 5,000–60,000 customers accounted for the remaining 20 percent of its sales. This 20 percent made up the B2C segment. For the B2B segment, Tata Steel initiated a Customer Value Management program.

Tata Steel revamped the distribution system for the B2C segment, which consisted mainly of the housing and construction sectors, on the Hub and Spoke model that would reduce logistics costs.

Bombay Dyeing

Distribution forms the key. Bombay Dyeing leverages its owned retail outlets in the country. It has a *network of over 600 franchise retail outlets*[18] spread over 300 towns and cities in India. The company also distributes its products through wholesalers—especially the long length sheeting.

It is a provider to other industry players as well. It provides material for fashion apparel manufacturers, canvas fabric to shoe manufacturers, disposals to those in medical industry, etc. It also sells directly to hotels and those in hospitality industry.

The company does not go for extensive promotion. Since it has distribution outlets in the form of mail-order houses, the houses promote the product under their own brand names.

For products that are not distributed under such houses, the company promotes them under the name Bombay Dyeing and not under the numerous brands it has in each product category.

M&M

One of the major strengths of M&M is its strong distribution network for its tractor division,[19] consisting of dealers for sales and service of tractors and spare parts. The dealer network is managed by 28 area offices, situated in all major cities and covering all the principal states.

Apollo Tyres

It is the only tyre company with more than 100 sales and service offices in India. Apollo Tyres has a strong 7,000-dealer network and is the largest in the country. Out of these, there are over 3,500 exclusive outlets under the brand name "Apollo Tyre World" and "Apollo Radial World."[20]

A strong distribution network is essential for the company's success in the industry. A robust network ensures the availability of the product at major locations especially in the replacement market.

Besides strong distribution network, another key success factor is strong brand recall. Apollo goes for celebrity endorsements to have top of the mind recall.

Exide Industries

Exide's sales and distribution network is spread throughout India and its factories are geographically distributed at strategic locations around the country. The advantages of having such a huge network are as follows: (*i*) Multilocation to hedge supply risks to customers; (*ii*) Strategically located near markets; (*iii*) Logistically efficient, considering 70 percent raw materials are imported; and (*iv*) Proximity to ports—cost efficiency in exports.

Exide has 25 offices, 100 Exide care centers, 25 Exide power centers, 5,734 dealers, and 291 marketing staff.[21]

Siemens Ltd

Siemens has a wide presence across the country, where its operations include 12 manufacturing plants and 19 sales offices.

Siemens operates in the core business segments of energy, industry and buildings, information technology, communication, transportation, health care, and lighting (Table 3.7). The company has the capability to integrate diverse products, systems, and services into turnkey solutions across the life cycle of a project.

In the energy sector, the services of the company ranges from power plants to meters and in the industry sector, the company builds airports, as well as produce contactors. In transportation, the company is involved from high-speed trains, right down to safety relays, whereas in lighting, it illuminates large stadiums and also manufactures small light bulbs. In health care, it executes complete solutions for hospitals, as also provide "in- the canal" hearing aids. It is also a major player in telecommunications.

Within the transmission and distribution department, the company has a "Centre of Excellence" that acts as a hub for working on high-voltage direct current projects all over the world. The Centre of Excellence operates as a profit center within the department.

TABLE 3.7 Siemens—Business Segments

Division	Products	Market segments
Industry products and solutions	Automation and drives, industrial solutions and services, and building technology	Building, electrical, and automation
Energy	Power generation, power transmission, and distribution systems	Power projects in power companies
Health care	Medical equipment and solutions including hearing aids	Hospitals
Information and communication	Networks—enterprises, public communication; information technology	Enterprises and carrier markets
Transportation	Transportation systems and automotive systems	Railways
Lighting products and solutions	Incandescent and fluorescent ones	Domestic and industrial lighting

Source Author (based on company's website).

Execution Excellence Theme 4

It is your Work in life that is the ultimate seduction.

—Pablo Picasso

Suresh Rajpal[1] (President at HP India) and Ravi-Raj Sagar examine the fundamental causes of business excellence and recommend that process improvement is one area where improvements will directly impact customer satisfaction.

The key traits required in an organization to achieve excellence are:

1. Having customer insights
2. Focusing business strategies on customer value
3. Commitment to quality
4. Upgrading knowledge and processes
5. Management by facts and feedback

In the Indian scenario, it is mainly the MNCs, driven by their global processes, which are driving business excellence (Figure 4.1). The authors opine that the same culture needs to be cultivated by the Indian companies, be they large or medium ones.

The quest for operational efficiencies was made by the companies in a bid not only to contain costs but also to optimize product quality. Various management techniques like benchmarking, Total Quality Management, JIT inventory management, BPR,

FIGURE 4.1 Business Model—Execution Excellence

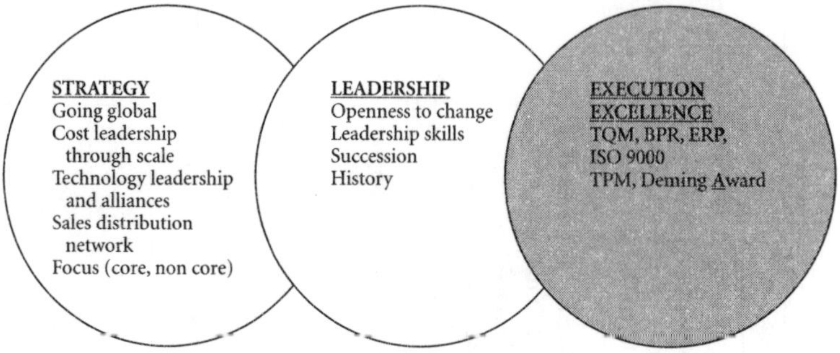

STRATEGY
Going global
Cost leadership through scale
Technology leadership and alliances
Sales distribution network
Focus (core, non core)

LEADERSHIP
Openness to change
Leadership skills
Succession
History

EXECUTION EXCELLENCE
TQM, BPR, ERP,
ISO 9000
TPM, Deming Award

SCM, or customer and employee surveys were deployed by the companies to sharpen operations.

What the reader can expect to read in this section is to understand how the companies pursued operational efficiencies as a part of their growth strategy. In this section, the reader would draw lessons growth from Tata Steel, Tinplate, Tata Chemicals, Indian Hotels, Bombay Dyeing, M&M, Apollo Tyres, Sundaram Fasteners, Kirloskar Brothers, etc.

TATA STEEL

Tata Steel's achievement of becoming the lowest-cost producer of steel was mostly attributed to its implementation of Total Operational Performance (TOP), a program that focused on improving operational practices and rationalizing procurement costs.

At the Tata Management Training center, group-wide training and value building exercises are conducted. Regular programs in quality and reliability; Project Top Gear—aimed at reducing production costs, improving quality, and building a seamless organization—have always been a focus. Tata Steel's Modernization Program from the year 1981 till 2002 is depicted in Table 4.1.

TABLE 4.1 Modernization Program

Phase	Period	Investment (₹ Billion)	Steps
I	1981–85	2.3	Installation of two 130t LD (Basic Oxygen Furnace) converters (a new technology of making steel in the place of open hearth furnaces which had gone beyond their life cycle). Six strand continuous billet caster—a first in an integrated steel plant in India—to replace ingot making (continuous casting was a major technological breakthrough in the steel industry in the 1960s).
II	1985–92	2.69	130t vacuum arc refining unit—against a first to produce higher quality steel. Installation of 0.3 Mtpa wire rod mill to enrich the product mix. Blending plant for raw materials to improve the sinter quality. Sinter plant of 2.5 Mtpa capacity to increase sinter usage in blast furnaces. Coke oven battery with 54 ovens using stamp charging technology—against a first in India. Waste recycling plant of 1 Mtpa capacity keeping ecology in view. Coal injection in blast furnaces—first in India—to reduce coke consumption.
III	1992–96	36	Installation of two more stamp charged coke oven batteries. Installation of a new 1 Mtpa blast furnace—the best blast furnace in India. Installation of another LD shop (LD2) with two 130t combined blown converters to eliminate open-hearths completely and to augment the production of continuously cast slabs from two single stand slab casters catering to the production of flat products. Installation of new hot strip mill (initially of 1 Mtpa capacity), to allow Tata Steel to enter the more profitable flat product market.
IV	1996–2002	12.62	Increase in hot metal and crude steel capacity. Third 130t vessel at LD2. Third-single stand slab caster to allow 100 percent continuous casting.

Source Author (based on company's website).

TOP and Improvement Initiatives

TOP was regarded as a program that will have a positive impact to the bottom line, with minimum investment, required in minimum time. Its objective was large improvements in the short term in throughput, quality, and cost. In the long run, TOP was expected to help the company to achieve high rates of performance improvement.

As the scale of operations was large, the entire company was divided into manageable units to facilitate the implementation of TOP. *A unit team, comprising a unit leader and two facilitators, worked full time for a period of 12 weeks known as a Wave.* Eight units worked simultaneously. The unit leader was responsible for the performance of that particular unit.

The whole Wave was divided into five phases. Phase I—two weeks, cost base was examined and the items that had the most impact on the bottom line were identified. Phase II—ideas were explored to reach the set targets. Phase III—ideas were generated to achieve the target output. On the basis of techno-economic feasibility, ideas were short-listed. Ideas were then grouped based on the capital expenditure required for implementing each idea. Phase IV began with the implementation of these ideas.

The Waves were first implemented in blast furnace and then adapted to shop floors. The TOP program enabled the company to broaden its attention from just producing volumes to costs and quality. It also helped the Tata Steel to improve customer satisfaction and loyalty. Tata Steel's Improvement Initiative undertaken from the year 1986 till 2003 are shown in Table 4.2.

In 1999, Tata Steel initiated a Total Productive Maintenance (TPM) program in its Tata Bearings Division. Later, the program was put into operation in other plants also. The basic element of TPM is to ensure that equipment is in good condition to minimize the chances of breakdown and to rectify defects in the initial stages before it becomes a major problem.

TABLE 4.2 Tata Steel—Improvement Initiatives

Year	Improvement initiative
1986	Value engineering
1989	Standardization program
1992	Quality improvement program
1995	JRD quality value
1997	Brand marketing
1999	Total productive maintenance
2000	Knowledge management
2001	Performance ethic program
2002	Six sigma
2003	Economic value added

Source Author (based on company's website).

Performance Ethic Program (PEP)

Between 1996 and 2000, Tata Steel took steps to reduce its manpower costs. The company adopted PEP, under which it planned to promote hardworking young people to higher positions depending on their performance, rather than following the convention of seniority. PEP had two core elements. First, it proposed a new organizational structure, which was expected to foster growth businesses, introduce more decision-making flexibility, clear accountability, and encourage teamwork among the managers and the workforce. Second, PEP introduced Performance Management System (PMS). It would identify and reward strong performers, and also offer development opportunities for each employee. PMS ensured that every employee's job profile was clearly defined. Through PMS, the company wanted to make performance appraisals transparent and fair and reward the good performers.

TINPLATE COMPANY OF INDIA LTD

In order to stay competitive, Tinplate Company of India Ltd (TCIL) reworked its strategies on the highly influential market factors of quality, cost, delivery, and customer sensitivity toward business transactions/services. The market survival challenge created the need to sweat assets by increasing the overall equipment efficiency (OEE), eliminate defects, and build a safe and conducive working environment for self-motivated employees with ample opportunities of continuous improvement and learning.

TPM

The top–down, bottom–up driven TPM initiative called for involvement of top management, down to frontline staffs. The effectiveness of TPM is measured by a matrix of P, Q, C, D, S, and M (production, quality, cost, delivery, safety, and morale).

TPM was initiated at TCIL in 2001–02 under the umbrella of Jishu Hozen Pillar (Autonomous Maintenance). Two manager model machines were selected under the guidelines of JIPM consultant. The objectives for selection of manager model machines were following: (i) managers as role model for frontline staffs to inculcate TPM as work culture and (ii) training of executives on Jishu Hozen Concepts to facilitate horizontal deployment.

Focused work on these manager model machines brought immense benefit to the company. Following the TPM methodology, eight pillars were created that worked under the guidelines of a JIPM consultant with time-bound action plan for TPM implementation. Senior level teams assumed the responsibility for various pillars (Jishu Hozen for planned maintenance, Kobestu Kaizen for education and training safety health and environment, and Hinshitsu Hozen for administration and initial flow control pillar).

During Phase I of the TPM journey, strong focus was given in manufacturing sector, where pillars like Jishu Hozen, Kobetsu Kaizen, planned maintenance, quality maintenance and education and training were provided attention. This has been achieved through the efforts of various small group activities (JH circles) under JH Pillar, cross-functional project teams of KK Pillar supported by planned maintenance and quality maintenance pillar. In order to enhance the knowledge and skill level of the employees, intensive training was provided through E & T Pillar. The success of manager model machines and implementation of proper 5'S' Kick–Off led to horizontal deployment of TPM culture all across the works. TPM was then initiated in areas like new projects (initial flow control), offices (administration), and safety (safety, health, and environment).

All 16 losses were mapped and loss structure had been prepared and displayed in various units of CRM and ETP under KK Pillar. Periodical audit of TPM circles by department and JH Pillar head had led to improvement in their respective areas. Each Pillar Heads review the activities of their respective pillar at regular intervals. This has helped in leakage control. Regular visit of JIPM consultant improved the 5S (Good Housekeeping) standard within the plant. This initiative led to self-inspection of various equipments resulting in reduction of downtime.

After one and a half years of progress under the guidance of JIPM consultant, TCIL challenged the JIPM TPM first-level award in 2005.

On April 5, 2005, TCIL cleared the TPM pre-audit and final TPM audit on October 5, 2005. The Tinplate Company of India Ltd was conferred with the prestigious TPM Award on February 16, 2006, at Pacifico, Yokohama, by Japan Institute of Plant Maintenance in a glittering ceremony.

TOP

TOP was instituted during 1999–2000 when the company wanted to focus on improving availability, quality, and throughput. Various

TOP teams were formed and a TOP Center was created at TCIL with the help of Tata Steel and McKinsey & Co.

The TOP process had three phases: Phase I being the Target Setting, Phase II being Idea Generation and Evaluation, and Phase III being the Implementation Planning. Each phase had a time-bound schedule and strictly adhered to. At the end of each phase, a presentation was made to the MD and other senior executives of the company and reviewed in detail by them. A lot of focus was given on correct evaluation of each idea and the savings yield and a very realistic schedule of implementation was drawn up by the TOP team with a complete agreement and syndication with various line managers. Thus the process not only involved the TOP team, but it involved each and everyone concerned directly or indirectly with the unit.

This made the program highly success-oriented. That is how it differed from various other improvement programs. The Wave is the time frame within which one or more units are taken. The first Wave of TOP at TCIL was launched with 6 Hi as the only unit. This unit began its operation on December 15, 1999, and ended on March 13, 2000. The second Wave was launched on March 13, 2000 with ETP and Annealing as two units. This wave was concluded on June 14, 2000, with the presentation of the final implementation plan. TCIL has already launched the third Wave with other important units such as degreasing, roll grinding shop, and CPL. The TOP process is shown in Figure 4.2.

Six Sigma

TCIL started its Six-Sigma journey in September 2002 with the help of consultant M/s ECS Limited. During the initial phase, the following three projects were selected as per their criticality to the organization's manufacturing:

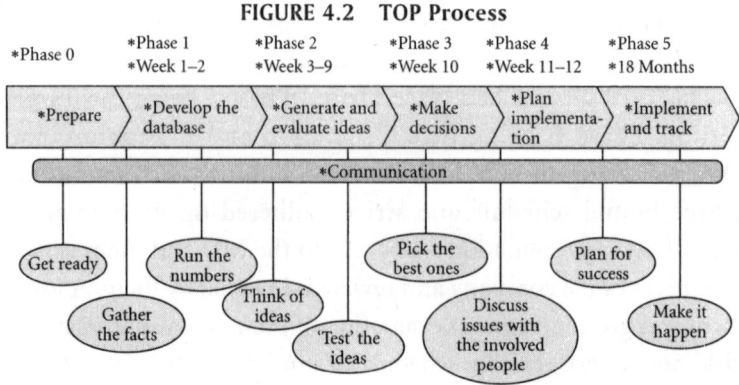

FIGURE 4.2 TOP Process

Source   http://www.tatatinplate.com/TOP.shtm (accessed August 29, 2011).

- Reduction in Off Gauge
- Reduction in Luider Band and Edge Pincher
- Enhancement of ETP uptime

Enhancement of ETP uptime was further broken into six small projects as follows:

- Metallic Roll Cleaning
- Hallden Shear setup time
- Rubber Roll abrading
- Rubber roll changing for less than 8 in. dia.
- Anode-related problem
- Sink/Upper motor failure

ECS and TCIL worked like a team complementing each other. Regular reviews by TOP management along with concerted efforts of Teams, TCIL achieved success in its projects.

During the second phase, TCIL had tied up with M/s Tata Motors Limited and under their guidance following projects made progress:

- Reduction in Off Gauge
- Process Defects at ETP
- Reduction in Power consumption at CRM and ETP
- Transit Damage and Rust

The above projects were carried out as per DMAIC methodology of Six Sigma. The team members were exposed to seven QC Tools, and statistical tools like FMEA (Failure Mode Effect Analysis), Test of Hypothesis, ANOVA (Analysis of Variance), and DOE (Design of Experiments). Thirty persons had been certified as Green Belts by M/s Tata Motors Limited.

Six-Sigma initiative had paid handsome dividends to TCIL.

TATA CHEMICALS (TCL)

In 1996, TCL received ISO 9001 certification. In 2002, the Chemicals Division at Mithapur was awarded the ISO 9001-2000 Migration certificate. In 2003, Mithapur became the first industrial township to be awarded the ISO 14001 certificate. During the same year, the fertilizer plant at Babrala got the ISO 14001 and OHSAS 18001 certificates.[2]

TCL takes the greatest possible care to ensure the safety, health, and welfare of its staff and communities living around its facilities. Environmental protection is an important component of its business philosophy. Stringent safety and occupational health programs are in place to ensure the well-being of employees and facilities at all locations. The safety management system is in line with the guidelines set by British Safety Council. Tata Chemicals Society for Rural Development, set up in 1979, looks into the benefit of the rural population in and around the company's plants and townships. Japanese 5-S and "Total Productive Maintenance" concepts have been implemented at Tata Chemicals to ensure the maintenance of quality standards and safety management norms.

INDIAN HOTELS CO LTD

In March 2001, IHCL launched an employee loyalty program called the "Special Thanks and Recognition Scheme" (STARS).[3] STARS as an initiative at Indian Hotels aimed at motivating employees to transcend their usual duties and responsibilities and have fun during work. This program also acknowledged and rewarded hardworking employees who had done excellent work.

The Taj Group had always believed that their employees were their greatest assets and the very reason for the survival of their business. *In 2000, to show its commitment to and belief in employees, the Taj Group developed the "Taj People Philosophy" (TPP), which covered all the people practices of the group.* The TPP considered every aspect of employees' organizational career planning, right from their induction into the company till their superannuation.

The TPP offered many benefits to the Taj Group. It helped the company boost the morale of its employees and improve service standards, which in turn resulted in repeat customers for many hotels in the group. The STAR system also led to global recognition of the Taj Group of hotels in 2002 when the group bagged the "Hermes Award" for "Best Innovation in Human resources" in the global hospitality industry. Out of the 120 applications received for the award for the year 2002, five were short-listed for the final round. The Taj Group won the award for the innovative "STAR" program.

STARS had five different levels. "Level 1" was known as the "Silver Grade." To reach this level, employees had to accumulate 120 points in three months. To attain "Level 2," known as the "Gold Grade," employees had to accumulate 130 points within three months of attaining the silver grade. To reach "Level 3," called the "Platinum Grade," employees had to accumulate 250 points within six months of attaining the gold grade. To attain "Level 4," employees had to accumulate 510 or more points, but below 760 points, to be part of the Chief Operating Officer's club. "Level 5," which was the highest level in STARS, enabled employees to be a part of the MD's club if they accumulated 760 or more points.

Points were granted to employees on the basis of parameters like integrity, honesty, kindness, respect for customers, environmental awareness, teamwork, coordination, cooperation, excellence in work, new initiatives, trustworthiness, courage, conviction, among others. Suggestions by employees that benefited the organization fetched them significant points. Such suggestions in each hotel of the Taj Group were examined by the general manager, the HR manager, and the training manager of the hotel. Suggestions could also be posted on the Web, which were constantly monitored. Employees could also earn points through appreciation by customers and "compliment a colleague" forums. Employees could also get "default points" if the review committee did not give feedback to the employee within two days of his/her offering a suggestion for the betterment of the organization. In such cases, the employee concerned was awarded "20 default points." Hence, in an indirect manner, the system compelled the judges of the review committee to give feedback to employees as early as possible.

BOMBAY DYEING

Processes are looked at with a view to achieving cost efficiency. It initiated measures to reduce its fuel, power, and raw material costs and shed workforce. In 1996, the company cut its workforce by 5 percent through a VRS and began restructuring its textiles division. The gain so far has been a 5 percent rise in productivity. During 1996–99, the across the board restructuring under the guidance of Warwick focused on product development, processes, quality, delivery, performance, and marketing.[4]

DMT division at Bombay Dyeing had been able to reduce the consumption of catalysts, save energy, and improve reliability by embracing TQM. It notched up a 90 percent conversion factor and 93 percent capacity utilization in 1996–97. Given that the plant is a secondhand one, the achievements are significant. Besides, the DMT division is evolving performance guidelines based on Malcolm Baldridge Award criteria and at the same time implementing ISO 9004 standards for continuous improvement.

The company had been carrying out R&D in the following specific areas with an objective of increasing customer satisfaction and improving the business viability: (*i*) process optimization/recipe modification/introduction of new dyes and chemicals for "cost economy," (*ii*) process standardization, (*iii*) process development, and (*iv*) product development.

M&M

M&M had set up Mahindra Research Valley[5] that serves as a principal engineering research and product development facility. In 1975, the company started its own in-house development of diesel vehicles. Since then, the company had been upgrading its technical know-how and launching new products regularly.

Quality is a driving force at the company with a philosophy of delivering value for money to its customers. The quality theme cuts across products, one's work, and interactions with others.

The bottom line is improved by controlling costs—lowering cost production facilities at Nagpur plant, shifting production to satellite plants/skid plants geared to meet regional requirements, implementing supply chain management techniques for significant reduction in pipeline stocks, reengineering working capital costs by reducing dealer stocks, adoption of lean manufacturing techniques, etc.

BPR Implementation

In 1994, a major restructuring exercise was initiated as a part of a BPR program. M&M's decision to undertake BPR implementation was largely influenced by its ambition to become a leading tractor manufacturer in the world. This was accompanied by a decision to focus on enhancing productivity and delivering world-class quality at the least possible cost. The company also undertook total quality management initiative. Various other initiatives such as supplier upgradation, strategic and global sourcing, product development, channel management, and lean manufacturing were also taken up.

BPR refers to a complete overhaul of the way an organization does its business. Instead of focusing on improving or modifying processes, it focuses on reinventing the way the company carries out its business. BPR can be categorized into "Process Improvement," "Process Redesign," and "Business Transformation."

Process improvements involve improving processes that are part of a single business function and are not cross-functional. They result in small improvements to the existing process, usually through eliminating non-value-added activities. Process Redesign on the other hand, involves the total redesign of an end-to-end process. This usually results in considerable performance improvement in terms of cost, quality, and cycle time. Business Transformation is the highest degree of BPR and focuses on reinventing the business through a top–down reappraisal and redesign of the total business.

A typical BPR implementation is divided into three phases of two stages each as shown in Table 4.3.

M&M's workforce resisted the attempt to reengineer the organization. Soon after the senior staff began working on the shop floor, the first signs of the benefits became evident. Around 100 officers produced 35 engines a day as compared to the 1,200 employees producing 70 engines in the pre-BPR days.

TABLE 4.3   BPR Implementation Phases

Phase I	Phase II	Phase III
1. Business Understanding	3. Business Process Identification	5. Process Redesign
2. Project Planning & Training	4. Process Envisioning	6. Process Implementation

Source   Author (based on company's information and business research).

Prior to BPR, HR has not been a key element of strategy formulation. From a multilayered structure, the company adopted a flat structure, reducing the number of layers to just five under the president. M&M also implemented a performance management system, where a significant part of the compensation package, up to 30–35 percent, was linked to performance.

M&M worked on the principle of cellular manufacturing. In this type of manufacturing, plant layout is reorganized drastically and workers are required to do multitasking through multi-machine running. The plant and machinery layout at the company had to be revamped to reduce nonproductive activities and introduce cellular manufacturing. To enhance productivity, M&M moved from a batch to a modular process and implemented TPM and Kaizen.

M&M also adopted the "Platform Concept," focusing on customer requirements. It requires the formation of cross-functional teams consisting of people from R&D, manufacturing, processing, marketing, etc. These teams jointly develop the product, keeping in mind the end customer. This was a shift from the traditional form of product development that was product/function centric.

Continuing with the BPR exercise, IT solutions were integrated with an ERP package from SAP.

In 1997, following Mckinsey's recommendations, the farm equipment division undertook "Project Vishwajeet," a major restructuring exercise, where the tractor business was divided into 38 business units classified under five business divisions. The hierarchy structure in each of these divisions was limited to just five layers to ensure autonomy and clear accountability.

The company created history in 2004 by becoming the first tractor company in the world to bag the coveted Deming Prize, instituted by the Japanese Union of Scientists and Engineers (JUSE) that has become a synonym for quality and excellence.

Strategic sourcing had been a key part of vendor development. The M&M way involves asking one vendor to fit the tyres on the wheels after providing him the tyres. What comes to the plant is a fully assembled piece that can be fitted straight onto the vehicle.

APOLLO TYRES

Apollo Tyres adopted cost management by modernizing equipment and improving processes, reducing energy consumption, improving scrap recovery, and by implementing the ERP system. The ERP helped the company generate vital cost data to formulate its price strategies after assessing internal and external influences on manufacturing cost.

Apollo Tyres R&D Center at Limda, well equipped with the latest sophisticated testing and analytical equipment available in the world, focused its R&D effort to cater to the emerging needs of the OEM, domestic replacement market, and export market, a move that continues to give it a considerable leverage over the competition.

The R&D has a team of highly qualified rubber/chemical/textile technologists and scientists who are fully committed toward achieving the corporate objective of excellence and growth. The focus is on development of high performance radial passenger car tyres, alternate sources of raw materials, optimization of material usage, process improvements, developmental work by reverse engineering, development of new/improved tyre compounds, and constructions to enhance the performance and optimize cost of products. Other areas of focus include development of energy-efficient tyre, further enhancement of mileage and durability of tyres, tyres with higher speed capability, efficient utilization of raw materials, and cost optimization of existing products. Fine tuning and optimizing the process to improve productivity and adopting latest technological improvements is an ongoing process.

The company's efforts to absorb and adapt the most modern technology supplied by the technical collaborators have paid rich dividends. Several new products were developed and commercialized. Further, there were considerable product improvements and several innovations in product design as well as process. This has resulted in consistent performance in a highly competitive market. Because of the adoption of the latest technology, the company was able to achieve substantial reduction in the cost and improvement in quality.

Along with in-house development of products and processes, the company also has a strategic alliance with Michelin, a global leader in the tyre industry. A passenger car radial tyre Technical Assistance Agreement has been signed with M/s Michelin Research Asia B.V.[6] in November 2003, enabling the company to have access to world-class technology.

KIRLOSKAR BROTHERS

Formal quality processes began in the Kirloskar Group during the 1980s. In 1987, the company started an intra group Ravi Kirloskar Quality Award initiative. It went in for ISO 9000 certification during the 1990s.

Technology Alliances

Way back in the mid 1920s, when India was a net importer of almost every industrial product, Laxmanrao Kirloskar was the first Indian to manufacture world-class diesel engines and electric motors at Kirloskar Brothers. He sourced the know-how from a British company and integrated the technology by adapting it to local conditions making it a technology leader.

Technology through strategic tie-ups has been at the heart of Kirloskar's growth strategy. Somewhere along, the group took its eyes off cost control and ever since it has been banking on its quality-driven brand equity alone to fight the competition.

Kirloskars have been cautious about JVs, especially after the Cummins controversy in the 1990s. More often than not, tie-ups have been restricted to filling technology gaps. There are two reasons why a group like Kirloskars could afford to have that approach. One, the Kirloskar Group's own reverse engineering R&D skills are strong. It took care to upgrade its technology even when a protected market gave it the option of not doing so. Second, it had demonstrated skills in skillfully locating technology and integrating sub-technologies into its products. As once explained by Kirloskar, the company has the basic engineering skills and there is a lot that they can do themselves, with a little bit of help from consultants.

Post Cummins,[7] there have also been a new generation of alliances: (*i*) Mysore Kirloskar—JV with $ 6 billion Snyder General to manufacture pollution control equipment in 1992, (*ii*) Mysore Kirloskar—JV with $ 7.2 billion Toyoda Automatic Loom Works—Holding Co. of Toyota and a textile machinery manufacturer, and (*iii*) Toyota JV.

In 1996, the Kirloskar Brothers bagged a critical assignment for developing a pump for use in a nuclear reactor. In a market that is value conscious, Kirloskar's low cost and one-off design capabilities have worked as differentiators.

SUNDARAM FASTENERS LTD

Sundaram Fasteners Ltd (SFL) became the first Indian company to achieve ISO 9000 certification with the support of CII's TQM

Division in February 1991. This was a role model, a benchmark for others to follow. Although they had established a reputation as a reliable supplier with accent on quality, their cost competitiveness was always under threat, especially from the emerging economies.

Around the time the Government of India launched the famous economic reforms program in July 1991, Sundaram Fasteners worked with CII and the government to prepare the approach paper for setting up the Quality Council of India which today is a reality.

The group companies shared their knowledge by leveraging collective learning for greater individual benefits. The division embraced TQM first with an idea of improving the performance to survive and prosper in a competitive environment. Their TQM journey started in 1998 and decided to challenge Deming Prize only in 2002 when they decided to undergo TQM diagnosis by the Deming Prize Committee.[8]

Although TQM is synonymous with participation, involvement, accountability, ownership, and empowerment, the division also formed a TQM Council comprising senior management to facilitate in cascading the vision down the line and aligning all the activities toward realizing the vision. It is a company-wide effort at continuous quality improvement of all processes, products, and services through total employee involvement that results in increasing customer satisfaction and loyalty, and improved business results.

They benchmarked themselves against the best practices to improve in the area of energy, efficiency, and output to input ratio. They are on par with the best with regard to external failures, product life-cycle management, process control, productivity, and surface utilization.

General Motors has about 30,000 suppliers worldwide and every year there are about 150–80 suppliers in the fray for "The Supplier of the Year" Award. SFL has got this award many times. They supply to about 28 different plants of GM in North America.

As a supplier, basically, they have to ensure zero-defect and not default in dispatches to any of the plants. They have a warehouse in North America and dispatch from this to the various plants every week. They supply around 4 Mi radiator caps to GM every year. Naturally, they are expected to be world-competitive and are world-competitive. They have been achieving year after year, these zero-defect and on-time deliveries. To attain this, they have been upgrading technology to maintain the high standards of quality and delivery.

When they had put up the plant, they worked out the basics and also planned how it should be in about five years. They also worked out the TQM technology and the TPM technology to ensure this zero defect. It is very difficult to compete with 30,000 suppliers around the world and they are the only suppliers for GM from India. GM does not source any other products from India other than from SFL. They also had a lot of problems while using TPM technology.

The Deming Award had considerably enhanced Sundaram Fasteners status in the domestic and the export markets and had helped them become the largest exporter of automotive castings from India.

TPM is a 10-year process and they were able to achieve it in five years. TPM is about reducing breakdowns, downtimes, and zero accidents. This enhances the efficiency to 90 percent and has a tremendous impact on the employee's moral. It is a 10-year process and if one achieves TPM in the first four years, one gets the TPM excellence award. If this is continued for 2–3 years, one gets a special award and then a world-class award. They have practiced it and continue to do so.

GAMMON INDIA LTD

Gammon is the only Indian Construction Company to have been accredited with ISO 9001 certification for all fields of Civil

Engineering Works including design; it stands out as gateway for technological and engineering excellence in Civil Engineering fields.

GIL has presence in all areas of civil construction. GIL has executed many multi-ferrous civil engineering works from cotton godowns, bridges, flyovers, bitumen and concrete roads, marine structures, cooling towers, chimneys, tunnels, and dams.

The company has specialization in bulk storage structures, energy projects and high-rise structure, ground engineering and environmental protection, hydraulic works and irrigation projects, industrial structures, marine structures, tunnel engineering, public utility structure, and transport engineering.

The company provides start-to-end solutions like the builders and contractors, reinforced concrete specialists, engineers, architects, surveyor's estimators, and designers.

Gammon India Ltd made the longest river bridge in the world across the mighty Ganges at Patna, the tallest bridge in Asia, the longest span cantilever bridge in India across river Jadukata, the longest road bridge in India across the open sea, and the first cable-stayed bridge in India.

Leadership Theme 5

Know Thyself.
—Scribes of Delphi, via Plato

What the reader can expect to read in this chapter is to understand how the companies emphasized on leadership development and change management to support their growth. In this chapter, what stands out are the best practices with respect to the people processes of the Tata Group companies be it Tata Steel, Tata Chemicals, Indian Hotels, etc., based on Tata Business Excellence Model. Ultimately it is people first and strategy next that drives growth. It is this consideration that makes the leadership piece come in the center of the Business Model as shown in Figure 5.1.

TATAS

In 1991, Ratan Tata took over as the head of the Tata Group from JRD Tata. Increased liberalization meant more competition. In the first six years since he took over as chairman in 1991, he spent much of his energy reining in the various fiefdoms that made up the Tata empire, undoing what his predecessor JRD has done. In 1983, Tata attempted to reorganize companies on the basis of synergies. In 1992, he again announced plans to refocus the group as well as

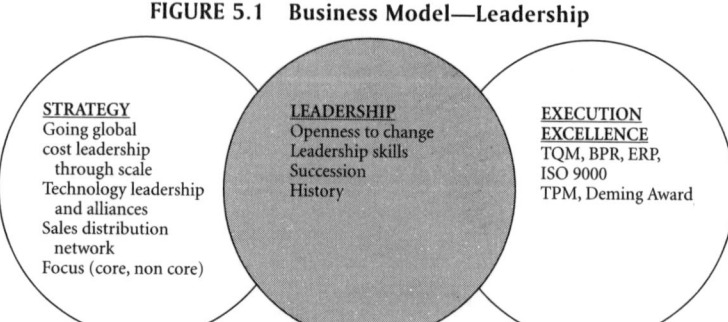

FIGURE 5.1 Business Model—Leadership

STRATEGY
Going global
cost leadership
  through scale
Technology leadership
  and alliances
Sales distribution
  network
Focus (core, non core)

LEADERSHIP
Openness to change
Leadership skills
Succession
History

EXECUTION EXCELLENCE
TQM, BPR, ERP,
ISO 9000
TPM, Deming Award

individual companies. He did not get much success in the earlier two initiatives. In 1997 he sought the assistance of McKinsey to help redraw his business portfolio.

The Tata Group consisted of nearly 90 companies in diversified businesses like steel, truck making, power generation, hotels, computers, consulting, and consumer goods. But more than 60 percent of group revenues came from only five companies—Tata steel, Tata Motors, Indian Hotels, Tata Electric, and Tata Chemicals. Ratan Tata undertook measures like restructuring of the group, concentrating on seven core businesses, expanding into telecommunications and initiating efforts to globalize different businesses of the group.

The future of Tata Group was in the success of its restructured operations and getting clear business focus. First on the target was the culture of the organization that was institutionalized in the organization since its birth. The relation between the management and employees witnessed a seesaw change—it became more of a practical than a munificent one. To safeguard Tata's interests within these companies, Ratan decided to raise the conglomerate's stake in all the group companies to minimum 26 percent. With Ratan sitting at the helm of Tata, an era of corporate management came up. He made sure that his troops meet the performance targets—and in setting targets he followed the erstwhile "GE Way" vision, which was to be either number one or two in terms of market share in that industry. And in that vision, the shareholder's wealth became pristine. From Tata Steel (where the workforce reduced from 80,000 in 1992 to around 35,000 in 2006) becoming the lowest cost steel producer in the world to hiving off stakes in many industries, from TOMCO to the Ambassador hotel chain, from TCS acquiring Chinese operations, to newfound Corus deal, from telecom to infrastructure, Tata Group leads like very few! How different parameters related to the Tata Group fared over a period from 2000 to 2006 is shown in Table 5.1.

TABLE 5.1 Tata Group—Performance on Various Parameters[1]

Parameters (Figures in ₹ billion)	2000	2006
M Cap	342	2202
Revenues	410	764
Net profits	30	98
Promoter stake	26%	30%

Leadership Skills and Openness to Change

By playing the role of a hands-on CEO, Ratan Tata has reversed the role of key investor and strategic advisor that JRD played.

The Tata Group believes that executives should become CEOs by the age of 45 years so that they get time to implement their plans. The Tata Group Mobility Plan is in place. The former Tata Tea MD Krishna Kumar recently took over as the MD of Indian Hotels in 1997.

Business Portfolio

The group has a presence in as many as 25 industries ranging from infotech to knitwear.

- **Core** (our study companies): TISCO, Tinplate, Tata Chemicals, and Tata Electric.
- **Other core:** TELCO, Tata Tea, TCS, TCE, Tata Refractories, Tata Tetley, Tata Infotech, Tata IBM, Tata Exports, Tata Telecom, and Tata Timken.
- **Noncore:** ACC, Goodlass Nerolac, Merind, Timex Watches, TEC, Rallis, Nelco, Forbes Gokak, Tata Finance, Eureka Forbes, Tata McGraw Hill Publishing, Tata Donnelly, Lakme, and Titan.

They are rarely first movers, but often, using their size and muscle, have come from behind to overtake early leaders. TISCO and Tata Motors have leveraged on economies of scale and capitalized on Tata brand name as a differentiator. Coming to the Tata's business portfolio, TISCO holds a 15 percent market share in the steel industry; Tata Chemicals, while its soda ash business is secure, the company's urea project is clearly a question mark; Indian Hotels is a cash cow—consolidation and not growth is its target; Tata Electric Co. which holds a nonexclusive license of supplying power in Mumbai—one of the fastest growing regions in the country—until 2014; Tata Motor's small car project—Indica is a potential cash cow.

History of the Tata Group

1868–1918: Jamsetji Nusserwanji Tata laid the foundation of the House of Tata by starting a private trading firm in 1868. The years from 1868 to 1918 saw the establishment of the first "swadeshi" (indigenous) Indian textile mill; the birth of Tata Sons; and the opening of the first Indian luxury hotel, the Taj Hotel, Mumbai. This period also witnessed the historic foundation of the Tata Iron and Steel Company and the Tata Hydro-Electric Power Supply Company.

1919–68: The years saw the Tata Group reach for the skies with their first commercial aviation mission, new ventures in chemicals, investment, electronics, and automobiles. And the Tatas diversified into exports, putting India on the global map with their offices abroad. The concept of consultancies was explored in several fields.

1969–78: The years saw the Tata Group undertake aeronautical space projects and enter sectors such as publishing, precision instruments, and computer hardware.

1979–88: The years saw Indian civil aviation celebrate its 50th year. Tata Engineering took another significant leap with its passenger cars. Tata Telecom was established.

1989–98: The period saw sectors such as information technology taking the lead and Tata Consultancy Services established itself as a force to be reckoned with. Tata Engineering launched India's first truly indigenous car, the Indica. Tata Quality Management services instituted the JRD Quality Value (QV) Award, and Ratan Tata took over from JRD Tata as the Group's chairman.

1998–2003: Far reaching changes have taken place in the Tata Group from 1999. The new Tata Group corporate mark and logo were unveiled; Tata Tea gained control of the Tetley Group, UK, following a cross border acquisition by an Indian company; a "group executive office" was set up to provide long-term direction to the group; and a "group corporate office" was established to guide the group's strategy for the future.

Tata Steel

In recent years, steel was considered as a sunset industry and a value destroyer worldwide. Today the industry is characterized by strong demand growth and consolidation. Tata Steel is aiming at 15 MMT by 2010 from the present 5 MMT and to 30 MMT by 2015. It has made two overseas acquisitions, Natsteel and Millenium Steel, in the last two years.

Tata Power

Tata Power generates and supplies power to bulk consumers in the Mumbai metropolitan area. In April 2000, Andhra Valley Power Supply Company Ltd and Tata Hydro-Electric Power Supply Company Ltd were amalgamated with Tata Power.

Tata Power is a dominant private sector player in the power sector in the country. The company operates four thermal and three hydroelectric plants in and around Mumbai, with an aggregate capacity of 1797 MW supplying power to the Mumbai Licensed area.

The company also supplies power to TISCO and ACC through captive power plants and has set up an 81 MW independent power project in Belgaum, Karnataka. It has built a fiber optic network in Mumbai and also has an electronics division that manufactures electrical equipment. Tata Power has diversified outside the Mumbai license area, by acquiring a distribution circle in Delhi during its recent privatization exercise and is also implementing a 400 KV 1,200 km transmission line between Bhutan and Delhi with Power Grid Corporation Ltd.

Power sector became a mess with SEBs for 52 long years since 1951. The Electricity Act 2003 has attracted Indian private companies like Reliance Energy and Tata Power. It has also attracted global giants like AES, Daewoo Power, and Electricite de France.

According to the "Indian Electricity Sector—Opportunity and Challenges" report by FICCI and E&Y, "With historical GDP growth rates of 5–6% per annum and energy demand growth rates of 6% per annum, the energy deficit and peak deficit are currently around

8% and 12% respectively."[2] And an unbelievable 44 percent of household electricity demand goes unmet!

The Government of India's latest plan is to set up seven "Ultra Mega Power Projects" of 4,000 MW each. There is a need for an investment of $ 200 billion.

Thermal and nuclear contribute 56 percent and 3 percent. Thermal is the pick due to the available coal reserves in India. The nuclear will be 40,000 MW by 2020 from the current 20,000 MW. And the complete ratifying of the nuclear deal with the US would surely give this sector a big boost.

Indian Hotels Co. Ltd

In 1902, Jamsetji Tata, the founder of the Tata Group, formed the IHCL. Till 1965, it owned and managed two hotels, viz., the Taj Mahal Hotel and the Green's Hotel. In 1972, Taj Intercontinental Hotel was opened. In 1979, IHCL put up a hotel of international standards in Colombo, Sri Lanka. In 1986, IHCL took over Hotel Chandela at Khajuraho on leave and license basis. The same year, IHCL commissioned the Jai Mahal Palace Hotel in Jaipur. In 1995, two new hotels of associated companies were commissioned, viz., a 50-room Taj Garden Retreat at Varkala (new Trivandrum), Kerala and a 100-room business-class hotel Taj Residency at Nasik, Maharashtra. It also undertook to set up two new luxury hotels in Mumbai and one in Chennai. In 2003, IHCL renovated and upgraded its leading leisure hotel properties in Kerala, Goa, Rajasthan, and Tamil Nadu.

Tata Chemicals

In 1927, Kapil Ram Vakil set up Okhamandal Salt Works. In 1937, the Tatas approached to take over the Salt Works. TCL got incorporated on January 23, 1939.

Today, TCL is the chemical arm of the Tata Group, India's foremost business conglomerate. TCL is India's leading manufacturer of inorganic chemicals in the country.

TCL started operations in 1943, recovering minerals and sea water and then converting them to basic chemicals like soda ash, caustic soda, chlorine, sodium bicarbonate, bromine, salt, and urea that find application in different areas like agriculture, animal nutrition, construction, food products, glass, metals, pharmaceuticals, soaps, detergents, textiles, and leather.

The chemical industry is mainly concentrated in the western part of the country, mainly in the states of Maharashtra and Gujarat. It also has a significant presence in the states of Tamil Nadu and West Bengal. The different segments of the Indian chemical industry are organic and inorganic chemicals, plastics and petrochemicals, drugs and pharmaceuticals, fertilizers, specialty chemicals, dyes and dye-intermediates, agrochemicals, etc.

Indian chemicals sector produces a range of chemicals that can be broadly classified into two categories—inorganic chemicals and organic chemicals. Inorganic chemicals include chemical groups like the Chlor-alkali group (caustic soda, soda ash), inorganic acids (sulphuric acid, hydrochloric acid), and industrial gases (chlorine, argon). Major organic chemicals include chemical groups like organic acids (formic/acetic acid), anhydrides (acetic anhydrides), and alcohols (methanol).

The major players in the inorganic chemical sector are Tata Chemicals, Gujarat Alkalies & Chemicals Ltd, GHCL, Kanoria Chemicals, and Sree Rayalaseema Alkalies. The basic chemicals produced in the industry are soda ash, caustic soda, liquid chlorine, calcium carbide, acetic acid, methanol, formaldehyde, phenol, and acetone. These chemicals are inputs for several downstream industries such as fertilizers, detergents, paints, pesticides, polyesters, plastics, synthetic rubber, drugs, paper, etc.

The Indian chemical industry evolved through a number of phases. In the early years, after Independence, the focus was mainly on chemicals that protect crops and improve health. In the 1970s, the Indian government established the public sector company to develop a downstream petrochemical industry. In the 1980s, the chemical industry passed through consolidation.

Post liberalization in 1991, when the economy was opened to the foreign players, a number of MNCs came up with major investment plans in the country along with domestic players. The monopoly of the public sector companies gradually decreased.

On April 1, 2003, Hindustan Lever Chemicals Ltd, Unilever Group Company, merged with TCL with a post-merger shareholding of 25 percent for the Tata Group and 8 percent for the Unilever Group.

Tinplate Company

Born in 1922, out of a commitment to make India self-sufficient in manufacturing of tinplate, The Tinplate Company of India Ltd, an associate of Tata Steel, has pioneered the tinplate industry in India.

The site chosen was Golmuri, Jamshedpur. The first steel plate of Tinplate gauge was rolled on December 18, 1922, at the Hot Dip Plant (HDP), producing Hot Dip Tinplate from tin bars supplied by Tata Steel and this continued till 1979, albeit with capacity enhancements. For 50 years, TCIL thus almost single-handedly built up the Indian tinplate industry.

To keep pace with technological developments, TCIL was the first to set up a combination line capable of producing both Electrolytic Tinplate (ETP) and Tin Free Steel (TFS). This plant, the first of its kind in India, was commissioned in 1978 and commenced production in January 1979. In 1982, Tata Steel bought the shareholding of Burmah Oil, the then major shareholder, and took over the management of the company.

In 1991–92, TCIL undertook backward integration to set up a Cold Rolling Mill (CRM) for production of TMBP Coils based on Hot Rolled Coil supplies from Tata Steel which was also setting up its Hot Strip Mill (HSM) at the same time. The CRM was thus a strategic fit for TCIL with Tata Steel. The CRM was commissioned in 1996–97 but with heavy time and cost overruns, the company started incurring severe losses. A turnaround strategy was developed with the objective of ensuring revival and setting fundamentals right, and was implemented during the financial years of 1997–2001. The basic elements of this strategy were: operational improvements, financial restructuring, and HDP phase-out and downsizing.

Since April 1998, TCIL operates under a conversion arrangement with Tata Steel for its business. Today, TCIL is the only indigenous manufacturer of value-added tinplate and TFS for processed food, battery, dairy product, beverage, and soft drink crown caps in both single reduced and double reduced forms. The establishment of the Solution Centre, in December 2005, provided further impetus to its business purpose of being a cost-effective metal packaging solution provider with focus on innovation and consumer convenience.

The solution center will facilitate the process of building solutions for end-use customers, i.e., fillers/food processors, complement the efforts of can fabricators across the country, and develop R&D capabilities. TCIL with its continuing yen for quality, productivity, cost-effectiveness, and customer service, looks forward to the future with confidence.

TATA BUSINESS EXCELLENCE MODEL[3]

Tata Business Excellence Model (TBEM), derived from the Malcolm Baldrige Model of Business Excellence, is the business model followed by the Tata Group of companies to achieve business results. TBEM has a strong approach toward robust systems and processes, with the belief that more efficient and robust processes facilitate quicker adjustment to change, faster improvement, and thus higher competitiveness.

TBEM comprised core values like customer-driven excellence, focus on future, organization agility, management by fact, managing for innovation, valuing employees and partners, and visionary leadership among others. It was broadly classified into two sections—"strategy development and deployment" (allotted 550 points) and "business performance/results" (allotted 450 points). Strategy development and deployment was further classified into six key management areas, such as customer and market focus, human resources, information and analysis, leadership, process management, and strategic planning.

TBEM aimed at establishing a link between business performance and individual performance. Tata Steel was the first and is only Tata Group company to achieve the JRD QV Award in 2000, having scored 616 points out of 1,000 points on the TBEM scale.

The JRD QV Award was given to the Tata Group for achieving excellence in quality.

There are four categories of JRD QV Awards (Table 5.2).

Leadership

Tata group identifies leadership as "leadership that delivers." In order that the leadership is not limited to a few individuals, and lest it should be viewed as a one time performance, a "Leadership System" has been developed to guide the leadership (Figure 5.2). Leadership at Tata group is built on a strong ethical foundation defined in the Tata Code of Conduct (Figure 5.3) and guided by its core values—customer focus, passion for engineering, integrity, and corporate citizenship. This constitutes the rigid base that does not move.

TABLE 5.2 Categories of JRD QV Awards

Award	Points
Recognition for serious adoption	450–500
Recognition for active promotion	500–600
JRD QV Award	>600
Sustained Excellence Award	For Tata Group companies that achieved sustained performance growth for three years following the receipt of JRD QV Award.

Source Abad (2005).

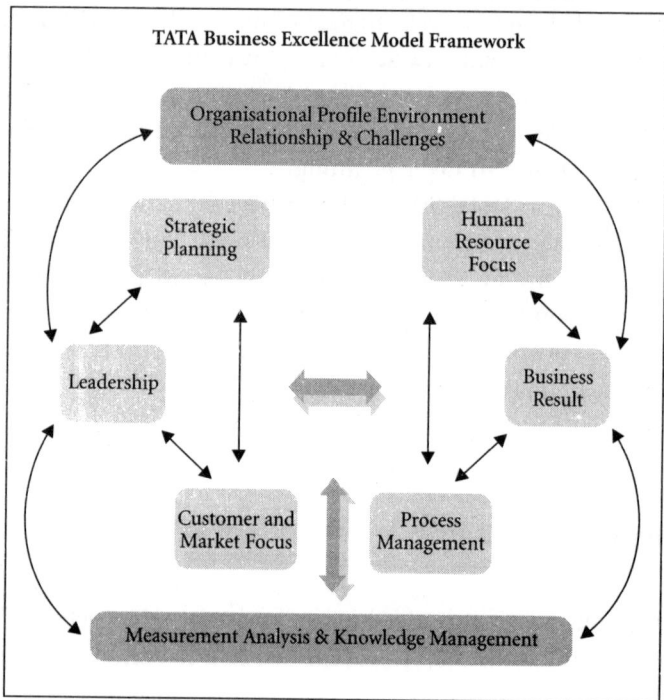

FIGURE 5.2 Tata Business Excellence Model

Source Abad (2005).

Strategic Planning

The success and growth of the business depends on how well the strategic planning process is executed. The clear articulation, communication, and execution of the strategic direction in three distinct

FIGURE 5.3 Tata Code of Conduct

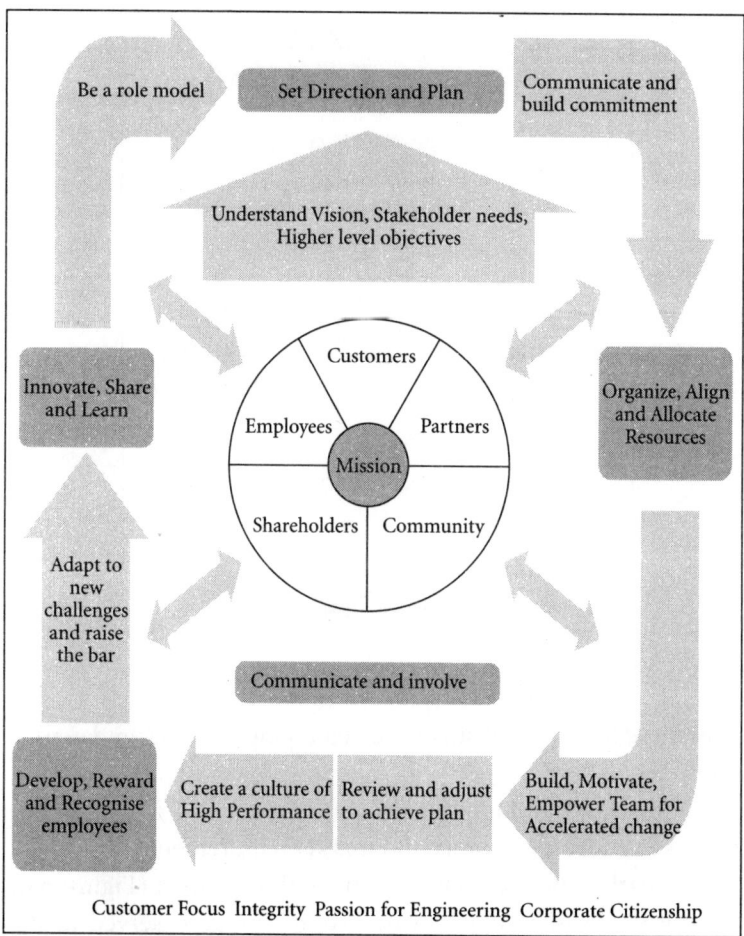

Source   Abad (2005).

phases—"think," "develop," and "deploy"—result in consistent performance in the market place (Figure 5.4).

Customer and Market Focus

Tata's customer-driven excellence is directed toward customer retention and loyalty, market share gain and growth, which demands

FIGURE 5.4 Strategic Planning Process

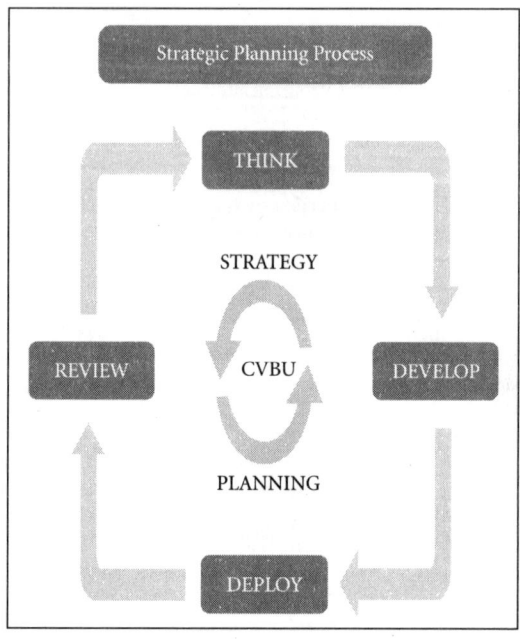

Source Abad (2005).

constant sensitivity to changing and emerging customer and market requirements.

The market development process (Figure 5.5) is the anchor process to address customer and market requirements.

The market and customer segmentation process (Figure 5.6) intrinsically ensures that a wide product range is served to the customer base to suit their diverse needs.

Measurement, Analysis, and Knowledge Management

Tata's information management and performance measurement system (Figure 5.7) takes inputs from Enterprise Process Model, Leadership System, and Strategic Planning process for determining the business objectives. The data is then analyzed and a balanced

Figure 5.5 Market Development Process

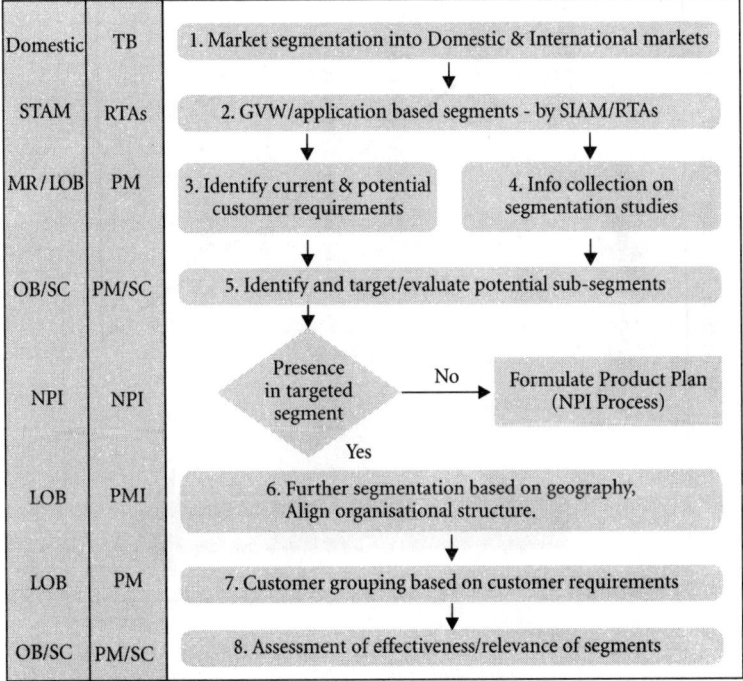

Source Abad (2005).

FIGURE 5.6 Market and Customer Segmentation Process

Domestic	TB	1. Market segmentation into Domestic & International markets
STAM	RTAs	2. GVW/application based segments - by SIAM/RTAs
MR/LOB	PM	3. Identify current & potential customer requirements / 4. Info collection on segmentation studies
OB/SC	PM/SC	5. Identify and target/evaluate potential sub-segments
NPI	NPI	Presence in targeted segment — No → Formulate Product Plan (NPI Process); Yes ↓
LOB	PMI	6. Further segmentation based on geography, Align organisational structure.
LOB	PM	7. Customer grouping based on customer requirements
OB/SC	PM/SC	8. Assessment of effectiveness/relevance of segments

Source Abad (2005).

FIGURE 5.7 Information and Performance Management Process

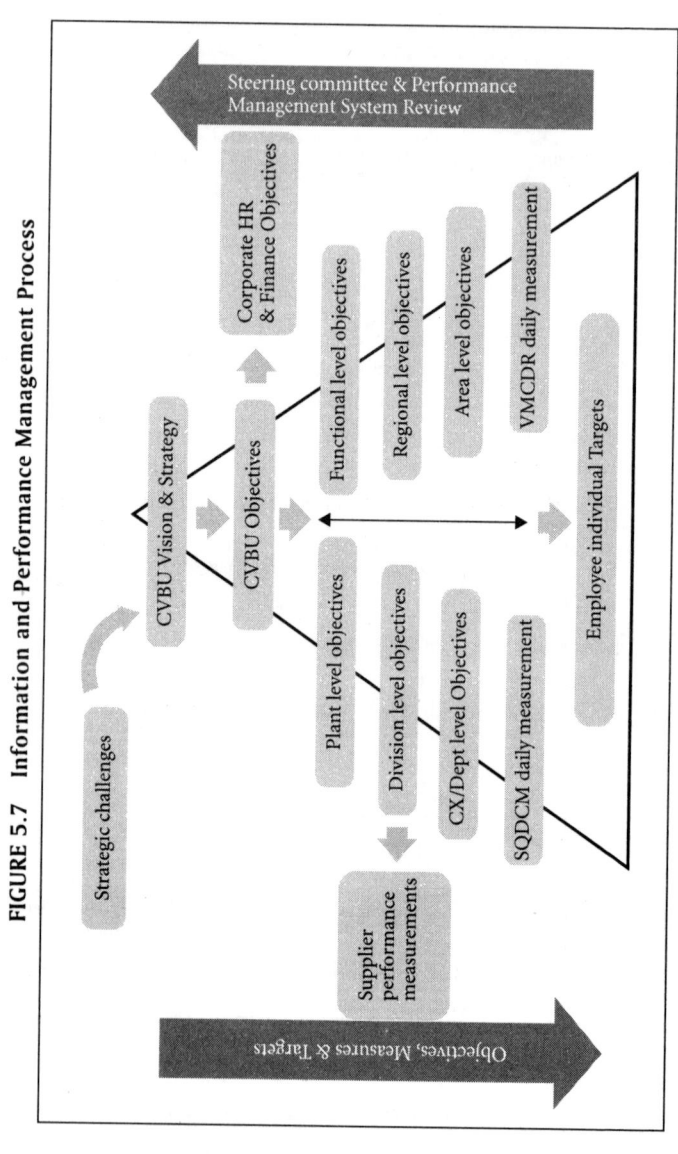

Source Abad (2005).

scorecard is used as a performance measurement tool to deploy the strategies drilled from the organization level down to the individual's level. Analysis supports a variety of purposes, such as planning, reviewing the overall performance, improving operations, change management, and comparing the performance with competitors or with "best practices" benchmarks.

Human Resource Focus

All major HR processes that are aligned to Tata's vision and mission, have a four-level planning and execution structure, which are a benchmark against best companies to support Tata's journey toward world leadership position. The company has a well-defined transparent Performance Management System to track, retain, and refine the people asset. This in turn creates a high performance culture.

The Organization Health Survey (OHS) (Figure 5.8 and Figure 5.9), which is done annually, helps to arrive at specific action plans that strike the desired balance between business needs and employee well-being.

Process Management

TBEM views organization as a collection of processes which help to deliver value to its stakeholders. Tata's have an evolved framework of processes called "Enterprise Processes Model" (Figure 5.10) to achieve systematic growth.

Conclusion

It may be noted that the adoption of best practices alone does not ensure success; the inculcation of these practices in the philosophy

FIGURE 5.8 OHS Survey 1

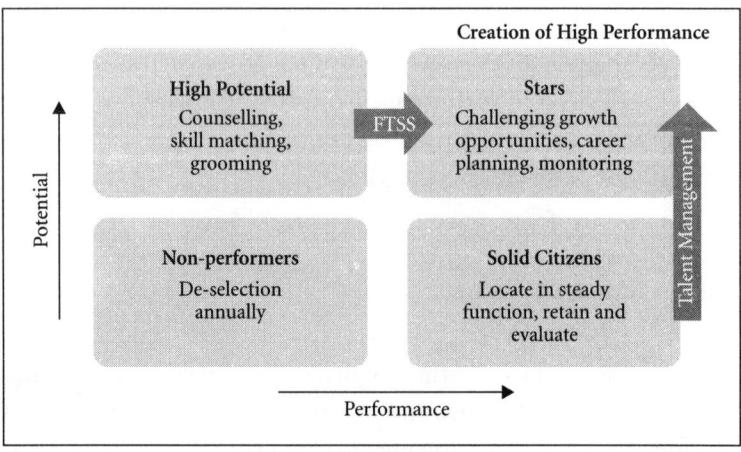

Source   Abad (2005).

FIGURE 5.9 OHS Survey 2

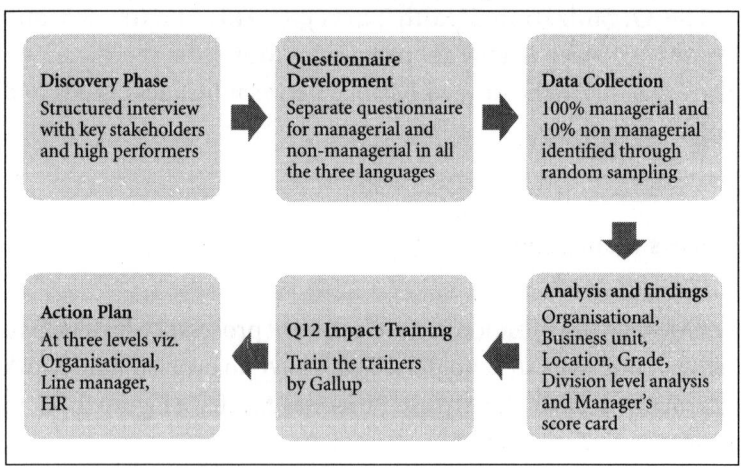

Source   Abad (2005).

of an organization and their timely execution puts the organization on the path of becoming the best. Becoming the best requires continuous improvements and religious fanatic adherence to the principles.

FIGURE 5.10 Enterprise Process Model

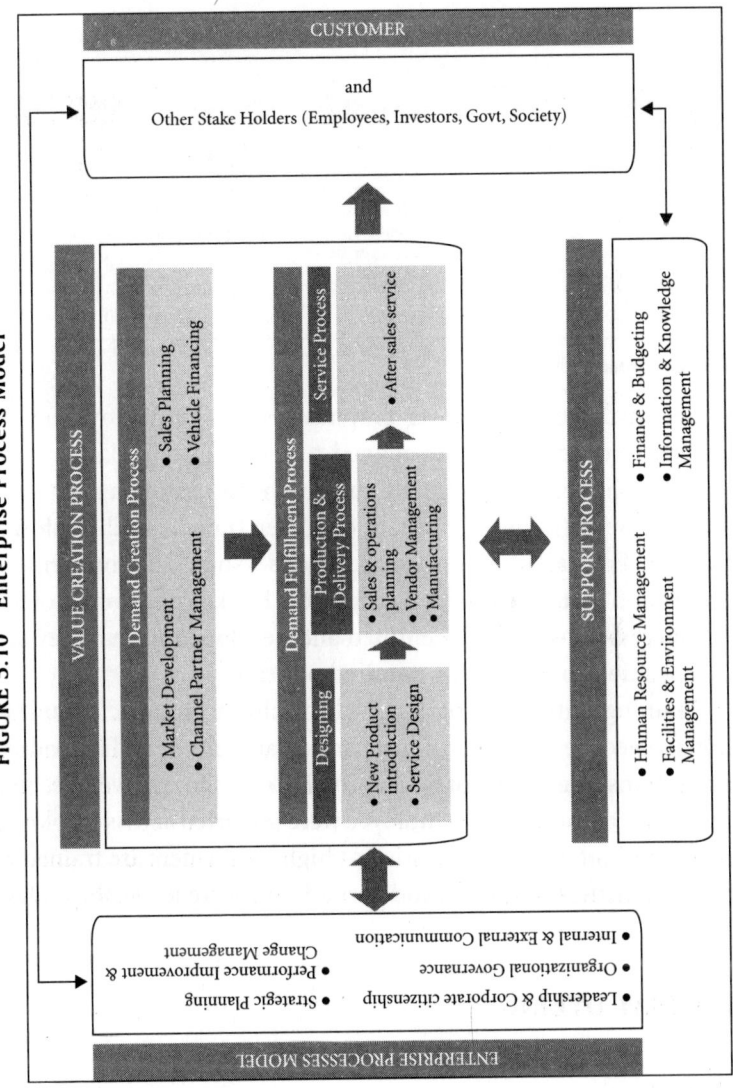

Source: Abad (2005).

The future is a moving target. Hence realignments and midcourse corrections will be the norm. The challenge is to remain the best within the fast-changing environment (Figure 5.11).

FIGURE 5.11   Overall Approach to Process Management

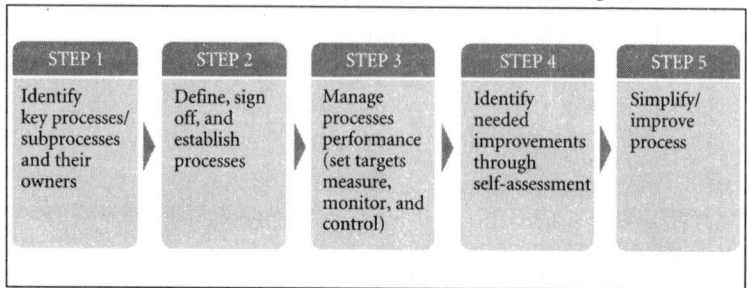

Source   Abad (2005).

For instance, Tata Power emphasizes on the deployment of human resources processes aligned to the TBEM. To induct and attract fresh talent, three separate trainee schemes are implemented—Management trainee, Graduate engineer trainee, and Diploma trainee. For talent retention and leadership development, a Succession Planning Process is deployed. For key positions, potential successors would be identified and developed so that they are in a position to occupy the required position.

Training initiatives are designed to achieve strategic organizational objectives, meet divisional performance needs and individual aspirations aligned to organizational goals. On an average, five man-days of training per employee were imparted across employee segments and divisions. Consistent high performers are trained at reputed institutes in India and abroad for future leadership roles.

BOMBAY DYEING

History

In 1879, Bombay was next to New Orleans as the world's largest cotton port. It was at this time that Nowrosjee Wadia set his sights on India's mushrooming textile industry. On August 23, in a humble redbrick shed, he began a small operation where cotton yarn spun in India was dip-dyed by hand in three colors and laid out in the sun to dry. Thus, Bombay Dyeing & Manufacturing Co. Ltd was born.

From a modest beginning, the company had grown into one of India's largest producer of textiles. It manufactures cotton textile goods, nonwoven fabrics, and DMT. The textile products are sold under the trade name "TEXSPRING," "SPRINGTEX," etc. The manufacturing operations include spinning, weaving, bleaching, dyeing, printing, mercerizing, sanforizing, tebilizing, Hecowa, and other finishings. The daily production exceeds 300,000 meters of fabric. Facilities are available to produce bleached fabric up to 120 in., dyed and printed fabric up to 98 in., and grey fabric up to 124 in.

In 1979, the company started sales in Indonesia through an incorporated company named P.T. Five Star Industries Ltd.

In 2002, the company acquired 51 percent stake in Proline India and changed its readymade garment business to Proline.

The DMT business has a market share of 75 percent and contributes a lot to the earnings.

Leadership Skills and Openness to Change[4]

The Wadia group may be family-owned but it is CEO managed. The day-to-day operations of the companies and the SBU are left to the CEOs and the SBU heads. At times, Wadia becomes a hands-on chairman. If Wadia is visionary, he is also overambitious. His penchant for controversy is legendary. He spends his time strategizing for his friend Ratan Tata, fighting against satraps like Russi Mody, Darbari Seth, and Ajit Kerkar (former MD of Indian Hotels). He has fought Dhirubhai Ambani and also the government.

At one time, Bombay Dyeing was perceived as a competitor to RIL. Today RIL's turnover is at least four times that of Bombay Dyeing.

For Bombay Dyeing, the strategy of leveraging its brand name and retail distribution system is likely to help it combat its competitors, many of whom are highly fragmented. As for exports, the company will have to focus on higher value-added products to increase its presence in the international markets. Individually, the prospects of Bombay Dyeing are bright.

By hiring Warwick, Bombay Dyeing has shown its willingness to change and shift from its status quo; Bombay Dyeing is incorporating modern management techniques and setting standards for itself.

Business Portfolio

The portfolio at Bombay Dyeing comprises:

- *Core*: Bombay Dyeing—Textiles, DMT; Britannia.
- *Noncore*: Bombay Burmah, Citurgia Chemicals, and National Peroxide.

While Bombay Dyeing's textiles and DMT businesses are related, the others are nowhere near the core. To acquire and nurture cash rich companies like Britannia Industries, it has never looked for synergy or integration in its portfolio.

Bombay Burmah Trading Corporation (₹ 1,110 million), National Peroxide (₹ 880 million), and Citurgia chemicals (₹ 820 million) qualify as dogs with reference to the BCG Matrix.

Bombay Dyeing and Britannia Industries account for almost 87 percent of the aggregate turnover. The former is a cash cow while the latter is a star.[5]

Bombay Dyeing has only itself to blame for the decline. After setting up the DMT unit 15 years ago, the company did not make any serious efforts at integration—either backward or forward. It has neither a refinery nor any plant to make PSF (polyester staple fiber).

Arch rival, RIL, on the other hand has naptha to fabrics facilities. It cracks naptha at its Hazira plant to make the building blocks (ethylene, propylene, xylene, and benzene) which in turn yield several intermediates, including paraxylene the raw material for PTA and DMT. Thus, while RIL saved on costs because of the in-house production of paraxylene, Bombay Dyeing had to rely on imports that not only squeezed its margins but also exposed it to the vagaries of the currency markets. Integration would also insure Bombay Dyeing against price fluctuations in the international market. Unless it does that, the group could find all its petrochemical ventures unviable.

For the Wadia Group, business beyond Indian shores has been a way of life for over a hundred years. The activities of the Group span several countries in the Far East. Group companies in textiles, chemicals, agro-based industries, electronics, light engineering, laminates, health care, and more recently in processed foods have some of the best brand names supported by complementary distribution networks in India. The demonstrated ability to manage well diverse business, using professional management and financial acumen has resulted in the Group enjoying a fine reputation in the market place. The guiding principles for the Group have been fair and ethical dealings, trust, and integrity.

HINDALCO

GD Birla set up his first business in 1912 in Kolkata. It is a diversified group from rubber gloves and textiles to cement and aluminum. The flagship is Grasim Industries that makes cement, sponge iron, and viscose staple fiber. Hindalco set up in 1958 is part of the Birla empire that three generations of Birlas had built with foresight and care.

History

On December 15, 1958, Hindalco was incorporated in Mumbai by the Birlas in collaboration with the Kaiser Organization of USA. Hindalco commenced operations in 1962 with an aluminum facility at Renukoot in eastern Uttar Pradesh. In 1967, the company set up its own captive power plant at Renusagar. Over the years, it grew into the largest integrated aluminum manufacturer of the country.

It is a flagship company of the Aditya Birla Group. It is structured into two strategic businesses—aluminum and copper—and is an industry leader in both the segments. A nonferrous metals powerhouse, close to global scale, the company's integrated operations and operating efficiency have positioned Hindalco as India's largest integrated player in aluminum.

The Aditya Birla Group is India's first truly multinational corporation. Global in vision, rooted in Indian values, the group is driven by a performance ethic pegged on value creation for its multiple stakeholders. A $ 6.5 billion conglomerate, it is anchored by an extraordinary force of 72,000 employees belonging to over 20 different nationalities. Over 30 percent of its revenues come from operations across the world. The group's products and services offer distinctive customer solutions. Its 66 state-of-the-art manufacturing units and sectoral services span India, Thailand, Indonesia, Malaysia, Philippines, Egypt, Canada, Australia, and China. The Group is a dominant player in all of the sectors in which it operates—viscose staple fiber, nonferrous metals, cement, viscose filament yarn, branded apparel, carbon black and insulators, chemicals, fertilizers, sponge iron, insurance and asset management, and financial services.

Openness to Change

Way back in 1974, Aditya Birla set up the group's first overseas venture in Thailand. A year later, he set up the first textile mill in Philippines which exported to the US, South Korea, Australia, and China.

Leadership Skills[6]

Kumar Mangalam Birla proved to be as capable a change agent as his father Aditya Birla. Luckily for him, a doting Basant Kumar threw all his weight to help his grandson.

Political connectivity, a controlled economy, and surplus cash spawned a conglomerate whose tentacles were just beginning to extend overseas when Aditya Birla died. With such an inheritance, the only challenge left for the young Birla is to push ahead with the globalization of his empire. And the only way he can do so is by expanding his manufacturing bases in Asia, where the business downturn of the 1990s makes the timing for this push perfect. Kumar Mangalam Birla can set out to conquer the world with the very commodities businesses that have made him impregnable at home.

Aditya Vikram Birla[7]

Very early in his career, long before the word "globalization" came into our everyday lexicon, Aditya Vikram Birla had foreseen the winds of change and staked the future of his business on a competitive, free market–driven economic order. At a time when India's economy was glued with bureaucracy and taped with controls, his was rather a lone voice. He also acted decisively and with conviction. He had this ambition of doing something "really big" even when he was doing his post graduation from MIT. He learnt his lessons initially while establishing the Eastern Spinning Mills, a group company.

He was an ardent advocate of liberalization and professional management. To him professional management was "good management"—a key driver of progress, prosperity, and economic health. For him, globalization meant more than just geographic reach. He believed that a business could be global even whilst being based in India. He single-mindedly put together the building blocks to make his Indian business a global force. It is this vision that is his enduring legacy to Indian business. It is a vision that prompts the Indian entrepreneur to take a longer stride; a vision that makes the Indian entrepreneur dare and maybe even dream; a vision that sounds a new India in the making.

He thought that excellence is an ever-moving target and believed in leadership, innovation, productivity of men and machines, quality, project management, system perfection, delegation and decentralization, participative management by consensus and consultation knowledge integration program, entrepreneurship, skills development, and human resources development.

He built up the plants and gradually increased the capacities. He also successfully diversified the business outside India. He also used the financial innovations effectively to leverage on his company's strengths by going in for GDR issues, etc.

Kumar Mangalam Birla[8]

At the outset of 1990s, the Birla empire was struck by two storms—one was the competitive scenario post liberalization and the other was the death of the legendary A.V. Birla in 1995.

Kumaramangalam Birla, an MBA from London Business School, was just beginning to grapple with the complexities of the ₹ 150,000 million Group at the age of 28, when in 1995 he lost his father, Aditya Vikram Birla. Kumar's ascension coincided with the economic downturn. Initially, his soft and shy approach led critics to comment that he lacked the business acumen and aggressiveness of his father. Over the years, he proved himself by driving productivity and profitability.

In a marked departure from the past, he hired senior people from outside, as he believed that sustainable advantage would come from constantly reinventing the group and getting people who can think out of the box on the bus. Kumar Birla made BMCL, modeled after GE Capital, the apex strategic decision-making body for catalyzing the transfer of best practices across group companies. He led growth through organic and inorganic route. In 2000, the Group acquired Indal from Alcan for a little over Rs 10,000 million. Bringing Indal into the Group's fold has helped position the Hindalco–Indal combine in every link of the value chain from metals to downstream products, accounting for over 70 percent market share. In 2003, Grasim acquired Larsen & Toubro's cement business.

Kumar Birla brought in a new breeze in the organization. He not only introduced stricter and new age management concepts, but also restructured and streamlined the operations of the group. He changed the recruitment policy of the company and instituted a retirement policy which helped in bringing a much younger, energetic, and dynamic workforce to the group companies. He laid stress on empowering the group as a whole, rather than resting powers with individual companies. He changed the way business was done within the Birla Group.

Changes[9]

In order to do away with the "babu culture," Kumar Birla launched a 360-degree feedback program that allowed managers to question even his leadership style. The Group took bold HR initiatives, spearheaded by the former Hindustan Lever Santrupt Mishra by roping in the US-based firm Hay Management Consultants to rationalize its job profile.

Kumar Birla also introduced a pathbreaking retirement policy that saw 325 senior executives between the ages of 62 and 65 step down after years of service. They have been replaced by 190 young executives.

The Cash Value Added method replaced the old partha system that focused only on production. The Cash Value Added method emphasizes three aspects: profitability, asset productivity, and growth.

Under his leadership, the Birla Group has grown five times in size through acquisitions and foray into sectors like telecom, subsequently de-risking the business portfolio of the family which was mainly in commodities. Despite taking hits in sectors like cement (because of foreign companies like Lafarge, Holcim taking over Indian companies), today the A.V. Birla group's operations extend to new age businesses like MFs, insurance, and dozens of others. How different parameters related to the Aditya Birla Group fared over a period from 2000 to 2006 is shown in Table 5.3.

TABLE 5.3 Aditya Birla Group—Performance on Various Parameters[10]

Parameters (Figures in ₹ billion)	2000	2006
M Cap	109	535
Revenues	125	270
Net profits	9	30
Promoter stake	21%	27%

Source Compiled by author from various sources.

Business Portfolio

More than 80 percent of the group's revenues come from cash cows of textiles (including VSF and VFY), cement, carbon black, aluminum, and fertilizers and one star oil refining. All of them are commodities, and even though tariff barriers are falling, the group's leadership position does not face a threat from global players. Prices of aluminum are linked to the LME. But Hindalco's low freight costs make it more attractive to local users.

The core business of the Group are Hindalco; Kesoram Industries; Grasim—VSF, cement, and textiles; Century Textiles—cement, VFY, and Textiles; and Century Enka.

COROMANDEL FERTILISERS

The Murugappa family members have all been professionally trained. They continue to seek assistance from outside consultancies like that of McKinsey.

Business Portfolio

The core business comprises CFL, EID Parry, TI, Parry Agro, CIFCO, Parry Confectionery, and Carborundum Universal. While the noncore business consists of Parry Engineering and Coromandel Engineering.

The Farm Inputs group includes CFL and EID parry's fertilizers and pesticides division. There are nine business groups. The group is the market leader in four—bonded abrasives, chains, sanitary ware, and confectionery.

MAHINDRA & MAHINDRA

History

On October 2, 1945, Mahindra & Mohammed was formed and later renamed as Mahindra & Mahindra Ltd (M&M). Initially, it started steel trading business with suppliers from the UK. In 1949, M&M started the assembly of the Jeep (Multi Utility Vehicle—MUV), becoming the sole four-wheel drive manufacturer in the country. Five years later, it went in for a technical and financial collaboration with Willys-Overland Corporation. In 1956, the company went public and got its shares listed on the Bombay Stock Exchange.

In 1963, M&M diversified into the Tractor business by setting up a joint venture with International Harvestor Co., USA, under the name International Tractor Co. of India (ITCI). This company was later merged with M&M in 1977 to become its tractor division. It went on to become a market leader in the Indian tractor market, with a market share of around 27 percent, a position that the company has never relinquished since 1983. In 1965, the company started manufacture of Light Commercial Vehicles (LCVs). In 1994, the company went global with the formation of Mahindra USA Inc., for distribution of tractors in the USA. M&M accounts for more than 70 percent of revenues.

Started by Kailash Chandra Mahindra (1894–1963) and Jagdish Chandra Mahindra (1891–1950), the leadership was taken over by Keshub Mahindra, Kailash Chandra's son, in 1964. He had three daughters. It is now Anand Mahindra, his nephew who is in charge.

Leadership Skills and Openness to Change[11]

In the early 1990s, the group's response was to replace M&M's top management team with a more pro-change one: executive director R.K. Pitamber, 65, took over as Managing Director (MD), and Anand Mahindra, nephew of Keshub Mahindra, aged 42, took over as Deputy MD.

In 1994, BPR was introduced as an experiment at M&M's Igatpuri plant, with the prime intention of increasing productivity. With Lucas Engineering systems of the UK, BPR was seen as the only way of attacking the company's age-old problem of manufacturing inefficiencies, poor productivity, long production cycles, and suboptimal output. This new system of production, which involved the relocation of machine tools, was so efficient that the company was able to reduce its staff since one person could operate four to five machines, increasing production and reducing inventory levels.

It has started making an impact on the balance sheet. Employee costs as a percent of net sales came down from 12 percent in 1994 to 9 percent in 1997 and inventory dropped from 18 percent to 12 percent. These are the benefits that came from implementation at Nashik and Igatpuri and not yet from Kandivli facility.

In 1997, Anand Mahindra visited the dealers in rural India. Subsequently M&M influenced its dealers to sell not only tractors but also seeds, fertilizers, farm equipment.

Business Portfolio

The Mahindra's have spent the post-liberalization 1990s, like every other business family, trying to build an empire that spans everything from hotels to telecom, resorts to software, advertising to engineering consultancy.

The core business of the group comprises M&M—Tractors, Mahindra USA, M&M Utility Vehicles, Mahindra Hellenic, Mahindra Sintered, Mahindra Exports, and Mahindra Engineering.

The noncore business of the group consists of Mahindra Realty & Infrastructure, Mahindra Holiday resorts, Mahindra Ugine Steel, Mahindra British telecom, Mahindra BT International, etc.

The group's six strategic business units are automotive, farm equipment, infrastructure, trade and financial services, telecom and software, and auto components.

While the farm equipment and utility vehicles businesses are both stars that require substantial investments to protect them, all the other businesses are question marks. But one question mark with star potential is auto components.

M&M is a premier leader in the automobile industry with unparallel leadership in farm equipment (tractors and implements) as well as the MUV/SUV segment. One of the main reasons for the extraordinary performance of the company has been the presence of leadership and adept management.

The leaders have developed a culture and spirit that goes beyond products and profits. More important than profitability is to provide customers value for money. M&M has always stuck to its core philosophy of providing the customers with quality products at competitive prices. The core values of M&M are (*i*) good corporate citizenship, (*ii*) professionalism, (*iii*) customer first, (*iv*) quality focus, and (*v*) dignity of the individual.

The drive to bring a change in the organization has been internal with the company committing the resources for constant innovation in the products, services, and processes. This is the reason that explains for the company's preparedness in the liberalization era. The achievement motivation has been high and the company has shown self-confidence in facing competitive forces. The efforts and initiatives taken by the company have been aligned to the core.

M&M has never sat back on its laurels and let the future slip by. Complacency was never allowed to settle in. The company aimed at goals that were out of its comfort zone, like, e.g., going global and setting up manufacturing units abroad. The Deming Award is another testimony for its spirit of pursuing "good enough never is."

Today, M&M is the flagship company of the ₹ 62,000 million Mahindra Group, one of the most respected groups in the country. The Group has presence in vehicles, farm equipment, steel, information technology, trade, financial related services, and infrastructure development. How different parameters related to the Mahindra Group fared over a period from 2000 to 2006 is shown in Table 5.4.

M&M has kept its core competencies intact.

TABLE 5.4　M&M—Performance on Various Parameters[12]

Parameters (Figures in ₹ billion)	2000	2006
M Cap	36	191
Revenues	54	121
Net profits	4	13
Promoter stake	22%	23%

Source　Compiled by author from various sources.

APOLLO TYRES

History

Incorporated on September 28, 1972, by Mathew T. Marattukalam, Jacob Thomas, and his associates, subsequently after two years the company was taken over by Raunaq Singh and his associates. The tyre project was implemented in 1976 and commercial production started in 1977 with an installed capacity of 420,000 each of tyres and tubes.

The company had technical collaboration with General Tire International Co., USA, which was later taken over by Continental Gummi Werke GmbH, West Germany. This collaboration expired in 1987.

In the early 1970s, the MNCs and the Indian tyre majors dominated the tyre industry. Despite incurring heavy losses in the initial years, primarily because the production capacities were higher compared to the market demand, Apollo came back as a strong player backed by strong production and marketing strategies. With state-of-the-art technology and goal-oriented management, Apollo came to be recognized as a respected name in the Indian tyre industry in nylon as well as radial tyre segments.

In 1987, the company acquired interest in Gujarat Tyres Ltd for implementing an industrial license to manufacture automobile tyres and tubes in Gujarat state. The company set up a plant with a capacity of 0.675 million tyres per annum at Limda, Baroda, in Gujarat, at an estimated cost of ₹ 1,690 million.

In 1994, a new plant in Pune was commissioned. The company entered into an agreement with Continental AG, Germany, for setting up a passenger car radial tyre factory. It is the single-largest tube and flaps manufacturing unit and started production in 1996. The entire production was captively consumed and outsourcing of tubes came down considerably.

In 1998, a plant to manufacture radials was set up in Vadodara. Premier Tyres, its subsidiary, set up another radials plant at Ropar in Punjab to cater to the tractor and earthmovers segments.

Openness to Change

If there is one word that sums up the history of Apollo Tyres—India's largest manufacturer of truck tyres—it is resilience.

Started in 1973, for a company nationalized in the sixth month of its operations in 1977, tossed back to its promoters five years later with its net worth eroded five times, and besieged by four years of board room battles between promoter Raunaq Singh, 80 and his son Onkar Singh Kanwar, 55; Apollo has shaped up remarkably well.

Like its domestic rivals, Apollo was caught off guard by the opening up of the market. Tariff barriers had lulled tyre companies into complacency. Kanwar reacted in the only way he possibly could—by bolstering marketing efforts rather than investing in radial technology—and he was quick.

Earlier Apollo would resort to discounts for perking up a sluggish market. Not anymore. Instead, it is building a secondary value chain directed solely at its customers. Instead of relying on dealers, Apollo is now servicing its large customers directly with the help of its 100 offices nationwide.

There has been a focus on retooling organizational skills with the help of management consultants. The exercises involved relocating or inducting human capital and scrapping old functions, or creating new ones. Non-MBA employees were positioned to attend management programs while MBA managers were trained in leadership and communication skills. Further, Apollo de-layered its 12 management layers to reduce to half.

Family Dynamics

The family owns 22 percent which is 4 percent less than what it needs to block a special resolution. Kanwar has managed to stall his father Raunaq Singh's bid to transfer his holdings to his other children.

Kanwar is the undisputed CEO. He manages by consensus. His younger son, Neeraj Kanwar, heads strategic planning while the elder Raaja Kanwar looks after the Apollo International, the company's export arm.

All major proposals are filtered through a five-member corporate executive committee which comprises the heads of marketing, HR, manufacturing, finance, and R&D. While Kanwar has the power to veto any decision, he rarely does so.

Leadership Skills

While one saw the group as a paternalistic organization, which put the family first, the other relies more on professionals and empowerment. Kanwar believed in reposing a lot of faith in his people. As long as people deliver, they had carte blanche. Kanwar loosened his control and allowed professionals to run the company.

Kanwar believes that people are central to his process of strategy planning—a tyre manufacturer like Apollo needs both technologists and marketers.

The fear of competition has been well embedded in the organization's psyche. Competitiveness is something that the CEO has constantly drummed into his people. With the transnationals like Groupe Michelin coming in, things are not going to be the same again.

Business Portfolio

The core business of the Group comprises Apollo Tyres and Premier Tyres, while the noncore business consists of Apollo Finance.

KIRLOSKAR BROTHERS

History

The group is 117 years old. Laxmanrao Kirloskar started his bicycle assembly business in 1880, a time when there was hardly any industrial activity in India except for the manufacture for cotton textiles. By the time India became independent, the group had become the first manufacturer of engineering products like diesel engines and electric motors. During the last three decades, however, the Kirloskars have not entered any new product lines.

The group is sharply focused on critical engineering products like engines, motors, and compressors. Paradoxically, while the Kirloskar Group was the first in the country to make electric motors, machine tools, diesel engines, and centrifugal compressors—and has dominant position in most of these businesses—its margins are under pressure because of several process inefficiencies that have not been weeded out over the years. In many ways, the group is reminiscent of German companies of the mid-1960s which had excellent engineering skills but abysmal financial controls.

The group is rising from two decades of desolation. The first, leading to the 1990s, saw death wipe out almost the entire second generation of the ₹ 26,950 million Kirloskar Group. The next, in the early 1990s, saw a shaky family mount a search for an effective alternative to the group head, Shantanurao Laxmanrao Kirloskar (SLK) who by then was an ageing octogenarian. While SLK did manage to anoint his nephew Vijay, before he died in 1994, at the age of 91, the group paid dearly for its preoccupation. It missed the liberalization bandwagon.

In 1990, they lost control of Kirloskar Cummins to their collaborator, the $ 5.3 billion Cummins Engine.

The strengths typically have been native technological strengths, a focus on appropriate technology and strong brand. They built the business with commitment and integrity. Their name commands a high degree of loyalty among its customers. Where the group did err was in not managing its finances as well as its product quality.

Openness to Change

False sense of complacency due to its premier position in the market, the Group has been slow to change. A phobia had kept it from getting into JVs in its core businesses. The group was headed by different family members, depriving the group of professional and objective views. In 1990, they lost control of Kirloskar Cummins to their collaborator, the $5.3 billion Cummins Engine. Post Cummins there have also been a new generation of alliances, such as (*i*) Mysore Kirloskar—JV with $6 billion Snyder General to manufacture pollution control equipment in 1992, (*ii*) Mysore Kirloskar—JV with $7.2 billion Toyoda Automatic Loom Works—holding company of Toyota and a textile machinery manufacturer, and (*iii*) Toyota JV.

As for the JV with Toyota, the Kirloskars do not suffer from the delusion of being equal partners. An important part of the Japanese model is the vendor's close relationship with the car maker. Apart from holding a 26 percent equity stake, the Kirloskars would supply a range of components to the JV.

Family Dynamics

The 1980s witnessed the sudden death of brother Ravikant and his sons Chandrakant and Shrikant. The departed Chandrakant left behind his sons Atul and Vikram. The departed Shrikant left behind his sons Sanjay and Rahul. While Vijay Kirloskar acted as the Group Head, Atul Kirloskar functioned as the VC and MD of Kirloskar Oil Engines and Vikram Kirloskar became the CEO of Mysore Kirloskar.

Business Portfolio

The flagship of the group is Kirloskar Oil Engines—market share at 56 percent over 1987–97. The second-largest company, Kirloskar Electric, had market shares ranging between 16 percent and 80 percent in various product categories.

The group had a high degree of conceptual synergy. There are sources of mechanical power (like electric motors and diesel engines) and pumps, compressors, alternators, and machine tools that are driven by these power sources. There are also transformers and switchgear that fit upstream and downstream from motors to alternators. For much of this product range, the market is one since all industrial units need a broad range of these products.

Kirloskar Institute of Advanced Management studies typically had been providing the supply of managers to the group. The group HRD system had lent support for sharing best practices within the group.

SUNDARAM FASTENERS[13]

Four sons of T.V. Sundaram Iyengar, T.S. Rajam, T.S. Krishna, T.S. Srinivasan, and T.S. Santhanam, then successfully led TVS into the fields of vehicle dealerships, auto parts, auto financing, and manufacturing of two-wheelers.

Suresh Krishna is the chairman and managing director at SFL. Under his leadership, SFL became the first company in the Indian engineering industry to set up a fully owned manufacturing subsidiary in China. He is also the chairman of Sundaram Clayton Ltd, Upaasana Finance Ltd, Sundaram Telematics Ltd, Sundaram Non-Conventional Energy Systems Ltd, Sundaram Numeric Ltd, and Unipaat TVS Ltd. Also, he is a director at Lucas TVS, TV Sundaram Iyengar & Sons Ltd, and TVS Sewing Needles Ltd.

Under the competent leadership and relentless perfectionism of Venu Srinivasan, T.S. Srinivasan Group today boasts of successful companies like TVS Motors, TVS Electronics, Sundaram Clayton, and India Nippon among others. Venu Srinivasan is also a board director at SFL. He is the grandson of TVS founder—T.V. Sundaram Iyengar. An engineering graduate and MBA from Purdue University, he started his career as a car mechanic at their own TVS Garage. He is the Chairman of TVS Suzuki and Sundaram Clayton. His passion for excellence made Sundaram Clayton win the Demings Award, a global quality benchmark. He is credited with pioneering the TQM efforts based on the Japanese Model in India, long before the other enterprises embraced it. How different parameters related to the TVS Group fared over a period from 2000 to 2006 is shown in Table 5.5.

The family accord has not suffered either.

TABLE 5.5   TVS Group—Performance on Various Parameters

Parameters (Figures in ₹ billion)	2000	2006
M Cap	8	35
Revenues	39	44
Net profits	2	1
Promoter stake	59%	57%

Source   See Note 10.

EXIDE INDUSTRIES

Leadership

Exide Industries is led by Satya Brata Ganguly, the chairman and managing director. He has built a superior executive team around him. In spite of batteries being in the OGL, he and his team has achieved near monopoly in the battery business, which speaks of his leadership abilities. He is a level 5 leader with paradoxical blend of fierce will and personal humility. They are stubborn yet they are humble. Ganguly inspires standards and has been instrumental in making Exide into one of the best companies of India.

Human Resources Management

Exide had 3,860 permanent employees as at the end of March 2004. The training needs for the managerial category of employees is assessed by the HR department at the beginning of the year and a number of programs are organized with both in-house and external experts to deliver need-based training. The company has also a system of annual appraisals with nonperformers being singled out for guidance and monitoring. A system of succession planning has commenced in the current year and is expected to ensure that performers have a fast career growth path.

GAMMON INDIA LTD

History

The company was established by late John C. Gammon in 1919 is a firm of civil engineers and contractors, which in 1922 was incorporated as a private limited company under the name of J.C. Gammon (Bombay) Pvt. Ltd The firm went public in 1962 and was rechristened as Gammon India Limited.

The first work carried out by J.C. Gammon was the construction of reinforced concrete pile foundations for Gateway of India. Since then, the Company has executed many multi-ferrous civil engineering works from cotton godowns to bridges/flyovers, marine structures, cooling towers, chimneys, tunnels, and dams in India and in the Middle East. Gammon is the pioneer of prestressed concrete in India.

Striving for excellence and perfection, the company has many firsts to its credit. The company has introduced prestressed concrete in India as early as in 1941 followed by the first prestressed concrete bridge in 1949.

Gammon has to its credit the longest river bridge in the world across the mighty Ganges in Patna, the tallest bridge in Asia, the longest span cantilever bridge in India across River Jadukata, the longest road bridge in India across the open sea, and first cable-stayed bridge in India. The company pioneered cantilever construction, pre-cast segmental bridge construction.

Today, the company can claim for the largest numbers of bridges and flyovers built in India. With over 80 years of tradition in the field of construction, Gammon is a name that is inextricably woven into the fabric of India. Gammon India Limited, the only Indian Construction Company to have been accredited with ISO 9001 certification for all fields of Civil Engineering Works including design, stands out as gateway for Technological and Engineering excellence in Civil Engineering fields. This has led Gammon to the position of one of the leading engineering and construction companies in India. Gammon today can be rightly referred to as "Builders to the Nation."

John C. Gammon, the founder, joined the Public Works Department of India as Assistant Engineer in 1910, after a First Class Honors in Engineering from London, and brief stint in the reinforced concrete department of Messrs Leslie & Co., Kingston. He soon became reinforced concrete expert and contributed his genius to the structures of the Science College, the Prince of Wales Museum, and the Customs House in Bombay. After the First World War and demobilization, he returned to India in 1919 and gave foundation to the prestigious Gateway of India and many other structures that won him recognition, here and abroad.

In 1922, he established J.C. Gammon Ltd. He continued to expand his horizon across the Commonwealth, Asia, and West Africa. And though the activities spread far and wide, Gammon India continued to root, the source where J.C. Gammon first sowed the seed of his remarkable vision.

From monuments and bridges to reservoirs and jetties, his innovative vision and engineering skill, his intuitive understanding of the materials and systems of construction sought and fought answers to some of the most challenging examples in civil engineering projects. His abiding faith in people and their abilities inspired them to meet the challenge after challenge.

Gammon had several firsts to credit. The RCC pile foundation for the Gateway of India, the thin shell structure of the Meerut

Garages, the colloidal grouting process at Mundali Weir, the hyperbolic cooling towers at Sabarmati are but a few achievements. Bridges like Bonum and Patalgang, which were built by him, have stood the test of time as monuments to his ingenious skill.

LARSEN & TOUBRO

History

Founded in 1938 by two Danish engineers, Henning Holk Larsen and Soren Kristian Toubro, as a partnership firm, Larsen & Toubro became a private limited company in 1946 and a public limited one in 1950. Larsen & Toubro (L&T) is one of the largest engineering conglomerates in South East Asia.

Beginning with the import of machinery from Europe, L&T rapidly took on engineering and construction assignments of increasing sophistication. Today, the company sets engineering benchmarks in terms of scale and complexity.

It manufactures a wide range of engineering products like earthmoving, industrial and chemical machinery, switchgears, valves, and welding alloys. L&T diversified into shipping, acquiring two bulk carriers from Japan in 1981–82. In 1983–84, it commenced operations at its 1-Mtpa cement plant at Awarpur, Maharashtra. The company is taking various steps to exit from its noncore areas to enhance the focus on its core businesses—Engineering & Construction, High End Manufacturing, Electrical & Electronics, Information Technology, and Engineering Services. Much awaited, extensively deliberated demerger of cement business to UltraTech Cemco has been effective from April 1, 2003, and now L&T is purely a EPC contractor with interests in electrical and electronics, ready mix concrete, and power (through subsidiary).

L&T is a technology-driven engineering and construction organization, and has additional interests in manufacturing, services, and Information Technology.

A strong, customer-focused approach and the constant quest for top-class quality have enabled the Company to attain and sustain leadership in its major lines of business across seven decades.

SIEMENS LTD

History

Siemens was founded in Berlin by Werner von Siemens in 1847. As an extraordinary inventor, engineer, and entrepreneur, Werner von Siemens made the world's first pointer telegraph and electric dynamo, inventions that helped put the spin in the industrial revolution. He was the man behind one of the most fascinating success stories of all time—by turning a humble little workshop into one of the world's largest enterprises.

As Werner had envisioned, the company he started grew from strength to strength in every field of electrical engineering. From constructing the world's first electric railway to laying the first telegraph line linking Britain and India, Siemens was responsible for building much of the modern world's infrastructure.

Siemens is today a technology giant in more than 190 countries, employing some 440,000 people worldwide. Their work in the fields of energy, industry, communications, information, transportation, health care, components, and lighting had become essential parts of everyday life.

While Werner was a tireless inventor during his days, Siemens today remains a relentless innovator. With innovations averaging 18 a day, it seems like the revolution Werner started is still going strong.

India Operations

The company was incorporated on March 2, 1957 as a private limited company under the name "Siemens Engineering and Manufacturing Company of India Private Limited." When the company was incorporated at its repair shop, switchboard manufacture was being carried on at Worli, Mumbai. The Company entered into a collaboration agreement with two foreign companies, viz., Siemens & Halske AG and Siemens–Schuckertwerke AG of West Germany. Later these companies were merged with Siemens AG in 1970.

In 1967, the name of the Company was changed from Siemens Engineering & Manufacturing Co. of India Ltd to Siemens India Ltd. In 1987, the name of the company again changed from Siemens India Ltd to Siemens Ltd.

The company manufactures switchboards, switch gear, different types of motors up to 315 KW, assembly of railway signaling equipment, X-ray, and other electromedical equipment, installation, testing and commissioning of electrical plant and equipment undertaking repair work of motors, generators, transformers, calorific and measuring instruments, certain household appliances and marine electrical equipment, and selling of products manufactured by the Company as well as those of its licensees.

People Strengths

Employees have been a key pillar in their success. The company well recognizes this aspect which is embedded in its Four Point Program. It is their belief that employees have to be given the right environment for their talents to bloom and they need to be nurtured as one of their most important assets. Their constant endeavor has therefore been to provide people with an enabling atmosphere where they are motivated to deliver their best.

A number of initiatives have been taken by the company to address their employees needs. We have several programs aimed at tapping employee potential and developing key talent. Increased transparency right across the organization has been one of the key achievements of their relationship. The company believes that its employees must be on the same plane of awareness with regard to information about the organization and events that affect them.

Some initiatives in this direction include a leadership continuity plan. Their dialogue process has proved to be very successful and employees are being given higher responsibility with higher targets for delivery. The company has a highly performance-driven team with an entrepreneurial spirit. Interestingly, through their suggestion scheme, their employees have contributed directly to the bottom line of our Company. This has come about through tangible and measurable suggestions received from employees that have resulted in savings.

Social Responsibility

Despite the company's sights firmly on the growth path, it has not lost sight of its social commitments. It has been amongst the first to lend a helping hand to the unfortunate. Its long-term commitments continue unhindered be it in providing relief to the victims of tsunami in India and Sri Lanka or in tendering to the children of St Catherines High School, Mumbai, India.

Frequently Asked Questions 6

It is your Work in life that is the ultimate seduction.
—Pablo Picasso

1. Did you select the companies?
2. Why did you limit your research to publicly traded companies?
3. Why did not any IT companies appear in the study set?
4. Why did not any public sector companies appear in the study set?
5. Which are the companies and what made them succeed in the pre- and post-1991 liberalization era of the Indian industry?
6. Why did you term these companies as "Excellent Companies" instead of "Great Companies?"
7. How did some of these study companies compare with those companies that got selected in other surveys?
8. Would you like to reference any other international works which in your opinion are inspirational?

1. Did you select the companies?

We did not select the companies. Our methodology selected the 23 companies. Our companies were (*i*) publicly traded, listed companies since 1974; (*ii*) have been in existence since 1974; (*iii*) showed positive profits consistently; and (*iv*) had a market capitalization (365 days average) of ₹ 500 million in 2002.

The market capitalization was the "365 days average" market capitalization for a company.

The final list of 23 companies performed three times above the general market returns computed as OSPI by taking the average of the "compound annual total returns" for all the 144 short-listed companies.

2. Why did you limit your research to publicly traded companies?

Publicly traded companies have the advantage of easily accessible data. Privately held companies have limited information available which would be problematic from a study viewpoint.

3. Why did not any IT companies appear in the study set?

We have selected 1974 as the cutoff year, i.e., only those companies make the cut which were established and listed prior to 1974. *We decided that a period of minimum 30 years* should be taken so as to eliminate any element of personal bias and make sure that "onetime wonders" were not considered.

Hence many good companies in the Indian scenario, especially the *IT power horses* (Infosys, Wipro, etc.) couldn't make the cut. As a result, even though some of these companies have been performing very well consistently, they still couldn't make it to our list.

4. Why did not any public sector companies appear in the study set?

Also many *good public sector units* like Indian Oil, Hindustan Petroleum, etc., and several good public sector banks could not make the cut as they went in for IPO and listing only after the 1991 economic reforms.

5. Which are the companies and what made them succeed in the pre- and post-1991 liberalization era of the Indian industry?

It is interesting to note that the companies that have qualified as good to excellent companies belong to different industries and have stuck to their respective core businesses. The industries range from textiles, hotels, sugar, power, automotives, chemicals, tires, fasteners, aluminum, etc. Another interesting feature is that these companies have existence of 40 years or more, possibly because of the screening criteria adopted by us in our study that the companies should have been listed from the year 1974.

Most of the above companies have gone global, while sticking to a business that they knew best. A few companies like Indian Hotels and Bombay Dyeing went global in 1979, almost 12 years before the 1991 Economic Reforms. Even companies like Tata Power, that has served the domestic market since ages, have started going global.

Exception to the companies going global are companies in the power generation and distribution, like Ahmedabad Electricity, etc. (now part of the Torrent Power), where there is so much of unmet demand in the country and also Bajaj Hindusthan that is in an agro-based industry like sugar.

Quite a few Tata Group companies find their place, viz., Indian Hotels, Tata Power, Tata Chemicals, Tata Steel, and Tinplate Company. Tata Power stuck to its knitting in power business and remained as a single business company, Tata Chemicals as dominant business, M&M as related diversifier in metal-based companies, and Siemens as a related diversifier in electricity companies. Hindalco, Tata Steel, and Apollo Tyres pursued a dominant vertical strategy.

A study of these companies led us to propose a business model that is based on strategy, execution excellence, and leadership that provides a compelling explanation of their exceptional performance.

6. Why did you term these companies as "Excellent Companies" instead of "Great Companies?"

India is a young democracy that achieved its economic freedom from 1991. Unlike America, India is not as mature in terms of its economic growth. India earned its right to freedom and self-determination in 1947 while America got it way back in 1776. It is this context and backdrop that makes us to refer to the Indian companies as "Excellent" instead of "Great." Most of the Indian companies do not figure in the top global companies. It is also this consideration that prompts us to refer to them as "Excellent."

Twenty years later, when a similar analysis is carried out at a time that India would have attained developed nation status, perhaps it would become more meaningful to refer to those then companies that would have satisfied our current screening criteria as "Great."

7. How did some of these study companies compare with those companies that got selected in other surveys?
You can find the answer to this question in Chapter 7 and Appendix B.

8. Would you like to reference any other international works which in your opinion are inspirational?
Yes. I would recommend reading the works of Tom Peters, *In Search of Excellence* (1982), and Jim Collins, *Good to Great* (2001). Please read a synopsis on the two books in Appendix C.

Wrapping It Up 7

Vision without action is merely a dream. Action without vision just passes time. But vision with action can change the world.
—Joel Arthur Barker

Toward the end of this research work, it is interesting to see that our research companies are getting listed in several surveys that get carried out in our country. Here we take reference to three recent surveys that figured some of our research companies.

FIRST SURVEY

Our following research companies got listed in the BT 500 companies (India's most valuable companies), a methodology adopted by *Business Today* on average market capitalization between April 1 and September 30, 2005, as shown in Table 7.1.

The ranking is based on average market capitalization in the period between April 1, 2005, and September 30, 2005. BT 500 isn't the only corporate listing around. Others rank companies on sales alone and still others for hybrid listings.

TABLE 7.1 Study Companies in BT 500—India's Most Valuable Companies[1]

Company	Rank	Avg. Mar Cap H1 2005–06 (₹ million)
Hindalco	20	119,413.5
Sundaram Fasteners	137	13,914.7
SKF India	181	11,027.4
Tata Power	28	78,261.0
Tata Steel	10	206,378.8
Indian Hotels	59	34,648.0
Gammon India	85	22,722.5
Tata Chemicals	56	37,862.9
Coromandel Fertilisers	301	5,602.3
Bombay Dyeing	144	13,749.3
M&M	36	68,177.9
Kirlsokar Brothers	143	13,749.8
Exide Industries	151	13,185.3
KEC International	229	8,417.8
Bajaj Hindusthan	108	17,784.7
Apollo Tyres	192	10,314.5

SECOND SURVEY

If we examine the statistics of performance of the top 100 companies operating in India during the period 1991–2002, we will notice that a large number of companies had dwindling performance and slipped to lower ranks, while during the same period a few companies not only sustained but also surpassed many others to achieve much higher rank within the list.

Only 27 companies remained among the top 100, while 73 companies which were among the top 100 companies in market capitalization in the year 1991, were no more in the list and were replaced by other companies in the year 2001. During this period, some companies that were at much lower ranks moved up significantly.

Thirteen of the companies in our study figure in the top 100 of the *Business Today* rankings of 1991 and 2002 that was based on market capitalization as shown in Table 7.2.

THIRD SURVEY

Our following six study companies (see Table 7.3) got listed in the 100 most profitable companies, a methodology adopted by *Business & Economy*, September 22–October 5, 2006 issue:

Tata Steel—Rank 17
Hindalco—Rank 25
M&M—Rank 36
Tata Power—Rank 37
Indian Hotels—Rank 69
Tata Chemicals—Rank 77

The companies were chosen from BSE 500 index. The BSE index represents 93 percent of the total market capitalization on BSE. It virtually covers all possible sectors. In total, 17 sectors were

TABLE 7.2 Study Companies in Top 100 of the BT Rankings[2,3,4]

Company name	BT rank 1991 (based on market capitalization)	BT rank 2002 (based on market capitalization)
Hindalco	11	18
L&T	14	23
Siemens	37	56
Tata Power	47	32
Tata Steel	1	20
Tata Chemicals	25	–
SKF Bearings	28	–
Apollo Tyres	45	–
Coromandel Fertilisers	91	–
M&M	–	45
Indian Hotels	–	65
Novartis	–	79
Motor Industries	20	–

identified: agriculture, capital goods, consumer durables, textiles, FMCG, banking, telecom, health care, housing related, IT, media and publishing, metal and mining, oil and gas, power, transport equipment, chemicals and petrochemicals, and other diversified.

Four defining parameters were considered for the shortlist of 100. These are cash earnings per share (EPS), adjusted ROCE, ROA, and market capitalization. Equal weightage was attached to all the four parameters.

The absolute figures for the past three financial years were taken into account, thereby discounting down the effects of any windfall gains or abrupt losses that companies may have had in the recent short term. Two additional details like dividend yield and PAT/sales ratio have been given as details with performance summary and profile commentaries. Only 25 percent weight has been given to market capitalization as it moves more by market dynamics than by true fundamental or technical analysis. Moreover, some leading companies that were not listed on BSE 500 were also left out.

TABLE 7.3   100 Most Profitable Companies[5]

Company	Adj. ROCE avg.	CEPS avg.	ROA avg.	M Cap avg.	Final score
Tata Steel	0.29	78.68	0.29	22,009.04	5,522.07
Hindalco	0.11	13.71	0.11	14,803.37	3,704.32
M&M	0.18	30.67	0.18	8,754.51	2,196.38
Tata Power	0.07	36.71	0.07	8,673.71	2,177.64
Indian Hotels	0.05	44.74	0.05	4,167.43	1,053.07
Tata Chemicals	0.09	26.15	0.09	3,745.78	943.03

Jagdish Sheth mentions that as India integrates into the world economy, there is a need for it to reposition itself as a country.[6] From the domestic-oriented, self-sufficient license raj, it has come a long way to become a global-oriented economy focusing on those key sectors of the economy where it has a resource advantage over other nations. The objective is to offer better products at lower prices. Exports to the most demanding markets, after all, are the key to success for a globally competitive economy. To achieve this objective, India needs to reengineer itself in the following areas of industrial policy, international trade, domestic industry, and national infrastructure. Of these, domestic infrastructure is the weakest link. The Indian industries reposition themselves from the diversified domestic corporations to focused global enterprises. To be a global hub, they need quality and reputation and must, therefore, invest in design and research, create brand equity, increase productivity, leverage human capital, get access to low-cost capital, and organize supply chain.

CONCLUSION

Which are the companies and what made them succeed in the pre- and post-1991 liberalization era of the Indian industry?

Our research on "Which Indian companies succeeded in the pre- and post-1991 liberalization period and why?" adopted some of the methodologies applied by Jim Collins in his book *Good to Great* (2001).

We looked for companies that showed exceptional returns. We looked for companies that had cumulative returns at least three times the market over the years. A question arises here? Why three times the market? Three times the market because it exceeds the performance of most widely acknowledged companies. We took companies that were incorporated and listed before 1974 as these companies transcend the onetime wonders, as well as lucky breaks, and would exceed the normal tenure of most CEOs. To get a clearer understanding, please revisit Chapter 1.

Companies were identified that made the leap from good to excellent results and sustained those results since 1974. The good to excellent companies that made the final list attained extraordinary results averaging cumulative stock returns more than three times the OSPI since 1974.

The companies' performances were analyzed based on a number of parameters. An effort was made to determine those factors that made them perform and to understand what made these companies tick. We collected secondary data about these organizations from a variety of sources, and tried to then understand what separated these companies from the others. A case study method was adopted and an attempt was made to arrive at a business model.

TABLE 7.4 List of Study Companies

Sr. No.	Excellent companies
1	Ahmedabad Electricity Company (now Torrent Power)
2	Apollo Tyres Ltd
3	Bajaj Hindusthan
4	Bombay Dyeing and Manufacturing Ltd
5	Coromandel Fertilisers Ltd
6	Exide Industries
7	Gammon India Ltd
8	Hindalco Industries Ltd
9	Indian Hotels Co. Ltd
10	KEC International Ltd
11	Kirloskar Brothers Ltd
12	Larsen & Toubro Ltd
13	Mahindra & Mahindra Ltd
14	Motor Industries Co. Ltd
15	Novartis India Ltd
16	SKF Bearings India Ltd
17	Siemens Ltd
18	Sundaram Fasteners Ltd
19	Surat Electricity Company (now Torrent Power)
20	Tata Chemicals Ltd
21	Tata Iron & Steel Co. Ltd
22	Tata Power Co. Ltd
23	Tinplate Co. of India Ltd

Many other good companies in the Indian scenario, all the IT powerhouses (Infosys, Wipro, etc.), couldn't make the cut because they did not meet the criteria of minimum 25 years of operation and public trading/listing for 25 years. As a result, even though some of these companies have been performing very well consistently, they still couldn't make it to our list of top companies. Also many good public sector units like Indian Oil, Hindustan Petroleum, etc., and several good public sector banks could not make the cut as they went in for IPO and listing only after the 1991 economic reforms.

As said earlier, the companies that have qualified as good to excellent companies have existence of 40 years or more, possibly because of our screening criteria that the companies should have been listed from the year 1974. The other interesting feature is that these companies belong to different industries and have stuck to their respective core businesses. The industries range from textiles, hotels, sugar, power, automotives, chemicals, tyres, fasteners, aluminum, etc.

Most of the companies have global operations, while adhering to a business that they knew best. Companies like Bombay Dyeing and Indian Hotels went global in 1979, 12 years before the 1991 economic reforms. Companies like Tata Power, which served the domestic market since ages, have started going global. Tata Power's power systems division has emerged as a major player in the EPC transmission business in the country. It has won the largest transmission line construction export contract in Bangladesh against tough competition from domestic and international transmission line EPC companies.

There are a few exceptions to the companies going global which are into power generation and distribution, like Ahmedabad Electricity, etc. (now part of the Torrent Power), where there is a lot of unmet domestic demand. Bajaj Hindusthan, which is in an agro-based industry like sugar, is also an exception.

Quite a few Tata Group companies find their place, viz., Indian Hotels, Tata Power, Tata Chemicals, Tata Steel, and Tinplate Company. Tata Power stuck to its knitting in power business and remained as a single business company; Tata Chemicals as dominant business; M&M as related diversifier in metal-based companies; Siemens as a related diversifier in electricity companies. Hindalco, Tata Steel, and Apollo Tyres pursued a dominant vertical strategy.

A study of these companies made the research work propose a business model that is based on strategy, execution excellence, and leadership that provides a compelling explanation of their exceptional performance.

THE BUSINESS MODEL CONSISTS OF THREE THEMES

Strategy

Going global, cost leadership through scale, technology leadership and alliances, sales distribution network, focus (core, noncore) (Figure 7.1).

Execution Excellence

TQM, BPR, Six Sigma, ERP, e-business (process, people, and productivity); responsiveness to change: shop floor, R&D, IT, and HRM; structure; operating mechanisms.

Leadership

Change management, professionalism, culture, succession planning, internal stability, passion to win, will, vision, and values.

Jim Collins methodology was used with certain modifications to see if there are certain Indian companies that have demonstrated transition from good to great. While Jim Collins referred to those exceptional companies as "Good to Great," this study had referred to the exceptional Indian companies as "Good to Excellent."

India, unlike America, is a young democracy that has attained its economic independence from 1991. Unlike America, India is not

FIGURE 7.1 Business Model

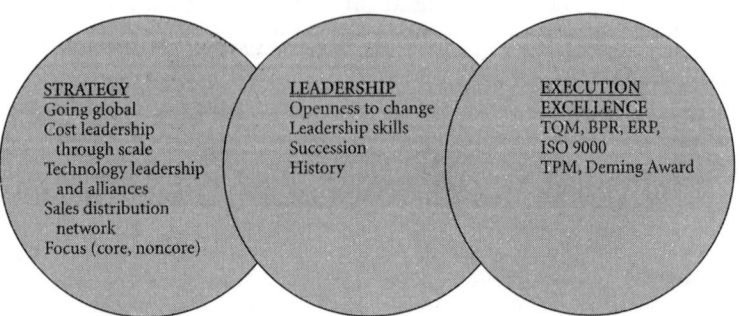

as mature in terms of its economic growth. India earned its right to freedom and self-determination in 1947 while America got it way back in 1776. It is this context and backdrop that makes us to refer to the Indian companies as "Excellent" instead of "Great." Most of the Indian companies do not figure in the top global companies. It is also this consideration that prompts us to refer to them as "Excellent."

Perhaps, 20 years later, when we carry out a similar kind of analysis at a time that India would have attained developed nation status, it would become more appropriate to refer to those then companies that would have satisfied our current screening criteria as "Great."

Appendix A
Chapter 1—Data

COMPARISON WITH JIM COLLINS METHODOLOGY

Our modifications and departures from Jim Collins Methodology are shown in the Table A.1.

TABLE A.1 Jim Collins vs. Our Methodology

Collins methodology	Our methodology
30 years' data Center for Research in Security Prices (CRSP)—University of Chicago	30 years' data Center for Monitoring Indian Economy (CMIE)—Prowess database
CUT 1 Universe to 1,435 companies—*Fortune* 500 listings of 1965, 1975, 1985, and 1995.	Universe (7,000 companies) to 144 companies from the CMIE Prowess data—based on existence since 1974 and a market capitalization exceeding ₹500 million.
CUT 2 Selecting 126 companies, founded after 1970, with compound annual total return to investors > 1.3 times average returns over 3 specific time periods: (*i*) 1985–95, (*ii*) 1975–95, and (*iii*) 1965–95.	Selecting 47 companies, with compound annual total return to investors > 1.3 times' average returns over 3 specific time periods: (*i*) 1996–2002, (*ii*) 1991–2002, and (*iii*) 1985–2002, and (*iv*) 1974–2002.
CUT 3 Applied the criteria of three times the average returns. Identified the transition point (*T* year), *X* period and	Litmus test is to look for three times above the OSPI curve:

(*Table A.1 continued*)

(*Table A.1 continued*)

Collins methodology	Our methodology
the Y period. From 126 companies came down to 19 companies. 11 elimination criteria were used: (*i*) there is no X period; (*ii*) no obvious shift to breakthrough performance; (*iii*) demonstrated a transition but an X period of < 10 years; (*iv*) terrible to average performance relative to the market; (*v*) transition after 1985; (*vi*) transition to increased performance but it is not sustained; (*vii*) wild swings with no clear X period, Y period, T year; (*viii*) data not available before 1975, making it difficult to identify X period; (*ix*) there is a transition pattern but the company demonstrated a period of such spectacular performance that the company is a great company that had fallen temporarily into difficult times, rather than a good company that became great. The classic example is Walt Disney (*x*) company is acquired or merged by the time of Cut 3 analysis (*xi*) mild transition but falls short of three times the market. **CUT 4** Find companies that made a transition, not industries that made a transition. To remove industry transition, CRSP analysis was repeated for the 19 companies, only this time against a composite industry index rather than the general stock market. This distilled the final list to 11 companies.	1. The company shows a transition to increased performance, but the rise in performance is not sustained. After the initial rise it goes flat or declines relative to the market until 2002. 2. The company demonstrates a volatile pattern of returns—large upward and downward swings. 3. The company falls for brief periods below the *three times* OSPI mark, demonstrating difficult times. 4. The company falls short of *three times* the market average returns.

Source Author.

TABLE A.2 List of 144 Companies (Listed before 1974)*

	Company name	Incorporation	M Cap (₹ million)
1	ABB Ltd	1949	11,375.7
2	Abbott India Ltd	1949	4,741.1
3	Ahmedabad Electricity Co. Ltd	1913	3,578.6
4	Alembic Ltd	1919	977.5

Table A.2 continued

Appendix A | 183

Table A.2 continued

	Company name	Incorporation	M Cap (₹ million)
5	Alfa Laval (India) Ltd	1937	4,258.3
6	Andhra Pradesh Paper Mills Ltd	1964	511.6
7	Andhra Valley Power Supply Co. Ltd [Merged]	1916	3,372.2
8	Andrew Yule & Co. Ltd	1919	824.1
9	Apollo Tyres Ltd	1972	4,078.1
10	Arvind Mills Ltd	1968	3,677.2
11	Ashok Leyland Ltd	1956	11,672.3
12	Asian Paints (India) Ltd	1945	21,135.9
13	Associated Cement Cos. Ltd	1936	25,408.3
14	Atlas Copco (India) Ltd	1960	2,045.5
15	BASF India Ltd	1943	3,044.1
16	BOC India Ltd	1935	1,267.1
17	Bajaj Auto Ltd	1945	48,042.9
18	Bajaj Hindusthan Ltd	1931	523.7
19	Bajaj Tempo Ltd	1958	1,358.2
20	Ballarpur Industries Ltd	1945	5,285.7
21	Balmer Lawrie & Co. Ltd	1924	1,305.1
22	Bata India Ltd	1931	1,849.2
23	Berger Paints India Ltd	1923	1,944.9
24	Bharat Forge Ltd	1961	6,833.8
25	Blue Star Ltd	1949	1,311.4
26	Bombay Burmah Trdg Corpn Ltd	1863	546.6
27	Bombay Dyeing & Mfg Co. Ltd	1879	1,804.0
28	Brooke Bond Lipton India Ltd [Merged]	1912	43,548.6
29	Burroughs Wellcome (India) Ltd	1912	1,983.7
30	Cabot India Ltd	1962	768.2
31	Ceat Ltd	1958	1,102.3
32	Century Enka Ltd	1965	2,395.1
33	Chennai Petroleum Corpn Ltd	1965	4,495.7
34	Chettinad Cement Corpn Ltd	1962	1,322.6
35	Cipla Ltd	1935	54,945.7
36	Coates Of India Ltd	1947	642.5
37	Colour-Chem Ltd	1956	2,358.2
38	Coromandel Fertilisers Ltd	1961	1,350.7
39	Crompton Greaves Ltd	1937	2,440.5
40	Cummins India Ltd	1962	10,301.8
41	Dalmia Cement (Bharat) Ltd	1951	1,138.2
42	EIH Ltd	1949	10,408.7
43	Electrosteel Castings Ltd	1955	4,305.1
44	Engine Valves Ltd [Merged]	1954	948.4
45	Eveready Industries (India) Ltd	1934	805.3
46	Excel Industries Ltd	1960	831.3

Table A.2 continued

Table A.2 continued

	Company name	Incorporation	M Cap (₹ million)
47	Exide Industries Ltd	1947	2,821.8
48	FAG Bearings India Ltd	1962	861.7
49	Fertilisers & Chemicals, Travancore Ltd	1943	10,909.6
50	Finolex Cables Ltd	1973	4,063.4
51	Forbes Gokak Ltd	1919	794.1
52	Gammon India Ltd	1922	1,223.9
53	German Remedies Ltd [Merged]	1949	2,178.1
54	Glaxosmithkline Pharmaceuticals Ltd	1924	25,899.1
55	Godfrey Phillips India Ltd	1936	3,644.4
56	Goetze (India) Ltd	1954	580.3
57	Goodlass Nerolac Paints Ltd	1920	2,181.9
58	Goodyear India Ltd	1922	722.6
59	Gujarat Alkalies & Chemicals Ltd	1973	1,088.5
60	Gujarat State Fertilizers & Chemicals Ltd	1962	1,840.9
61	Gulf Oil Corpn. Ltd	1961	539.7
62	HEG Ltd	1972	1,150.4
63	Hindalco Industries Ltd	1958	45,741.1
64	Hindustan Construction Co. Ltd	1926	1,380.3
65	Hindustan Lever Ltd	1933	399,724.8
66	Hindustan Motors Ltd	1942	1,379.9
67	ITC Ltd	1910	160,404.2
68	India Cements Ltd	1946	3,066.0
69	Indian Aluminium Co. Ltd	1938	7,772.6
70	Indian Hotels Co. Ltd	1902	7,571.3
71	Indo National Ltd	1972	1,244.3
72	Ingersoll-Rand (India) Ltd	1921	6,467.4
73	JCT Ltd	1946	1,511.6
74	JK Corp Ltd	1938	531.0
75	JK Industries Ltd	1951	848.1
76	Jagatjit Industries Ltd	1944	1,545.1
77	Jindal Iron & Steel Co. Ltd	1972	1,969.3
78	KEC International Ltd	1945	541.5
79	KSB Pumps Ltd	1960	1,090.0
80	Kanoria Chemicals & Inds. Ltd	1960	677.8
81	Kennametal Widia India Ltd	1964	1,820.4
82	Kesoram Industries Ltd	1919	1,277.0
83	Kirloskar Brothers Ltd	1920	589.4
84	Kochi Refineries Ltd	1963	6,713.5
85	Lakshmi Machine Works Ltd	1962	1,168.7
86	Larsen & Toubro Ltd	1946	45,838.5
87	MRF Ltd	1960	3,689.3
88	Madras Aluminium Co. Ltd	1960	1,273.1
89	Madras Cements Ltd	1957	4,778.6

Table A.2 continued

Table A. 2 continued

	Company name	Incorporation	M Cap (₹ million)
90	Madura Coats Ltd	1974	2,545.7
91	Mahavir Spinning Mills Ltd	1973	1,501.6
92	Mahindra & Mahindra Ltd	1945	11,602.9
93	Malanpur Steel Ltd	1944	781.1
94	Mangalore Chemicals & Fertilizers Ltd	1966	642.5
95	Mcdowell & Co. Ltd [Merged]	1898	3,875.3
96	Merck Ltd	1967	4,606.9
97	Modi Rubber Ltd	1971	679.7
98	Monsanto India Ltd	1949	4,078.6
99	Motor Industries Co. Ltd	1951	10,118.5
100	Nelco Ltd	1940	748.5
101	Nestle India Ltd	1959	51,110.2
102	Novartis India Ltd	1947	7,857.7
103	Oriental Hotels Ltd	1970	1,199.4
104	Otis Elevator Co. (India) Ltd	1953	3,685.4
105	Parke-Davis (India) Ltd [Merged]	1958	2,136.0
106	Pfizer Ltd	1950	9,767.5
107	Pharmacia Healthcare Ltd	1946	802.1
108	Philips India Ltd	1930	4,532.4
109	Pidilite Industries Ltd	1969	5,549.7
110	Piramal Holdings Ltd	1958	530.2
111	Procter & Gamble Hygiene & Health Care Ltd	1964	8,995.9
112	Punjab Tractors Ltd	1970	8,694.1
113	Rallis India Ltd	1948	941.4
114	Ranbaxy Laboratories Ltd	1961	104,887.0
115	Raymond Ltd	1925	6,252.3
116	Reckitt Benckiser (India) Ltd	1951	7,931.6
117	Reliance Energy Ltd (Earlier BSES)	1929	30,143.5
118	Reliance Industries Ltd	1966	329,924.4
119	Rhone-Poulenc (India) Ltd [Merged]	1928	2,092.6
120	SKF Bearings India Ltd	1961	1,778.7
121	SRF Ltd	1970	1,562.9
122	Schenectady Herdillia Ltd	1963	571.4
123	Shaw Wallace & Co. Ltd	1946	1,778.3
124	Siemens Ltd	1957	9,769.0
125	Steelage Industries Ltd	1932	615.3
126	Sundaram-Clayton Ltd	1962	3,422.9
127	Sundram Fasteners Ltd	1962	3,099.2
128	Supreme Industries Ltd	1942	902.9
129	Surat Electricity Co. Ltd	1920	670.4
130	Swil Ltd	1962	692.4
131	Tata Chemicals Ltd	1939	9,918.5

Table A.2 continued

Table A.2 continued

	Company name	Incorporation	M Cap (₹ million)
132	Tata Hydro-Electric Power Supply Co. Ltd [Merged]	1910	2,246.6
133	Tata Investment Corpn. Ltd	1937	1,568.2
134	Tata Iron & Steel Co. Ltd	1907	47,743.6
135	Tata Motors Ltd	1945	46,742.4
136	Tata Power Co. Ltd	1919	21,963.5
137	Tide Water Oil Co. (India) Ltd	1922	1,215.3
138	Trent Ltd	1952	2,062.4
139	Tube Investments Of India Ltd	1949	1,951.3
140	Uniphos Enterprises Ltd	1969	3,448.3
141	Vardhman Spinning & General Mills Ltd	1962	759.8
142	Voltas Ltd	1954	1,649.6
143	West Coast Paper Mills Ltd	1955	761.7
144	Wimco Ltd	1923	1,164.5

Source Author.
Note *Market Capitalization was the 365 days average M-Cap in 2002.

TABLE A.3   Cut 3 Analysis Results—Table of 47 Companies

	Companies admitted in Cut 2	Outcome in Cut 3
1	Ahmedabad Electricity Co. Ltd	Selected
2	Apollo Tyres Ltd	Considered, Criterion 3
3	BASF India Ltd	Eliminated, Criterion 3
4	BSES Ltd	Criterion 4
5	Bajaj Hindusthan Ltd	Considered, Criterion 3
6	Ballarpur Industries Ltd	Eliminated, Criterion 3
7	Bharat Forge Ltd	Eliminated, Criterion 4
8	Bombay Dyeing & Mfg. Co. Ltd	Selected
9	Century Enka Ltd	Eliminated, Criterion 4
10	Coromandel Fertilisers Ltd	Selected
11	Cummins India Ltd	Eliminated, Criterion 3
12	Dalmia Cement (Bharat) Ltd	Eliminated, Criterion 4
13	EIH Ltd	Eliminated, Criterion 4
14	Eveready Industries (India) Ltd	Eliminated, Criterion 4
15	Exide Industries Ltd	Selected
16	Fertilisers & Chemicals, Travancore Ltd	Eliminated, Criterion 2, 3
17	Gammon India Ltd	Considered, Criterion 3
18	German Remedies Ltd [Merged]	Selected
19	Gujarat Alkalies & Chemicals Ltd	Eliminated, Criterion 3
20	HEG Ltd	Eliminated, Criterion 4
21	Hindalco Industries Ltd	Considered, Criterion 3

Table A.3 continued

Appendix A

Table A.3 continued

	Companies admitted in Cut 2	Outcome in Cut 3
22	Indian Aluminium Co. Ltd	Eliminated, Criterion 3
23	Indian Hotels Co. Ltd	Considered, Criterion 3
24	Jindal Iron & Steel Co. Ltd	Eliminated, Criterion 4
25	KEC International Ltd	Considered, Criterion 3
26	Kanoria Chemicals & Inds. Ltd	Eliminated, Criterion 4
27	Kesoram Industries Ltd	Eliminated, Criterion 3
28	Kirloskar Brothers Ltd	Selected
29	Larsen & Toubro Ltd	Considered, Criterion 3
30	Madras Aluminium Co. Ltd	Eliminated, Criterion 4
31	Mahindra & Mahindra Ltd	Considered, Criterion 3
32	Merck Ltd	Eliminated, Criterion 3
33	Motor Industries Co. Ltd	Considered, Criterion 3
34	Nelco Ltd	Eliminated, Criterion 4
35	Novartis India Ltd	Considered, Criterion 3
36	Oriental Hotels Ltd	Eliminated, Criterion 3
37	SKF Bearings India Ltd	Considered, Criterion 3
38	SRF Ltd	Eliminated, Criterion 4
39	Schenectady Herdillia Ltd	Eliminated, Criterion 4
40	Siemens Ltd	Considered, Criterion 3
41	Sundram Fasteners Ltd	Considered, Criterion 3
42	Surat Electricity Co. Ltd	Selected
43	Tata Chemicals Ltd	Considered, Criterion 3
44	Tata Iron & Steel Co. Ltd	Considered, Criterion 3
45	Tata Power Co. Ltd	Considered, Criterion 3
46	Tinplate Co. Of India Ltd	Selected
47	Voltas Ltd	Eliminated, Criterion 3

Source   Author.

Statistical Significance Test

$$Return_t = \beta_1 + \beta_2 Year_t + \beta_3 D_1 + \beta_4 D_1 Year_t + \upsilon_t$$

Where, $Return_t$ is shareholder average yearly returns, $Year_t$ is the year and D_1 is a dummy variable. It is 0 if the data is that of OSPI and 1 if it is of the company.

If the differential slope β_3 is statistically significant, we may reject the hypothesis that the two regressions have the same intercept. Similarly, if the differential slope β_4 is statistically significant, we may reject the hypothesis that the two regressions have the same slope.

$\beta_1 + \beta_3$ is the intercept of the company. Similarly, $\beta_2 + \beta_4$ is the slope of the company. β_1 is the intercept of OSPI × 3 and β_2 is the slope of OSPI × 3.

TABLE A.4: Statistical Significance Test

Company		β_1	β_2	β_3	β_4	$\beta_1 + \beta_3$	$\beta_2 + \beta_4$	F-Statistic	Comments[a]
Ahmedabad Electricity Co. Ltd	Coefficient	−3.406	1.030	4.663	−0.085	1.257	0.945	20.394	Same intercept and same slope (concurrent)
	t-value	(−1.086)	(5.646)	(1.052)	(−0.328)				
Bombay Dyeing & Mfg. Co. Ltd	Coefficient	−3.406	1.030	14.494	0.855	11.088	1.886	110.685	Different intercept (above OSPI × 3) and different slope (divergent)
	t-value	(−1.146)	(5.952)	**(3.447)**	**(3.494)**				
Coromandel Fertilisers Ltd	Coefficient	−3.406	1.030	1.558	0.415	−1.848	1.446	48.891	Same intercept and different slope (concurrent)
	t-value	(−1.269)	(6.591)	(0.410)	**(1.878)**[b]				
Exide Industries Ltd	Coefficient	−3.406	1.030	6.644	0.039	3.238	1.069	33.274	Same intercept and same slope (concurrent)
	t-value	(−1.234)	(6.411)	(1.702)	(0.172)				
	t-value	(−1.300)	(6.753)	**(3.046)**	**(2.963)**				
Kirloskar Brothers Ltd	Coefficient	−3.406	1.030	−2.729	1.551	−6.135	2.581	162.911	Same intercept (below OSPI × 3 before 1975) and different slope (divergent)
	t-value	(−1.338)	(6.952)	(−0.758)	**(7.399)**				
Surat Electricity Co. Ltd	Coefficient	−3.406	1.030	7.459	0.601	4.053	1.631	73.670	Different intercept and different slope (divergent)
	t-value	(−1.239)	(6.439)	**(1.919)**[c]	**(2.655)**				

Source   Author.

Notes   [a] 99 percent confidence; [b] 95 percent confidence; [c] 95 percent confidence. The figures in the parenthesis are the t-ratios. The bold ones are significant.

FIGURE A.1 Ahmedabad Electricity (Torrent Power)

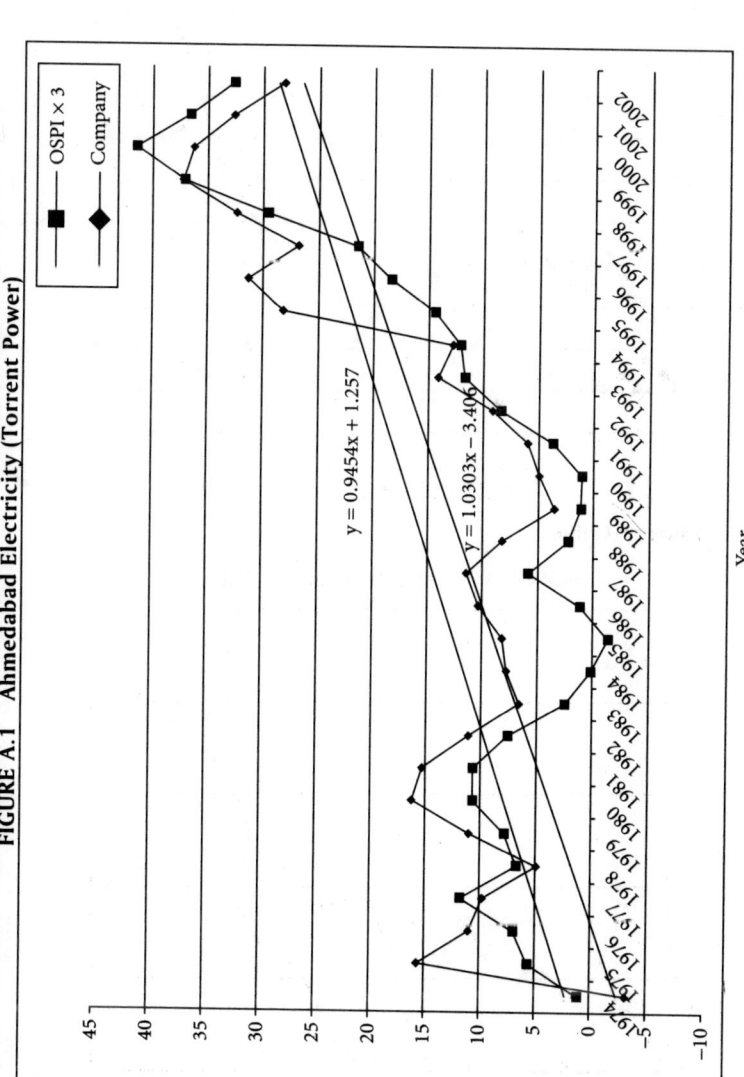

Source Author.

190 | Corporate Champions

FIGURE A.2 Apollo Tyres Ltd

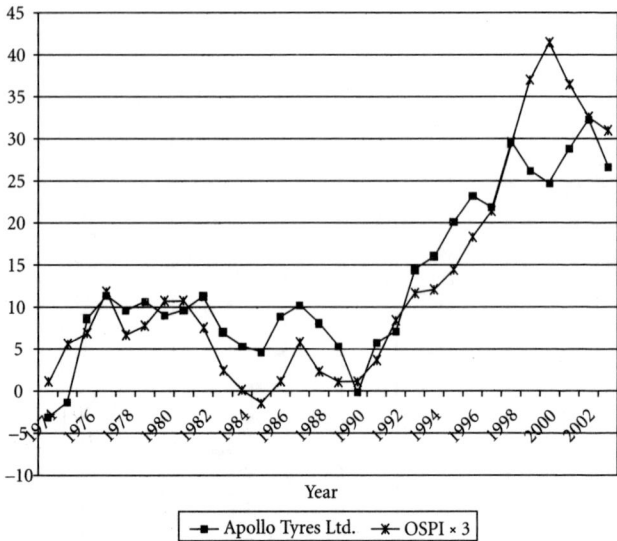

Source Author.

FIGURE A.3 Bajaj Hindusthan Ltd

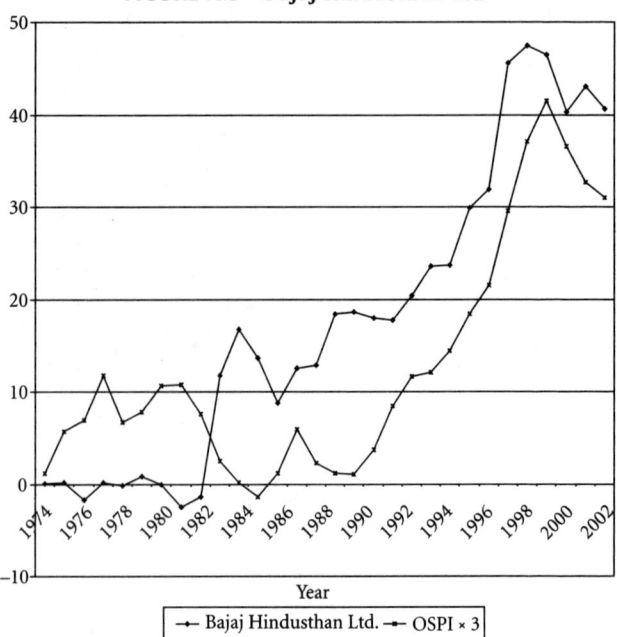

Source Author.

FIGURE A.4 Bombay Dyeing & Mfg. Co. Ltd

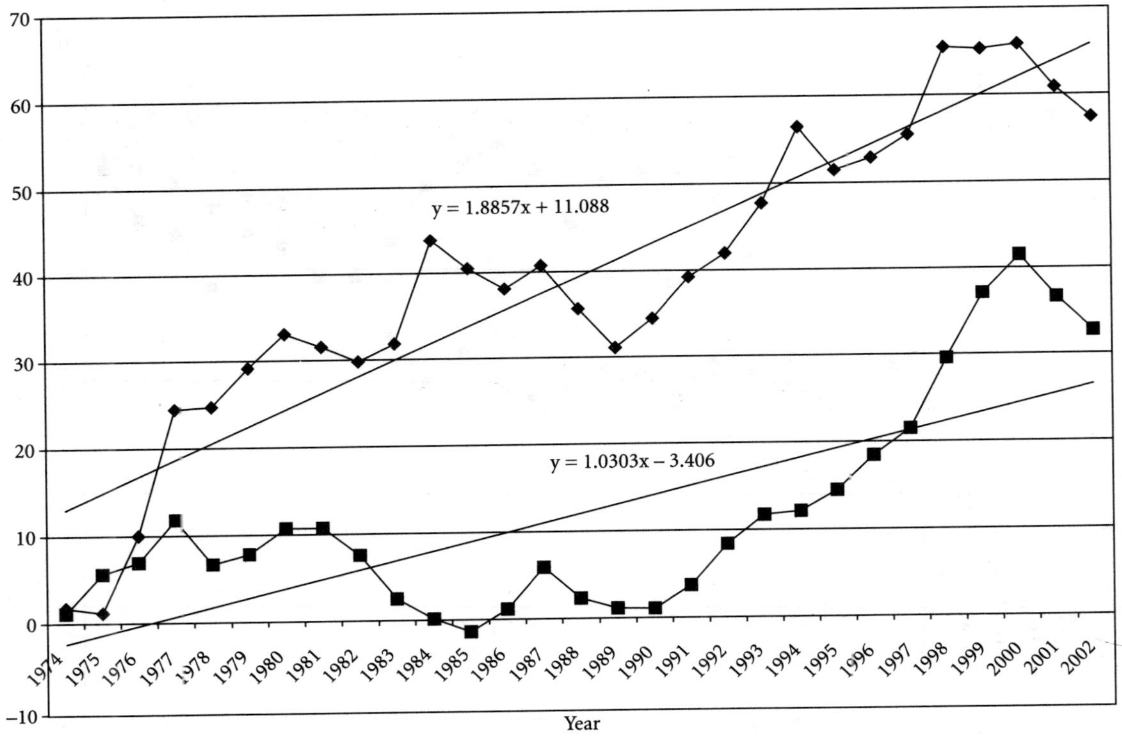

$y = 1.8857x + 11.088$

$y = 1.0303x - 3.406$

Year

Source Author.

FIGURE A.5 Coromandel Fertilisers Ltd

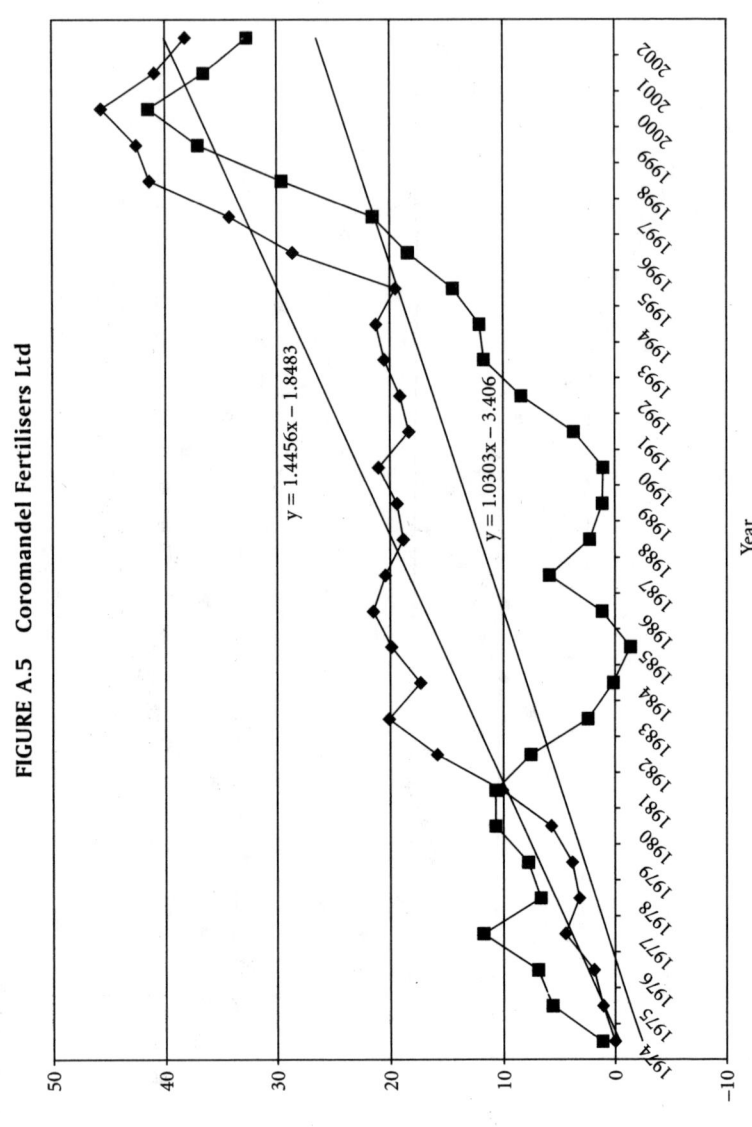

Source   Author.

FIGURE A.6 Exide Industries Ltd

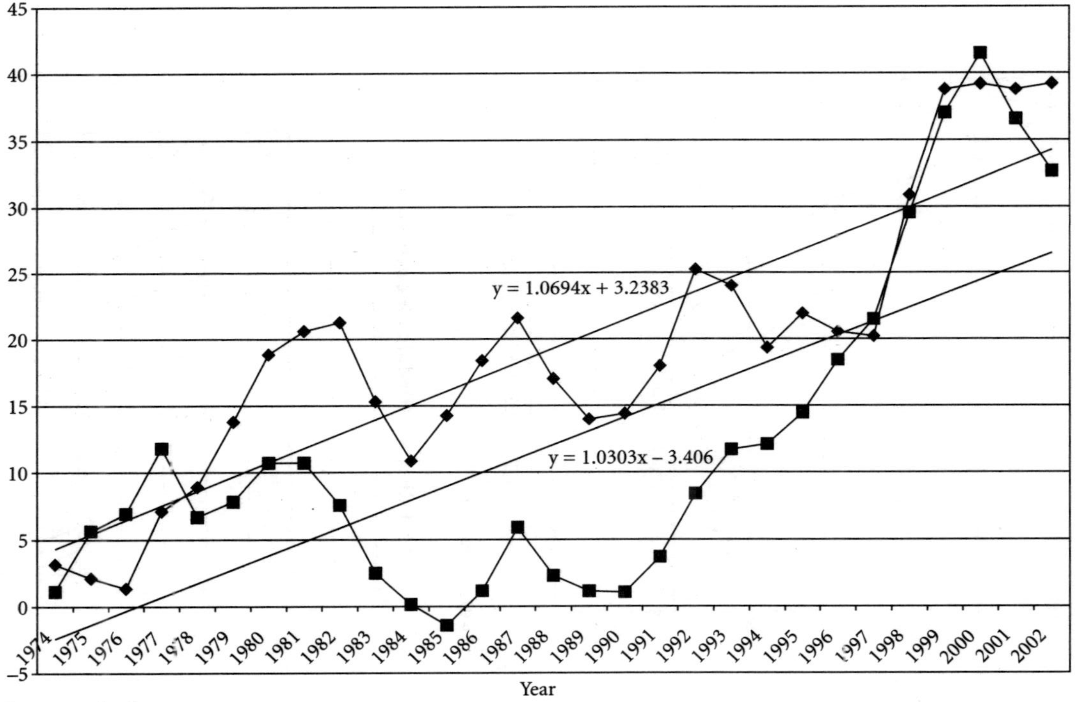

$y = 1.0694x + 3.2383$

$y = 1.0303x - 3.406$

Year

Source Author.

FIGURE A.7 Gammon India Ltd

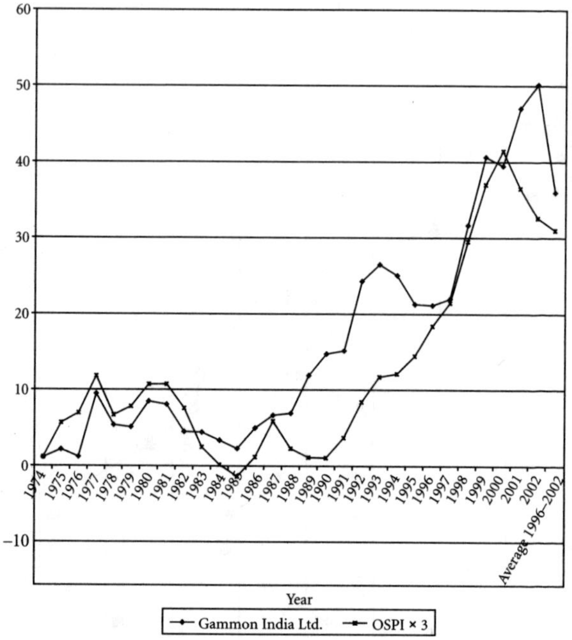

Source Author.

FIGURE A.8 Hindalco Industries Ltd

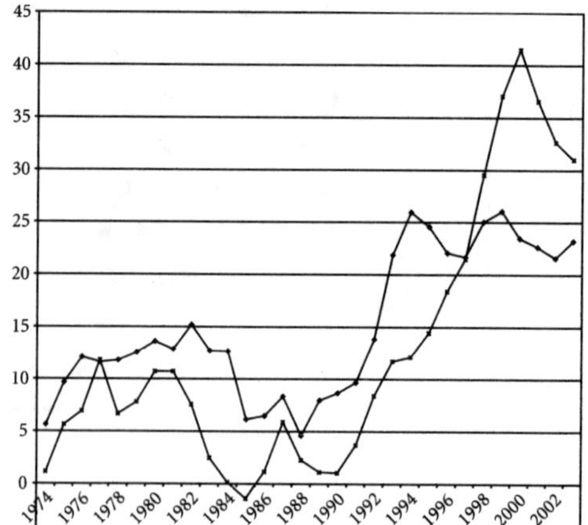

Source Author.

Appendix A | 195

FIGURE A.9 Indian Hotels Co Ltd

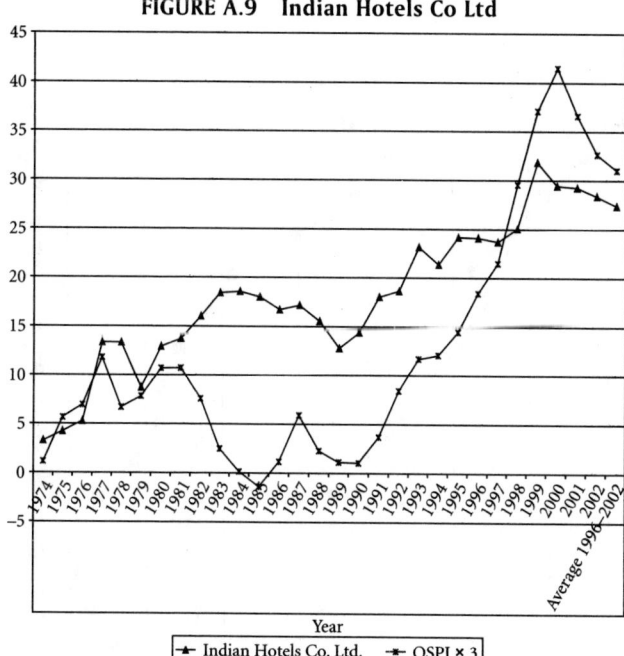

Source   Author.

FIGURE A.10 KEC International Ltd

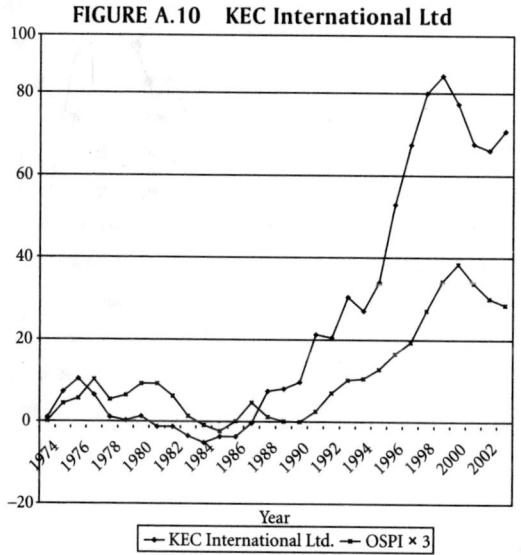

Source   Author.

FIGURE A.11 Kirloskar Brothers Ltd

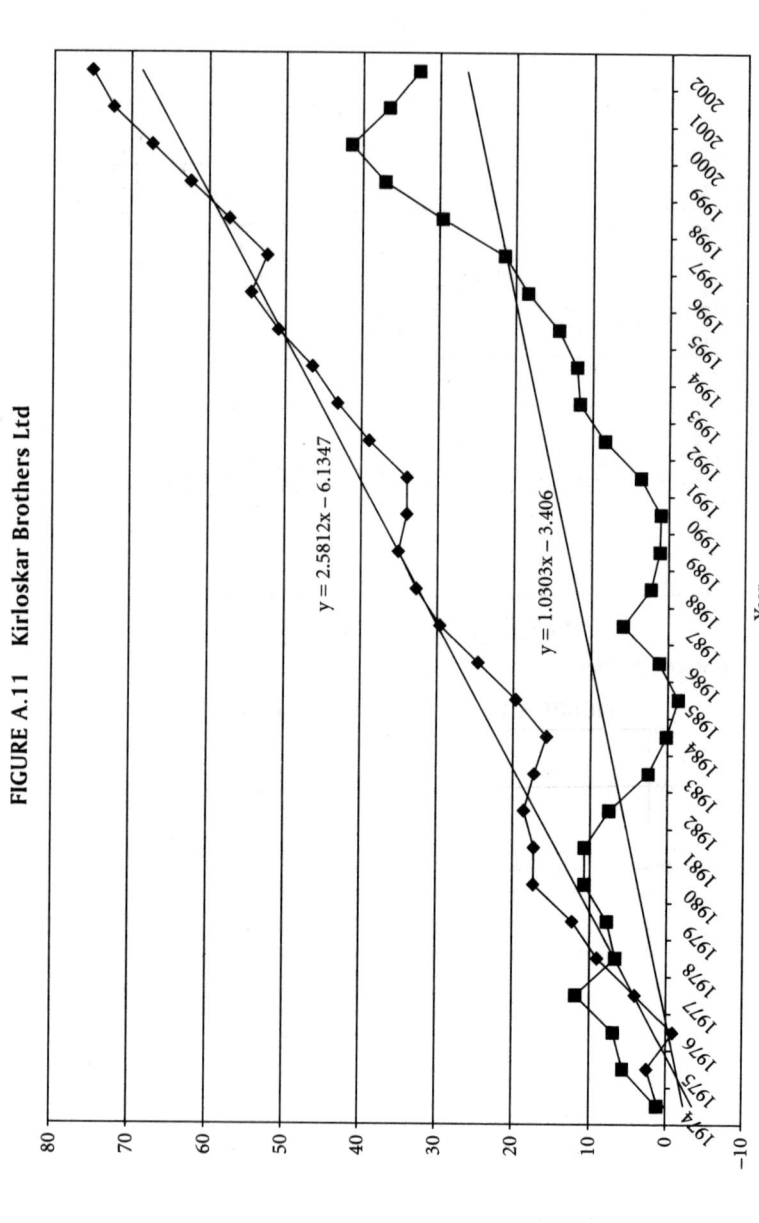

$y = 2.5812x - 6.1347$

$y = 1.0303x - 3.406$

Year

Source Author.

Appendix A | **197**

FIGURE A.12 Larsen & Toubro Ltd

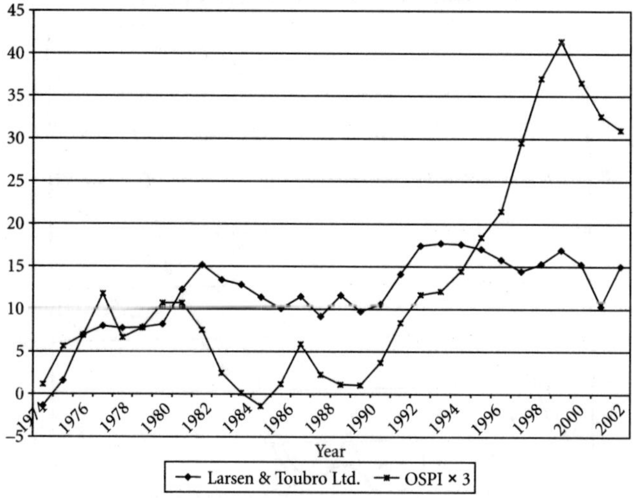

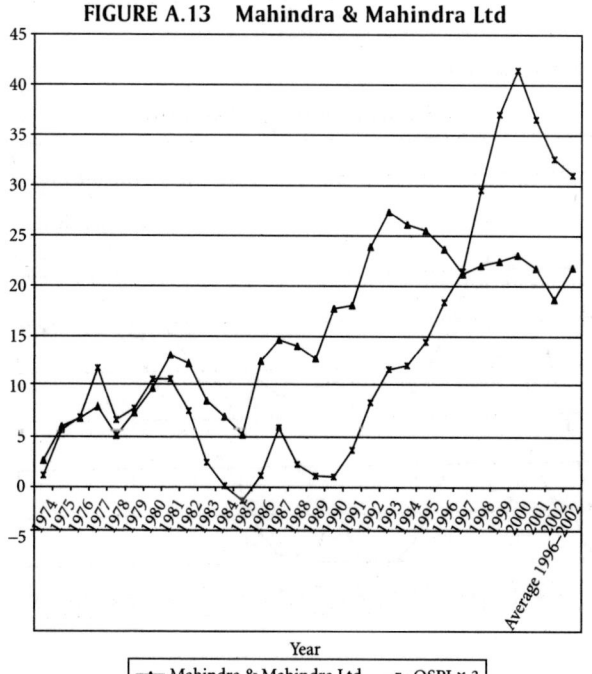

Source Author.

FIGURE A.13 Mahindra & Mahindra Ltd

Source Author.

FIGURE A.14   Motor Industries Co Ltd

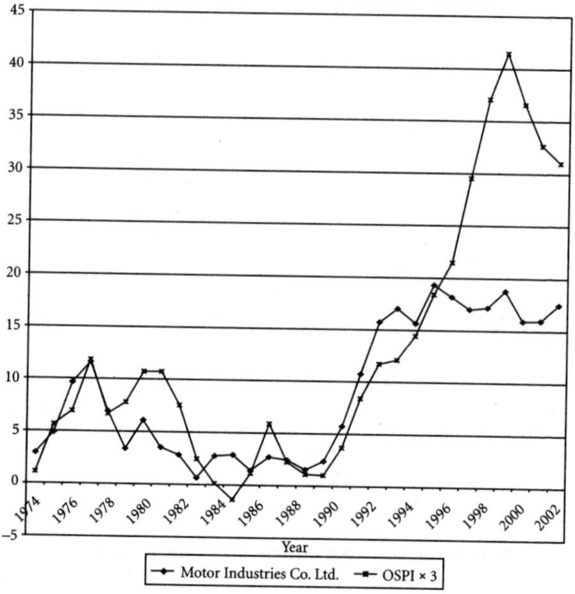

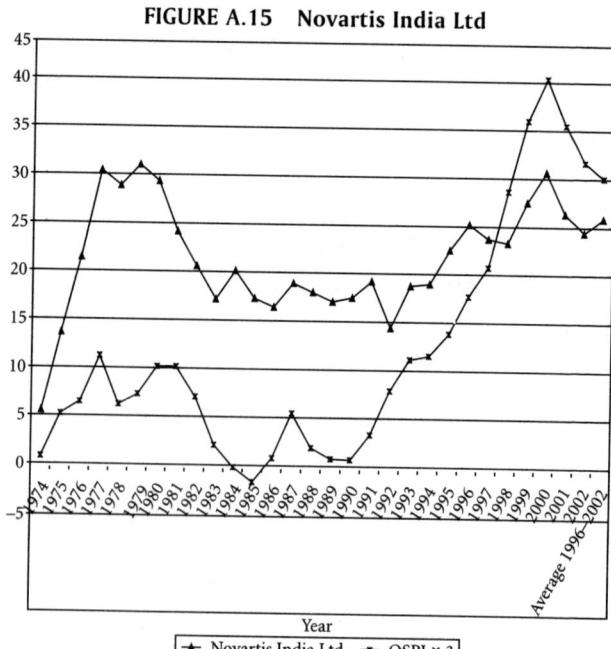

Source   Author.

FIGURE A.15   Novartis India Ltd

Source   Author.

Appendix A | 199

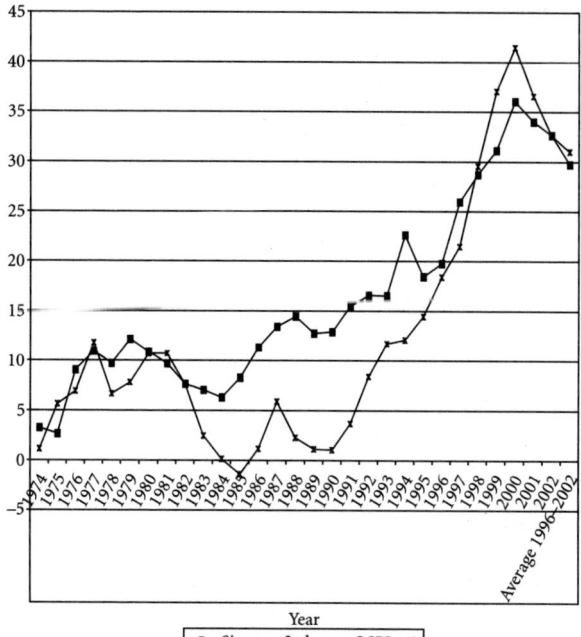

FIGURE A.16 Siemens Ltd

Source Author.

FIGURE A.17 SKF Bearings India Ltd

Source Author.

200 | Corporate Champions

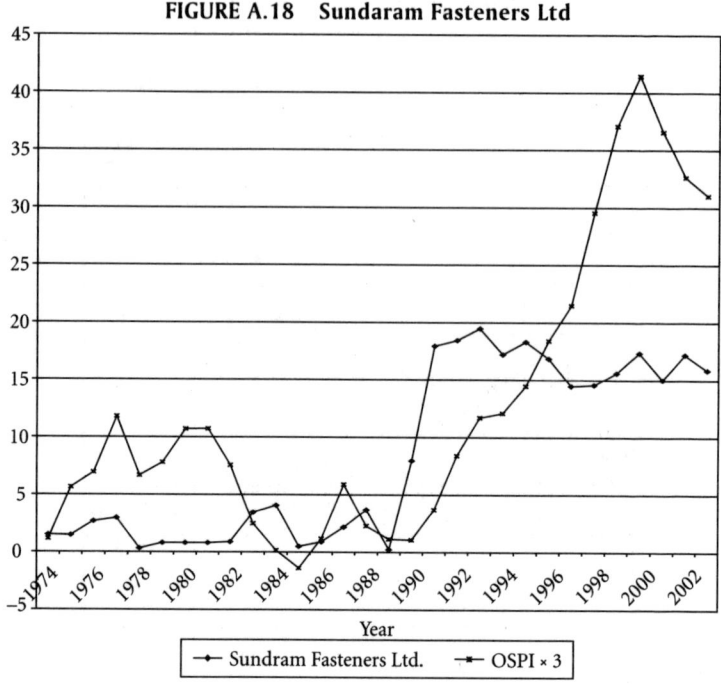

FIGURE A.18   Sundaram Fasteners Ltd

Source   Author.

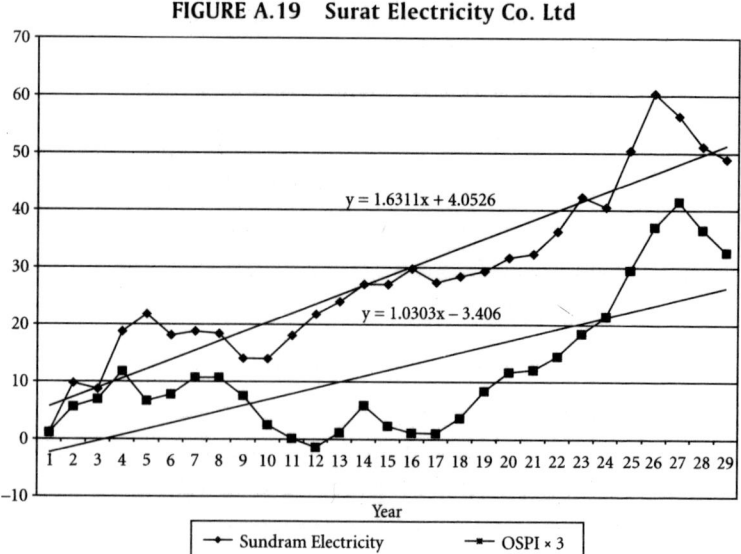

FIGURE A.19   Surat Electricity Co. Ltd

Source   Author.

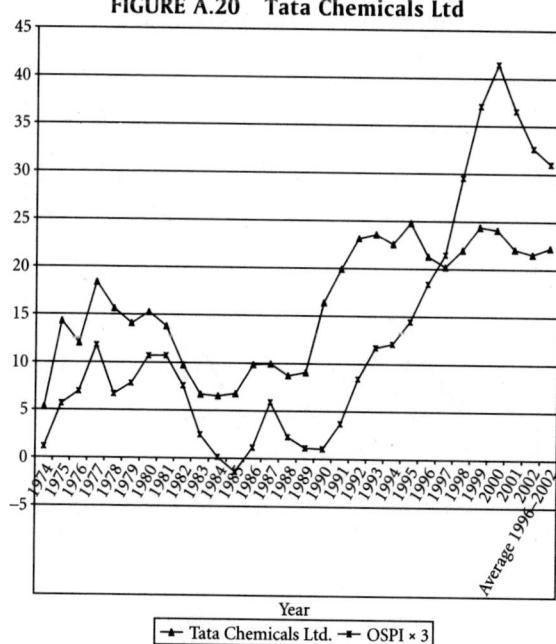

FIGURE A.20 Tata Chemicals Ltd

Source Author.

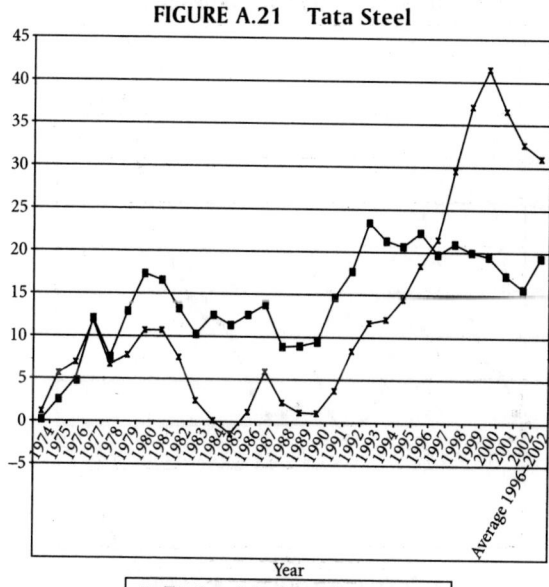

FIGURE A.21 Tata Steel

Source Author.

202 | CORPORATE CHAMPIONS

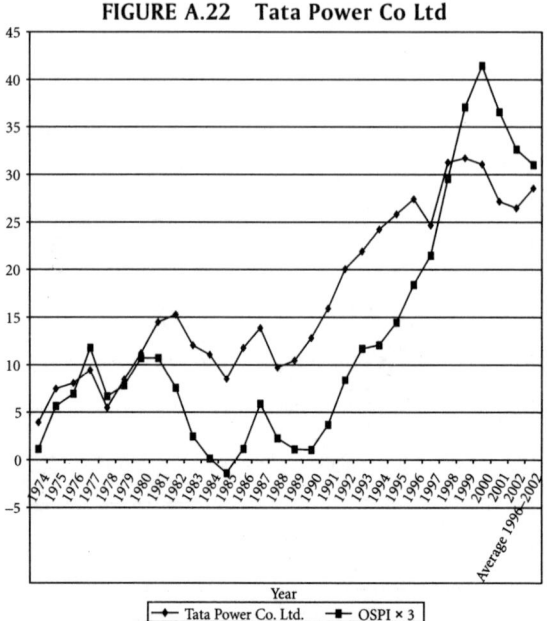

FIGURE A.22   Tata Power Co Ltd

Source   Author.

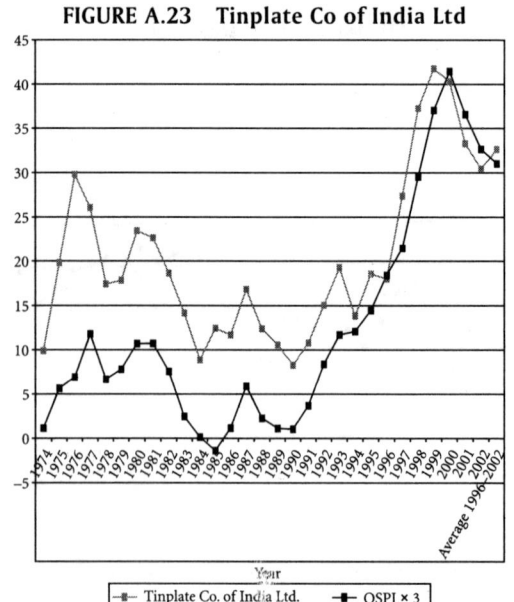

FIGURE A.23   Tinplate Co of India Ltd

Source   Author.

Appendix B
Chapter 6—Surveys

Review of literature was carried out to look for relevant studies in the Indian context. BT-AT Kearney has carried out a study on Best Managed Companies in India.[1] This study got published in *Business Today*, June 2003. The methodology adopted by BT-AT Kearney is different from the one adopted by this research work.

This study got published in *Business Today*, June 2003. Out of the 23 finalists, in the BT-AT Kearney Study, 16 agreed for an interview and a questionnaire. The 16 finalists are given in Table B.1:

TABLE B.1 Sixteen Finalists[2]

1	Reliance Industries
2	TVS Motor
3	Dr Reddy Labs
4	Sun Pharmaceuticals
5	HDFC Bank
6	ICICI Bank
7	Cadbury India
8	Asian Paints
9	Wipro
10	Infosys
11	Moser Baer
12	Satyam Computer
13	HPCL
14	Hindalco Industries
15	Gujarat Ambuja Cements
16	Britannia Industries

Table B.2 lists the differences in the methodology adopted by us and the BT-Kearney study.

TABLE B.2 Comparison of Methodologies

BT-Kearney study	Our methodology
CUT 1	
Universe of publicly listed companies no later than 1996, having minimum revenues of ₹1,000 million, minimum capitalization of ₹500 million, have declared a net profit at least two out of the past four years. Over 250 companies made the grade.	Universe of publicly listed companies from the CMIE Prowess Data—based on existence since 1974 and a market capitalization exceeding ₹500 million. *144 companies made the cut.*
CUT 2	
Twenty-three companies fell into the Quadrant 1 of Value Growth Matrix. These companies were termed as Value Builders because of their above industry average growth rates in Revenues and Market Value. The selection was based on quantitative criteria as well as qualitative ones (consistency of appearing in this quadrant over time; present size of operations; potential for future growth).	Selecting 47 companies, with compound annual total return to investors at >1.3 times' average returns over three specific times: (*i*) 1996–2002, (*ii*) 1991–2002, (*iii*) 1985–2002, and (*iv*) 1974–2002. We did not consider any qualitative criteria.
CUT 3	
A team of consultants from AT Kearney sought to meet the 23 companies to understand the strategic decisions that enabled the company to remain a value builder. (Seven companies refused to participate. These companies were HLL, Kodak, ONGC, Indian Oil, Zee Telefilms, Balrampur Chini, and Hero Honda.) The other 16 filled up a detailed questionnaire. The step was a qualitative evaluation based on the interviews and the responses.	Litmus test is to look for three times above the OSPI curve. Please note that once again at this stage we have not considered any qualitative criteria.
CUT 4	
	The research involved studying these companies and understanding the strategic decisions that made them such exceptional performers.

Source Author.

Appendix C
Chapter 6—Synopses of Two Inspirational Books

IN SEARCH OF EXCELLENCE BY TOM PETERS[1]

Quest for excellent companies that outperform the others has been a long one, with many bestsellers written using different methodologies. One of the most prominent of such writers is Tom Peters, who wrote a couple of best-selling books addressing this issue. His first book *In Search of Excellence* showed that excellent companies were exceptionally good on eight attributes:

1. A bias for action
2. Close to the customer
3. Autonomy and entrepreneurship
4. Productivity through people
5. Hands on, value driven
6. Stick to the knitting
7. Simple form, lean staff
8. Simultaneous loose-tight properties

Peters and Waterman examined 43 of *Fortune* 500's top-performing companies. They started with a list of 62 of the best-performing McKinsey clients and then applied performance measures to weed out what they thought to be the weaker companies.

Critics have pointed out that many of the companies that were studied fell from grace. But Kennedy and Duff[2] mention that the 43 companies have still outperformed the Dow Jones Industrial Average. If someone invested $10,000 in the excellence index 20 years ago, he would now have $140,050. An equivalent investment in Dow would have yielded $85,500.

Tom Peters himself, in an interview to Bogner, said he would not change any of those eight themes, but he would add to them: capabilities concerning ideas, liberation, and speed.[3]

Another major criticism for the book was that the book has too much of an internal focus and that it did not take into account external forces and unexpected environmental changes that could have a significant impact on organizational health and performance.[4]

In his sequel to this book, *Passion for Excellence*,[5] Tom Peters' principal advice is that excellence in organizational performance is the result of four attributes: care of customers via superior service and superior quality products, constant innovation, turned on people, and leadership. They say that these attributes should not be limited to the top management, but be present throughout and at all levels of the organization.

BUILT TO LAST BY JIM COLLINS AND JERRY PORRAS[6]

In 1995, Jim Collins and Jerry Porras wrote *Built to Last*. The book was based on the research of 18 visionary companies and 18 comparison companies spread over a life span of 90-plus years. The essential ideas that come out of their work are on clock building (not time telling), the genius of AND (not tyranny of OR), preserving the core ideology/stimulating progress and alignment of mechanisms/practices with the core ideology.

The genius of AND in visionary companies is that they preserve their core ideology and at the same time are aggressive on granting operational autonomy to individual employees. The essence of clock building is creating tangible mechanisms aligned to "preserve the core and stimulate progress." *Built to Last* emphasizes that visionary companies preserve their core ideology and stimulate progress through five tangible mechanisms. The mechanisms are:

1. Big, hairy, audacious goals
2. Try a lot of stuff and keep what works
3. Home-grown management
4. Cult-like culture
5. Good enough never is

Good to Great,[7] the prequel and not sequel (though this book came out later) to *Built to Last*, uses a very elaborate methodology, spread over 15,000 hours of research to address the issue of excellent companies.

Collins brought out what he termed as timeless "physics" of *Good to Great*. These are as follows:

1. Level 5 Leadership
2. First Who...Then What
3. Confront the Brutal Facts (Yet Never Lose Faith)
4. Hedgehog Concept
5. Culture of Discipline
6. Technology Accelerators

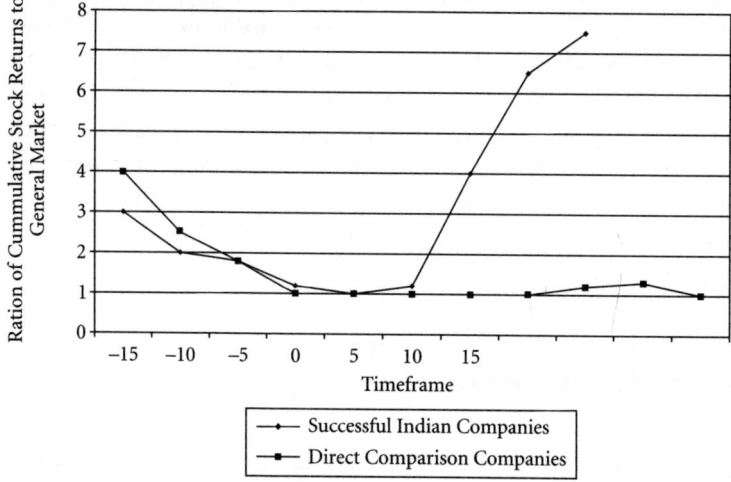

FIGURE C.1 Performance of Successful Companies vis-à-vis Others

Source Author.

As stated earlier, the theme behind our research is based upon Jim Collin's book *Good to Great*, which is all about transforming average companies to great companies. For years, this question preyed on the mind of Jim Collins. Are there companies that defy gravity and convert long-term mediocrity or worse into long-term superiority? And if so, what are the universal distinguishing characteristics that cause a company to go from good to great? Collins and his researched team selected 11 great companies and contrasted with their comparison companies (who they feel are average) to understand why some companies make the leap and some don't. Exhaustive research by Collins' team, which is nicely summarized in the appendices, elucidated the six basic characteristics (mentioned earlier) of the 11 great companies with each of the six elaborately described in individual chapters.

Level 5 Leadership

All of the great companies had leaders who were unexpectedly humble yet had a tenacious professional will whose primary concern was the health and growth of the company. This was compared to the control companies which often had charismatic leaders who make a big splash, looked after their self-interests first and in the end were unable to create sustained growth. The description of Ken Iverson, the dedicated and highly successful Nucor CEO, who still lived in a simple house with a carport and scraped ice off his car windows with a credit card sets the tone of the book which throughout emphasizes the "salt of the earth" nature of the companies leaders. The description of the control companies' CEOs who had a need for self-aggrandizement is reminiscent of the Tyco, Enron, Time Warner, and WorldCom CEOs.

First Who...Then What

This is another unexpected finding. The great companies did not formulate a great strategy first as did the control companies. Instead, the CEOs initially spent their energies hiring the best people for the job ahead and firing employees who they did not believe demonstrated the necessary personality traits and work ethic. By and large, these employee characteristics consisted of creative people who were self-motivated and did not need to be micromanaged.

Confront the Brutal Facts (Yet Never Lose Faith)

A Socratic style evident in all of the great companies is discussed, in which their status during the transition period is very honestly evaluated.

This honest appraisal leads to the fourth characteristic named the Hedgehog Concept.

The Hedgehog Concept

To quote directly from Collins, a Hedgehog Concept is a concept "to understand what your organization can be the best in the world at, and equally important what it cannot be the best at—not what it 'wants' to be the best at." It is "not a goal, strategy or intention; it is an understanding." It is also essential for the organization to build a culture of self-disciplined people (as getting disciplined people would limit the bureaucracy needed to compensate for lack of discipline) and uses technology wisely (avoid technology fad). Good to great transformation doesn't just happen with one single action or a grand program but instead follows a pattern of buildup and breakthrough. The organization is also able to confront the reality of the company's current situation, as the right decisions would follow subsequently. Simply put, the great companies used three questions to form a simple and direct growth strategy. These questions are:

1. What can we be the best in the world at?
2. What drives our economic engine?
3. What are we deeply passionate about?

Finally, the last two criteria discussed are entitled "A Culture of Discipline" and "Technology Accelerators." These chapters discuss the type of employees in the good to great companies.

Good to Great ends by identifying the concept that great companies exemplified the adage "slow and steady wins the race." They did not try and create an overnight turnaround, which in the end would have no sustainability but instead religiously followed the necessary path step by step, to make sure their company had a solid foundation with the appropriate employees, goals, attitudes, and technology in place.

Good to Great is truly an insightful book and a very well-researched one. Points are well presented using analogies and stories to back them up. The methodologies adopted by Jim Collins included:

Standards: Using tough benchmarks, Collins and his research team identified a set of elite companies that made the leap to great results and sustained those results for at least 15 years. How great? After the leap, the good to great companies generated cumulative stock returns that beat the general stock market by an average of seven times in 15 years, better than twice the results delivered by a composite index of the world's greatest companies, including Coca-Cola, Intel, General Electric, and Merck.

Comparisons: The research team contrasted the good to great companies with a carefully selected set of comparison companies that failed to make the leap from good to great. What was different? Why did one set of companies become truly great performers while the other set remained only good?

Over five years, the team analyzed the histories of all 28 companies in the study. After sifting through mountains of data and thousands of pages of interviews, Collins and his crew discovered the key determinants of greatness—why some companies made the leap and others didn't.

Findings: The findings of the *Good to Great* study will surprise many readers and shed light on virtually every area of management strategy and practice. Jim Collins' most important contribution was perhaps not just the findings but also the way he brought them out. The book is based on a very sound methodology and extensive research.

He based the selection of "Great" companies on the consistency of returns that their stocks give to an investor. "Great" companies meet the "3 times the market over 15 years from the transition point" standard of performance.

Appendix D
Profiles of Study Companies

Revolution means turning the wheel.
—Igor Stravinsky

You can accomplish anything in life, provided that you do not mind who gets the credit
—Harry S. Truman

INDIAN HOTELS COMPANY LTD

In 1902, Jamsetji Tata, the founder of the Tata Group formed the Indian Hotels Company Ltd (IHCL). Till 1965, it owned and managed two hotels, viz., the Taj Mahal Hotel and the Green's Hotel. In 1972, Taj Intercontinental Hotel was opened. In 1979, the IHCL put up a hotel of international standards in Colombo, Sri Lanka. In 1986, the IHCL took over Hotel Chandela at Khajuraho on leave and license basis. The same year, the IHCL commissioned the Jai Mahal Palace Hotel at Jaipur. In 1995, two new hotels of associated companies were commissioned, viz., a 50-room Taj Garden retreat at Varkala (new Trivandrum), Kerala, and a 100-room business class hotel Taj Residency at Nashik, Maharashtra. It also undertook to set up two new luxury hotels in Mumbai and one in Chennai. In 2003, the IHCL renovated and upgraded its leading leisure hotel properties in Kerala, Goa, Rajasthan, and Tamil Nadu.

Today, it is the largest hotel chain in South Asia, operating a total of 63 hotels with about 8,020 rooms in India and abroad with 51 hotels in India and 12 across eight countries. The Indian Hotels caters to a wide cross-section of travelers with its luxury, business, and leisure hotels (among them beach resorts, garden retreats, and palace hotels) making it the best hotel chain in the country. The IHCL has consistently been conferred a number of awards that highlights its position as one of the world's leading hotel chains. The 2003 World's Best Business Hotels—readers of *Travel & Leisure* named Taj Mahal Hotel, Mumbai, the winner. The Taj Hotels was voted the Best Hotel Group in India in the 2003 Selling Long Haul Travel Awards by Travel Agents, UK.

Indian Hotels owns its hotels either directly or through its subsidiaries or through its associates and partners. It has a 15 percent market share in the Four Star, Five Star, and Five Star Deluxe segments. As of 2004, it had a manpower strength of approximately 7,600 employees, out of which 1,400 were executives, 3,150 were bargainable staff, and 3,000 were probationers/trainees/apprentices and contract employees.

Indian Hotels has around 14 subsidiary companies.

TATA STEEL

In 1868, Jamshedji Nusserwanji Tata (J.N. Tata) founded Tata Group, one of the most respected corporate houses of India. From a single textile mill, the group went on to become an empire. In 1907, he established the Tata Iron and Steel Company (now called Tata Steel) at Jamshedpur in Bihar, India. The company commenced production in 1911 with a capacity of 0.1 million tons of mild steel. By 1958, its capacity had increased to 2 million tons. Over the years, Tata Steel acquired many companies. In 1973, it acquired some flux mines and collieries near Jharia, West Bokara in Jharkand. In 1983, it acquired the Indian Tube Co. Ltd, a manufacturer of seamless and welded tubes. In 1991, it acquired the ferrochrome unit of OMC Alloys Ltd near Bamnipal in Orissa.

In February 2007, Tata Steel acquired Corus Steel for $12.1 billion in a bidding process against the rival CSN, Brazilian Steelmaker. Corus makes nearly four times more steel than Tata Steel. Together, the combine becomes the fifth-largest producer in the world and the second in Europe. The combine will be the second-largest tin-plate maker in the world.

BOMBAY DYEING & MANUFACTURING CO. LTD

In 1879, Bombay was next to New Orleans as the world's largest cotton port. It was at this time that Nowrosjee Wadia set his sights on India's

D.1a

TABLE D.1 Financials of Indian Hotels Co. Ltd (₹ million)

Profit and loss	Mar. '92	Mar. '93	Mar. '94	Mar. '95	Mar. '96	Mar. '97	Mar. '98	Mar. '99
Sales	2,032.2	2,381.4	2,937.2	3,725	5,243	5,768.2	5,956.5	6,032.8
Other income	35.7	53.3	69.5	64.8	230	361.9	225.9	328.3
Change in stocks	08.6	0	0	0	0	0	0	0
Net sales	1,990.1	2,344.2	2,896.2	3,675.3	5,188.3	5,685.4	5,854.8	5,919.6
Total income	2,076.5	2,434.7	3,006.7	3,789.8	5,473	6,130.1	6,182.4	6,361.1
Raw material purchased	0	0	0	0	0	0	0	0
Cost of production	1,076.2	1,244.2	1,481.2	1,803.4	2,229.9	2,670.4	2,984.5	3,233.9
Selling cost	17.6	31.3	42.9	59.3	111.8	105.8	141.8	140.3
Cost of sales	1,085.2	1,275.5	1,524.1	1,862.7	2,341.7	2,776.2	3,126.3	3,374.2
Admin and other costs	471.7	536.1	619.6	722	875.9	1,023.5	1,093	1,085
Total costs	1,864.3	2,128.4	2,505.3	3,039.3	4,097.4	4,695.7	4,866.9	5,090.4
PAT	219.2	335.4	551.8	821.1	1,405.7	1,468.8	1,379.6	1,191.4
PBDIT	581.4	712.7	949.9	1,362.7	2,434.5	2,553.8	2,249.7	2,047.8
PBDT	381.1	523.1	815.8	1,187.8	1,999.4	2,076.6	1,963.8	1,779.8
PBIT	484.5	615	840.9	1,226	2,230.8	2,282	1,925.5	1,709.4
PBT	284.2	425.4	706.8	1,051.1	1,795.7	1,804.8	1,639.6	1,441.4
Cash flow from operations	0	0	0	1,255.9	2,136.5	2,246.9	2,149.3	1,281.8

D.1b

Balance sheet	Mar. '92	Mar. '93	Mar. '94	Mar. '95	Mar. '96	Mar. '97	Mar. '98	Mar. '99
Current liabilities	609.4	611.1	694.9	839.8	1,001.4	1,125.7	1,393.2	1,435
Sundry creditors	489.9	531.5	592.4	754.9	648.3	635.8	585.3	510.7
Creditors for cap. goods	0	0	0	0	0	0	0	0
Accrued interest	61.3	19.4	23.5	09.6	17.5	33.1	18.8	27.6
Other current liabilities	58.2	60.2	79	75.3	335.6	456.8	789.1	896.7
Provisions	75.3	113.3	169.8	277.3	421.6	500.6	500.9	585.3
Total liabilities	2,733.9	3,200.3	3,676.9	5,965.4	9,486.4	10,933.4	11,648.7	12,322.3
Gross fixed assets	1,944.4	2,106.8	2,346.4	2,935.9	3,840.1	5,001	5,814.8	6,656.7
Land and building	559	570.9	634	962.5	1,157.7	1,625.7	1,894	2,187.4
Plant and machinery	812.7	890.7	1,039.3	1,302.2	1,589.5	2,275.9	2,546.9	2,745.2
Other fixed assets	371.7	388.7	415	532.6	671.9	920.2	1,065.4	1,169.8
Capital work-in-progress	201	256.5	258.1	138.6	421	179.2	308.5	554.3
Net fixed assets	1,358.8	1,425.3	1,562.1	2,019.2	2,732.1	3,640.8	4,145.7	4,667.7
Investments	137.6	169.3	325.4	360.4	1,420.9	2,148	2,180.9	2,603.5
Inventories	80.6	117.9	117.2	129.9	136.3	175.3	203.3	229.7
Cash and bank balance	69	86.6	84.9	108.1	309.2	964.2	761.4	225.3
Advances	0	0	0	0	0	0	0	0

Receivables	1,087.9	1,401.2	1,587.3	3,347.8	4,887.9	4,005.1	4,357.4	4,596.1
Total assets (excl. reval. and dre)	2,669.6	3,136	3,606	5,882.8	9,389.6	10,810.1	11,514.9	12,163.8
Current assets	981.5	1,152.8	1,295.1	2,188.1	3,062.6	2,976.6	2,910.4	2,957.2
Quick assets	284.9	320.1	526.2	549	762	1,483.2	1,284.3	759
Current liabilities and prov. (incl. bank short)	684.7	725.1	865	1,458.9	1,962.5	1,693.8	1,894.1	2,102.3
Working capital	296.8	427.7	430.1	729.2	1,100.1	1,282.8	1,016.3	854.9
Current ratio	14.3	15.9	15	15	15.6	17.6	15.4	14.1
Debt–equity ratio	13.2	07.1	05.2	09.7	03.2	03	02	01.6
Solvency ratio	15	18.5	20.6	17.2	28.7	29.7	34	37.2
Quick ratio	04.2	04.4	06.1	03.8	03.9	08.8	06.8	03.6
ROCE	243.6	265.3	313.4	327.1	371.4	272.1	197.5	180.6

D.1c

Profit and loss	Mar. '00	Mar. '01	Mar. '02	Mar. '03	Mar. '04	Mar. '05	Mar. '06
Sales	6,186.8	7,067.7	6,001.5	5,901.9	7,009.6	8,863.5	11,257.8
Other income	473.5	346.5	323.7	360.6	314.1	428.7	640.7
Change in stocks	0	0	0	0	0	0	0
Net sales	6,070.5	6,933.9	5,880.3	5,764.4	6,866.2	8,696.2	10,980.8
Total income	6,660.3	7,414.2	6,325.2	6,262.5	7,323.7	9,292.2	11,898.5
Raw material purchased	0	0	0	0	0	127.3	11.3
Cost of production	3,802	4,325.7	4,022.8	4,004.3	4,739.7	5,469.1	6,313.9
Selling cost	163.9	225	451.7	295.1	327	374.7	333.2
Cost of sales	3,965.9	4,550.7	4,474.5	4,299.4	5,066.7	5,845.7	6,647.1
Admin and other costs	914	1,004.7	1,113.9	984.8	1,405	1,489.4	1,813.9
Total costs	5,569.1	6,498.3	6,608.3	6,214.4	7,332.8	8,492.2	10,138.4
PAT	1,132.3	1,167.9	807	404.8	606.5	1,058.6	1,837.8
PBDIT	2,043.9	2,404.2	2,147.6	1,517.7	1,726.7	2,587.5	3,949.7
PBDT	1,684.2	1,824.5	1,511.9	955.6	1,287.8	1,984.5	3,402.1
PBIT	1,667	1,952.6	1,672.7	1,127.9	1,240.9	2,019.8	3,290.7
PBT	1,307.3	1,372.9	1,037	565.8	802	1,416.8	2,743.1
Cash flow from operations	1,402.2	1,296.9	919.9	919.1	1,043.1	2,669.1	3,311.8

D.1d

Balance sheet	Mar. '00	Mar. '01	Mar. '02	Mar. '03	Mar. '04	Mar. '05	Mar. '06
Current liabilities	1,483.5	1,357.4	1,032.9	1,237.5	1,906.9	2,303.7	2,430.6
Sundry creditors	591.5	663.5	493.3	623.5	912.7	1,186.6	1,319.7
Creditors for cap. goods	0	0	0	0	0	0	0
Accrued interest	83.9	158.1	157	134.5	92.2	38.1	30.5
Other current liabilities	808.1	535.8	382.6	479.5	902	1,079	1,080.4
Provisions	527.9	513.4	399.7	878	929.7	1,546.3	1,504.2
Total liabilities	15,644.3	17,599.3	19,263.2	19,275.9	26,287.9	26,093.8	27,447.5
Gross fixed assets	8,297.3	9,280.5	9,204.5	9,670.1	11,408.5	12,573	13,248.3
Land and building	2,997.4	3,276.7	3,295.2	3,043.6	3,331.2	4,981.1	5,186.5
Plant and machinery	3,432.2	3,727.7	3,468.7	3,569.2	3,935.8	4,828.4	5,155
Other fixed assets	1,502	1,670.9	1,647.8	1,784.1	1,992.3	2,415.8	2,417.1
Capital work-in-progress	365.7	605.2	792.8	1,273.2	2,149.2	347.7	489.7
Net fixed assets	5,949.3	6,524.5	6,339.1	6,647.9	8,033	8,646.1	8,770.7
Investments	3,390.1	4,230.9	5,483.2	5,775	6,105.1	6,108.7	6,604.3

(Table D.1d continued)

(Table D.1d continued)

Balance sheet	Mar. '00	Mar. '01	Mar. '02	Mar. '03	Mar. '04	Mar. '05	Mar. '06
Inventories	192.8	180.7	154	169.7	203.2	238.3	258.5
Cash and bank balance	270.2	240.4	640.2	231.7	6,114.3	548	901.3
Advances	0	0	0	0	0	0	0
Receivables	5,707.8	5,668.4	6,274.4	6,193.6	5,594.6	10,305.3	10,628.4
Total assets (excl. reval. and dre)	15,371.1	16,723.7	18,937.6	18,831.7	25,782.3	25,543.8	26,822.6
Current assets	3,329.4	3,023.7	3,086	3,943.8	8,797.6	3,324.3	4,018.5
Quick assets	769.4	942.2	1,132.8	662.3	6,657.6	1,513	2,011.9
Current liabilities and prov. (incl. bank short)	2,191	2,945.8	1,708.5	3,330.1	4,193.8	4,233.9	4,017.4
Working capital	1,138.4	77.9	1,377.5	613.7	4,603.8	−918.2	−07.5
Current ratio	15.2	10.3	18.1	11.8	21	7.9	10
Debt–equity ratio	4.2	5.7	9.1	8.5	15.5	9	03.2
Solvency ratio	26.5	23.6	20.6	20.5	16	19.1	30.6
Quick ratio	3.5	3.2	6.6	2	15.9	3.6	5
ROCE	141	126.9	49.8	59.6	50.3	85	1,494

Source CMIE Prowess (accessed in 2006).

D.2a

TABLE D.2 Financials of Tata Steel (₹ million)

Profit and loss	Mar. '92	Mar. '93	Mar. '94	Mar. '95	Mar. '96	Mar. '97	Mar. '98	Mar. '99
Sales	3,084.45	3701.7	4102.7	4,993.39	6,349.35	6,919.4	7,012.35	6,885.12
Other income	102.82	101.71	52.16	44.58	76.18	150.52	117.16	96.73
Change in stocks	126.63	55.65	−39.74	−17.35	66.24	42.12	4.8	46.18
Net sales	2,895.18	3,428.49	3,791.83	4,521.64	5,729.02	6,196.08	6,252.71	6,143.44
Total income	3,313.9	3,859.06	4115.12	5,020.62	6,491.77	7,112.04	7,134.31	7028.03
Raw material purchased	829.99	992.79	782.19	1,131.17	1,397.47	1,381.64	1,590.26	1,501.43
Cost of production	2,326.46	2,860.61	2,940.31	3,379.03	4,156.86	4,711.22	5,005.01	5,052.74
Selling cost	263.22	307.14	336.05	466.82	570.35	638.11	641.57	602.22
Cost of sales	2,463.36	3,112.63	3,317.02	3,865.15	4682.78	5,307.85	5,633.64	5,613.94
Administrative and other costs	222.05	258.9	249.61	200.4	216.17	248.44	261.19	282.6
Total costs	3,127.99	3,975.46	4216.96	4,868.6	5898.71	6,818.89	7,161.26	7,194.66
PAT	200.55	119.1	180.84	264.19	565.79	469.21	322.08	282.23
PBDIT	618.75	539.61	603.77	808.1	1,212.74	1,260.45	1,030.38	1,058.26
PBDT	429.44	335.47	358.54	526.7	863.83	869.79	706.96	697.91
PBIT	453.86	324.24	426.07	545.84	915.13	933.62	687.15	676.08
PBT	264.55	120.1	180.84	264.44	566.22	542.96	363.73	315.73
Cash flow from operations	0	0	0	681.14	638.86	881.3	880.44	1,007.98

(*Table D.2a continued*)

(Table D.2a continued)

Balance sheet	Mar. '92	Mar. '93	Mar. '94	Mar. '95	Mar. '96	Mar. '97	Mar. '98	Mar. '99
Current liabilities	922.02	1,100.03	1,260.53	1,421.51	1,326.82	1,385.47	1,414.66	1,463.35
Sundry creditors	774.01	974.37	1,151.87	1,256.72	1,203.97	1251	1,296.61	1,340.17
Creditors for cap. goods	0	0	0	0	0	0	0	0
Accrued interest	29.33	23.84	26.33	31.8	25.59	22.01	22.28	32
Other current liabilities	118.68	101.82	82.33	132.99	97.26	112.46	95.77	91.18
Provisions	257.35	111.26	128.35	142.83	298.49	280.41	301.37	341.27
Total liabilities	4,789.08	6,261.84	7,347.26	7,835.11	9,209.78	9,920.87	1,1274.16	11,992.83
Gross fixed assets	4,025.77	5,462.74	6,439.94	6,962.89	7,408.46	7,850.82	8948.52	1,0032.17
Land and building	228.21	251.64	306.78	482.45	552	602.19	682.69	713.56
Plant and machinery	2,294.01	3,237.07	4,606.68	5,562.97	5,930.25	6,261.49	6,676.57	7,917.93
Other fixed assets	65.86	76.33	105.92	143.38	185.41	203.22	112.59	120.73
Capital work-in-progress	1,437.69	1,897.7	1,420.56	774.09	740.8	783.92	1476.67	1,279.95
Net fixed assets	2,877.8	4,107.25	4,924.39	5,213.48	5,393.56	5526.4	6,300.04	7,058.58
Investments	248.77	170.06	261.62	220.65	410.94	664.9	626.08	588.84
Inventories	798.33	973.21	835.35	865.34	1,076.57	1,021.11	1,039.7	1,016.51

Cash and bank balance	91.59	177.06	162.72	162.44	437.09	251.38	462.96	336.19
Advances	0	0	0	0	0	0	0	0
Receivables	772.2	827.77	1,127.25	1,341.87	1,723.63	2,178.76	1,948.4	1,874.18
Total assets (excl. reval. and dre)	4,615.71	6,216.01	7,288.26	7,774.73	9012.81	9554.1	10,242.7	10,711.81
Current assets	1,712.36	1,942.55	2,081.91	2,234.45	3,053.04	3,252.83	3,386.47	3,226.58
Quick assets	486.32	625.17	874.45	949.67	1,545.08	1,582.86	1,573.93	1,361.05
Current liabilities and prov. (incl. bank short)	1,364.32	1,691.26	1,608.53	1,713.38	2,188.86	2,060.34	2,304.65	2,545.16
Working capital	348.04	251.29	473.38	521.07	864.18	1,192.49	1,081.82	681.42
Current ratio	1.26	1.15	1.29	1.3	1.39	1.58	1.47	1.27
Debt–equity ratio	1.34	1.55	1.38	1.35	1.07	1.05	1.51	1.54
Solvency ratio	1.5	1.47	1.52	1.52	1.66	1.69	1.51	1.5
Quick ratio	0.36	0.37	0.54	0.55	0.71	0.77	0.68	0.53
Return on capital employed	15.51	7.67	7.95	9.49	15.16	12.81	8.44	6.58

D.2b

Profit and loss	Mar. '00	Mar. '01	Mar. '02	Mar. '03	Mar. '04	Mar. '05	Mar. '06
Sales	7,015.16	7,845.18	8,277.38	10,516.72	12,656.73	15,870.77	17,140.06
Other income	68.51	81.17	84.23	64.09	134.6	159.52	257.97
Change in stocks	−33.19	−56.74	−11.38	15.03	80.31	289.55	104.91
Net sales	6,188.03	6,892.05	7,347.82	9,409.6	11,395.35	14,403.47	15,079.58
Total income	7050.48	7,869.61	8,350.23	10,595.84	12,871.64	16,319.84	17,502.94
Raw material purchased	1,102.48	1,130.18	1,928.2	2064.91	2,243.97	2,026.02	2,472.14
Cost of production	4625.5	4,853.81	5,792.18	6,731.18	7,603.16	7,879.98	8,293.85
Selling cost	672.16	663.74	690.37	875.06	918.37	1,035.55	1,091.56
Cost of sales	5,359.11	5,575.34	6,530.18	7,569.61	8,446.46	8,649.12	9,272.01
Administrative and other costs	314.06	370.79	357.9	383.8	470.84	725.7	825.08
Total costs	7083.8	7,420.78	8,283.5	9,695.29	11,359.78	1,2915.1	14,038.34
PAT	422.59	553.44	204.9	1,012.31	1,746.22	3,474.16	3,506.38
PBDIT	1,291.98	1,507.16	1,179.5	2,208.25	3,548.99	6,165.92	6,144.35
PBDT	903.63	1,094.77	776.35	1,845.73	3,292.03	5,954.64	5,974.72
PBIT	865.44	1,015.43	654.75	1,637.31	2,923.88	5,547.14	5,410.39
PBT	477.09	603.04	251.6	1,274.79	2,666.92	5,335.86	5,240.76
Cash flow from operations	1,323.94	1,718.7	1,406.95	2,600.11	4,082.52	5,861.83	5,598.6

D. 2c

Balance sheet	Mar. '00	Mar. '01	Mar. '02	Mar. '03	Mar. '04	Mar. '05	Mar. '06
Current liabilities	1,492.55	1,696.38	1,647.82	1,881.02	2163.79	2640.04	2,781.41
Sundry creditors	1,345.65	1,566.75	1491.7	1,694.49	1937.86	2325.17	2,479.43
Creditors for cap. goods	0	0	0	0	0	0	0
Accrued interest	30.37	30.85	48.13	46.04	43.8	30.15	24.31
Other current liabilities	116.53	98.78	107.99	140.49	182.13	284.72	277.67
Provisions	1,122.41	1,297.89	393.37	2,292.36	2,181.59	2,648.56	2,488.12
Total liabilities	12,119.88	12,555.26	1,2809.64	1,3261.54	13,933.92	16,695.61	19,257.36
Gross fixed assets	10,668.33	11,258.17	11,742.44	12,393.79	1,3269.47	14,918.72	16,427.44
Land and building	688.3	824.32	976.65	998.83	1023.9	1,099.48	1,431.24
Plant and machinery	7,850.34	9,708.41	10,195.73	10,923.64	11,202.27	11,673.64	13,531.96
Other fixed assets	210.21	229.74	239.91	270.24	279.66	367.13	400.7
Capital work-in-progress	1,919.48	495.7	330.15	201.08	763.64	1,872.66	1,157.73
Net fixed assets	7,426.38	7,538.09	7543.7	7,543.8	7,857.85	9,094.84	9,849.81
Investments	818.89	850.83	912.74	1,201.56	2,201.42	2,463.25	4,100.91
Inventories	944.85	921.77	1,021.59	1,152.95	1,249.08	1,872.4	2,174.75
Cash and bank balance	232.87	239.78	220.45	373.12	250.74	246.72	288.39

(Table D.2c continued)

(*Table D.2c continued*)

Advances	0	0	0	0	0	0	0
Receivables	1,868.77	2,084.5	1,888.39	2,153.59	1,368.26	2,008.19	1,815.59
Total assets (excl. reval. and dre)	11,154.49	1,1489.1	11,632.98	12,835.34	13,738.12	16,436.77	18,929.07
Current assets	3,012.56	3,148.87	3,064.65	3906.86	4,124.86	4,478.44	4,994.27
Quick assets	1,222.09	1,271.82	1,116.84	1,598.17	2,255.76	1,838.08	1,930.5
Current liabilities and prov. (incl. bank short)	3,205.14	3,410.16	2582.12	4,352.89	4,486.73	5,413.99	5,326.01
Working capital	–192.58	–261.29	468.53	–446.03	–374.85	–935.89	–332.08
Current ratio	0.94	0.92	1.19	0.9	0.92	0.83	0.94
Debt–equity ratio	1.33	1.18	1.37	1.33	0.78	0.4	0.26
Solvency ratio	1.5	1.53	1.77	1.61	1.79	2.06	2.45
Quick ratio	0.38	0.37	0.43	0.37	0.5	0.34	0.36
Return on capital employed	8.72	13.35	7.63	21.31	37.53	63.23	49.98

Source CMIE Prowess (accessed in 2006).

mushrooming textile industry. On August 23, in a humble redbrick shed, he began a small operation where cotton yarn spun in India was dip dyed by hand in three colors and laid out in the sun to dry. Thus, Bombay Dyeing & Manufacturing Co. Ltd was born.

From a modest beginning, the company had grown into one of India's largest producer of textiles. It manufactures cotton textile goods, nonwoven fabrics, and DMT. The textile products are sold under the trade name "TEXSPRING," "SPRINGTEX," etc. The manufacturing operations include spinning, weaving, bleaching, dyeing, printing, mercerizing, sanforizing, tebilizing, Hecowa, and other finishings. The daily production exceeds 300,000 meters of fabric. Facilities are available to produce bleached fabric up to 120", dyed and printed fabric up to 98", and gray fabric up to 124".

In 1979, the company started sales in Indonesia through an incorporated company named P.T. Five Star Industries Ltd.

In 2002, the company acquired 51 percent stake in Proline India and changed its ready-made garment business to Proline.

The DMT business has a market share of 75 percent and contributes a lot to the earnings.

It is now more than a company that was born in 1879. A legacy was born that led to a rise of India's most respected business houses. For the Wadia Group, business beyond Indian shores has been a way of life for over a hundred years. The activities of the Group span several countries in the Far East. Group companies in textiles, chemicals, agro-based industries, electronics, light engineering, laminates, health care, and, more recently, in processed foods have some of the best brand names supported by complementary distribution networks in India. The demonstrated ability to manage well diverse businesses, using professional management and financial acumen, has resulted in the Group enjoying a fine reputation in the market place. The guiding principles for the Group have been: fair and ethical dealings, trust, and integrity.

MAHINDRA & MAHINDRA

On October 2, 1945, Mahindra & Mohammed was formed and later renamed as Mahindra & Mahindra Ltd (M&M). Initially, it started steel

D.3a

TABLE D.3 Financials of Bombay Dyeing & Manufacturing Co Ltd (₹ million)

Profit and loss	Mar. '92	Mar. '93	Mar. '94	Mar. '95	Mar. '96	Mar. '97	Mar. '98	Mar. '99
Sales	5,130.6	5,566.2	5,694.1	10,668.3	13,894.8	9,983	9,338.1	8,773.9
Other income	154.7	311.4	325.4	489.2	1,017.2	1,068.2	738.6	698
Change in stocks	160.7	56.1	22	330.3	68.4	−189.2	34.4	−23.9
Net sales	4,700.3	5,072.8	5,221.8	9,176.3	11,842	8,563.1	8,151.8	7,781.3
Total income	5,446	5,933.7	6,041.5	11,487.8	14,980.4	10,862	10,111.1	9,448
Raw material purchased	2,073.6	2,406.1	2,632.7	4,970.5	7,018.6	4,450.5	4,500.8	3,645.9
Cost of production	3,905.7	4,483.1	4,559.4	7,475.3	10,123.1	8,065.8	7,778.7	7,287.8
Selling cost	72.7	75.6	98.9	128.6	115.3	141.2	130.4	146.1
Cost of sales	3,856.3	4,550.7	4,773.5	7,377.5	10,146.8	8,373.8	7,891.6	7,420.7
Admin and other costs	176.3	186.3	197.6	337.8	407.5	411.9	438.2	425.7
Total costs	4,881.6	5,559.8	5,790.5	10,164.3	13,765.8	11,274.3	10,212.8	9,575.7
PAT	438.5	360	511.7	980.9	1,171	357	207.6	2.5
PBDIT	1,123.5	1,007.5	1,130.5	2,313.3	2,789.5	1,921.9	1,414	1,262.8
PBDT	844.8	693	783.4	1,523.8	1,630.8	853.2	737.3	534.2
PBIT	857.2	689.4	858.8	1,937.9	2,329.7	1,425.7	904.3	739.2
PBT	578.5	374.9	511.7	1,148.4	1,171	357	227.6	10.6
Cash flow from operations	0	0	0	1,614	4.8	1,763.7	−1,463.9	434

D.3b

Balance sheet	Mar. '92	Mar. '93	Mar. '94	Mar. '95	Mar. '96	Mar. '97	Mar. '98	Mar. '99
Current liabilities	687.8	706.2	985.7	2,086.1	1,769.5	2,793	1,204.5	1,079.2
Sundry creditors	626.8	632.2	926.4	1,637.8	1,416	2,240.8	754.4	720.3
Creditors for cap. goods	0	0	0	0	0	0	0	0
Accrued interest	50.2	60	31.3	177.3	289.4	500.6	383	296.9
Other current liabilities	10.8	14	28	271	64.1	51.6	67.1	62
Provisions	342.9	357.8	392.6	647.4	679.5	617.6	644.1	620
Total liabilities	4,715.3	6,109.3	9,562.7	14,548	17,829.5	16,515.3	15,190.9	14,912.2
Gross fixed assets	3,586.9	4,974.8	6,243.2	7,120.1	7,952.7	8,217.8	8,390	8,476
Land and building	199.2	220.1	245.7	284.2	332.3	345.7	344.9	351.4
Plant and machinery	3,036.8	3,660.8	5,832.2	6,636.1	7,481.1	7,672.7	7,774.1	8,050.7
Other fixed assets	27.6	28.7	29.1	28.8	40.6	42.2	42.6	44.1
Capital work-in-progress	323.3	1,065.2	136.2	171	98.7	157.2	228.4	29.8
Net fixed assets	1,877.7	2,959.6	3,968.4	4,486.4	4,909.9	4,671.1	4,337	3,914
Investments	542	494.1	2,068.6	5,335.9	6,206.9	5,571.1	4,230.1	4,219.4
Inventories	1,089	1,191.5	1,483.6	2,215.6	2,381.4	1,866.4	1,918.3	1,719.5

(Table D.3b continued)

(Table D.3b continued)

Balance sheet	Mar. '92	Mar. '93	Mar. '94	Mar. '95	Mar. '96	Mar. '97	Mar. '98	Mar. '99
Cash and bank balance	59.6	88.9	62	80.6	108.1	236.2	194.6	138
Advances	0	0	0	0	0	0	0	0
Receivables	1,146.9	1,375.1	1,980	2,429.5	4,223.2	4,117	4,374.3	4,623.4
Total assets (excl. reval. and dre)	4,378.5	5,697.6	9,127.7	13,937.6	16,886.4	15,661.7	14,193.1	13,727.5
Current assets	2,762.5	3,069.9	4,367.7	7,975.7	11,246.4	9,450.8	9,058.7	8,314
Quick assets	1,115.6	1,255.2	2,093.8	4,671.1	7,378.7	5,628.9	4,750.1	4,442.2
Current liabilities and prov. (incl. bank short)	1,712.4	2,195.2	2,917.7	4,152.7	6,371.1	4,986.1	4,821.4	4,022.5
Working capital	1,050.1	874.7	1,450	3,823	4,875.3	4,464.7	4,237.3	4,291.5
Current ratio	16.1	14	15	19.2	17.7	19	18.8	20.7
Debt–equity ratio	12.2	15.9	9.9	13.9	12.2	09.2	09.8	10.7
Solvency ratio	16.1	15.2	18.2	15.5	17	17.6	18.8	18.3
Quick ratio	06.5	05.7	7.2	11.2	11.6	11.3	09.9	11
ROCE	304.6	187.1	109.1	230.7	212.3	78.4	60.2	78.3

D.3c

Profit and loss	Mar. '00	Mar. '01	Mar. '02	Mar. '03	Mar. '04	Mar. '05	Mar. '06
Sales	9,619.1	9,419.3	8,959.2	9,589	10,116.8	11,486.1	11,220.5
Other income	709.3	681.9	292.8	278.6	188.6	112.5	123.7
Change in stocks	51.4	491.9	−283.5	−20.2	−274.4	128	−180.4
Net sales	8,631	8,385.7	8,093.6	8,707.6	9,092.8	10,295.9	10,180.6
Total income	10,379.8	10,593.1	8,968.5	9,847.4	10,031	11,726.6	11,163.8
Raw material purchased	4,311.2	4,721.5	3,522.9	5,093.9	5,266.6	7,104.2	5,851.5
Cost of production	7,857.1	8,489.6	7,768.4	7,844.2	8,077.2	9,656.9	9,133.6
Selling cost	139.4	258.6	285.4	260	255.8	243.3	252.7
Cost of sales	7,970.2	8,315.2	8,303.6	8,133.5	8,559.6	9,866.8	9,647.6
Admin and other costs	469.1	412.2	343.1	390.5	436	371.9	365.4
Total costs	10,125.5	10,481.4	9,658.6	9,612.2	10,369.8	11,629.8	11,248.6
PAT	431.6	−66.4	−779	329.9	535	265.6	613.4
PBDIT	1,576.1	1,182.7	−150.7	908.1	1,229.5	656.5	1,011.2
PBDT	892.3	465.5	−511.9	727	1,069.9	530.6	841.6
PBIT	1,129.7	650.8	−634	535.8	885.2	462.7	842.2
PBT	445.9	−66.4	−995.2	354.7	725.6	336.8	672.6
Cash flow from operations	1,219.8	−04.9	1,899.4	675.1	1,245.8	−47.3	246.4

D.3d

Balance sheet	Mar. '00	Mar. '01	Mar. '02	Mar. '03	Mar. '04	Mar. '05	Mar. '06
Current liabilities	1,309.9	1,245.5	1,194.6	729.4	870	748.9	675
Sundry creditors	1,027.4	1,138.3	1,112	675	825.2	695.9	591.6
Creditors for cap. goods	0	0	0	0	0	0	0
Accrued interest	210.2	23	04.9	04.2	05.3	05.7	05.7
Other current liabilities	72.3	84.2	77.7	50.2	39.5	47.3	77.7
Provisions	195.9	185.1	1,176.4	1,152.7	581.3	407.3	375.7
Total liabilities	14,228.7	13,975.3	9,364.9	9,829.9	9,488.2	8,365.1	11,477.3
Gross fixed assets	8,650.9	8,961.1	8,749.8	8,264.2	7,954	7,302.7	9,212.1
Land and building	361.2	525.1	537	523.1	492.5	461.2	380.6
Plant and machinery	8,188.1	8,262.8	8,067.8	7,603.1	7,331.7	7,009	6,747.5
Other fixed assets	46.5	69.7	74.2	76.9	68.8	73.7	76.1
Capital work-in-progress	55.1	103.5	70.8	61.1	61	593.9	2,750.7
Net fixed assets	3,576.8	3,463.1	2,967.9	2,540.4	2,222.5	1,914.8	3,993.7
Investments	4,382.8	3,229.1	1,435.1	3,004.5	3,602.5	2,411.9	1,680.2
Inventories	1,861.5	2,603.2	1,643.4	1,989.5	1,678.7	1,997.3	2,119.5
Cash and bank balance	105.6	191.6	98.9	67.7	68.4	55.1	333.4
Advances	0	0	0	0	0	0	0

Receivables	3,934	4,027.4	2,720.4	1,840	1,724.3	1,847.7	3,126.2
Total assets (excl. reval. and dre)	13,318.6	12,923.8	8,780.7	9,487.2	9,204	8,075.3	10,271.4
Current assets	4,633.8	8,056.5	3,740.6	5,877	6,135	5,432.1	5,706.5
Quick assets	905.5	3,664.6	758.5	2,892.7	3,629.9	2,544	2,461.2
Current liabilities and prov. (incl. bank short)	4,276.4	4,413.9	4,271.1	4,419.5	4,322.6	3,053.1	3,624.8
Working capital	357.4	3,642.6	−530.5	1,457.5	1,812.4	2,375.3	2,081.7
Current ratio	10.8	18.3	08.8	13.3	14.2	17.8	15.7
Debt–equity ratio	09.5	09.8	08.8	10.8	09.4	10.4	14.9
Solvency ratio	19.1	19	18.6	17.7	19.2	18.3	16.3
Quick ratio	02.1	08.3	01.8	06.5	08.4	08.3	06.8
ROCE	89.3	54.3	−38.7	100.8	60.7	35.8	65.6

Source CMIE Prowess (accessed in 2006).

trading business with suppliers from UK. In 1949, M&M started the assembly of the Jeep (multi-utility vehicle—MUV), becoming the sole four-wheel drive manufacturer in the country. Five years later, it went in for a technical and financial collaboration with Willys Overland Corporation. In 1956, the company went public and got its shares listed on the Bombay Stock Exchange.

In 1963, M&M diversified into the tractor business by setting up a joint venture with International Harvestor Co., USA, under the name International Tractor Company of India (ITCI). This company was later merged with M&M in 1977 to become its tractor division. It went on to become a market leader in the Indian tractor market, with a market share of around 27 percent, a position that the company has never relinquished since 1983.

In 1965, the company started manufacture of light commercial vehicles (LCVs).

M&M is a premier leader in the automobile industry with unparallel leadership in farm equipment (tractors and implements) as well as the MUV/SUV segment. One of the main reasons for the extraordinary performance of the company has been the presence of leadership and adept management.

The leaders have developed a culture and spirit that goes beyond products and profits. More important than profitability is to provide customers value for money. M&M has always stuck to its core philosophy of providing the customers with quality products at competitive prices. The core values of M&M are (*i*) good corporate citizenship, (*ii*) professionalism, (*iii*) customer first, (*iv*) quality focus, and (*v*) dignity of the individual.

The drive to bring a change in the organization has been internal with the company committing the resources for constant innovation in the products, services, and processes. This is the reason that explains for the company's preparedness in the liberalization era. The achievement motivation has been high and the company has shown self-confidence in facing competitive forces. The efforts and initiatives taken by the company have been aligned to the core.

M&M has never sat back on its laurels and let the future slip by. Complacency was never allowed to settle in. The company aimed at goals that were out of its comfort zone, like for instance going global and setting up manufacturing units abroad. The Deming Award is another testimony for its spirit of pursuing "good enough never is."

Today, M&M is the flagship company of the ₹62,000 million Mahindra Group, one of the most respected groups in the country. The Group has presence in vehicles, farm equipment, steel, information technology, trade, financial-related services, and infrastructure development.

APOLLO TYRES

Incorporated on September 28, 1972, by Mathew T. Marattukalam, Jacob Thomas, and his associates, subsequently after two years the company was taken over by Raunaq Singh and his associates. The tyre project was implemented in 1976 and commercial production started in 1977 with an installed capacity of 420,000 each of tyres and tubes.

The company had technical collaboration with General Tire International Co., USA, which was later taken over by Continental Gummi Werke GmbH, West Germany. This collaboration expired in 1987.

In the early 1970s, the MNCs and the Indian tyre majors dominated the tyre industry. Despite incurring heavy losses in the initial years, primarily because the production capacities were higher compared to the market demand, Apollo came back as a strong player backed by strong production and marketing strategies. With state-of-the-art technology and goal-oriented management, Apollo came to be recognized as a respected name in the Indian tyre industry in nylon as well as radial tyre segments.

In 1987, the company acquired interest in Gujarat Tyres Ltd for implementing an industrial license to manufacture automobile tyres and tubes in Gujarat state. The company set up a plant with a capacity of 0.675 million tyres per annum at Limda, Baroda in Gujarat at an estimated cost of ₹1,690 million.

In 1991, Apollo Tyres undertook exports of LCV and farm tyres in addition to truck tyres. In 1994, it emerged as the largest exporter of tyres.

There are several interesting facts worth noting on the company:

- It is the first tyre company in the country to get ISO 9001 certification in the year 1997.
- It is ranked 18th in the world tyre industry in terms of sales.

D.4a

TABLE D.4 Financials of Mahindra & Mahindra (₹ million)

Profit and loss	Mar. '92	Mar. '93	Mar. '94	Mar. '95	Mar. '96	Mar. '97	Mar. '98	Mar. '99
Sales	11,964.8	14,576.8	16,726.9	20,371.1	27,814.8	35,197.8	39,959.6	41,003.4
Other income	328.2	292.5	412.4	714.2	1,179	952	1,129	1,047
Change in stocks	115.5	197.9	150.3	−299.5	465	222.6	791.9	−689.5
Net sales	9,858.8	12,171.4	14,284.3	17,159.2	23,615.6	30,054.5	33,425.9	34,341.5
Total income	12,408.5	15,067.2	17,289.6	20,785.8	29,458.8	36,372.4	41,880.5	41,360.9
Raw material purchased	6,038.2	7,433.1	8,720.5	10,554.9	14,657.7	18,162.8	20,348.1	19,338.8
Cost of production	9,015.5	11,134.9	12,444.1	14,476.9	20,362.7	24,976.1	28,544.9	27,933.9
Selling cost	71.1	127.7	103.8	116	238	462.5	442.4	818.9
Cost of sales	9,003.9	11,046.7	12,414.8	14,887.1	20,193.7	25,292.4	28,192.8	29,381
Admin and other costs	576.2	614.6	811.7	930.3	1,329.5	1,730.3	2,099.2	20,65.6
Total costs	12,344.8	14,661.6	16,379	20,099.1	27,368.9	34,161	38,834.6	40,142.1
PAT	187.3	238.8	678.5	1,135.4	1,623.4	2,093.4	2,514.7	2,259.1
PBDIT	1,194.8	1,154.9	1,738.9	2,541.3	3,693.2	4,718	5,516.5	5,412.5
PBDT	536.1	560	1,176.5	2,094	3,211.7	3,913	4,287.6	3,893.9
PBIT	846	833.7	1,388.4	2,205.2	3,269.9	4,088.4	4,523.6	4,292.7
PBT	187.3	238.8	826	1,757.9	2,788.4	3,283.4	3,294.7	2,774.1
Cash flow from operations	0	0	0	2,025.8	3,769.7	4,502.8	764.1	4,765.8

D.4b

Balance sheet	Mar. '92	Mar. '93	Mar. '94	Mar. '95	Mar. '96	Mar. '97	Mar. '98	Mar. '99
Current liabilities	2,426.4	2,964.3	2,795.4	3,573.5	53,19.7	5,906.6	7,111.7	7,365.8
Sundry creditors	2,227.4	2,588	2,341.4	3,468.4	5,210	5,751.6	6,844.7	7,062.7
Creditors for cap. goods	0	0	0	0	0	0	0	0
Accrued interest	143.6	131.6	154.1	95.7	81.5	132.9	211.4	275.1
Other current liabilities	55.4	244.7	299.9	9.4	28.2	22.1	55.6	28
Provisions	199.3	192.6	342.4	448.1	787.5	1,249.5	1,050.8	1,338.9
Total liabilities	8,746.6	10,053.1	12,810.5	15,294.4	19,356.9	28,401.3	34,946.4	38,387.7
Gross fixed assets	4,706.7	5,117.5	5,236.1	6,246.3	8,131.2	11,464.2	14,265.4	16,146.4
Land and building	1,037.9	1,035.4	1,055.6	1,235.9	1,409.7	1,752.4	2,104.7	2,495.1
Plant and machinery	3,097.8	3,439.4	3,742.1	4,323.5	4,931	8,344.5	10,612.4	12,204.2
Other fixed assets	133	145.9	187.4	230	300.5	397	523.7	621.5
Capital work-in-progress	438	496.8	251	456.9	1,490	970.3	1,024.6	825.6
Net fixed assets	3,053.5	3,158.6	2,973.1	3,734.5	5,383.4	8,101	10,174.2	10,986.1
Investments	634.5	402.4	1,935.4	2,900.4	4,144.4	6,093.4	6,560.3	8,104.7
Inventories	2,389	2,614	3,192.4	3,519.1	3,917.9	4,474.8	5,148.7	4,369.9
Cash and bank balance	409.5	685.3	449.9	359.6	314.7	4,092.3	2,734.1	3,205.6
Advances	0	0	0	0	0	0	0	0

(Table D.4b continued)

(Table D.4b continued)

Balance sheet	Mar. '92	Mar. '93	Mar. '94	Mar. '95	Mar. '96	Mar. '97	Mar. '98	Mar. '99
Receivables	2,082.1	2,940.6	4,026.9	4,612.1	5,414.6	5,277.5	9,730.4	10,753
Total assets (excl. reval. and dre)	8,200.9	9,453.2	12,271.2	14,907.4	18,850.9	27,835.7	33,996.1	36,916.5
Current assets	5,158.5	5,844.3	8,043.1	8,689.9	7,844	15,008.3	18,507	18,745.5
Quick assets	1,791.5	1,958.7	2,810	3,459.8	2,109	8,216.7	8,764.4	10,979.4
Current liabilities and prov. (incl. bank short)	3,345.6	4,117.9	4,027.1	5,350.3	8,051.9	7,674.9	9,739.8	9,672.7
Working capital	1,812.9	1,726.4	4,016	3,339.6	−207.9	7,333.4	8,767.2	9,072.8
Current ratio	15.4	14.2	20	16.2	9.7	19.6	19	19.4
Debt–equity ratio	20.4	22.8	9.1	5.4	4.2	9.9	10.6	10.6
Solvency ratio	12.9	12.6	16.5	19.1	19.3	16	15.9	16
Quick ratio	5.4	4.8	7.0	6.5	2.6	10.7	9.0	11.4
ROCE	129.9	159.6	221.1	235.8	325.3	259.8	196.2	159.4

D.4c

Profit and loss	Mar. '00	Mar. '01	Mar. '02	Mar. '03	Mar. '04	Mar. '05	Mar. '06
Sales	43,190.8	42,761.8	39,345.4	44,982.5	58,870.9	76,495.2	92,730.9
Other income	1,258	1,133.3	900.9	1,210.2	1,342.7	1,895.4	1,975.3
Change in stocks	871.1	365.3	-597.2	-333	90.1	1,620.4	991.2
Net sales	35,317.6	35,065.2	32,430.5	36,965	49,125.3	65,759.5	81,119.1
Total income	45,319.9	44,260.4	39,649.1	45,859.7	60,303.7	80,011	95,697.4
Raw material purchased	21,318.2	21,938.3	18,547.2	22,704.2	31,342.4	44,565.9	53,599.2
Cost of production	29,576.2	31,115.1	27,205	31,692.2	41,111.3	54,865.1	66,295.6
Selling cost	1,109.3	1,665	2,059.8	2,247.3	2,888.1	3,896.5	4,599
Cost of sales	29,828.2	32,443.1	29,864	34,184.6	43,882.4	57,176.5	69,862.8
Admin and other costs	2,239.7	1,814.6	1,697	1,651.6	2,049	3,819.6	4,876.5
Total costs	42,251.2	43,274.4	39,853.9	45,561.7	57,346.1	72,976.7	88,070.5
PAT	2,634.8	1,205.6	969.1	1,455.3	3,405.2	5,126.7	8,571
PBDIT	6,152	3,813.7	3,555.3	4,788.1	6,732.5	9,236.7	13,451.9
PBDT	4,737.5	2,686.5	2,398.9	3,629.1	5,953.2	8,934.3	13,182.3
PBIT	4,919.3	2,412.8	2,161.5	3,129.3	5,071	7,579.1	11,694.6
PBT	3,504.8	1,285.6	1,005.1	1,970.3	4,301.7	7,276.7	11,425
Cash flow from operations	6,753.9	1,234.9	3,576.9	6,284	8,107.4	6,467.4	9,950.6

D.4d

Balance sheet	Mar. '00	Mar. '01	Mar. '02	Mar. '03	Mar. '04	Mar. '05	Mar. '06
Current liabilities	7,583.1	7,989.7	8,335.2	8,915	10,098.9	12,600.1	15,208.6
Sundry creditors	7,394.6	7,611.3	7,851	8,516.8	9,347.2	12,424.1	15,032.5
Creditors for cap. goods	0	0	0	0	0	0	0
Accrued interest	169.1	153.5	462	368.4	159.2	129	126.9
Other current liabilities	19.4	224.9	22.2	29.8	592.5	47	49.2
Provisions	1,419.5	1,302.4	2,174.2	2,033	2,942.8	4,196	4,722.1
Total liabilities	38,710.1	41,319.1	41,456.6	40,418.6	40,417.2	49,475.2	59,756.8
Gross fixed assets	18,589.3	22,332.8	24,170.7	24,909.7	25,391.8	27,812.9	30,332.6
Land and building	2,741.8	3,142.7	3,437.2	3,784.9	3,834.5	3,993.9	4,713.9
Plant and machinery	13,490.7	15,599.6	16,348.6	19,638.7	20,154.7	21,422.3	22,364.2
Other fixed assets	728.7	847.4	897.6	947.6	1,003.1	1,289.4	1,462.6
Capital work-in-progress	1,628.1	2,743.1	3,487.3	538.5	399.5	1,107.3	1,791.9
Net fixed assets	12,320	14,843.1	15,375.2	14,679.3	13,733.6	14,544.5	15,363.1
Investments	8,230.1	7,121.3	8,003.1	8,622.7	11,111.5	11,515.3	16,828.7

Inventories	5,155.5	5,525.4	4,690.4	4,567.4	4,997	7,598.4	8,787.3
Cash and bank balance	2,653.9	1,446.1	1,906	2,408.7	2,333.1	6,239.8	7,303
Advances	0	0	0	0	0	0	0
Receivables	8,799	10,147.1	10,724.3	9,140.3	7,648.4	8,737.5	10,674.9
Total assets (excl. reval. and dre)	36,789.8	38,416.6	40,651.6	39,192.7	39,189.2	48,022.9	58,442
Current assets	17,937.7	16,927.6	17,287.2	15,023	14,846.1	22,667.1	25,600.2
Quick assets	8,884.5	7,652.9	8,398.5	6,918	6,234.9	11,571.3	13,201.8
Current liabilities and prov. (incl. bank short)	9,747.1	11,444.1	11,997.8	11,177.6	14,519.3	17,639.3	20,307.9
Working capital	8,190.6	5,483.5	5,289.4	3,845.4	326.8	4,220.6	4,570.1
Current ratio	18.4	14.8	14.4	13.4	10.2	12.9	12.6
Debt–equity ratio	5.2	6.2	9.3	7.5	4.2	5.4	3.1
Solvency ratio	20	19.1	17.2	18.1	20.2	18.3	21.1
Quick ratio	9.1	6.7	7.0	6.2	4.3	6.6	6.5
ROCE	174.3	80.6	71.2	94.8	189.5	274.1	260.2

Source CMIE Prowess (accessed in 2006).

- It is the second-largest company with 15 percent market share operating in the truck and bus segment that accounts for 75 percent of its revenues.
- It is consistently rated as "Excellent" in quality audit by the collaborator M/s Continental AG.

Overall, it is the fourth-largest tyre player in India after companies like JK, MRF, and Ceat. The backbone of the company is its core values. The acronym "CREATE" stands for C: care for customer, R: respect for associates, E: excellence through teamwork, T: trust mutually, and E: ethical practices.

EXIDE INDUSTRIES

Incorporated on January 4, 1960, at Kolkata, under the name of Associated Battery Makers, Exide Industries has its main thrust on storage batteries, both for industrial sector and automobile sector. The company maintained its position as India's and South Asia's largest power Solutions Company. Its Haldia factory was set up in 1973 as a 100 percent export-oriented unit. In 1977, it started another factory near the export unit as the domestic demand increased. On August 25, 1995, the name of the company was changed to Exide Industries Ltd. In 1997, the Rajan Raheja–controlled Exide Industries became the country's largest automotive battery manufacturer and was exploring the acquisition route for stepping up production capacities. Shin-Kobe Electric Machinery Co. Ltd of Japan, the manufacturers of Hitachi have a technical collaboration with Exide Industries. The company manufactures products under brand names like Exide, Dynex, and Index. Of these, Exide is the largest-selling brand. The company's performance has ensured record sales of ₹13,320 million in the year ending on March 31, 2004. The share capital of the company is ₹710 million and had employees of 3,860 as on March 31, 2004.

TABLE D.5 Financials of Apollo Tyres (₹ crore)

D.5a

Profit and loss	Mar. '92	Mar. '93	Mar. '94	Mar. '95	Mar. '96	Mar. '97	Mar. '98	Mar. '99
Sales	362.26	502.34	686.82	749.03	1239.83	1416.59	1368.23	1154.31
Other income	11.38	10.02	6.06	3.83	14.61	13.95	4.37	3.82
Change in stocks	5.94	12.73	−10.14	16.85	6.43	2.65	−9.91	56.16
Net sales	276.07	391.78	527.04	570.88	963.78	1081.98	1067.8	896.18
Total income	379.58	525.09	682.74	769.71	1260.87	1433.19	1362.69	1214.29
Raw material purchased	147.64	231.06	292.54	354.68	657.92	657.31	602.66	534.41
Cost of production	203.02	323.39	422.46	472.84	810.36	900.02	834.55	729.12
Selling cost	11.45	17.83	26.43	31.83	29.29	44.14	50.71	61.34
Cost of sales	211.92	330.24	455.99	494.45	838.42	937.71	894.79	732.52
Administrative costs	16.51	19.48	22.92	22.48	32.39	35.27	39.97	44.79
Total costs	332.39	493.85	677.64	732.6	1216.06	13907	1317.92	1112.83
PAT	33.02	20.8	15.63	25.91	35.31	36.32	40.68	31.08
PBDIT	59.85	72.55	72.69	76.59	121.21	142.14	151.02	136.67
PBDT	43.04	40.47	37.94	41.86	53.4	61.86	76.53	66.38
PBIT	51.33	55.28	54.58	64.64	106.87	122.21	128.93	113.21
PBT	34.52	23.2	19.83	29.91	39.06	41.93	54.44	42.92
Cash flow from operations	0	0	0	75.91	51.53	115.26	113	157.9

D.5b

Balance Sheet	Mar. '92	Mar. '93	Mar. '94	Mar. '95	Mar. '96	Mar. '97	Mar. '98	Mar. '99
Current liabilities	70.79	94.83	105.87	154.07	204.98	191.83	229.48	190.95
Sundry creditors	62.47	85.14	99.11	146.32	189.02	174.63	215.95	180.25
Creditors for cap. goods	0	0	0	0	0	0	0	0
Accrued interest	8.06	7.33	5.71	6.4	12.99	11.96	10.57	8.95
Other current liabilities	0.26	2.36	1.05	1.35	2.97	5.24	2.96	1.75
Provisions	19.17	21.57	25.41	29.41	34.76	42.04	55.95	63.7
Total liabilities	385.05	458.82	479.22	569.65	743.33	762.26	843.04	855.81
Gross fixed assets	254.16	274.94	289.39	316.52	414.49	457.96	459.57	531.02
Land and building	37.64	41.21	41.24	46.6	59.59	63.78	63.51	66.76
Plant and machinery	206.17	225.86	236.24	251.01	295.76	346.47	348.57	386.38
Other fixed assets	4.86	7.5	9.94	12.91	30.92	40.92	42.81	44.16
Capital work-in-progress	5.49	0.37	1.97	6	28.22	6.79	4.68	33.72
Net fixed assets	186.32	187.92	182.63	204.69	287.52	310.31	308.73	357.99
Investments	8.48	8.52	14	18.78	30.13	27.61	27.56	27.59
Inventories	47.52	67.73	63.41	98.06	154.18	129.65	97.59	153.76

Cash and bank balance	21.19	26.66	36.08	59.5	38.55	34.6	38.43	57.37
Advances	0	0	0	0	0	0	0	0
Receivables	116.22	162.78	176.1	184.06	217.85	236.52	350.99	239.77
Total assets (excl. reval. and dre)	354.28	430.84	443.93	529.52	687.73	692.04	768.2	768.29
Current assets	168.91	238.2	261.02	330.97	394.86	384.9	483.46	448.23
Quick assets	80.41	108.01	153.11	159.04	152.44	165.01	290.22	183.87
Current liabilities and prov. (incl. bank short)	131.47	168.31	181.17	245.69	320.38	320.14	377.09	291.28
Working capital	37.44	69.89	79.85	85.28	74.48	64.76	106.37	156.95
Current ratio	1.28	1.42	1.44	1.35	1.23	1.2	1.28	1.54
Debt–equity ratio	1.03	1.22	1.19	1.27	1.48	1.34	1.17	0.99
Solvency ratio	1.62	1.51	1.51	1.45	1.39	1.44	1.47	1.6
Quick ratio	0.61	0.64	0.85	0.65	0.48	0.52	0.77	0.63
Return on capital employed	28.3	20.59	19.62	19.64	30.46	30.46	32.43	25.14

D.5c

Profit and loss	Mar. '00	Mar. '01	Mar. '02	Mar. '03	Mar. '04	Mar. '05	Mar. '06
Sales	1352.35	1458.69	1713.01	2028.98	2318.55	2662.53	3008.3
Other income	10.72	8.82	6.54	10.16	16.53	3.73	6.08
Change in stocks	6.58	37.64	−61.05	27.09	37.91	−24.72	88.74
Net sales	1064.98	1138.42	1373.47	1604.84	1906.8	2233.81	2609.97
Total income	1369.65	1505.15	1658.5	2066.23	2372.99	2641.54	3103.12
Raw material purchased	608.81	691.59	749.06	967.93	1206.18	1519.12	1846.08
Cost of production	808.33	955.76	1016.46	1282.05	1619.91	1863.75	2321.01
Selling cost	88.59	82.05	158.51	106.59	127.25	144.16	121
Cost of sales	893.53	1000.47	1237.25	1366.22	1709.74	2037.7	2359.86
Administrative costs	48.17	56.81	55.63	56.52	70.3	83.02	90.47
Total costs	1295.01	1440.31	1710.97	1932.15	2264.92	2611.96	2930.49
PAT	76.06	20.76	4.11	120.02	72.29	67.63	78.17
PBDIT	173.16	120.84	119.77	242.8	188.49	192.54	245.73
PBDT	120.66	51.71	54.38	200.45	150.82	141.7	179.16
PBIT	146.56	89.96	87.44	209.44	144.77	135.75	172.94
PBT	94.06	20.83	22.05	167.09	107.1	84.91	106.37
Cash flow from operations	101.88	70.97	214.01	200.24	160.07	109.15	102.43

D.5d

Balance sheet	Mar. '00	Mar. '01	Mar. '02	Mar. '03	Mar. '04	Mar. '05	Mar. '06
Current liabilities	249	273.69	279.13	222.57	310.59	380.14	415.72
Sundry creditors	237.85	265.16	271.94	214.4	292.97	366.64	406.04
Creditors for cap. goods	0	0	0	0	8.23	4.62	0.5
Accrued interest	8.7	6.34	1.33	0.37	5.39	5.84	6.92
Other current liabilities	2.45	2.19	5.86	7.8	4	3.04	2.26
Provisions	68.78	86.09	97.82	170.78	198.72	188.07	210.53
Total liabilities	1049.41	1139.1	1047.13	1181.31	1599.74	1794.37	2123.97
Gross fixed assets	616.17	655.62	676.68	775.91	1035.15	1223.63	1377.24
Land and building	93.64	99.84	102.61	104.6	141.86	160.22	173.57
Plant and machinery	453.99	495.64	513.74	557.9	751	892.35	1029.79
Other fixed assets	52.76	52.61	50.94	57.53	76.45	86.73	95.95
Capital work-in-progress	15.78	7.53	9.39	55.88	65.84	84.33	77.93
Net fixed assets	417.26	429.85	421.23	488.24	707.79	827.51	911.57
Investments	77.31	64.28	55.93	25.54	64.21	54.48	0.53
Inventories	185.01	212.58	142.06	216.48	262.66	330.12	419.41

(Table D.5d continued)

(Table D.5d continued)

Balance sheet	Mar. '00	Mar. '01	Mar. '02	Mar. '03	Mar. '04	Mar. '05	Mar. '06
Cash and bank balance	44.83	56.28	66.34	97.61	106.35	110.43	231.36
Advances	0	0	0	0	0	0	0
Receivables	310.74	361.37	344.89	344.01	448.75	462.24	545.32
Total assets (excl. reval. and dre)	951.53	1035.56	934.53	1027.83	1401.13	1595.89	1902.26
Current assets	539.74	663.57	589.92	692.35	848.63	899.79	1193.03
Quick assets	172.7	255.17	257.63	194.75	248.09	261.64	403.57
Current liabilities and prov. (incl. bank short)	419.62	502.08	478.2	511.07	692.55	860.91	992.02
Working capital	120.12	156.83	110.47	156.64	131.91	37.84	199.71
Current ratio	1.29	1.32	1.23	1.35	1.23	1.05	1.2
Debt-equity ratio	0.86	0.96	0.9	0.7	0.74	0.95	1.19
Solvency ratio	1.67	1.6	1.69	1.92	1.9	1.74	1.64
Quick ratio	0.41	0.51	0.54	0.38	0.36	0.3	0.41
Return on capital employed	23.51	14.95	16.32	36.99	20.75	14.37	18.11

Source CMIE Prowess (accessed in 2006).
Note 1 crore = 10 million.

Exide Industries Limited is the largest battery exporter from India. Batteries manufactured by Exide are exported across the world to various countries.

HINDALCO

On December 15, 1958, Hindalco was incorporated in Mumbai by the Birlas in collaboration with the Kaiser Organization of USA. Hindalco commenced operations in 1962 with an aluminium facility at Renukoot in eastern Uttar Pradesh. In 1967, the company set up its own captive power plant at Renusagar. Over the years, it grew into the largest integrated aluminium manufacturer of the country.

It is a flagship company of the Aditya Birla Group. It is structured into two strategic businesses—aluminium and copper—and is an industry leader in both the segments. A nonferrous metals powerhouse, close to global scale, the company's integrated operations and operating efficiency have positioned Hindalco as India's largest integrated player in aluminium.

The Aditya Birla Group is India's first truly multinational corporation. Global in vision, rooted in Indian values, the Group is driven by a performance ethic pegged on value creation for its multiple stakeholders. A $6.5 billion conglomerate, it is anchored by an extraordinary force of 72,000 employees belonging to over 20 different nationalities. Over 30 percent of its revenues come from operations across the world. The Group's products and services offer distinctive customer solutions. Its 66 state-of-the-art manufacturing units and sectoral services span India, Thailand, Indonesia, Malaysia, Philippines, Egypt, Canada, Australia, and China. The Group is a dominant player in all of the sectors in which it operates—viscose staple fiber, nonferrous metals, cement, viscose filament yarn, branded apparel, carbon black and insulators, chemicals, fertilizers, sponge iron, insurance and asset management, and financial services.

D. 6a

TABLE D.6 Financials of Exide Industries (₹ million)

Profit and loss	Mar. '92	Mar. '93	Mar. '94	Mar. '95	Mar. '96	Mar. '97	Mar. '98	Mar. '99
Sales	2,489	2,433.5	2,603.4	2,996.2	3,583.4	5,113	5,660.6	8,180.1
Other income	16.7	15.7	28.2	29.2	30.1	14.1	29.5	21
Change in stocks	−39.9	56.7	−53.9	02.8	61.4	−06.6	134	130.4
Net sales	1,957.7	1,868.7	1,998.8	2,245.3	2,785.8	3,987.5	4,425.7	6,453.6
Total income	2,465.8	2,505.9	2,577.7	3,028.2	3,674.9	5,120.5	5,824.1	8,331.5
Raw material purchased	1,103.4	1,107.3	1,048.5	1,274.5	1,818	2,339.6	2,568.9	3,328.4
Cost of production	1,440.9	1,431.5	1,459.2	1,745.6	2,132.9	2,997.5	3,368.2	4,898.8
Selling cost	98.2	99.6	115.6	163.3	227.4	270	360.7	446.3
Cost of sales	1,574.4	1,480.7	1,641	1,908.1	2,301.5	3,269.2	3,673.2	5,241.5
Admin and other costs	80.5	85.1	97.5	98.4	131.8	150.7	189.2	253.9
Total costs	2,376.7	2,349.3	2,533.5	2,928	3,406.1	4,821.9	5,470.6	7807
PAT	137.3	112	79.4	101.4	204.1	309.3	233.6	398.7
PBDIT	353.8	358.9	300.2	306.4	440.4	708.7	790	1,327.8
PBDT	263.3	246.4	190.8	186.8	280.2	489.2	464.7	805.8
PBIT	327.8	330.7	269.8	272	379.3	585.8	586.4	975.7
PBT	237.3	218.2	160.4	152.4	219.1	366.3	261.1	453.7
Cash flow from operations	0	0	0	0	327.4	256.3	768.7	437.8

D. 6b

Balance sheet	Mar. '92	Mar. '93	Mar. '94	Mar. '95	Mar. '96	Mar. '97	Mar. '98	Mar. '99
Current liabilities	494.4	328.5	350.2	473.5	685	801.6	1,556.5	955.7
Sundry creditors	455.7	286.3	310.4	461.4	627.5	698.9	1,398.5	802.8
Creditors for cap. goods	0	0	0	0	0	0	0	0
Accrued interest	05	08	06.8	07.8	11.2	14.8	51.7	44
Other current liabilities	33.7	34.2	33	04.3	46.3	87.9	106.3	108.9
Provisions	52.3	50.5	35.1	66.1	69.2	92.3	101.5	132.1
Total liabilities	1,948.8	2,055.1	2,158.2	2,424.8	3,318.6	4,552.1	7,227.9	7,946.7
Gross fixed assets	1,015.1	1,035.8	1,065.1	1,232.9	1,798.5	2,623.2	4,718.6	5,537
Land and building	449.3	457.1	459.4	475.2	529.3	647.5	1,417	1,604.3
Plant and machinery	544.8	540.5	576.6	657.4	1,028.7	1,859.8	3,060.2	3,740.8
Other fixed assets	17.1	19.4	22.5	29.6	40.3	54.3	97.1	121.9
Capital work-in-progress	03.9	18.8	06.6	70.7	200.2	61.6	144.3	7
Net fixed assets	672.5	668.5	656.8	779.6	1,273.8	2,005.2	3,884.9	4,369.1
Investments	02.7	02.7	02.7	03.9	06.9	11.3	61.6	11.6
Inventories	573.8	662.3	555.2	569.7	881.4	1,018.3	1,521.6	1,713.4

(Table D.6b continued)

(Table D.6b continued)

Balance sheet	Mar. '92	Mar. '93	Mar. '94	Mar. '95	Mar. '96	Mar. '97	Mar. '98	Mar. '99
Cash and bank balance	14.1	46.9	60.3	33	89.4	46	47	87
Advances	0	0	0	0	0	0	0	0
Receivables	685.7	674.7	883.2	1,027.1	1,041.5	1,460.3	1,700.7	1,742.1
Total assets (excl. reval. & dre)	1,494.9	1,618.3	1,723.9	1,977.9	2,880.6	4,157.1	6,847.4	7,570.8
Current assets	1,244.7	1,365	1,496.5	1,629.2	2,011.6	2,524.5	3,207.1	3,542.5
Quick assets	405.9	522.4	735	770.2	790.6	1,114.4	1,204.7	1,411
Current liabilities and prov. (incl. bank short)	696.4	627.6	656.4	798	1,079.4	1,220.3	2,800.5	1,520.7
Working capital	548.3	737.4	840.1	831.2	932.2	1,304.2	406.6	2,021.8
Current ratio	17.9	21.7	22.8	20.4	18.6	20.7	11.5	23.3
Debt–equity ratio	05.5	08.9	10.1	11	11	11.9	21.8	13.2
Solvency ratio	16.9	16.8	16.4	15.4	15.5	15.6	13.1	15.9
Quick ratio	05.8	08.3	11.2	09.7	07.3	09.1	04.3	09.3
ROCE	447.6	356.1	279.2	235.4	253.6	244.2	169	193.2

D. 6c

Profit and loss	Mar. '00	Mar. '01	Mar. '02	Mar. '03	Mar. '04	Mar. '05	Mar. '06
Sales	9,464.3	9,537.2	9,899.7	11,000.6	12,155.2	14,925.3	17,643.2
Other income	62.4	42.8	32.3	68.5	90.9	67.1	91.1
Change in stocks	55.2	–06.1	110.2	102.7	15.3	90.8	181.1
Net sales	7,649.7	7,688.4	7,960.3	8,819.1	9,675.7	11,857.1	13,816.6
Total income	9,581.9	9,573.9	10,042.2	11,171.8	12,261.4	15,083.2	17,915.4
Raw material purchased	4,134.4	3,581.4	3,785.4	4,341.1	5,180.8	7,028.1	7,997.2
Cost of production	5,734.7	5,818.2	6,092.8	6,630.6	7,243.1	9,457.3	10,737.3
Selling cost	558.2	675.8	866.2	884.2	842.1	977.7	1,169.2
Cost of sales	6,355	6,469.2	6,869.4	7,460.2	8,083	10,380.5	11,826.8
Admin and other costs	257.5	267.9	268.1	258.3	310.8	290.4	335.6
Total costs	9,050.3	9,167.7	9,632.7	10,570.2	11,476.3	14,275.2	16,761.8
PAT	488.9	415.5	314.2	523.3	728.6	772.8	1,007.3
PBDIT	1,501.2	1,421.2	1,314.2	1,648.9	1,867.4	1,842.5	2,352.9
PBDT	947.3	912.4	872.7	1,278.7	1,586.8	1,703	2,121.8
PBIT	1,105.3	994.3	870	1,193.5	1,328.4	1,309.8	1,804.9
PBT	551.4	485.5	428.5	823.3	1,147.8	1,170.3	1,573.8
Cash flow from operations	1,130.3	1,547.8	1,751	1,762.9	2,004.5	1,321.2	2,781.5

D. 6d

Balance sheet	Mar. '00	Mar. '01	Mar. '02	Mar. '03	Mar. '04	Mar. '05	Mar. '06
Current liabilities	1,064.5	946.8	1,143.6	1,270.1	1,711.6	1,701.1	2,186.3
Sundry creditors	969.3	851.7	1,070.9	1,197.2	1,624.4	1,662.1	2,107.9
Creditors for cap. goods	0	0	0	0	0	0	0
Accrued interest	11	09.6	21.1	10.6	20.2	11.4	07.5
Other current liabilities	84.2	85.5	51.6	62.3	67	27.6	70.9
Provisions	127.2	59.5	124.6	160.7	387.4	502.1	629.5
Total liabilities	9,319.8	9,244	8,734.5	8,538.8	8,694.1	10,571.5	11,815.2
Gross fixed assets	6,630.3	7,119	7,204.8	7,555.6	8,077.2	8,610.6	8,884.3
Land and building	1,803.7	1,925.1	1,938.1	1,977.7	2,002.6	2,055.2	2,078.7
Plant and machinery	4,496	4,363.7	5,092.5	5,409.7	5,926.5	5,621	5,805.4
Other fixed assets	203.8	805.7	124.7	128.6	133	896.5	938.1
Capital work-in-progress	126.8	24.5	49.5	39.6	15.1	37.9	62.1
Net fixed assets	5,239.7	5,238.6	4,959.4	4,818	4,775.1	4,842.7	4,574.5

Investments	23.3	200.3	190.3	190.3	198.7	1,116.2	2,785.4
Inventories	1,964.3	1,791	1,712.2	1,803.9	2,123.4	2,275.8	2,417.2
Cash and bank balance	30.1	61.7	37.8	26.6	12.5	361.9	173.7
Advances	0	0	0	0	0	0	0
Receivables	1,967.5	1,872.2	1,778	1,659.7	1,519.6	1,946.2	1,814
Total assets (excl. reval. and dre)	8,359.6	8,370.7	7,942.6	7,857.3	8,077.7	9,981.6	11,317.4
Current assets	3,934.4	3,697.4	3,500.3	3,390.1	3,654.5	5,490.6	4,404
Quick assets	1,593.8	1,505.4	1,403.5	1,318.2	1,259.4	2,843.1	1,645.8
Current liabilities and prov. (incl bank short)	2,640.9	1,944.4	2,707.9	2,512.6	2,693.4	3,870.4	3,378.5
Working capital	1,293.5	1,753	792.4	877.5	961.1	1,620.2	1,025.5
Current ratio	14.9	19	12.9	13.5	13.6	14.2	13
Debt–equity ratio	13.6	14.2	13	09.5	05.9	06.8	05.7
Solvency ratio	15.7	15.7	17	18.5	19.8	19.7	19.8
Quick ratio	06	07.7	05.2	05.2	04.7	07.3	04.9
ROCE	186.2	163.3	154.7	250.9	290.8	244.2	270.7

Source CMIE Prowess (accessed in 2006).

D.7a

TABLE D.7 Financials of Hindalco (₹ million)

Profit and loss	Mar. '92	Mar. '93	Mar. '94	Mar. '95	Mar. '96	Mar. '97	Mar. '98	Mar. '99
Sales	8,566.2	9,769.4	9,238	11,318	14,241.7	13,163.2	16,719.1	20,145.3
Other income	303.5	516.9	663.3	1,178	1,709.3	1,408.3	1,200.5	1,304.2
Change in stocks	142.7	−75.6	53.8	198	135.9	173.3	150	352.5
Net sales	6,550.2	7,560.4	7,511.3	9,572.6	12,535.4	11,649.5	14,742.7	17,680.1
Total income	9,012.4	10,210.7	9,955.1	12,694	16,086.9	14,744.8	18,069.6	21,802
Raw material purchased	2,280.5	2,500.7	2,164.2	2,293.2	2,391.3	2,991.4	3,176.3	3,844.5
Cost of production	4,930.7	5,235.7	5,133.1	5,736.9	6,552	6,880.9	8,699.2	10,318.3
Selling cost	113.8	175.6	205.3	221	290.5	406	407.3	525.7
Cost of sales	4,922.7	5,535	5,313.4	5,831.1	6,800.8	7,361.5	9,025.8	10,633.3
Admin and other costs	121.2	174	210.6	228	471.3	429.1	437.8	513.3
Total costs	8,007.9	9,231.3	8,359.1	9,662.5	11,998.7	11,195.2	13,031.1	15,914.2
PAT	880.4	1,155	1,597	2,919.5	4,011.4	3,903	4,962.1	5,667.8
PBDIT	2,041.4	2,840.9	2,979.1	5,110.5	7,384.3	6,014.4	7,339.4	9,223.1
PBDT	1,711	2,297.4	2,490.6	4,629	6,759.8	5,521.2	6,612.8	8,383.8
PBIT	1,830.8	2,471	2,710.5	4,781	7,035.9	5,591.2	6,558.7	7,977.1
PBT	1,500.4	1,927.5	2,222	4,299.5	6,411.4	5,098	5,832.1	7,137.8
Cash flow from operations	0	0	0	4,089	4,755.2	3,456.3	5,736	6,883.8

D. 7b

Balance sheet	Mar. '92	Mar. '93	Mar. '94	Mar. '95	Mar. '96	Mar. '97	Mar. '98	Mar. '99
Current liabilities	803.4	748.4	629.7	936.9	1,234.2	1,564.2	1,576.3	1,566.6
Sundry creditors	647.5	572.9	419.6	694	988.1	1,161.7	1,054.2	1,220.1
Creditors for cap. goods	0	0	0	0	0	0	0	0
Accrued interest	42.2	99.5	81.7	99.3	86	48.2	86.2	80.8
Other current liabilities	113.7	76	128.4	143.6	160.1	354.3	435.9	265.7
Provisions	247.6	283.2	348.2	343	369.1	443.8	507.9	2,060.2
Total liabilities	7,514.4	18,341.8	20,588	27,501.6	32,518.8	36,056.8	42,248.4	58,869.8
Gross fixed assets	5,666.8	18,673.8	19,700.4	22,116.3	25,044.5	30,811.4	36,205	52,004.7
Land and building	778.4	1,729.8	1,851	1,906.2	2,081.1	2,529	3,230.4	5,082.3
Plant and machinery	4,577.2	15,873	16,970.4	17,580.9	18,687.1	23,532.9	30,804.7	44,704.6
Other fixed assets	69.3	350	410.2	521.8	641.2	777.8	907.3	1,069.7
Capital work-in-progress	241.9	721	468.8	2,107.4	3,635.1	3,971.7	1,262.6	1,148.1
Net fixed assets	2,374.6	11,822.3	11,892.7	13,291	15,183	19,848.9	23,871.9	35,718.4
Investments	2,104.6	2,627	4,920.9	8,414.6	8,364	8,492.7	10,093.6	10,628.5
Inventories	1,123.3	1,443.6	1,427.1	1,639.2	1,836.4	2,461.9	2,767.2	3,156.7
Cash and bank balance	96	261.6	191.5	228.8	1,434.3	259.2	410.2	1,082.3

(*Table D. 7b continued*)

(Table D.7b continued)

Balance sheet	Mar. '92	Mar. '93	Mar. '94	Mar. '95	Mar. '96	Mar. '97	Mar. '98	Mar. '99
Advances	0	0	0	0	0	0	0	0
Receivables	1,814.9	2,186.3	2,154.8	3,927	5,700.1	4,993.1	5,105.1	8,236.4
Total assets (excl. reval. and dre)	7,139	9,930.3	12,867.5	20,344.5	25,982.1	30,162.1	36,906.3	41,036.8
Current assets	3,434.3	4,103.7	6,106.3	9,556.6	11,402	9,660.6	9,241.8	14,624.7
Quick assets	1,948.4	2,004.9	4,161.9	7,244.7	8,058.1	5,273.4	4,564.8	7,714.8
Current liabilities and prov. (incl. bank short)	1,346.4	1,495.3	1,210.4	1,882	2,539.8	2,803.8	2,482.4	3,869.3
Working capital	2,087.9	2,608.4	4,895.9	7,674.6	8,862.2	6,856.8	6,759.4	10,755.4
Current ratio	25.5	27.4	50.4	50.8	44.9	34.5	37.2	37.8
Debt–equity ratio	7.5	5.9	3.3	2.9	2.7	2.4	2.8	2.1
Solvency ratio	19.5	22.9	32.8	37.2	39.2	41.5	38.9	48.4
Quick ratio	14.5	13.4	34.4	38.5	31.7	18.8	18.4	19.9
ROCE	341.9	332.9	263.8	310.2	330.2	205.6	207.6	211.8

D.7c

Profit and loss	Mar. '00	Mar. '01	Mar. '02	Mar. '03	Mar. '04	Mar. '05	Mar. '06
Sales	23,093.7	25,857.9	26,620.7	549,907	68,198.5	104,637.1	124,834.3
Other income	1,360.5	1,159.5	1,458.7	1,679.6	1,604	1,104.6	1,511.6
Change in stocks	39.6	−88.8	193	236.8	1,019.4	2,556.5	11,242.8
Net sales	20,324.2	22,766.5	23,329.8	49,809	62,057.7	95,032.7	113,960
Total income	24,493.8	26,928.6	28,272.4	56,907.1	70,822	108,298.2	137,588.7
Raw material purchased	3,958.2	4,538.2	4,899.1	25,803.5	30,511.6	53,528.2	70,862.8
Cost of production	11,077.4	12,210.4	13,504.8	37,056	47,490.7	72,968.4	87,242.2
Selling cost	622.5	717.9	698.8	−1,727.3	1,429.9	2,424.3	2,540.1
Cost of sales	11,669.1	12,977.3	14,170.3	39,045.8	49,168.3	75,209.6	90,037.1
Admin and other costs	611	670.4	757.9	1,261.1	1,106.9	2,065.6	2,990.7
Total costs	18,125.2	20,563.3	22,288.5	50,616.4	62,448.3	95,264.8	110,511.7
PAT	6,123.7	6,780.8	6,860	5,821.4	8,389.3	13,293.6	16,555.5
PBDIT	10,563.5	11,868.6	12,056.3	13,024.4	17,406.6	26,039.7	28,220.5
PBDT	9,965.8	11,232.4	11,594.6	11,638.8	15,631.2	24,390.1	26,223.8
PBIT	9,206.4	10,438.1	10,511.7	10,379.5	14,232.1	21,407.1	23,053.7
PBT	8,608.7	9,801.9	10,050	8,993.9	12,456.7	19,757.5	21,057
Cash flow from operations	9,176.9	10,161.6	9,614.6	12,005.7	12,717.9	17,049.9	10,067.8

D.7d

Balance sheet	Mar. '00	Mar. '01	Mar. '02	Mar. '03	Mar. '04	Mar. '05	Mar. '06
Current liabilities	1,536.3	1,807.3	2,480.7	7,065.9	8,964.1	16,483.7	21,995.7
Sundry creditors	1,197.2	1,357	1,836.4	5,800.9	7,704.8	14,274.6	19,745.3
Creditors for cap. goods	0	0	0	0	0	0	0
Accrued interest	72	152.8	268.7	582.5	557.3	715.4	604.8
Other current liabilities	267.1	297.5	375.6	682.5	702	1,493.7	1,645.6
Provisions	740.5	1,039.5	1,059.9	1,474.4	1,792.9	8,698.3	9,531.7
Total liabilities	60,362	66,647.4	74,898.4	102,992.4	1,149.7	151,144.9	189,081.1
Gross fixed assets	53,449.6	56,315	63,117.4	64,490.2	71,043.7	99,556.4	110,815.4
Land and building	5,435.2	5,619	6,433.3	5,726.7	6,893.6	8,963.3	10,027.1
Plant and machinery	45,432.2	46,284	48,426.8	48,349.7	57,196.3	74,349.7	89,027.8
Other fixed assets	1,483.2	1,629.6	1,815.9	2,389.7	2,277.2	3,013.6	3,431.3
Capital work-in-progress	1,099	2,782.4	6,441.4	8,024.1	4,676.6	13,229.8	8,329.2
Net fixed assets	34,349.5	34,344.4	38,269.1	48,432.7	51,931.6	69,038.5	75,764.3
Investments	11,329.4	19,175.4	19,852.7	26,484.3	33,772.1	37,021.5	39,713.2

Inventories	3,283.4	3,473.5	3,771.7	10,022.2	11,913.5	23,745.2	40,950.9
Cash and bank balance	3,260.9	2,605.7	3,757.7	2,940.1	2,279.1	4,009.7	9,173.7
Advances	0	0	0	0	0	0	0
Receivables	8,138.8	7,005.7	9,043.5	14,811.3	14,889.9	17,009.5	22,903
Total assets (excl. reval. and dre)	45,537.6	53,027.1	63,046.3	101,755.5	114,750.3	151,051	189,021.1
Current assets	13,059.6	13,029.9	14,645	27,276	40,969	71,352.4	100,312.4
Quick assets	7,423.8	6,657.5	8,303.7	10,952.4	20,957.5	39,153.9	49,923.7
Current liabilities and prov. (incl. bank short)	2,953.5	3,102.5	4,103.7	12,983.6	12,096.2	27,012.7	33,358
Working capital	10,106.1	9,927.4	10,541.3	14,292.4	28,872.8	44,339.7	66,954.4
Current ratio	44.2	42	35.7	21	33.9	26.4	30.1
Debt-equity ratio	01.5	01.6	02.1	03.9	03.7	05	05.1
Solvency ratio	60.4	57.4	49.9	32.6	31.7	23.9	23.5
Quick ratio	25.1	21.5	20.2	08.4	17.3	14.5	15
ROCE	228.7	219.3	187.5	167	153.6	185.6	169.8

Source CMIE Prowess.

TINPLATE COMPANY OF INDIA

Born in 1922, out of a commitment to make India self-sufficient in manufacturing of tinplate, The Tinplate Company of India Ltd, an associate of Tata Steel, has pioneered the tinplate industry in India.

The company was incorporated in 1920 and the site chosen was Golmuri, Jamshedpur. The first steel plate of tinplate gauge was rolled on December 18, 1922, at the Hot Dip Plant (HDP) producing Hot Dip Tinplate from tin bars supplied by Tata Steel and this continued till 1979, albeit with capacity enhancements. For 50 years, TCIL thus almost single-handedly built up the Indian tinplate industry.

It is today the largest indigenous producer of tin-coated and tin-free steel sheets in India, enjoying 35–40 percent market share and undoubtedly the industry leader for 85 years. The company exports about 20–25 percent of its production directly to end-users (can-makers) and its products are well accepted in the markets of Southeast Asia, the Middle East, and some developed countries in Europe.

Headquartered in Kolkata, the Company's works is located at Jamshedpur, Jharkhand. There are presently eight zonal offices and a distribution network with 15 stocking points.

TABLE D.8 Financials of Tinplate Company of India Ltd (₹ million)

D. 8a

Items	2005	2004	2003	2002	2001
Total income	2,665.7	3,088.2	2,428.9		
PBT	321.3	213.4	20.2		
PAT	304.8	213.4	20.2		
Equity	1,412.4	1,412.4	1,412.4		

D.8b

Key ratios	2005	2004	2003	2002	2001
Gross profit margin (PBIDTM) percent	271.7	201.9	196.8		
Total assets	2,738	2,865.3	2,785.9		
D/E ratio	14.9	22.7	27.4		
LT D/E ratio	13.5	21.3	25.7		
Current ratio	8.3	8.2	7.8		

Source CMIE Prowess.

GAMMON INDIA

The company was established by late J.C. Gammon in 1919 as a firm of civil engineers and contractors which in 1922 was incorporated as a private limited company under the name of J.C. Gammon (Bombay) Pvt. Ltd. The firm went public in 1962 and was rechristened as Gammon India Limited.

The first work carried out by J.C. Gammon was the construction of reinforced concrete pile foundations for Gateway of India. Since then, the Company has executed many multi-ferrous civil engineering works from cotton godowns to bridges/flyovers, marine structures, cooling towers, chimneys, tunnels, and dams in India and in the Middle-East. Gammon is the pioneer of prestressed concrete in India.

Striving for excellence and perfection, the company has many firsts to its credit. The company has introduced prestressed concrete in India as early as in 1941 followed by the first prestressed concrete bridge in 1949.

Gammon has to its credit the longest river bridge in the world across the mighty Ganges at Patna, the tallest bridge in Asia, the longest span cantilever bridge in India across the river Jadukata, the longest road bridge in India across the open sea and first cable-stayed bridge in India. The company pioneered cantilever construction, pre-cast segmental bridge construction.

Today, the Company can claim the largest numbers of bridges and flyovers built in India. With over 80 years of tradition in the field of construction, Gammon is a name that is inextricably woven into the fabric of India. Gammon India Limited, the only Indian construction company to have been accredited with ISO 9001 certification for all fields of civil engineering works including design, stands out as gateway for technological and engineering excellence in civil engineering fields. This has led Gammon to the position of one of the leading engineering and construction companies in India. Gammon today can be rightly referred to as "Builders to the Nation."

LARSEN & TOUBRO

Founded in 1938 by two Danish engineers, Henning Holk Larsen and Soren Kristian Toubro, as a partnership firm, Larsen & Toubro (L&T) became a

D. 9a

TABLE D.9 Financials of Gammon India (₹ million)

Profit and loss	Mar. '92	Mar. '93	Mar. '94	Mar. '95	Mar. '96	Mar. '97	Mar. '98	Mar. '99
Sales	813.7	855	1,016.3	1,223.5	1,517.2	1,749.5	2,157.5	3,283.4
Other income	69.5	40.5	27.1	33.8	40.9	24.8	19.1	19.2
Change in stocks	−16.4	46.1	−11.1	−25.3	−13.2	85.7	06.5	09.5
Net sales	800.1	853.1	1,015.2	1,220.5	1,514.2	1,744.8	2,156	3,282.3
Total income	866.8	941.6	1,032.3	1,232	1,544.9	1,860	2,183.1	3,312.1
Raw material purchased	334.4	394.1	470.9	603.8	656.1	897.9	1,047.6	1,807.7
Cost of production	704.5	744	854.7	1,008.5	1,205.8	1,499.1	1,843.8	2,933.2
Selling cost	22.6	13.9	0	0	0	0	43.8	0
Cost of sales	727.1	757.9	854.7	1,008.5	1,204.6	1,498.8	1,888.2	2,933.2
Admin and other costs	77.7	77.9	82.4	112.2	133.5	108.2	109	151.8
Total costs	892.7	913.9	1,018.7	1,201	1,457.7	1,740.9	2,149.9	3,205.3
PAT	27.9	06.8	26.4	43.6	64.7	46.8	71.4	100.1
PBDIT	122.3	103.6	127.8	158	226.7	212.3	261.7	269.3
PBDT	53	28.9	54.6	67.9	125.2	90.1	142	173.2
PBIT	102.2	83	106.9	133.7	195.7	176	222.6	220.2
PBT	32.9	08.3	33.7	43.6	94.2	53.8	102.9	124.1
Cash flow from operations	0	0	0	0	237.7	183.2	285.4	194.2

D. 9b

Balance sheet	Mar. '92	Mar. '93	Mar. '94	Mar. '95	Mar. '96	Mar. '97	Mar. '98	Mar. '99
Current liabilities	1,514.9	1,336.2	1,341.6	1,473.2	1,625.4	1,658.5	1,654	1,252.6
Sundry creditors	218.5	430.2	475.4	438.2	394.5	466.7	502.4	589
Creditors for cap. goods	0	0	0	0	0	0	0	0
Accrued interest	48.5	73.6	59.6	58.4	68.3	34	54.4	61.7
Other current liabilities	1,247.9	832.4	806.6	976.6	1,162.6	1,147.8	1,097.2	601.9
Provisions	116.4	118.5	128.5	123.2	155	161.9	160.6	182.5
Total liabilities	1,459.8	1,416.4	1,478.5	1,603.5	1,928	2,038.1	2,093	3,259.9
Gross fixed assets	583.5	579.8	632.3	696.7	782.9	843.5	975.7	1,920.6
Land and building	27.8	21.2	50.5	50.5	50.5	49.9	55.9	865.9
Plant and machinery	477.1	453.4	487.6	534.9	590.9	541.9	685.5	855.6
Other fixed assets	70.7	76.3	89.7	106.9	135.2	146.9	153.3	186.1
Capital work-in-progress	7.9	28.9	4.5	4.4	6.3	4.8	81	13
Net fixed assets	188.7	196.6	230.3	270.8	339.1	365.7	462.2	1,375.2
Investments	11.8	12.2	15	16.8	86.2	73.7	75.2	169.1
Inventories	220.8	273.1	264	380.6	344.2	398.9	391.5	451.2
Cash and bank balance	251.4	154.3	127.2	93.5	202.5	123.4	144.6	145.6
Advances	0	0	0	0	0	0	0	0

(Table D. 9b continued)

(Table D. 9b continued)

Balance sheet	Mar. '92	Mar. '93	Mar. '94	Mar. '95	Mar. '96	Mar. '97	Mar. '98	Mar. '99
Receivables	787.1	780.2	842	841.8	956	1,076.4	1,019.5	1,118.8
Total assets (excl. reval. and dre)	1,400.3	1,346.8	1,395.2	1,501.9	1,793.7	1,863.9	1,841.5	2,202.8
Current assets	1,151.8	1,111.4	1,134.5	1,234.1	1,424.8	1,488.9	1,496.1	1,624.2
Quick assets	492.5	217.8	389.6	325.8	470.4	371.4	479.9	495.6
Current liabilities and prov. (incl. bank short)	1,694.6	1,492.3	1,519.3	1,680.3	1,900.5	1,995.7	1,919.3	1,555.1
Working capital	-542.8	-380.9	-384.8	-446.2	-475.7	-506.8	-423.2	69.1
Current ratio	6.8	7.4	7.5	7.3	7.5	7.5	7.8	10.4
Debt–equity ratio	9.7	6.7	7.7	8.7	12.5	12	9.3	6
Solvency ratio	8	8.9	9.1	8.8	8.9	8.9	9.5	14.2
Quick ratio	2.9	1.5	2.6	1.9	2.5	1.9	2.5	3.2
ROCE	242.5	210.6	371.6	403.4	481.7	286.1	284.3	274.8

D. 9c

Profit and loss	Mar. '00	Mar. '01	Mar. '02	Mar. '03	Mar. '04	Mar. '05	Mar. '06
Sales	4,516.7	5,037.6	5,146.7	7,272.1	11,204.9	8,725.8	14,709
Other income	496	62.8	54.8	60.3	87.8	99.4	302.4
Change in stocks	256.3	−254.1	473.7	514	584.7	570.6	1,121.5
Net sales	4,513.5	5,028.5	5,127.4	7,242.9	10,992.9	8,546	14,293.6
Total income	4,822.6	4,846.3	5,675.2	7,846.4	11,877.4	9,395.8	16,132.9
Raw material purchased	2,456.8	2,293.9	2,967.5	3,633.8	3,557.1	3,614.3	5,602.9
Cost of production	4,073.6	4,565	4,331.2	6,234.8	9,724.3	7,440.9	12,316.5
Selling cost	10.5	01.5	07.4	06.9	10.5	11.1	04.7
Cost of sales	4,084.1	4,567	4,339.7	6,242.2	9,735.2	7,453.7	12,321.8
Admin and other costs	163	160.9	210	182.9	210.7	180.2	345.7
Total costs	4,424.3	4,957.4	5,008.9	7,156.7	10,955.8	8,395.8	13,991.5
PAT	121.6	148.7	191.9	188.1	292.7	381.4	1,042.6
PBDIT	366.6	461.1	755.2	1,062.2	1,290.5	1,129.7	2,334.3
PBDT	231	291.6	428.5	500.9	695.8	632.8	1,517.6
PBIT	299.4	371.2	637.7	892.9	1,091.1	965.2	1,963.3
PBT	163.8	201.7	311	331.6	496.4	468.3	1,146.6
Cash flow from operations	346.4	61.9	941.1	1,041.9	866.9	274.9	−414.5

D. 9d

Balance sheet	Mar. '00	Mar. '01	Mar. '02	Mar. '03	Mar. '04	Mar. '05	Mar. '06
Current liabilities	1,649.6	1,543.9	2,712.3	3,894	4,881	4,947.5	4,970.3
Sundry creditors	689	864.3	1,457.1	1,857.2	2,287.4	3,029.6	2,530.3
Creditors for cap. goods	0	0	0	0	0	0	0
Accrued interest	85.8	83.5	120.6	168.5	308.7	313.9	248.5
Other current liabilities	874.8	596.1	1,134.6	1,868.3	2,284.9	1,604	2,191.5
Provisions	235.3	339.7	399.2	339.4	321.4	436.1	418.5
Total liabilities	4,064.9	4,399.7	6,623	8,365.3	9,939.2	12,737.6	16,714.5
Gross fixed assets	2,215.8	2,510.3	3,265.1	3,897.9	4,190.2	4,633	5,493.3
Land and building	865.8	865.8	865.8	866	866.2	866.2	867.7
Plant and machinery	1,095	1,316.7	1,815.9	2,474.1	2,752.4	3,070.8	3,793.2
Other fixed assets	234.1	246.9	385.6	467.7	523.5	567.9	759.2
Capital work-in-progress	20.9	80.9	197.8	90.1	48.1	128.1	73.2
Net fixed assets	1,588.8	1,779.8	2,411.9	2,868.9	2,953.1	3,224.8	3,770.6
Investments	177.5	172.6	157.1	768.9	805	896.3	1,161.9
Inventories	823	592.4	1,231	1,830.7	2,675	3,494.4	4,705.9
Cash and bank balance	188.5	110.1	396.8	245.6	279.4	728	1,342.6

Advances	0	0	0	0	0	0	0
Receivables	1,287.1	1,744.8	2,425.7	2,649.2	3,214.6	4,380.3	5,717.2
Total assets(excl. reval. and dre)	2,966.8	3,262.9	5,423.5	7,127.4	8,735.8	11,472.2	15,383.2
Current assets	2,256.9	2,330.5	3,752.4	4,608.7	6,142.4	8,080.6	11,501.6
Quick assets	480.1	605.1	1,223.3	1,189.4	1.449	2,327.3	3,143
Current liabilities and prov.(incl.bank short)	2,024.9	2,043.6	3,711.5	4,813.4	6,122.4	6,783.6	5,388.8
Working capital	229.3	284.2	37.7	−209.4	15.9	1,292.9	6,108.7
Current ratio	11.1	11.4	10.1	09.6	10	11.9	21.3
Debt–equity ratio	08.7	10.1	13.5	14.9	14.4	09.3	02
Solvency ratio	13.4	13.7	13.1	12.7	12.7	14.6	23.9
Quick ratio	02.4	03	03.3	02.5	02.4	03.4	05.8
ROCE	288.6	253	352.7	385.9	425	272.3	254.4

Source CMIE Prowess (accessed in 2006).

private limited company in 1946 and a public limited one in 1950. L&T is one of the largest engineering conglomerates in Southeast Asia.

L&T is a technology-driven engineering and construction organization and one of the largest companies in India's private sector. It has additional interests in manufacturing, services, and information technology.

A strong, customer-focused approach and the constant quest for top-class quality have enabled the company to attain and sustain leadership in its major lines of business across seven decades.

L&T believes that progress must necessarily be achieved in harmony with the environment. A commitment to community welfare and environmental protection constitute an integral part of the corporate vision.

SIEMENS INDIA LTD

The company was incorporated on March 2, 1957, as a private limited company under the name "Siemens Engineering and Manufacturing Company of India Private Limited." When the company was incorporated at its repair shop, switchboard manufacture was being carried on at Worli, Mumbai. The company entered into a collaboration agreement with two foreign companies, viz., Siemens & Halske AG and Siemens-Schuckertwerke AG of West Germany. Later these companies were merged with Siemens AG in 1970.

In 1967, the name of the company was changed from Siemens Engineering & Manufacturing Co. of India Ltd to Siemens India Ltd. In 1987, the name of the company again changed from Siemens India Ltd to Siemens Ltd.

The company undertakes the manufacture of switchboards, switch gear, different types of motors up to 315 KW; assembly of railway signaling equipment, x-ray, and other electromedical equipment; installation, testing, and commissioning of electrical plant and equipment; repair work of motors, generators, transformers, calorific and measuring instruments, certain household appliances, and marine electrical equipment; and selling of products manufactured by the company as well as those of its licensees.

D. 10a.

TABLE D.10 Financials of Larsen & Toubro (₹ million)

Profit and loss	Mar. '92	Mar. '93	Mar. '94	Mar. '95	Mar. '96	Mar. '97	Mar. '98	Mar. '99
Sales	14,174.9	21,538.8	27,389	32,695.4	42,635.6	53,184.2	57,403.7	73,500.9
Other income	276.8	494	433.2	874.4	949.5	1,398	1,219.2	1,709.3
Change in stocks	3,564.6	595.9	−171.8	263.2	773.3	1,070.1	258.9	1,586.3
Net sales	12,664	19,760.4	25,469	30,362.7	39,676.1	49,667.6	53,356.9	68,920.7
Total income	18,016.3	22,628.7	27,650.4	33,833	44,358.4	55,552.3	58,881.8	76,796.5
Raw material purchased	5,005.8	6,842.6	6,895.3	8,471.4	12,334.4	12,911.8	12,773	21,830.9
Cost of production	8,868.4	16,241.4	20,465.6	23,822.9	29,877.3	36,904.9	39,525	52,444.7
Selling cost	1,004.3	879.9	1,035.8	1,350.1	2,334.2	4,127.2	4,922	5,971.2
Cost of sales	9,742	16,795.2	21,530.1	25,138.8	32,075.4	40,613.2	44,283.3	58,537.5
Admin and other costs	827.6	1,076.3	1,449.5	1,717	2,653	3,258.6	3,951.7	4,685
Total costs	13,566.6	21,050.6	26,132.2	30,943.7	39,994.6	50,581.9	54,762.8	71,462
PAT	1,020.6	1,188.3	1,956.4	2,773.6	3,886.9	4,113.5	5,314.4	4,707.4
PBDIT	3,153.9	3,339.1	4,026	5,623.1	7,591.4	9,063	10,111	11,274.6
PBDT	2,102.8	2,570.9	3,134.4	4,362.9	5,694.7	6,487	8,216	8,130.3
PBIT	2,506.7	2,589	3,189	4,528.8	6,193.6	7,307	7,795.4	8,366.7
PBT	1,455.6	1,820.8	2,297.4	3,268.6	4,296.9	4,731	5,900.4	5,222.4
Cash flow from operations	0	0	0	3,703.5	2,694.3	4,713.2	5,909.4	4,417.1

D. 10b

Balance sheet	Mar. '92	Mar. '93	Mar. '94	Mar. '95	Mar. '96	Mar. '97	Mar. '98	Mar. '99
Current liabilities	15,660.2	20,262.9	26,359.4	28,649.9	35,703.1	43,226.5	58,319.2	71,506
Sundry creditors	1,899.9	2,936.5	4,281.6	5,434.3	7,092.3	8,876.2	9,280.7	10,517.2
Creditors for cap. goods	0	0	0	0	0	0	0	0
Accrued interest	363.3	230.4	160.1	135	151.4	428.5	672.1	726.9
Other current liabilities	13,397	17,096	21,917.7	23,080.6	28,459.4	33,921.8	48,366.4	60,261.9
Provisions	787.5	1,317.6	1,216.8	1,593.3	2,082.1	2,604	2,832.1	2,838.2
Total liabilities	30,768.6	38,514.1	47,856.5	57,997.8	77,881.5	96,681.8	123,539.2	144,993.7
Gross fixed assets	11,416.8	15,075.2	19,339.6	24,529.8	33,822.6	45,141.4	54,910.8	58,747
Land and building	2,521.3	2,765.4	3,275.3	3,749.6	4,467.8	7,183.4	8,163.9	9,817.9
Plant and machinery	7,631	9,482.4	13,223.7	16,312	22,305.2	29,048.3	32,920.4	41,409.4
Other fixed assets	745.6	898.1	1,128.8	1,288.3	1,586.8	1,977.5	2,138.4	2,577.9
Capital work-in-progress	518.9	1,929.3	1,711.8	3,179.9	5,462.8	6,932.2	11,688.1	4,941.8
Net fixed assets	7,202.4	10,118.4	13,580.4	17,680.1	25,529.8	34,982.8	42,973.7	45,547.7
Investments	1,474.8	579.5	935.6	3,271.4	1,520.3	1,424.3	3,482.4	5,518.6
Inventories	15,575.6	19,255.2	24,195.5	26,048.3	31,833.4	40,516.9	54,319.7	70,423.4

Cash and bank balance	619.5	719.4	794.3	961.7	4,937.7	2,777.9	3,943.3	2,716.2
Advances	0	0	0	0	0	0	0	0
Receivables	5,733.3	7,711.9	8,238.6	9,902.3	13,917.3	16,846.7	18,660.6	20,623.4
Total assets (excl. reval. and dre)	29,889.7	37,706	47,106.5	57,264	77,173.4	96,016.2	122,924.9	144,398.3
Current assets	23,347.3	28,165.1	34,030.3	39,755.1	51,427.8	59,498.7	76,339.2	92,447.5
Quick assets	4,483.6	4,391	5,291.2	7,593.3	12,201.4	10,141.2	11,300.6	10,300.5
Current liabilities and prov. (incl. bank short)	17,020	22,989.2	29,498.9	33,432.9	42,142.1	50,364.1	66,826	81,670.4
Working capital	6,327.3	5,175.9	4,531.4	6,322.2	9,285.7	9,134.6	9,513.2	10,777.1
Current ratio	13.7	12.3	11.5	11.9	12.2	11.8	11.4	11.3
Debt–equity ratio	07	02	03.4	03.2	04	06.5	08.4	09.2
Solvency ratio	13.6	15.5	14.5	15.6	15.7	14.6	13.8	13.4
Quick ratio	02.6	01.9	01.8	02.3	02.9	02	01.7	01.3
ROCE	204.7	183.7	189.8	217.9	206.2	182.6	131.6	126.7

D. 10c

Balance sheet	Mar. '00	Mar. '01	Mar. '02	Mar. '03	Mar. '04	Mar. '05	Mar. '06
Current liabilities	67,517.5	23,300.2	26,869.1	34,350	39,351.8	47,609.2	58,962.8
Sundry creditors	11,254.5	12,531.8	15,074.6	20,903.5	20,604.7	33,079.7	40,626.1
Creditors for cap. goods	0	0	0	0	0	0	0
Accrued interest	906.2	1,029	838	663.1	273.9	225.1	81.5
Other current liabilities	55,356.8	9,739.4	10,956.5	12,783.4	18,473.2	14,304.4	18,255.2
Provisions	2,748.1	2,712.2	2,873.2	4,292.6	6,879.7	7,957.5	10,153.7
Total liabilities	148,644.8	108,640.4	107,019.7	115,285.7	89,600.2	110,032.4	132,151.5
Gross fixed assets	60,660.7	64,412	62,404.1	63,049.2	19,643.5	20,784.6	25,511.1
Land and building	9,752.7	10,827.2	11,326.6	11,850.1	6,702.3	6,294.8	6,639.2
Plant and machinery	43,439.3	46,852.2	44,538.1	44,918	10,060.6	12,987.6	14,422.7
Other fixed assets	5,050.1	5,410.7	5,488.3	5,555.1	2,618.3	1,561.1	1,588.6
Capital work-in-progress	2,418.6	1,321.9	1,051.1	726	262.3	658.2	2,860.6
Net fixed assets	45,887.3	46,709.9	42,643.2	40,488.7	10,089.4	10,767.7	15,942.6
Investments	8,235.8	8,254.6	9,178.1	11,687.3	9,737.1	9,699.7	20,278

Inventories	68,517.1	25,370.5	25,220.3	25,900.1	18,123	22,612.6	22,102.7
Cash and bank balance	2,208.5	1,388.8	2,044.8	3,205.3	3,752.7	8,280.2	5,832
Advances	0	0	0	0	0	0	0
Receivables	23,434.4	26,481.5	26,603.8	32,455.6	46,120.1	56,970.9	66,347.7
Total assets (excl. reval. & dre)	147,876.6	107,824.9	106,023.8	114,242.5	88,812	109,324.5	131,638
Current assets	92,367.1	51,092.2	51,162.3	57,267.7	66,678.8	86,451.5	99,378.8
Quick assets	10,965.3	10,330.3	11,499	16,045.4	30,563.1	36,176.8	47,584.4
Current liabilities and prov. (incl. bank short)	81,938.5	37,100.9	36,841.6	46,806.9	50,968.4	61,337.8	72,042.2
Working capital	10,428.6	13,983	14,282.5	10,460.8	15,710.4	25,101.5	27,308
Current ratio	11.3	13.8	13.9	12.2	13.1	14.1	13.8
Debt–equity ratio	10.5	10.9	10.7	09.2	04.9	05.6	03.2
Solvency ratio	13.4	15.7	16.5	16.2	14.9	14.7	15.7
Quick ratio	01.3	02.8	03.1	03.4	06	05.9	06.6
ROCE	123.2	115.2	123.7	146.8	220.5	276	298.1

D. 10d

Profit and loss	Mar. '00	Mar. '01	Mar. '02	Mar. '03	Mar. '04	Mar. '05	Mar. '06
Sales	74,382.3	75,593.2	81,258.8	87,825.4	99,219.6	133,990.2	150,427.3
Other income	1,622.2	1,928.9	2,217.6	2,870.3	3,834.7	2,189.9	3,275.6
Change in stocks	−129.8	2,859.4	590.8	11,056.3	4,325.9	868.4	−1,060.9
Net sales	68,868.5	70,390.1	76,191.3	82,199.6	96,158.5	131,343.2	147,483.7
Total income	75,874.7	80,381.5	84,067.2	101,752	107,380.2	137,048.5	152,642
Raw material purchased	10,320.2	11,266.7	11,627.8	18,868.8	24,545.1	56,856.1	59,943.8
Cost of production	52,591.8	52,716	56,884.5	62,692.9	81,853.3	113,157.5	124,624.4
Selling cost	6,905.6	7,312.5	8,204.9	8,918.5	2,661.2	4,327	3,929.3
Cost of sales	58,331.2	59,774.7	65,566.5	71,495.1	84,415.5	117,185.7	129,139.2
Admin and other costs	4,358.6	4,943.7	4,913.2	4,923.9	5,262.1	5,986.4	7,476.9
Total costs	73,584.1	75,710.9	80,629.5	86,811.1	98,277.7	131,471.6	145,875.6
PAT	3,416.3	3,150.6	3,468	4,331	5,327.5	9,838.5	10,116
PBDIT	11,728.6	12,031.2	11,801.1	12,143	11,711.3	16,840.3	18,391.8
PBDT	6,753.1	6,517.9	7,255.5	8,261.7	8,979.8	13,997.7	15,178.4
PBIT	8,796.8	8,899.9	8,550.4	9,097.3	10,866	15,898.6	17,246.9
PBT	3,821.3	3,386.6	4,004.8	5,216	8,134.5	13,056	14,033.5
Cash flow from operations	3,915.8	6,336.3	12,774.4	12,189.9	4,572.3	3,932.3	16,989

Source CMIE Prowess (accessed in 2006).

TABLE D.11 Financials of Siemens India Ltd (₹ million)

D. 11a

Profit and loss	Mar. '92	Mar. '93	Mar. '94	Mar. '95	Mar. '96	Mar. '97	Mar. '98	Mar. '99
Sales	4,371.7	5,282.6	6,752.2	8,739.7	10,747	n.a.	17,773.4	10,420.5
Other income	69.4	104.8	105.2	239.8	167.2	n.a.	363.3	165.2
Change in stocks	307.5	104.7	168.7	488.1	817.6	n.a.	-1,188.5	-340.4
Net sales	4,329.1	5,234.1	667.9	8,662.5	10,677.5	n.a.	17,683.5	10,336.5
Total income	4,748.6	5,492.1	7,026.1	9,467.6	11,731.8	n.a.	16,948.2	10,245.3
Raw material purchased	958.8	1,297.1	1,619.3	2,288.8	3,670.1	n.a.	2,860.4	1,687.1
Cost of production	3,627.3	4,243.4	5,443.5	7,401.6	8,379.7	n.a.	14,532.8	8,644.8
Selling cost	42.8	78.4	75.7	97.6	201.4	n.a.	653	72.4
Cost of sales	3,573.3	4,169.6	5,469.1	7,294.2	8,426.8	n.a.	15,481.5	8,887.2
Admin and other costs	408.2	514.6	680	865.9	1,228	n.a.	1,988.3	1,423
Total costs	4,305.5	5,170.8	6,620.7	8,705.2	10,562.7	n.a.	18,887.1	10,946.5
PAT	164.7	248.2	276.3	351.2	372.4	r.a.	-1,556.3	-560.2
PBDIT	547.6	806.3	849	1,102.4	1,662.7	r.a.	620.9	553.4
PBDT	437.2	609.4	698.6	863.5	1,038.3	n.a.	-669	30.9
PBIT	446.1	686.3	674.7	819.1	1,210.8	n.a.	-228.9	-07.9
PBT	335.7	489.4	524.3	580.2	586.4	n.a.	-1,518.8	-530.4
Cash flow from operations	0	0	0	853.1	613.2	n.a.	3,011.4	369.8

D. 11b

Balance sheet	Mar. '92	Mar. '93	Mar. '94	Mar. '95	Mar. '96	Mar. '97	Mar. '98	Mar. '99
Current liabilities	2,148.8	2,178.9	2,724.1	3,777	5,873.3	n.a.	6,739.9	5,914
Sundry creditors	1,750.9	1,637.8	2,228.4	3,048.8	4,896.1	n.a.	4,688.2	4,742.8
Creditors for cap. goods	0	0	0	0	0	n.a.	0	0
Accrued interest	19.6	21	18.3	27	28.2	n.a.	39.7	33.4
Other current liabilities	378.3	520.1	477.4	701.2	949	n.a.	2,012	1,137.8
Provisions	271.5	285.6	340.1	401.5	413.2	n.a.	444	679.2
Total liabilities	4,287.3	5,018.5	6,589.7	9,302.2	13,660.9	n.a.	12,586.6	10,660.2
Gross fixed assets	1,509.4	1,741.3	2,225.2	3,765.2	5,356	n.a.	5,677.4	5,259.9
Land and building	285.5	339.8	424.5	576.7	1,070.3	n.a.	1,472.2	1,498
Plant and machinery	942.4	1,072.9	1,337.1	1,763.8	2,089.2	n.a.	1,985.9	2,028
Other fixed assets	172.6	227.8	321.1	1,149.3	1,629.9	n.a.	1,862.8	1,539.2
Capital work-in-progress	108.9	100.8	142.5	275.4	566.6	n.a.	356.5	194.7
Net fixed assets	614	737.7	1,063.9	2,319.3	3,459.8	n.a.	3,523.3	3,019.2
Investments	55.6	91.3	145	174.2	208.9	n.a.	459.7	423.9
Inventories	1,429.8	1,612.5	1,824.8	2,426.6	3,447.3	n.a.	2,029.8	1,507.1

Cash and bank balance	05.3	38.8	122.2	194.9	187.7	n.a.	94.6	143.2
Advances	0	0	0	0	0	n.a.	0	0
Receivables	2,182.1	2,537.7	3,433.8	4,187.2	6,357.2	na	6,479.2	5,566.8
Total assets (excl. reval. and dre)	4,225.2	4,953.7	6,439.6	9,154.4	13,458.9	n.a.	1,226	10,358.4
Current assets	3,624.1	4,211.5	5,313.9	6,809.7	9,945.5	n.a.	8,443.6	6,921.9
Quick assets	686.8	1,097	1,818.8	2,493.5	3,612.2	n.a.	3,952.1	2,583.4
Current liabilities and prov. (incl. bank short)	2,829.7	3,434.5	3,723.7	5,648.4	8,005.9	n.a.	9,931.2	7,480.9
Working capital	794.4	777	1,590.2	1,161.3	1,939.6	n.a.	−1,487.6	−559
Current ratio	12.8	12.3	14.3	12.1	12.4	n.a.	08.5	09.3
Debt–equity ratio	07.6	10.7	04.5	09.5	15.7	n.a.	19.9	12.5
Solvency ratio	13.4	13.3	16	14	12.7	n.a.	11.7	12.1
Quick ratio	02.4	03.2	04.9	04.4	04.5	n.a.	04	03.5
ROCE	308.7	440.2	292.9	236.5	259.2	n.a.	147.1	65.6

D.11c

Profit and loss	Mar. '00	Mar. '01	Mar. '02	Mar. '03	Mar. '04	Mar. '05	Mar. '06
Sales	10,993.5	11,426.6	12,520.4	13,855.5	15,261.8	19,302.1	28,961.5
Other income	256.6	417.9	444.5	368.4	603.5	754.3	1,537.4
Change in stocks	−159.3	−305.3	−56.8	−08.1	342.8	463.9	1,270.8
Net sales	10,929.3	11,335.7	11,791.2	13,096.2	14,378.3	18,052.3	27,023.8
Total income	11,090.8	11,539.2	12,908.1	14,215.8	16,208.1	20,520.3	31,769.7
Raw material purchased	1,854.4	1,836.8	3,087.2	2,007	2,670.1	3,690	5,406.3
Cost of production	8,829.2	9,702.7	10,168.9	11,207.5	12,294.4	15,263.6	23,321.9
Selling cost	124.5	128	127.3	125.8	236.4	147.7	242.3
Cost of sales	9,062.7	10,022.9	10,259.7	11,385	12,327.9	15,343.3	23,193.9
Admin and other costs	1,694.1	1,002.3	953.3	944.5	1,017.8	1,182.5	1,769.3
Total costs	11,134	11,251.7	12,325.8	13,597	14,857.6	18,450.2	27,966.9
PAT	351.2	840	687.2	865.6	1,393.8	1,513.7	2,547.5
PBDIT	1,124.4	1,413	1,453.9	1,773.5	2,297.1	2,482.6	4,009.2
PBDT	841.2	1,324	1,336.2	1,681	2,231.3	2,421.1	3,922.6
PBIT	664.2	975.6	1,081.9	1,396.9	2,047.6	2,234.4	3,717.7
PBT	381	886.6	964.2	1,304.4	1,981.8	2,172.9	3,631.1
Cash flow from operations	2,780.5	1,988.3	498.5	1,690.6	1,168.4	2,537.9	3,473.4

D.11d

Balance sheet	Mar. '00	Mar. '01	Mar. '02	Mar. '03	Mar. '04	Mar. '05	Mar. '06
Current liabilities	5,988.6	6,247.6	5,765.7	6,421.8	6,532.8	9,299.6	12,759
Sundry creditors	4,581.3	4,677.2	4,257.1	5,151.1	5,412.2	5,421.2	9,439.6
Creditors for cap. goods	0	0	0	0	0	0	0
Accrued interest	37.4	02.5	0	0	0	0	0
Other current liabilities	1,369.9	1,567.9	1,508.6	1,270.7	1,120.6	3,878.4	3,319.4
Provisions	678	745.2	689.6	495.9	3,934.3	5,892	7,474.6
Total liabilities	9,609.2	10,250.1	9,860.9	10,947.9	15,570	19,527	28,255.8
Gross fixed assets	5,544.1	5,521.6	5,466.2	5,476	5,524.9	5,523.3	5,367
Land and building	1,649.3	1,667.7	1,669.1	1,645.3	1,590.2	1,646.3	1,629
Plant and machinery	2,189.2	2,175.9	2,869.8	2,128.3	2,246.3	2,415.1	2,373.4
Other fixed assets	1,594.9	1,637.2	881.1	1,656.7	1,667.5	1,400	996.8
Capital work-in-progress	110.7	40.8	46.2	45.7	20.9	61.9	367.8
Net fixed assets	2,839.2	2,450.1	2,176.9	1,941.6	1,820.2	1,928.5	2,237.4
Investments	411.5	613.5	510.5	370.1	972.9	1,289.2	3,302.6
Inventories	1,198.2	806	725.8	759.1	1,215.9	1,698.3	3,284.1

(Table D. 11d continued)

(Table D. 11d continued)

Balance sheet	Mar. '00	Mar. '01	Mar. '02	Mar. '03	Mar. '04	Mar. '05	Mar. '06
Cash and bank balance	772	2,244.4	885.7	2,026.7	2,584.7	4,309.9	4,855.1
Advances	0	0	0	0	0	0	0
Receivables	4,388.3	4,136.1	5,240.4	5,541.5	8,661.2	9,971.6	14,136.9
Total assets (excl. reval. and dre)	9,400.7	10,164.3	9,651.7	10,762.9	12,107.9	15,530.1	23,133.5
Current assets	6,381.7	7,186.5	5,891.9	7,262.3	11,686.8	15,409	22,378.8
Quick assets	2,995.4	4,863	3,329.3	4,692.9	5,407.9	8,236.2	11,675.7
Current liabilities and prov. (incl. bank short)	7,080.4	7,162.5	6,458	6,949.8	10,467.1	15,191.6	20,233.6
Working capital	−698.7	24	−566.1	312.5	1,219.7	217.4	2,145.2
Current ratio	09	10	09.1	10.4	11.2	10.1	11.1
Debt–equity ratio	05.1	01.5	00.1	00.2	00.1	0	0
Solvency ratio	12.6	13.9	15.4	15.8	17.2	13.8	15.3
Quick ratio	04.2	06.8	05.2	06.8	05.2	05.4	05.8
ROCE	150.3	259.4	323.1	321	373.1	413.5	516.8

Source CMIE Prowess.

COROMANDEL FERTILISERS

Incorporated in 1964, Coromandel Fertilisers (CFL) was the result of the synergistic efforts of E.I.D. Parry India Limited, now belonging to the ₹42,000 million Murugappa Group—one of the leading business houses in India and two major US corporations—Chevron Chemical Company and International Minerals and Chemical Corporation (IMC). This brought to India world-class technology for the production of high analysis fertilizers. In 1995, Chevron Chemical Company disinvested their stake in favor of E.I.D. Parry and IMC in end 1998. After effecting buyback of 20 percent of CFL's total shares in which the promoters did not participate, the Group's stake has gone up to 78.34 percent. The Indian Financial Institutions hold about 7.59 percent equity, the remaining 14.07 percent being held by the public.

Ever since production commenced in 1967, Coromandel has been an active partner of the Indian farmer in the field, helping him in his efforts to produce more from small landholdings. It has played a crucial role in assisting India achieve self-sufficiency in food grain production.

TABLE D.12 Coromandel Fertilisers—Chronology

Year	Happenings
1964	Company was set up jointly by E.I.D Parry, Cheveron Chemical Company & International Minerals and Chemical Corporation.
1967	Production started at 0.25 million TPA.
1985	Capacity enhanced to 0.3 million TPA.
1995	Capacity increased to 0.4 million TPA.
2000	Commissioned to increase capacity to 0.6 million TPA.
2003	The merger of the Farm Inputs Division (FIND) of E.I.D Parry (India) Limited with the company.

Source Author.

Consequent to the merger of the Farm Inputs Division of E.I.D. Parry (India) Ltd with Coromandel Fertilisers Limited, a new organizational structure is in place. Policies and processes have also been streamlined in support of the above. The company has also taken various steps to improve the capability of not just its people but also people processes. The industrial relations climate continues to be cordial. A long-term four-year settlement was reached at the Navi Mumbai unit. Settlement on productivity-linked bonus and incentive was also signed resulting in improvements in productivity and reduction in costs.

CFL has for long been under the shackles of limited growth. It has grown equally with the industry. In 1995, its market share was around 4 percent and in 2003, its market share is still around 4 percent although in absolute terms its increased terms its revenue has increased. But, now CFL is changing its color. It is trying to "break free" and trying to grow through consolidation. It has acquired Godavari Fertilizers and also merged with the FIND business of E.I.D Parry (India). However, there are some inherent problems in mergers and acquisition. It remains to be seen how effectively CFL will cope up with these problems.

KEC INTERNATIONAL LTD

Incorporated in 1945 as Kamani Engineering Corporation, KEC International is today the largest power transmission EPC company in India and one of the largest in the world. In 1982, it came under the fold of the RPG Enterprises Group. In 1984, the name was changed from Kamani Engineering Corporation Ltd to KEC International Ltd.

KEC's main business areas are design, manufacture, supply, and construction of turnkey projects of power transmission lines of voltages up to 800 KV and in the execution of railway electrification projects, setting up substations and power distribution networks, optical fiber cable installations, turnkey telecom infrastructure services, and maintenance of power transmission lines. Its core competencies lie in design, engineering, manufacturing of towers, tower-testing capabilities, and project management.

The company has a client base spread over 20 countries and over 75 percent of its projects are executed overseas with a strong presence in the Middle East, Africa, and Pacific Rim countries. In India, the company has a market share of 30 percent.

More than 70 percent of its business and contracts are outside India. Therefore, it faces stiff competition globally rather than just domestically. Globally, the market is fragmented and dominated by regional players.

There is intense competition between Indian, Spanish, Italian, French, Turkish, Saudi, Korean, Japanese, and Chinese companies. The market has huge opportunities in the Middle East, Africa, and Southeast Asia.

TABLE D.13 Financials of Coromandel Fertilisers (₹ million)

D.13a

Profit and loss	Mar. '92	Mar. '93	Mar. '94	Mar. '95	Mar. '96	Mar. '97	Mar. '98	Mar. '99
Sales	2,727.2	2,305.8	2,748.7	3,032.7	3,323.5	3,742	4,704.5	4,834.4
Other income	52	37.3	34.9	42.4	51.7	43.7	53.6	53.7
Change in stocks	45.1	374.4	−208.2	−43.6	161	416.4	40.8	−300.1
Net sales	2,722	2,298.9	2,741.9	3,028.7	3,318.5	3,738	4,692.9	4,797.2
Total income	2,824.3	2,717.5	2,575.4	3,031.5	3,536.2	4,202.1	4,798.9	4,588
Raw material purchased	1,587.9	1,622.7	1,432.3	1,493.2	1,674.2	1,836.8	2,027.9	2,316.1
Cost of production	2,314.6	2,329.8	2,236.2	2,483.2	2,735.5	3,256.3	3,784.7	3,343.1
Selling cost	118.4	138.3	139.1	174.9	159.3	270.7	242.8	208.3
Cost of sales	2,390.8	2,073	2,611.4	2,696.2	2,730.6	3,134.7	3,958.5	3,859.9
Admin and other costs	67.3	68.2	52.5	72.3	174.3	92.6	111.9	114.8
Total costs	2,688.8	2,337.3	2,876.5	2,962.8	3,121	3,537.6	4,401.1	4,402.9
PAT	94.9	17.2	−19.3	144.9	233.6	292.3	343.7	468.7
PBDIT	355	250.6	193.1	356.2	493.1	675	747.3	967.4
PBDT	221.7	66.7	19.5	193	329.8	478.2	574.7	785.3
PBIT	314.2	202.1	154.3	308.1	433.4	598.6	658.3	853.8
PBT	180.9	18.2	−19.3	144.9	270.1	401.8	485.7	671.7
Cash flow from operations	0	0	0	0	374.7	843.6	348.5	729.3

D.13b

Balance sheet	Mar. '92	Mar. '93	Mar. '94	Mar. '95	Mar. '96	Mar. '97	Mar. '98	Mar. '99
Current liabilities	453.4	436.8	790.7	781.7	835.7	1,038.2	768.6	998.2
Sundry creditors	437	431.1	784.7	778.5	833.5	1,027.3	762.1	989.9
Creditors for cap. goods	0	0	0	0	0	0	0	0
Accrued interest	7.3	05.6	6	3.2	2.2	10.5	5.9	07.3
Other current liabilities	9.1	00.1	0	0	0	0.4	0.6	01
Provisions	28.2	0	0.8	25.9	56.3	90	136	204.1
Total liabilities	3,064.9	3,144.9	3,278.8	3,396.3	3,411.6	4,058.5	4,032.9	4,672.7
Gross fixed assets	4,236.1	4,420.2	4,512.1	4,653.7	4,781.2	5,069	5,351.2	4,964.2
Land and building	438.2	452.6	452.5	453.4	457.1	458.7	562.3	576.8
Plant and machinery	3,676.3	3,687.2	3,679.7	3,993.4	4,154.3	4,373.9	4,614.9	4,307.2
Other fixed assets	54.7	46.2	45.3	40.4	50.4	63.9	68.9	36.9
Capital work-in-progress	66.9	234.2	334.6	166.5	119.4	172.5	105.1	43.3
Net fixed assets	1,646.7	1,657.7	1,588.6	1,569	1,595.2	1,793.8	1,985.2	2,146.5
Investments	119.7	99.6	47	153.2	21.3	2.3	02.3	2.3
Inventories	300.2	758.2	784.9	717.6	871.3	1,210.8	1,225.5	988
Cash and bank balance	2.9	3.9	08.9	30.5	21.8	126.2	48.3	69.1

Advances	0	0	0	0	0	0	0
Receivables	995.4	625.5	849.4	926	902	925.4	771.6	1,466.8
Total assets (excl. reval. and dre)	1,951.7	2,156.9	2,486.9	2,753.8	2,954.4	3,711.4	3,730.3	4,423.1
Current assets	1,418	1,487.1	1,690.1	1,827.2	1,816.4	2,164.2	2,017.2	2,525.7
Quick assets	347.5	250.8	304.9	448.5	361.9	232	139.3	248.5
Current liabilities and prov. (incl. bank short)	829.7	890.8	1,229.5	1,304	1,382.6	1,969.7	1,546.1	1,871.9
Working capital	588.3	596.3	460.6	523.2	433.8	194.5	471.1	653.8
Current ratio	17.1	16.7	13.7	14	13.1	11	13	13.5
Debt–equity ratio	09	12.1	12.4	12.2	09.1	09.8	8	06.7
Solvency ratio	16.6	15.8	14.5	14.8	15.8	15.4	17.3	17.7
Quick ratio	04.2	2.8	2.5	3.4	02.6	01.2	0.9	01.3
ROCE	315	167.9	89.4	218.1	307	334.8	344.6	370.6

D.13c

Profit and loss	Mar. '00	Mar. '01	Mar. '02	Mar. '03	Mar. '04	Mar. '05	Mar. '06
Sales	6,062.7	6,149.9	6,667	5,932.3	12,643.1	15,822.3	19,086.2
Other income	62.5	75.9	56.4	99.9	86.5	101.3	260.2
Change in stocks	126.3	05.8	–115.5	199.9	–276.1	–192.9	1,158.8
Net sales	6,054.2	6,100	6,622.7	5,893.5	12,334.5	15,479.2	18,713.5
Total income	6,251.5	6,231.6	6,607.9	6,232.1	12,453.5	15,730.7	20,505.2
Raw material purchased	2,761.6	3,573.4	3,469.4	3,437.6	7,229.4	9,325.6	13,762.5
Cost of production	4,941.8	4,783.8	4,950.9	4,912.1	9,709	12,929.8	17,058.1
Selling cost	288.4	437.9	525.3	564.7	1,206.4	1,159.2	1,309.1
Cost of sales	5,092.5	5,205.8	5,581.3	5,292.8	11,196.5	14,333.8	17,242.3
Admin and other costs	129	113.6	159.4	142.3	242	306.1	338.1
Total costs	5,679.5	5,770.5	6,311.9	5,797.4	12,329.5	15,578	18,613.2
PAT	480.5	528.8	455.4	270.3	431.1	691.9	835.5
PBDIT	1,038.9	1,064.9	1,154.7	749.8	1,339.9	1,648.6	1,920
PBDT	838.2	849.3	977.8	620.9	1,052.7	1,446.9	1,662.5
PBIT	916.2	919.4	982.3	593.8	1,013.5	1,297.6	1,549.2
PBT	715.5	703.8	805.4	464.9	726.3	1,095.9	1,291.7
Cash flow from operations	1,060.7	517.5	1,639.5	–04.1	1,973.5	1,323.8	–157.7

D.13d

Balance sheet	Mar. '00	Mar. '01	Mar. '02	Mar. '03	Mar. '04	Mar. '05	Mar. '05
Current liabilities	891.9	984.2	709.4	787.5	2,463.8	2,716.3	4,982.5
Sundry creditors	883.4	971.6	693.9	767.5	2,325	2,589.9	4,753.1
Creditors for cap. goods	0	0	0	0	0	0	0
Accrued interest	07.6	11.4	11.6	8.7	41.4	33.5	57.5
Other current liabilities	0.9	1.2	3.9	11.3	97.4	92.9	171.9
Provisions	251.4	164.4	296.5	254	394.3	449	576.5
Total liabilities	4,807.2	5,500.2	4,735.4	5,623.7	10,081.1	10,586.2	14,979
Gross fixed assets	5,368.2	3,592.4	3,229.3	3,327.6	6,474.6	6,718.2	6,832.7
Land and building	567.3	219.8	223.6	235.2	601.1	634.8	591.8
Plant and machinery	4,327.4	3,201.5	2,900.5	2,964.9	5,641.3	5,730.6	5,945.3
Other fixed assets	69.8	95.8	101.7	95.9	213.2	230.8	239
Capital work-in-progress	403.7	75.3	3.5	31.6	19	122	56.6
Net fixed assets	2,421.9	2,500.4	2,226.9	2,182.2	3,843.3	3,775.2	3,636.7
Investments	02.3	06.3	29.8	126.5	1,361.7	1,348.8	1,618.1
Inventories	1,076.8	1,116.6	1,018.3	1,248.3	1,969.6	1,911	3,953.1
Cash and bank balance	62.8	58.1	64.2	101.1	29	328.4	243.3

(Table D. 13d continued)

(Table D. 13d continued)

Balance sheet	Mar. '00	Mar. '01	Mar. '02	Mar. '03	Mar. '04	Mar. '05	Mar. '06
Advances	0	0	0	0	0	0	0
Receivables	1,243.4	1,818.8	1,392.6	1,959.4	2,860	3,202.6	5,502
Total assets (excl. reval. and dre)	4,582.6	5,500.2	4,735.4	5,623.7	10,013.5	10,524.5	14,979
Current assets	2,383	2,993.5	2,490.2	3,308.8	4,850.1	5,442	9,533.4
Quick assets	296.6	743.1	864.9	1,353.6	1,548.3	1,278.7	1,271
Current liabilities and prov. (incl. bank short)	1,728.5	2,364.5	1,419	2,134.8	3,326.1	3,195	6,736.9
Working capital	654.5	629	1,071.2	1,174	1,524	2,234.1	2,783.6
Current ratio	13.8	12.7	17.5	15.5	14.6	17	14.2
Debt–equity ratio	07.4	08.4	5.2	7.7	8.9	07.1	09.7
Solvency ratio	17.6	17.5	22.3	19.9	17.2	18	15.3
Quick ratio	01.7	03.1	6.1	6.3	4.7	4	1.9
ROCE	331.2	287.8	314	191.3	224.2	157.6	206.5

Source CMIE Prowess (accessed in 2006).

Following joint ventures were established for manufacture and construction of transmission line projects:

TABLE D.14 KEC—Joint Ventures, 1995–97

Year	Countries
1995	Vietnam, Malaysia
1996	Brazil
1997	Saudi Arabia (Al Sharif KEC Ltd)

Source Author.

Till the year 2000, KEC had been continuously making profits. But between the years 2001 and 2003, the company incurred losses. The losses were as high as ₹650 million in the year 2002. The nonexecution of projects and delayed payment on some overseas projects had pushed the company into the red, even as fixed costs had increased. The company turned around in 2004 and made a net profit of ₹252.8 million as against a loss of ₹95.4 million in the previous year. The company achieved total sales of ₹8,270 million as compared to ₹7,480 million during the previous year. Significant steps taken by the company to achieve the turnaround were: (*i*) created a SBU structure with a clear accountability and focus; (*ii*) interacted continuously with customers, suppliers, bankers, and employees; (*iii*) undertook all-round cost-effective and rationalization measures for its operations that included VRS; and (*iv*) working capital reduction.

The company is the recipient of Engineering Export Promotion Council's Award for Highest Exports in Capital Goods. Its workforce is spread over in 12 countries with strength of around 2,300. KEC credo is that no project is complete till the customer is totally satisfied.

SUNDARAM FASTENERS

Originating as a transport company in 1911, the TVS Group now comprises over 29 companies that operate in diverse fields like automotive component manufacturing, automotive dealerships, and electronics. Today, the Group is India's leading supplier of automotive components and one of the country's most respected business conglomerates.

D.15a

TABLE D.15 Financials of KEC International Ltd (₹ million)

Profit and loss	Mar. '92	Mar. '93	Mar. '94	Mar. '95	Mar. '96	Mar. '97	Mar. '98	Mar. '99
Sales	1,026.3	1,779.9	2,641.8	4,162.7	4,326.3	6,621.4	6,847.3	10,709
Other income	58	48.8	55.3	95	261.2	226.5	520.1	337.4
Change in stocks	36.7	08.6	26.7	15.4	−85.3	47.4	−20.3	27.2
Net sales	967.5	1,680.1	2,537.5	3,977.6	4,187.6	6,492.5	6,727.7	10,572
Total income	1,121	1,837.3	2,723.8	4,273.1	4,502.2	6,895.3	7,347.1	11,073.6
Raw material purchased	435.7	722.4	1,330.6	2,116.8	1,547.6	2,771.8	2,991.6	5,771.7
Cost of production	863.8	1,251.8	1,943.9	3,205.2	3,215.3	5,032.1	5,560	8,588.2
Selling cost	32.4	89	148.4	105	126	253.7	221.4	431.4
Cost of sales	861.9	1,344.2	2,067.4	3,296.3	3,403.1	5,234.9	5,804.6	9,005
Admin and other costs	77	97.2	121.3	204	290.1	409.9	414.8	656.9
Total costs	1,113.4	1,748.4	2,545.9	3,995.3	4,356.5	6,509.5	7,199.5	10,876
PAT	50.4	84.8	167	300.7	337.3	385.5	238.5	259.4
PBDIT	206.1	337.2	460.3	659.8	895.6	1,215.3	1,165.1	1,502.4
PBDT	90.4	141.5	292.1	449.4	496.9	602.4	365	469.7
PBIT	166.1	292	419.9	610.6	833	1,065.1	1,060.3	1,334.6
PBT	50.4	96.3	251.7	400.2	434.3	452.2	260.2	301.9
Cash flow from operations	0	0	0	−375.4	536.5	242.5	590.4	325

D.15b

Balance sheet	Mar. '92	Mar. '93	Mar. '94	Mar. '95	Mar. '96	Mar. '97	Mar. '98	Mar. '99
Current liabilities	902.9	791	1,166.3	1,673.9	2,216.4	2,999.1	4,084.1	5,366.7
Sundry creditors	713.6	607.7	892.4	1,222.6	1,678.7	2,353.4	3,297	4,123.4
Creditors for cap. goods	0	0	0	0	0	0	0	0
Accrued interest	14.2	14.9	12.5	13.9	27.8	52.2	40.7	43.3
Other current liabilities	175.1	168.4	261.4	437.4	509.9	593.5	746.4	1,200
Provisions	36.5	55.3	72.6	126.7	158.8	150.3	129.3	193.5
Total liabilities	2,109.5	2,319.7	2,927.8	5,868.7	7,129	9,272.7	11,684.7	14,578.8
Gross fixed assets	528	600.7	668.6	774	1,487.5	1,932.8	2,303.7	2,458.2
Land and building	119.5	120.3	120.8	130.5	476.6	524.4	998	1,017.3
Plant and machinery	337.4	350	400.4	438.6	767.5	828.8	948.2	1,047.6
Other fixed assets	65.3	75.1	87.9	118.8	216.2	224.7	336.4	364.5
Capital work-in-progress	5.8	55.3	59.5	86.1	27.2	354.9	21.1	28.8
Net fixed assets	325.2	357.9	391	454.1	1,105	1,402.2	1,686.4	1,687
Investments	12.4	17.6	84.3	1,065.3	1,128.7	1,204.9	1,336.8	1,582.6
Inventories	288.1	306.7	432.8	599.1	625.1	720.2	632.8	796.2

(*Table D. 15b continued*)

(Table D. 15b continued)

Balance sheet	Mar. '92	Mar. '93	Mar. '94	Mar. '95	Mar. '96	Mar. '97	Mar. '98	Mar. '99
Cash and bank balance	331.6	296.8	313.6	414	194	343.6	446.7	948.1
Advances	0	0	0	0	0	0	0	0
Receivables	1,142.9	1,334.3	1,701.2	3,329.7	4,050.2	5,582.8	7,165.7	9,159.6
Total assets (excl. reval. and dre)	2,012.5	2,265.9	2,889	5,832.2	7,074.8	9,198.5	11,171	14,038.5
Current assets	1,763.8	1,938.9	2,449.9	3,961.9	4,224.5	5,852	7,262	9,691.9
Quick assets	718.5	904.1	1,206.1	2,096.8	2,131.5	2,125.9	3,596.4	4,718.9
Current liabilities and prov. (incl. bank short)	1,265.4	1,224.2	1,287.2	2,031	2,431.2	3,586.2	5,168.9	6,969.7
Working capital	498.4	714.7	1,162.7	1,930.9	1,793.3	2,265.8	2,093.1	2,722.2
Current ratio	13.9	15.8	19	19.5	17.4	16.3	14	13.9
Debt–equity ratio	11.5	7.6	7.9	07.8	8.2	11.3	17	20.2
Solvency ratio	13.5	15.6	14.7	16.3	15.7	14.5	13	12.5
Quick ratio	5.7	7.4	9.4	10.3	8.8	5.9	7	6.8
ROCE	115.1	310.2	303.9	211.8	179	208.9	175.6	188.3

D.15c

Profit and loss	Mar. '00	Mar. '01	Mar. '02	Mar. '03	Mar. '04	Mar. '05
Sales	9,768.5	5,259	5,094.8	7,415.9	8,275.9	12,493.7
Other income	451.6	419.6	337.6	151	94.9	220.4
Change in stocks	−82.5	86.7	−23.8	7.9	41.3	55.5
Net sales	9,678.2	5,169.1	5,010.7	7,274	8,136.6	12,202.9
Total income	10,137.6	5,765.3	5,408.6	7,574.8	8,412.1	12,769.6
Raw material purchased	4,437.8	1,690.5	2,405	3,096.1	3,404.4	6,164.4
Cost of production	7,668.6	4,474.6	4,294.4	5,904.4	5,493.8	9,730.4
Selling cost	385.5	193.8	372.3	300.9	866.7	604.6
Cost of sales	8,114.8	4,585.9	4,688.1	6,198.9	6,345.6	10,319
Admin and other costs	747.8	484.6	554.7	345.8	476.9	501.6
Total costs	10,249.7	6,470.9	6,373.1	7,736.7	7,964.4	12,343.5
PAT	86.3	−470.7	−643.8	−95.4	252.8	422.6
PBDIT	1,538.1	989.1	527.2	1,069.6	1,356.1	1,755.2
PBDT	286.5	−321.4	−517.4	24.6	353.5	782.7
PBIT	1,381.6	839.8	402.4	954.7	1,255.4	1,654.7
PBT	130	−470.7	−642.2	−90.3	252.8	682.2
Cash flow from operations	−263.6	−25.2	151	1,415.9	1,584.9	2,479

D.15d

Balance sheet	Mar. '00	Mar. '01	Mar. '02	Mar. '03	Mar. '04	Mar. '05
Current liabilities	4,939.7	3,190.3	3,438.8	4,845.8	5,630.3	107.7
Sundry creditors	4,039.9	2,362.9	2,125.6	3,430.8	4,081	104.8
Creditors for cap. goods	0	0	0	0	0	0
Accrued interest	159.2	59.9	114.4	21.4	17.8	0
Other current liabilities	740.6	767.5	1,198.8	1,393.6	1,531.5	2.9
Provisions	48.4	69.3	99.9	76	186.7	33.8
Total liabilities	14,622.5	13,078.2	13,190.6	14,236.9	14,048.5	3,139.2
Gross fixed assets	2,524.9	2,510.1	2,517.5	3,141	2,721	472.3
Land and building	1,035.1	1,034.7	1,022.8	1,620.7	1,257	462
Plant and machinery	1,100.5	1,192.1	1,204.7	1,211	11,856	023
Other fixed assets	375.4	270.5	266.8	265.4	238.7	8
Capital work-in-progress	13.9	12.8	23.2	43.9	39.7	0
Net fixed assets	1,619.2	1,481.1	1,384.8	1,924.7	1,480.3	456.6
Investments	1,319.3	1,260.6	1,023.4	1,023.3	965.5	0

Inventories	478	408.3	322.4	438.8	507.7	0
Cash and bank balance	256.7	258.9	191.6	463.7	403.4	4
Advances	0	0	0	0	0	0
Receivables	10,600.7	9,378.9	9,616.9	9,967.6	10,251.1	2,675.3
Total assets (excl. reval. and dre)	14,198.9	12,608.2	12,679.6	13,389.3	13,370.7	2,588.9
Current assets	9,145.5	7,948.7	7,759	8,090.6	8,381	2,679.3
Quick assets	4,161.4	2,377.7	2,901.4	3,574.5	3,283.5	04
Current liabilities and prov. (incl. bank short)	6,099.9	7,156.5	5,607	6,831.3	7,995	141.5
Working capital	3,045.6	792.2	2,152	1,259.3	386	2,537.8
Current ratio	15	11.1	13.8	11.8	10.5	189.3
Debt–equity ratio	21.2	27.8	38	35	32.8	1.1
Solvency ratio	12.6	12.5	12.1	11.9	11.6	87.4
Quick ratio	6.8	3.3	5.2	5.2	4.1	0.3
ROCE	165.3	75.3	16.7	129.2	236.2	405.5

Source CMIE Prowess (accessed in 2006).

Established in 1962 and headquartered in Chennai, Sundaram Fasteners Ltd (SFL) is one of the leading manufacturers of auto components and an exporter of high-tensile fasteners with a strong presence in international markets. SFL is the largest manufacturer with over 70 percent market share. Initially, SFL manufactured a wide range of fasteners that included high-tensile fasteners. Later it expanded its range to cold formed/extruded parts for auto and non-auto applications, powder metal parts, precision formed gears, iron powders, radiator caps, gear shifters, tyre carriers, and other automotive components. The company manufactures gear shifter assemblies in technical collaboration with Dura Automotive Systems, a US-based manufacturer.

SFL has five plants in Chennai, Hosur, Madurai, Medak, and Pondicherry. The two plants at Madurai and Chennai that manufacture fasteners contribute to 80 percent of sales. It is the first Indian company to get an ISO certification. SFL has been winning the Supplier of the Year awards from General Motors and has won TPM awards from the JIPM.

SFL has been focusing on new markets and customers for its growth in exports while stepping up supplies to its existing customers. The company has been making supplies to Daimler Benz, AG, Germany (through Kamax); Cummins Engine Company Inc., USA; and General Motors Corporation, USA, that contributed to its growth and profits.

SFL is the largest manufacturer and exporter of high-tensile fasteners with export in sales accounting for ₹7,750 million in the year 2004–05. SFL produces the largest range of fasteners in the country and has the largest library of tools in the sector. Apart from the Original Equipment (OE) market, the company has a presence in the replacement and export market. In the OE sector, its clientele include auto majors such as Tata Motors, Maruti Udyog, Baja Auto, and Mahindra & Mahindra.

In recent years, SFL acquired Autolec Industries Ltd, the largest manufacturer of water and oil pumps in India.

Milestones

1962—Incorporated as a private limited company under the name Kasjax Engineering Ancillaries Pvt Ltd.

1965—Name changed to Sundaram Fasteners (P) Ltd when the company began to focus and manufacture fasteners.

1982—Company went public.

1992—Entered into an agreement with General Motors that led to the creation of EOU for manufacture of radiator caps, oil filler caps, and petro filler caps.

1997—SFL signed an agreement with General Motors to supply its entire requirement of radiator caps. It set up a warehouse in Tory (Michigan), on line with all GM plants, supplying parts just in time.

1998—Technical collaboration agreement with Dura Automotive Group, USA, for the manufacture of gear shifters and parking brake assemblies for automobiles.

2000—Awarded the ACMA (Automotive Component Manufacturer's Award) Export Trophy for 1999–2000 for Excellence in export Performance; won the GM's Supplier of the Year Award for the fifth consecutive year.

2003—The company's subsidiary, TVS Autolec, in which SFL had 51 percent equity stake, was amalgamated with the company; Cramlington Precision Forge Ltd (CPFL), a 100 percent subsidiary of SFL, has acquired the precision forgings of Dana Spicer Europe Ltd (DSEL).

2004—Opened its first offshore facility in Haiyan county of China.

TATA CHEMICALS

In 1927, Kapil Ram Vakil set up Okhamandal Salt Works. In 1937, the Tatas approached to take over the Salt Works. Tata Chemicals Ltd (TCL) got incorporated on January 23, 1939.

TABLE D.16 Financials of Sundaram Fasteners Ltd

D.16a

Items	2004	2003	2002	2001	2000
Sales	774.7	519.4	433.2	424.2	431.9
PBT	88.57	66.86	43.33	42.16	51.65
PAT	59.20	45.93	31.97	34.46	44.05
Revenue earning in forex	172.86	97.67	82.37	75.97	65.75
Equity Capital	10.51	10.22	10.22	10.22	10.22

D.16b

Key ratios	2004	2003	2002	2001	2000
Gross profit margin (PBIDTM) percent	14.74	16.80	16.38	16.72	17.80
Net profit margin (APATM) percent	7.64	8.84	7.38	8.12	10.20
D/E ratio	0.93	0.45	0.65	0.67	0.79
LT D/E ratio	0.45	0.02	0.03	0.22	0.48
Current ratio	1.39	1.12	1.01	1.25	1.56

Source CMIE Prowess.

Today, TCL has an annual turnover of ₹35,000 million and is the chemical arm of the Tata Group, India's foremost business conglomerate. TCL is India's leading manufacturer of inorganic chemicals in the country.

TCL started operations in 1943, recovering minerals and sea water and then converting them to basic chemicals like soda ash, caustic soda, chlorine, sodium bicarbonate, bromine, salt, and urea that find application in different areas like agriculture, animal nutrition, construction, food products, glass, metals, pharmaceuticals, soaps, detergents, textiles, and leather.

On April 1, 2003, Hindustan Lever Chemicals Ltd, Unilever Group Company, merged with TCL with a post-merger shareholding of 25 percent for the Tata Group and 8 percent for the Unilever Group.

TCL is now in the process of expanding its operations globally. The demand outlook for the soda ash business, especially from the glass segment, remains strong, both domestically and globally. The "salt" business continues to receive good business at both the distributor and the consumer end. TCL is raising long-term resources for its expansion and raising borrowing limits.

D.17a

TABLE D.17 Financials of Tata Chemicals Ltd (₹ million)

Profit and loss	Mar. '92	Mar. '93	Mar. '94	Mar. '95	Mar. '96	Mar. '97	Mar. '98	Mar. '99
Sales	3,484.2	4,147.5	5,043.8	7,701.7	15,153.7	15,985.2	16,435.3	14,619.6
Other income	568.9	674.1	740.6	425.2	447.8	415.5	250.3	251.7
Change in stocks	53.2	−54.3	85.7	−129.3	174.6	−213.6	602.7	−243.7
Net sales	2,956.9	3,560.3	4,364.2	6,696.7	14,025.6	14,777.6	15,261.6	13,566.8
Total income	4,106.3	4,767.3	5,870.1	7,997.6	15,776.1	16,187.1	17,288.3	14,627.6
Raw material purchased	459.2	996.1	905.6	1,566.7	2,018.2	2,657.1	3,101.1	2,309.3
Cost of production	2,118	2,465.8	2,846	4,286.6	6,747.6	8,005	8,644.1	7,664.2
Selling cost	63.4	56.6	135.6	182.8	549	692.2	978.2	1,058.3
Cost of sales	2,128.2	2,576.7	2,895.9	4,598.7	7,122	8,910.8	9,019.6	8,966.7
Admin and other costs	180.5	277.4	432.9	447.8	404.8	462.5	585.2	471.9
Total costs	3,634.7	4,313.3	4,679.2	8,367.9	11,836.3	13,993.9	13,989.7	13,429.2
PAT	597.5	749.5	2,765.8	2,866.5	3,923.1	2,499.6	2,886.3	1,816.7
PBDIT	1,672.7	1,901.4	3,668.7	4,319.4	8,009.7	7,046.5	7,177.7	5,731.1
PBDT	1,162.5	1,398.9	3,042.4	3,327.2	5,192	4,020.5	4,472.6	3,259.8
PBIT	1,407.7	1,639.1	3,442.1	3,859.3	6,960.8	5,905.6	6,026.4	4,569.6
PBT	897.5	1,136.6	2,815.8	2,867.1	4,143.1	2,879.6	3,321.3	2,098.3
Cash flow from operations	0	0	0	148.8	5,026.1	5,267.6	7,371.8	5,510.2

D.17b

Balance sheet	Mar. '92	Mar. '93	Mar. '94	Mar. '95	Mar. '96	Mar. '97	Mar. '98	Mar. '99
Current liabilities	853.2	1,711.9	2,562.2	1,689.9	1,814.8	1,764.8	1,892.9	1,481.1
Sundry creditors	534.6	1,337.8	2,083.9	1,274.4	1,405.1	1,362.7	1,572.9	1,211.7
Creditors for cap. goods	0	0	0	0	0	0	0	0
Accrued interest	310.3	365	464.1	394.7	383.6	373.9	281.9	221
Other current liabilities	8.3	9.1	14.2	20.8	26.1	28.2	38.1	48.4
Provisions	264.5	319.9	677.5	786.4	1,240	1,362	1,310.6	1,329.2
Total liabilities	11,063.3	16,747.6	24,010.7	28,081.8	31,685.8	33,639.3	34,425.6	35,273.3
Gross fixed assets	6,979.7	11,935.8	19,456.2	20,974.7	22,447.5	24,179.9	25,979.4	27,399.5
Land and building	602.2	673.6	897.3	1,815.3	2,041.4	2,209.7	2,571.9	2,715.9
Plant and machinery	2,822	3,019.7	4,111	15,329.4	18,268.2	19,464.2	20,241.9	21,321.9
Other fixed assets	366.3	408.2	682.6	889	958	1,063.1	785.8	815.5
Capital work-in-progress	3,189.2	7,834.3	13,765.3	2,941	1,179.9	1,442.9	2,379.8	2,546.2
Net fixed assets	5,117.9	9,830.8	17,193	18,303	18,760.3	19,396.2	20,074.1	20,347.9
Investments	3,519.6	3,777.8	2,951.6	2,697.4	3,508.8	2,591.2	2,581.5	2,625.8

Inventories	884.9	1,070.6	1,197.9	2,078.7	2,184	2,162.8	3,023.8	2,555.5
Cash and bank balance	157.3	264.5	192.8	53.4	37.8	53.2	77.6	102.8
Advances	0	0	0	0	0	0	0	0
Receivables	1,316.4	1,722.4	2,424.5	4,929.8	7,184.9	9,395.6	8,611	9,619.2
Total assets (excl. Reval. and dre)	10,988.5	16,646	23,245.3	27,588.2	31,211.7	32,344.4	32,505.6	32,818.6
Current assets	4,932.2	6,158.8	3,939.8	6,940.6	9,568.9	11,749.4	12,030.7	12,608.3
Quick assets	3,260.5	4,209	1,255.9	2,479.2	3,945.8	4,049.6	3,122.5	780.2
Current liabilities and prov. (incl. bank short)	1,722.3	2,621.8	4,066.6	3,692.1	4,395.3	5,116.6	7,092.3	6,970.5
Working capital	3,209.9	3,537	−126.8	3,248.5	5,173.6	6,632.8	4,938.4	5,637.8
Current ratio	28.6	23.5	09.7	18.8	21.8	23	17	18.1
Debt–equity ratio	17	19	15.3	14.7	11.8	11.3	9.6	09.4
Solvency ratio	15	14.3	15.4	1.6	17.3	17.9	19.6	20.4
Quick ratio	18.9	16.1	03.1	06.7	9	7.9	4.4	1.1
ROCE	149.3	136.1	126.2	123.9	272.9	212.6	215.7	160.2

D.17c

Profit and loss	Mar. '00	Mar. '01	Mar. '02	Mar. '03	Mar. '04	Mar. '05	Mar. '06
Sales	15,194.2	14,700	13,962.8	16,129.9	26,327.9	30,979.1	36,382.3
Other income	443.5	423.2	998	672.9	646.6	533.6	940.5
Change in stocks	110	−9.1	−285	44.8	216.8	−410.5	874.4
Net sales	14,230.6	13,821	13,201.1	15,213	25,242.1	29,826.4	35,028.5
Total income	15,747.7	15,114.1	14,675.8	16,847.6	27,191.3	31,102.2	38,197.2
Raw material purchased	3,580	3,566.5	2,795.7	3,380.7	11,734.6	13,258.2	15,190.1
Cost of production	8,818	9,476.9	8,654.1	9,430.8	18,907.8	21,810.3	26,954.5
Selling cost	2,716.5	2,459.5	1,609.4	2,264	2,495.8	2,930	3,361.9
Cost of sales	11,441.2	12,114.7	10,634.7	11,797.3	21,301.2	25,164.5	29,460.4
Admin and other costs	1,789.4	1,412	674.3	909.1	1,113.1	1,135.4	1,340.7
Total costs	15,655.4	15,640.3	14,028.4	15,356	25,347.2	29,341.5	34,328
PAT	1,172.9	1,649.5	1,268.2	1,965.8	2,205.3	3,405.5	3,530.3
PBDIT	4,924.4	5,166.9	4,667.4	5,236	5,567.4	6,728.2	7,200.2
PBDT	2,669.2	3,189.3	3,332.7	4,225	4,954	6,403.9	6,802.3
PBIT	3,689.7	3,838.5	3,335.3	3,866.7	4,125.9	5,351.2	5,810.9
PBT	1,434.5	1,860.9	2,000.6	2,855.7	3,512.5	5,026.9	5,413
Cash flow from operations	6,782.1	4,790.3	5,540.3	5,721.6	5,713.4	6,076.6	3,436.7

D.17d

Balance sheet	Mar. '00	Mar. '01	Mar. '02	Mar. '03	Mar. '04	Mar. '05	Mar. '06
Current liabilities	1,798.5	1,184.4	1,244.6	1,624.3	3,590.3	4,810.9	4,654
Sundry creditors	1,480.6	979.9	943.2	1,355.7	3,290.2	4,538.2	4,275.2
Creditors for cap. goods	0	0	0	0	0	0	0
Accrued interest	261.6	145.7	172.9	152.8	89.5	26.4	92.4
Other current liabilities	56.3	58.8	128.5	115.8	210.6	246.3	286.4
Provisions	2,146	3,003.5	2,920	1,178.2	1,448.1	3,101.3	3,273.6
Total liabilities	34,575.8	35,105	35,010.6	31,811.9	37,659.1	44,858.2	47,560.4
Gross fixed assets	28,448.8	28,123.8	28,598.9	28,349	30,702.5	30,120.4	31,231.3
Land and building	1,581.2	1,663.9	1,812.9	1,838.9	2,198.8	2,141.1	2,196.9
Plant and machinery	23,201.1	23,619.3	24,099.2	23,989	25,734.4	25,842	26,570.7
Other fixed assets	2,542.9	2,376.7	2,352.1	2,407.5	2,491.6	2,653.9	2,654.6
Capital work-in-progress	1,123.6	463.9	334.7	113.6	277.7	542	867.7
Net fixed assets	20,224.4	18,843.6	18,146.7	16,844.1	17,414.5	15,623.9	15,509.7
Investments	2,084.4	4,282.2	5,556.8	5,690.2	6,269.4	9,387.4	11,183.7

(Table D. 17d continued)

(Table D. 17d continued)

Balance sheet	Mar. '00	Mar. '01	Mar. '02	Mar. '03	Mar. '04	Mar. '05	Mar. '06
Inventories	2,683.7	2,700.4	1,980.7	1,807	4,398.4	4,886.4	5,608.2
Cash and bank balance	68	141	90.7	211	726.9	7,516.7	460.6
Advances	0	0	0	0	0	0	0
Receivables	8,977.6	8,716.8	8,874.9	7,043.8	8,626.9	7,235.4	14,546.6
Total assets (excl. reval. and dre)	31,617.1	32,007.5	31,530.3	28,011.3	34,259.3	43,136.8	46,805.2
Current assets	11,831.6	13,342.1	15,103.7	11,449.4	14,481.8	25,111.3	16,192.3
Quick assets	3,094.8	3,792.7	5,669	4,007.4	4,221.7	16,628.7	7,318.5
Current liabilities and prov. (incl. bank short)	8,120.7	7,707.1	7,220.7	6,284.7	9,940.9	13,112.2	14,414
Working capital	3,710.9	5,635	7,883	5,164.7	4,538.4	11,996.6	1,775.8
Current ratio	14.6	17.3	20.9	18.2	14.6	19.2	11.2
Debt–equity ratio	8.4	6	7	5	3.8	6.6	6.7
Solvency ratio	20.8	24.7	27.3	38.4	36.7	22.2	21.5
Quick ratio	3.8	4.9	7.9	6.4	4.2	12.7	5.1
ROCE	143.9	93.1	122.2	152.4	160.4	160.8	181.3

Source CMIE Prowess (accessed in 2006).

BAJAJ HINDUSTHAN

History

Bajaj Hindusthan was incorporated on November 23, 1931, by Jamnalal Bajaj and was named Hindusthan Sugar Mills Ltd. Besides being a respected businessman, Jamnalal Bajaj was a confidante and disciple of Mahatma Gandhi.

The first factory of the company was located at Gola Gokarannath in Lakhimpur Kheri district in the Terai region of Uttar Pradesh, India, an area rich in sugarcane. The factory started with a crushing capacity of 400 tons of sugarcane per day. Subsequently, the capacity was increased in stages to reach its current level of 13,000 TCD. The distillery unit at Gola Gokarannath set up by the company commenced production during the last years of the War in 1944. During the first few years, the major output was in the form of power alcohol as an additive to petrol, which was then in short supply. In fact, the unit was the first to supply the alcohol-mixed petrol to the army.

In 1967, a new company—Sharda Sugar & Industries Ltd—was established as a subsidiary of Hindusthan Sugar Mills Ltd. A sugar factory with a cane crushing capacity of 1,400 TCD was set up in 1972 at Palia Kalan, a large cane supply center at a distance of about 70 km from Gola Gokarannath. This was done primarily to help the cane growers of the area to supply their cane to the new factory. The capacity was increased in stages to reach its present level of 11,000 TCD.

In 1988, Hindusthan Sugar Mills Ltd was renamed as Bajaj Hindusthan. In the year 1990, Sharda Sugar & Industries Ltd was amalgamated with Bajaj Hindusthan.

The company set up a new distillery unit at Palia Kalan with a capacity of 60 KL/day that commenced production since February 2004.

Today, Bajaj Hindusthan has a crushing capacity of 24,000 TCD—comprising 13,000 TCD at Gola Gokarannath and another 11,000 TCD at Palia Kalan. The Gola Gokarannath unit has the single largest distillery in India with a capacity to manufacture 100 KL/day of rectified spirit and 85 KL/day of ethanol. The Palia Kalan unit has a capacity of 60 KL/day of rectified spirit or ethanol. With this, the company has emerged as the largest producer of ethanol in India.

Sugar industry

Sugar is produced in over 100 countries across the globe. Approximately 75 percent of it is produced from sugarcane. Beet sugar has gone down from 40 percent in 1990 to 25 percent in 2003. The reason that can be sited is that the cost of sugar from cane is less than the cost of sugar from beet.

About 70 percent of the worldwide production is consumed in the country of origin. The balance 30 percent is traded in the world markets. Almost 33 percent of export is controlled by Brazil, 15 percent the EU, 13 percent Thailand, and 12 percent Australia. Even though India is the second-largest producer of sugar in the world, it is not involved in large exports as it is also the largest consumer of sugar in the world. With 506 sugar factories located throughout the country (2002 figures), the sugar industry is among the largest agro-processing industries in India.

In the past, the government permitted only small-sized units of 1,250 TCD and 2,500 TCD and expansions for 5,000 TCD and above were discouraged. As a result, the industry has grown horizontally. The sugar industry is highly fragmented with organized and unorganized players. The unorganized players mainly produce *gur* and *khandsari*, the less refined forms of sugar. The government de-licensed sugar sector in August 1998.

The government went for a phased deregulation of the sugar industry. The compulsory levy obligation of the sugar factories was reduced from 40 percent to 30 percent from January 1, 2000. This was further reduced to 15 percent from February 1, 2001, and 10 percent from March 1, 2003. Sugar prices are the lowest in India when compared to the leading sugar-consuming countries in the world.

TABLE D.18 Operating Divisions of Bajaj Hindusthan

Process	Key points
Sugarcane procurement	Total of 0.141 million hectares of cultivable land under their command area, covering 1,344 villages. Has 95 centers and purchases canes from 0.114 million farmers.
Sugar extraction by-products	Molasses, bagasse, and fly ash

Source Author.

During the 1970s, the company forayed into cement business, which it later sold during the 1990s and stuck to its core business of sugar.

FIGURE D.1   Sugar Production Value Chain

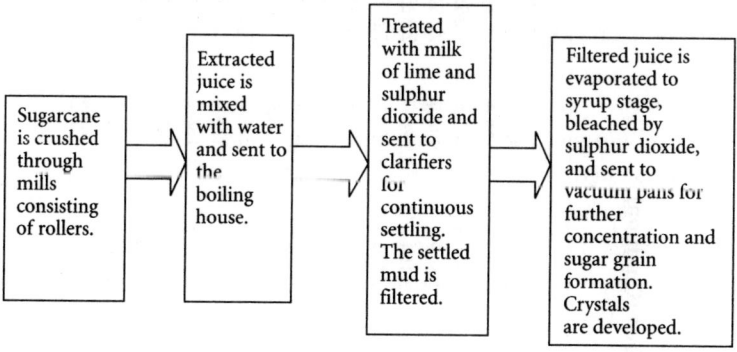

Source   Author.

CONCLUSION

Today, Bajaj Hindusthan has a crushing capacity of 24,000 TCD. It has the single-largest distillery in India at Gola Gokarannath. Along with its Palia Kalan unit, the company has emerged as the largest producer of ethanol in India.

SKF INDIA

History

In 1964, a rolling bearing factory was started in Pune, India, by SKF Bearings India. Another bearing factory was opened in Bangalore in 1989.

SKF India is a 54 percent subsidiary of SKF Sweden, the leading global supplier of rolling bearing and seals. SKF has its roots in Sweden. In 1907,

D.19a

TABLE D.19 Financials of Bajaj Hindusthan (₹ million)

Profit and loss	Mar. '92	Mar. '93	Mar. '94	Mar. '95	Mar. '96	Mar. '97	Mar. '98	Mar. '99
Sales	1,330.3	2,102.1	2,106.9	1,392.6	1,732.5	2,028.9	2,535.3	2,982.7
Other income	18.4	22.2	24.1	45	43.3	27.2	31.6	30.7
Change in stocks	287.9	69.5	−132.7	293.8	378.5	240.5	261.8	−84.3
Net sales	1,184	1,834.7	1,929	1,299.9	1,619.6	1,908.5	2,359.1	2,794
Total income	1,636.6	2,193.8	1,998.3	1,731.4	2,154.3	2,296.6	2,828.7	2,929.1
Raw material purchased	666.1	965.1	905	1,002.8	1,453.3	1,550.7	1,649.2	1,697
Cost of production	1,342.4	1,775.7	1,484.7	1,352.5	1,894.7	2,008.8	2,144	2,191.2
Selling cost	76.1	130	69.1	15.1	25.8	27.3	31.2	32.6
Cost of sales	1,145.9	1,804.4	1,669.8	1,089.7	1,542.5	1,802.4	1,908.1	2,311.4
Admin and other costs	55.9	51.7	52.1	48.5	59.2	55.9	66.1	61.4
Total costs	1,530.3	2,391.8	2,067.7	1,372.6	1,903.9	2,226	2,435.6	2,842.6
PAT	−144.4	−255.6	953.5	133	−141	−178.4	128.8	186.5
PBDIT	156.4	135.9	1,185.2	365.6	145.1	168.2	525.4	576.4
PBDT	−25.8	−132.4	1,017.3	223.9	−44.2	−79	256.3	355.4
PBIT	37.8	12.7	1,121.4	274.7	48.3	68.9	414	467.6
PBT	−144.4	−255.6	953.5	133	−141	−178.3	144.9	246.6
Cash flow from operations	0	0	0	0	−29.1	64.4	249.5	537.6

D.19b

Balance sheet	Mar. '92	Mar. '93	Mar. '94	Mar. '95	Mar. '96	Mar. '97	Mar. '98	Mar. '99
Current liabilities	694.5	892.1	436.5	449	594.1	723.2	561.6	431.8
Sundry creditors	406.8	4,262	218.2	331.6	467.9	600.5	430.8	289.8
Creditors for cap. goods	0	.0	0	0	0	0	0	0
Accrued interest	192.3	330.2	26.4	12.1	16.5	18.1	96.6	96.5
Other current liabilities	95.4	135.7	191.9	105.3	109.7	104.6	34.2	45.5
Provisions	7.7	2.4	26.9	20.3	01	0.1	40.2	100.5
Total liabilities	2,755.8	2,986.4	2,601.9	2,683.5	3,093.3	3,252.9	3,394.8	3,328.3
Gross fixed assets	2,431.7	2,480.4	1,702.2	1,831.8	1,883.3	2,053.4	2,130	2,216.4
Land and building	223.3	254.5	209.6	227.5	232	249.6	265.5	277
Plant and machinery	1,728.5	1,717.3	1,367.1	1,507.3	1,531.4	1,626	1,759.1	1,837
Other fixed assets	617	64.4	57.1	61	64.1	78	84.8	95.9
Capital work-in-progress	418.2	444.2	68.4	36	55.8	99.8	20.6	6.5
Net fixed assets	1,643.9	1,555	1,199.1	1,228.5	1,170.7	1,236.6	1,193.2	1,167.2
Investments	2.3	02.3	2.5	2.5	152	2	2	2

(Table D. 19b continued)

(Table D. 19b continued)

Balance sheet	Mar. '92	Mar. '93	Mar. '94	Mar. '95	Mar. '96	Mar. '97	Mar. '98	Mar. '99
Inventories	881.8	906.4	712.3	1,010.5	1,400.7	1,632.6	1,890.5	1,788.1
Cash and bank balance	37.5	66.5	70.9	29.9	51.1	49.8	92.5	110.8
Advances	0	0	0	0	0	0	0	0
Receivables	181.5	226.6	588.3	385.2	295.3	311.8	200	247.2
Total assets (excl. reval. and dre)	2,441.7	2,507.3	2,430.6	2,530.1	2,957.6	3,130.7	3,236.7	3,125.4
Current assets	1,101.8	1,200.5	1,372.5	1,426.6	1,747.4	1,990	2,164.6	2,146.4
Quick assets	97.7	162	91.2	38.8	103.1	90.2	99	127.6
Current liabilities and prov. (incl. bank short)	1,077.6	1,319.4	840.2	1,027.9	1,522.4	1,895.8	2,052.9	1,920.1
Working capital	24.2	−118.9	532.3	398.7	225	94.2	111.7	226.3
Current ratio	10.2	9.1	16.3	13.9	11.5	10.5	10.5	11.2
Debt–equity ratio	62.1	151.2	9.3	8.1	13.6	19.2	18.7	14.5
Solvency ratio	11.1	10.4	17.2	18.2	15.1	13.6	14.1	15.4
Quick ratio	0.9	1.2	1.1	0.4	0.7	0.5	0.5	0.7
ROCE	0.4	0.6	166.3	133.6	41.7	57.9	336.9	354.5

D.19c

Profit and loss	Mar. '00	Mar. '01	Mar. '02	Mar. '03	Mar. '04	Mar. '05	Mar. '06
Sales	2,613.4	3,295.1	n.a.	6,204.5	4,582.7	5,276.2	8,914.6
Other income	41.1	42	n.a.	66.7	73.3	41	69.4
Change in stocks	453.1	427.5	n.a.	−1,578.4	94.7	−467.2	−706.3
Net sales	2,288.8	3,036.2	n.a.	5,908.8	4,206.3	4,997.7	8,462.2
Total income	3,107.6	3,764.6	n.a.	4,692.8	4,750.7	4,850	8,277.7
Raw material purchased	1,954.9	2,508.1	n.a.	2,995.7	3,169.6	2,799.1	4,611.3
Cost of production	2,429	3,109.8	n.a.	3,894.6	3,879.9	3,591.4	5,728.3
Selling cost	16.8	32.1	n.a.	38.5	37.6	48.8	143.1
Cost of sales	2,023.6	2,699.9	n.a.	5,488	3,822.8	4,107.4	6,566.9
Admin and other costs	74.9	81.1	n.a.	95.3	82.9	117.4	144.2
Total costs	2,594	3,265.9	n.a.	6,116.7	4,419.8	4,813	7,616.5
PAT	69.9	40.1	n.a.	62.1	283.5	610.2	1,404.5
PBDIT	351.7	373.7	n.a.	484	556.3	1,110.8	2,208.5
PBDT	185.5	152.1	n.a.	269.8	433.7	969.7	2,056.4
PBIT	240.8	266.1	n.a.	299.8	421.2	919.9	1,857.5
PBT	74.6	44.5	n.a.	85.6	348.6	778.8	1,705.4
Cash flow from operations	141.2	0.6	n.a.	1,694	202	1,657.4	1,742.3

D.19d

Balance sheet	Mar. '00	Mar. '01	Mar. '02	Mar. '03	Mar. '04	Mar. '05	Mar. '06
Current liabilities	711.3	734	n.a.	340	344.1	656.7	549.8
Sundry creditors	552.6	630.8	n.a.	239.2	327.4	532	266.4
Creditors for cap. goods	0	0	n.a.	0	0	86.7	247.3
Accrued interest	103.1	12.3	n.a.	5.1	9.9	25.6	18.6
Other current liabilities	55.6	90.9	n.a.	95.7	6.8	12.4	17.5
Provisions	45.9	92.2	n.a.	99.2	47.6	61.2	436.7
Total liabilities	3,699.9	4,213.2	n.a.	2,515.1	3,693.9	5,741.3	12,682.7
Gross fixed assets	2,250.3	2,439.3	n.a.	2,432.4	3,340.8	5,869.6	12,786.3
Land and building	281.7	302.3	n.a.	263.1	267.7	586.6	1,131.5
Plant and machinery	1,867	1,985.5	n.a.	2,003.8	2,124.1	3,271.5	5,015.4
Other fixed assets	98	107.5	n.a.	140.4	160.7	225.5	405
Capital work-in-progress	3.6	44	n.a.	25.1	788.3	1,786	6,234.4
Net fixed assets	1,061.5	1,141.3	n.a.	1,108.1	1,892.6	4,232.8	10,797.3
Investments	2	48.8	n.a.	32.1	13.2	12.2	62.2

Inventories	2,240.1	2,668.1	n.a.	1,190.1	1,270.9	774.1	555.5
Cash and bank balance	51.5	40.6	n.a.	32.3	123.2	39.4	58.3
Advances	0	0	n.a.	0	0	0	0
Receivables	335.4	309.5	n.a.	152.5	394	682.8	1,209.4
Total assets (excl. reval. and dre)	3,421.6	3,978	n.a.	2,475.6	3,693.9	5,700	12,682.7
Current assets	2,627	3,033.7	n.a.	1,354.9	1,758.1	1,496.3	1,823.2
Quick assets	92.5	106.6	n.a.	51.6	346	317.7	236.9
Current liabilities and prov. (incl. bank short)	2,331.7	2,775.7	n.a.	1,282.7	1,603.5	1,550.3	1,743.6
Working capital	295.3	258	n.a.	72.2	154.6	−54	79.6
Current ratio	11.3	10.9	n.a.	10.6	11	9.7	10.5
Debt–equity ratio	14.7	18.2	n.a.	9	14.8	23.4	8.3
Solvency ratio	15.1	14.2	n.a.	19.6	16.9	14.6	20.8
Quick ratio	0.4	0.4	n.a.	0.4	2.2	2	1.4
ROCE	178	224.1	n.a.	333.2	267.7	292.1	255.5

Source CMIE Prowess (accessed in 2006).

Sven Wingquist, a bright young Swedish engineer, developed the world's first self-aligning ball bearing in Gothenburg, Sweden. The company grew rapidly with the opening of branch offices in Germany and France and appointment of agents in Finland, Switzerland, Belgium, Denmark, Austria, and Australia. In 1911, SKF established another factory in Luton, UK. By 1912, it had representatives established in 32 overseas centers, mostly within Europe and in cities such as Tokyo, Melbourne, and Mexico.

Over the years, SKF made acquisitions in Sweden, Germany, the US, Finland, and Austria.

SKF India manufactures a product range comprising about 60 sizes of deep groove ball bearings, 70 sizes of taper roller bearings, textile machinery components, automotive specials, bearing accessories like housings, sleeves, etc., to cater to the needs of the automotive, electrical, and industrial OEMs and after market customers. Its associate company, CR Seals India Pvt Ltd, a wholly owned subsidiary of SKF Sweden, offers customers complete sealing solutions based on CR's leading-edge technology.

It is a market leader in the domestic bearing industry with around 30 percent market share in the organized market. The company derives 50 percent of its sales in OEs and after market from the automobile sector and the balance from the industrial sector. While 60 percent sales are for OEs, the balance 40 percent is for the aftermarket.

The company has an installed capacity of 71 million ball and roller bearings. In addition to the manufacture, SKF offers integrated mechanical and engineering services, preventive and predictive maintenance.

The company has a development center in Bangalore to develop new products.

Industry overview

India has a relatively strong base for the manufacture of bearings. There are about 12 large and medium units that together turn out over 100 million bearings every year. Almost all the units have foreign collaboration. The Indian bearing industry makes around 500 types of bearings as against over 30,000 types of bearings being used by the Indian industry. Majority of these are only of standard types and are used mostly in low-technology areas like fans, electric motors, water pumps, and automobiles. As a consequence of a small range being manufactured in the country, there is a big dependence on imports by the industrial units.

The bearings industry comprises of organized large players, small players, and imports.

In the organized segment, there are more than 20 manufacturers with an installed capacity of approximately 200 million numbers. The capacity utilization was 75 percent in FY 2000. The capacity utilization could be higher but for stiff competition from the unorganized sector in small bearings and imports (legal as well as illegal) in large bearings.

The organized large players are SKF Bearings, FAG Precision, Tata Timken, NBC, NRB Bearings, etc. The bearings industry can be segmented into ball and roller bearings. Roller bearings are of four types—taper, cylindrical, spherical, and needle roller bearings. The distribution of production is ball bearings (54 percent), taper roller bearings (30 percent), cylindrical roller bearings (7 percent), needle roller bearings (6 percent), and spherical roller bearings (3 percent). SKF, FAG Precision, and NBC dominate the ball bearings segment. SKF, Tata Timken, and NBC dominate the taper roller bearing segment.

The small players generally manufacture small bearings used in automobiles. These players are competitive compared to large players because of excise benefits (and evasion). Further, some of these players manufacture spurious items and sell them under known brand names. They have a regional presence and constitute about 10 percent of the market with volumes at around 50 million numbers.

Imports are high as the demand for numerous sizes of bearings that are not made in the country is high. Around 70 percent of the total bearing requirement in terms of volumes is imported.

The bearings industry is highly capital intensive in nature. As bearings are the critical component of machinery, the bearings manufacture requires high degree of precision and quality. This necessitates heavy investment in sophisticated machines for manufacturing and quality control at all stages of production. It may be noted that the precision requirement is more for large bearings.

Operating divisions

With an aim to provide customer focus, the company has organized itself into five business units where each BU is responsible for sales, marketing, manufacturing, and product development with support functions in their respective area.

TABLE D.20 Major Players in the Bearings Industry

Company	Collaborator
SKF Bearings	SKF, Sweden
National Engineering	NTN, Japan
NRB Bearings	Torrington, USA and Nadella, France
FAG Precision Bearings	FAG, Germany
Tata Timken	Timken, USA
Bimetal Bearings	Clevite, USA

Source Author (based on business research).

TABLE D.21 Bearings Industry—Operating Divisions

Division	Products	Customer group
Automotive business	Wheel hub bearings, taper roller bearings, seals, special automotive products, complete repair kits for the vehicle service market.	Cars, light trucks, heavy trucks, bus, vehicle component industries, vehicle service market.
Industrial business	Wide range, in particular spherical and cylindrical roller bearings, angular contact ball bearings.	Railways, linear motion and precision technologies, coupling and lubrication systems.
Electrical business	Deep groove ball bearings, seals.	Manufacturers of electric motors, household appliances, electrical components for the automotive industry, power tools, office machinery, and two-wheelers.
Service business	Knowledge-based service solutions to optimize asset efficiency—mechanical services, predictive and preventive maintenance, condition monitoring, decision support systems and performance-based contracts.	Industrial after market through distributors, industrial customers.
Textile machinery component business	Precision textile machinery components.	OEM customers, spindle manufacturers, drafting conversion manufacturers, help textile mills to modernize existing machines.

Source Author (based on business research).

Products

The major users of bearings are automobile, general engineering, railways, and electrical equipments. The percentage share by user segment is as follows—automobile (45 percent), general engineering (28 percent), heavy industries including railways (21 percent), and electrical equipment and others (6 percent). The growth of the bearing industry is determined by growth rates of the end-user segments.

The growth of the replacement market is dependent on the growth in machinery and equipment "stock" in the country and its maintenance. The life of engineering products is around 12 to 15 years. Thus, the stock of machinery and the demand from the replacement is expected to grow by approximately 3 percent.

TABLE D.22 Bearings Category, Market Share, and Competition

Category	Market share	Competition
Ball bearings	37 percent	FAG Precision, NBC
Taper roller bearings	23 percent	Tata Timken, NBC

Source Author (based on website and business research).

Exports

India has been exporting low-value small bearings in small quantities. The country is not competitive when it comes to large-sized bearings in the export market due to the following reasons: (*i*) international market is highly quality conscious and in the past the quality of bearings manufactured in India was not of international standard except for a few big manufacturers, (*ii*) relatively small size of operation of existing players which makes it difficult to adhere to timely delivery schedules, (*iii*) high cost of production, and (*iv*) ensured domestic market for the existing players.

SKF and Tata Timken have started exports to neighboring countries and are planning to export to developed countries as well.

Conclusion

SKF Bearings India has been able to leverage on the technical expertise of the parent company SKF, which gave it an edge in product design and

D.23a

TABLE D.23 Financials of SKF India (₹ million)

Profit and loss	Mar. '92	Mar. '93	Mar. '94	Mar. '95	Mar. '96	Mar. '97	Mar. '98	Mar. '99
Sales	3,049.6	3,217.4	3,400.2	3,986.1	4,514.5	4,867	4,334.9	4,081.8
Other income	112.9	65.7	69.4	95.9	89.1	83.3	76.3	43.3
Change in stocks	250.9	5.1	-3	30.9	14.4	416.5	-137.9	-107.2
Net sales	2,355.1	2,500.3	2,759.6	3,195	3,763.5	4,047.3	3,677.3	3,531.7
Total income	3,413.4	3,288.2	3,439.6	4,112.9	4,618	5,366.8	4,273.3	4,017.9
Raw material purchased	1,303.3	897.9	1,090	1,207.5	1,532	1,442.2	1,058.4	1,141.2
Cost of production	1,976.5	2,161.5	2,307.6	2,415.1	2,831.8	3,376.4	2,911.9	2,804.4
Selling cost	0	6.1	0.4	5.8	4.1	20.1	30.2	16
Cost of sales	1,803	2,107.1	2,323.6	2,399.8	2,866.4	2,963.9	3,076.9	2,931.4
Admin and other costs	110.4	104.4	166.5	195.2	227.5	274.3	312.8	272
Total costs	2,959.2	3,308.4	3,469.1	3,808.3	4,362.9	4,638.8	4,343.9	4,013.1
PAT	206.5	28.1	36.4	291.1	244.9	292.9	58.9	-442.7
PBDIT	780.2	690.1	637.4	994.6	1,073.4	1,202.5	727.8	197.9
PBDT	478.9	310.3	300.4	714.9	805.4	916.6	461.2	-61.7
PBIT	557.8	407.9	374.8	713.3	762.9	873.8	355.5	-183.1
PBT	256.5	28.1	37.8	433.6	494.9	587.9	88.9	-442.7
Cash flow from operations	0	0	0	826.1	983.2	628	845	926.3

D.23b

Balance sheet	Mar. '92	Mar. '93	Mar. '94	Mar. '95	Mar. '96	Mar. '97	Mar. '98	Mar. '99
Current liabilities	839.3	484.2	489	527.4	622.3	763.2	690.5	697.6
Sundry creditors	712	415.1	419.7	228.6	294.5	285.8	275.7	279.3
Creditors for cap. goods	0	0	0	0	0	0	0	0
Accrued interest	80.3	68.1	64	68.1	58.3	65.2	86.5	94.6
Other current liabilities	47	1	5.3	230.7	269.5	412.2	328.3	323.7
Provisions	69.1	65.2	89.6	107.4	113	135.7	27.6	0
Total liabilities	4,083.2	3,988.4	3,896.8	4,024.6	4,126	4,809	4,773.4	4,742.5
Gross fixed assets	2,973.7	3,305.3	3,399.9	3,541	3,818.9	4,118.9	4,749.5	5,250.5
Land and building	189	190.8	205.6	211.1	215.4	217.9	223.6	240.5
Plant and machinery	2,576.5	2,891.5	2,948.3	3,215	3,353.8	3,588.3	4,076.7	4,554.9
Other fixed assets	23.7	25.4	35.1	36.4	36	37.4	46.1	51.9
Capital work-in-progress	184.5	197.6	210.9	78.5	213.7	275.3	403.1	403.2
Net fixed assets	2,178.1	2,227.5	2,060.5	1,924.2	1,913.6	1,918.2	2,183	2,309.1
Investments	31	31	39.8	48.1	48.4	30.1	30	30
Inventories	1,045.7	844.4	835.5	887.5	1,000.3	1,461.9	1,155.1	1,113.8
Cash and bank balance	171.4	72.8	94.6	88.3	116.9	99	124.3	114.4

(Table D.23b continued)

(Table D.23b continued)

Balance sheet	Mar. '92	Mar. '93	Mar. '94	Mar. '95	Mar. '96	Mar. '97	Mar. '98	Mar. '99
Advances	0	0	0	0	0	0	0	0
Receivables	657	812.7	862.8	1,076.5	1,046.8	1,299.8	1,281	1,175.2
Total assets (excl. reval. and dre)	4,053	3,988.4	3,891.5	4,007	4,072.8	4,757.1	4,664.7	4,628.8
Current assets	1,800.1	1,710.9	1,772.7	1,930.4	2,122.4	2,805.8	2,580.3	2,433.4
Quick assets	563.5	737.2	722.6	800.2	843.8	1,042.2	955.4	896.1
Current liabilities and prov. (incl. bank short)	1,319.5	879.4	994.3	1,027.2	1,281.5	1,572.4	1,189.3	1,354.4
Working capital	480.6	831.5	778.4	903.2	840.9	1,233.4	1,391	1,079
Current ratio	13.6	19.5	17.8	18.8	16.6	17.8	21.7	18
Debt–equity ratio	18.6	20.9	18.2	14.3	11.8	12.5	13	20.6
Solvency ratio	13.8	13.9	14.3	15.3	16.2	15.7	16.1	14
Quick ratio	4.3	8.4	7.3	7.8	6.6	6.6	8	6.6
ROCE	230	121	113	236.4	259.7	293.5	106.7	106.6

D.23c

Profit and loss	Mar. '00	Mar. '01	Mar. '02	Mar. '03	Mar. '04	Mar. '05	Mar. '06
Sales	3,352.4	4,544.1	4,493.7	5,085	5,624.1	6,985.6	9,234.1
Other income	55.9	26.5	55.9	29.9	572	49.6	94.6
Change in stocks	−29.7	206.6	−35.9	−37.5	−872	107.4	309.4
Net sales	2,782.6	371	3,639.1	4,161	4,789.1	6,008.7	7,970.8
Total income	3,378.6	4,777.2	4,513.7	5,077.4	5,594.1	7,142.6	9,638.1
Raw material purchased	902.9	1,454.5	1,116.9	1,389.6	1,638.2	2,392.9	2,607.8
Cost of production	2,261.7	3,196.5	3,092.5	3,225	3,793	4,708.5	6,659.2
Selling cost	11.2	20.4	26.7	25.2	4.2	59.2	62
Cost of sales	2,312.6	3,014.2	3,094.1	3,302.5	3,872	4,677.2	6,392.8
Admin and other costs	208.2	321.7	316.8	440	454.9	489.9	592.6
Total costs	3,347.8	4,506.6	4,586.5	4,924.1	5,446.5	6,527.7	8,651.8
PAT	98.2	68.5	89.7	208.8	322	566.1	640.7
PBDIT	656.9	814.1	742.4	740.4	872.1	1,209.4	1,303.1
PBDT	411.7	491.3	477.7	608.4	798.1	1,169.2	1,297.6
PBIT	355.4	409	410.8	466.4	606.6	949.8	1,043.8
PBT	110.2	86.2	146.1	334.4	532.6	909.6	1,038.3
Cash flow from operations	680.2	556.8	929	916.8	894.4	984	1,388.3

D.23d

Balance sheet	Mar. '00	Mar. '01	Mar. '02	Mar. '03	Mar. '04	Mar. '05	Mar. '06
Current liabilities	801	938.1	946	931.8	923.8	1,633.9	1,498.6
Sundry creditors	325.6	251.9	309.9	355.9	432.9	805.5	1,013.9
Creditors for cap. goods	0	0	0	0	0	0	0
Accrued interest	71.8	43	34	27.3	7.9	05.5	5.7
Other current liabilities	403.6	643.2	602.1	548.6	483	822.9	479
Provisions	31.4	106.5	73.4	1,513.2	1,802.5	357	440.4
Total liabilities	4,673.5	4,661.6	4,489.8	5,501.7	5,527.7	4,789.9	5,548.6
Gross fixed assets	5,430.8	5,534.2	5,400.1	5,327.3	5,407.5	5,416.2	5,865.1
Land and building	243	228.4	227.1	226.8	221.9	231.7	231.4
Plant and machinery	4,783.7	5,010.1	4,944.7	4,912.7	4,962.5	5,026.5	5,177.1
Other fixed assets	50.5	57.1	78.8	82.9	84.7	89.3	96.6
Capital work-in-progress	353.6	238.6	149.5	104.9	138.4	68.7	360
Net fixed assets	2,257.6	1,978.9	1,688.4	1,459.3	1,286.1	1,172	1,474.4

Investments	30	30.1	43	43	21.3	0	0
Inventories	991.6	1,162	1,075	1,040	942.1	1,250.7	1,391.9
Cash and bank balance	126.4	170	361.8	466.4	573.7	1,002.5	1,114.8
Advances	0	0	0	0	0	0	0
Receivables	1,267.9	1,320.6	1,197.6	2,423.1	2,623.5	1,212.6	1,486.5
Total assets (excl. reval. and dre)	4,603.3	4,547.2	4,450.6	4,052.2	3,934	4,786.1	5,424.3
Current assets	2,386.7	2,682.7	2,656.1	3,951.2	4,139.3	2,987.6	3,993.2
Quick assets	1,083.5	1,076.7	1,183.5	1,211.4	1,297.3	1,260.2	2,138.9
Current liabilities and prov. (incl. bank short)	1,435.6	1,785.4	1,180.1	2,500.1	2,765.7	1,574.9	1,939
Working capital	951.1	897.3	1,468.2	1,451.1	1,373.6	1,412.7	2,054.2
Current ratio	16.6	15	22.5	15.8	15	19	20.6
Debt–equity ratio	17.6	15.6	7.7	4.5	2.2	0.2	0
Solvency ratio	14.3	14.5	18.5	21.5	24.7	23.3	29.9
Quick ratio	,7.5	6	10	4.8	4.7	8	11
ROCE	93.1	132.7	97.6	151.9	193.5	346.9	357.5

Source CMIE Prowess (accessed in 2006).

quality control. Better products and high quality made SKF Bearings the market leader in its segment.

The big trigger could come when the present SKF Sweden develops the Indian counterpart into global outsourcing base. The company would then be looking at tapping export opportunities as the Indian operations are very cost-effective with a 30–35 percent lower cost structure with comparable quality standards.

TATA POWER CORP. LTD

History

Tata Power generates and supplies power to bulk consumers in the Mumbai metropolitan area. In April 2000, Andhra Valley Power Supply Company Ltd and Tata Hydro-Electric Power Supply Company Ltd were amalgamated with Tata Power.

Tata Power is a dominant private sector player in the power sector in the country. The company operates four thermal and three hydroelectric plants in and around Mumbai, with an aggregate capacity of 1,797 MW supplying power to the Mumbai licensed area.

The three hydel plants at Bhira, Bhivpuri, and Khopoli have been awarded ISO 9001:2000 certification in recognition of institution of Quality Management System.

The company also supplies power to TISCO and ACC through captive power plants and has set up an 81 MW independent power project in Belgaum, Karnataka. It has built a fiber optic network in Mumbai and also has an electronics division that manufactures electrical equipment. Tata Power has diversified outside the Mumbai license area, by acquiring a distribution circle in Delhi during its recent privatization exercise and is also implementing a 400 KV, 1,200 km transmission line between Bhutan and Delhi with Power Grid Corporation Ltd. The outside license area sales are to MSEB, Madhya Pradesh SEB, etc.

During 2004–05, the company acquired 100 percent equity in Duncans North Hydro Power Company Ltd (DNHPC). DNHPC is developing a 330 MW run of the river hydro project at Shrinagar in Uttaranchal.

DNHPC has been renamed Alaknanda Hydro Power Company Ltd with a capital outlay for the project at ₹16,280 million and is expected to be completed in 2008.

Sales distribution

North Delhi Power Ltd (NDPL) is the company's first venture in retail distribution outside its license area. The company has applied for parallel distribution licenses in seven areas of MSEB that are contiguous to its Mumbai license area. The company has also expressed interest in taking franchises in Gujarat for power distribution.

The 400 KV transmission project is the first public–private joint venture transmission project with 51 percent equity participation from the company and 49 percent from Power Grid Corporation of India Ltd. The scope of work involves establishment of 400 KV transmission lines as a part of the transmission system associated with Tala Hydro Project in Bhutan, NE connector and northern region transmission system on build, own, operate, and transfer basis.

The company has set up a wholly owned subsidiary, viz., Tata Power Trading Company Ltd (TPTC) with the objective of entering into power trading business at national level. TPTC has applied to CERC for interstate trading license and the same is expected to be issued shortly.

Other businesses

Power systems division of the company has emerged as a major player in the EPC transmission business in the country. The division has won the largest transmission line construction contract in Bangladesh against stiff competition from Indian and international transmission line EPC companies. The division has enhanced its customer base with contracts from Damodar Valley Corporation, Power Grid Company of Bangladesh, and Zambia Electricity Supply Company. Power Grid Corporation of India continues to be the major customer for the division. The division has also extended its product portfolio by entering into sub-transmission and substation EPC businesses.

Strategic electronics division executed two major turnkey systems for the Indian army. Several systems developed by the division were displayed in the Republic Day Parade 2004 by DRDO. These were Pinaka (MBRL) Launcher, subsystems of AGNI and PRITHVI, Samyukta Entity workposts, and AKAS launchers.

Tata Power Broadband (TPBB) continued with its "Carriers' Carrier" business model, offering services to carriers, telecom service providers, and bulk users of IP bandwidth. TPBB has created India's first Dense Wave Division Multiplexing (DWDM) technology–based optic fiber network and has launched MPLS (Multi Protocol Label Switching)–based services during 2003–05. MPLS Virtula Private Networks were the major driver of IP demand. TPBB assisted the network rollout of Tata Teleservices Ltd (Maharashtra) by offering reliable fiber connectivity and very high speed bandwidth on its multi-ring architecture. TPBB is working toward enabling the retail broadband offering of VSNL. In essence, the customers are served for fiber, bandwidth, and IP/MPLS VPN requirements in Mumbai and Pune.

The company is into energy business through its wholly owned subsidiary, Tata Petrodyne Ltd, engaged in the business of exploration and production of oil and gas.

Outlook

Power sector became a mess with SEBs for 52 long years since 1951. The Electricity Act 2003 has attracted Indian private companies like Reliance Energy and Tata Power. It has also attracted global giants like AES, Daewoo Power, and Electricite de France.

According to the *Indian Electricity Sector—Opportunity and Challenges* report by FICCI and E&Y, "With historical GDP growth rates of 5–6 percent per annum and energy demand growth rates of 6 percent per annum, the energy deficit and peak deficit are currently around 8 percent and 12 percent respectively." And an unbelievable 44 percent of household electricity demand goes unmet!

The GOI's latest plan is to set up seven "Ultra Mega Power Projects" of 4,000 MW each. There is a need for an investment of $200 billion.

Thermal and nuclear contribute 56 percent and 3 percent. Thermal is the pick due to the available coal reserves in India. The nuclear will be 40,000 MW by 2020 from the current 20,000 MW. The complete ratifying of the nuclear deal with the US would surely give this sector a big boost.

Strategy

Tata Power enjoys a near monopoly status in the Mumbai metropolitan area as it has the license to supply electricity to bulk buyers and distributors in the Mumbai metropolitan area, such as BSES, BEST, and end-users having a power requirement exceeding 1,000 KVA. The company attained its near monopoly status as a result of the regulations of the old Electricity (Supply) Act, 1948, according to which the distribution licensees in the region had to necessarily depend on Tata Power for purchase of electricity.

However, the open access provisions in the Electricity Act 2003 pose a threat to Tata Power's dominance in the Mumbai metropolitan area. The Act allows distributors to expand their generation capacity and gives them the freedom to select their power supplier in a free and competitive market. Currently, a major portion of the company's sales, nearly 70 percent of the total generation, are to distributors such as Reliance Energy Ltd (REL is the erstwhile BSES) and BEST in the Mumbai Metropolitan area. Since REL is exploring the purchase of power at lower cost from other sources, Tata Power is also looking to sell its power to other buyers through the Power Trading Corporation and its subsidiary Tata Power Trading Company Ltd. REL is working on the feasibility of evacuating self-generated power from North India (Dadri—3,740 MW, expected to be commissioned by around 2007–08).

Tata Power possesses certain advantages that strengthen its market position in the segment, such as depreciated plants, fully captive production, and higher operational reliability resulting from technologies such as islanding and higher HT/LT ratio. In 2003–04, the company's islanding system operated successfully on four occasions during grid failures/disturbances in the western region, thereby ensuring uninterrupted power supply to Mumbai. The company is also allowed to supply power directly to end-users having a power requirement exceeding 1,000 KVA. Till now, the company had been directly supplying electricity to the railways, BARC, textile mills, airports, etc. Now, it is also targeting commercial and industrial users, and big housing complexes having a high power requirement on a collective basis. Tata power and REL are competing head on for consumers having a requirement for more than 1,000 KVA but less than 2,000 KVA, as REL has a license to supply up to 2,000 KVA.

The power reforms represent both an opportunity and a threat to the company's existing business. The Electricity Act 2003 offers Tata Power large scope for expansion. The company has already made inroads into the distribution business; North Delhi Power Ltd (NDPL), in which Tata Power has management control, has already commenced operations. NDPL supplies power to areas in the northwestern part of Delhi, catering to around 800,000 registered customers. Tata Power is also bidding for the distribution circles in Gujarat, Uttar Pradesh, Rajasthan, Madhya Pradesh, and Maharashtra.

Tata Power has acquired a 51 percent stake in a joint venture with Power Grid Corporation for the 400 KV Tala transmission project. This is the first across the state transmission line project with private sector participation.

The company's captive power plants (CPP) are characterized by steady, secured demand since the output is used for captive consumption. After entering into a contract with the Jharkhand State Electricity Board (JSEB) to supply power, the company is implementing an expansion plan at its Jojobera plant. With the steady growth in ACC and TISCO, and with the expected increase in purchases by JSEB and KPTCL, Tata Power's CPP and IPP businesses are expected to grow at a faster rate than the existing businesses in the license area.

The estimated value of the announced and under implementation expansion plans is around ₹167,630 million.

With power sector reforms and the emergence of free and competitive markets, players with better operational and cost-efficiencies will be able to become leaders in the sector. Tata Power has a high fuel cost on account

TABLE D.24 Announced and Under Implementation Power Projects

Project name	Project status	Project cost (₹ million)
Dholpur Power Project	Announced	30,000
Jamshedpur Coal based Power project	Announced	4,800
Pir Pau Jetty Project	Proposed	2,000
Sonbhadra Power Project	Announced	80,000
Vile Thermal Power Project	Announced	40,000
Jojobera Power Project—120 MW	Under implementation—to be completed in October 2005	3,900
Tala Project with Powergrid (51 percent equity stake)	Financial closure	1,830
Uttaranchal project (100 percent equity)	Acquired (to be completed in three years)	4,950
Investment in SPV for power trading	Soon to be invested	20 to 250
Estimated total capital expenditure		**167,630**

Source Author (based on business research, 2005).

of the higher usage of liquid fuels. However, the company is reducing its fuel costs by altering its fuel portfolio through the increased usage of coal for power generation. To counter the problem of tight domestic coal supply, in the long term, the company is looking at acquiring a stake in coal mining companies in Australia and Indonesia. Further, the greenfield expansions of Tata Power will use coal or gas as a fuel. Tata Power is also planning to bring in more gas by way of agreements with Petronet LNG and is studying the feasibility of acquiring a 26 percent stake in Indonesia's largest coal producer, Adaro.

TABLE D.25   Peer Comparison of Power Sector Companies

		Tata Power	REL	AEC	CESC	SEC
PLF	Percent	77.6	86.0	68.8	78.3	n.a.
T&D losses	Percent	6.2	13.4	16.6	17.2	13.0
Purchase tariff p.u. purchased	₹	3.2	3.4	3.7	3.4	2.7
Fuel cost per unit generated	₹	1.4	1.1	1.4	1.0	n.a.
Debtors and bills disc (as days gross and traded sales)	Days	69	60	72	115	n.a.
Operating margins	Percent	30.9	22.6	14.3	38.1	11.3

Source   Author (based on business research, 2005).

Global Compact, announced by the UN Secretary General in January 1999 at the World Economic Forum in Davos, is aimed at a partnership between the developmental agencies and the corporate sector to address issues of globalization. The Compact requires businesses to adhere to nine principles in the areas of human rights, labor standards, and environment. Pursuant to the Tata Group signing the Compact, the company adopted the Global Reporting Initiatives (GRI) which makes it easier for the company to assess its total performance—economic, environmental, and social.

AHMEDABAD ELECTRICITY COMPANY LTD (NOW PART OF TORRENT POWER)

Founded in 1913, Ahmedabad Electricity Company (AEC) is an integrated power generation, transmission, and distribution company. It was set up by a UK-based company named M/s Killick Nixon Ltd.

D.26a

TABLE D.26 Financials of Tata Power Corp. Ltd (₹ million)

Profit and loss	Mar. '92	Mar. '93	Mar. '94	Mar. '95	Mar. '96	Mar. '97	Mar. '98	Mar. '99
Sales	5,546.7	7,589.8	9,498.1	10,599.2	11,698.1	11,913.7	12,053.2	11,591.8
Other income	55.8	150.8	187.1	375.4	744.2	734.1	880.7	999.6
Change in stocks	43.8	8.6	74.1	−104.9	11	59.6	40.8	50.7
Net sales	5,462.7	7,502.7	9,400.1	10,497.7	11,567.9	11,767.5	11,882.9	11,403.2
Total income	5,646.3	7,749.2	9,759.3	10,869.7	12,453.3	12,707.4	12,974.7	12,642.1
Raw material purchased	2,168.8	2,588.9	2,953.1	3,558.5	4,139.4	50,418	4,756.7	4,157.3
Cost of production	4,425.9	5,954	7,599	8,335.8	7,812	9,076.6	8,429.3	8,188.2
Selling cost	30	22.4	29.6	30.7	106.4	117.7	40.2	52.1
Cost of sales	4,455.9	5,976.4	7,628.6	8,366.5	7,919.6	9,195	8,469.5	8,240.3
Admin and other costs	130.1	185.6	253.4	306.2	398.2	429	403.4	354.1
Total costs	5,344.5	7,053	8,801.1	9,781.2	10,216	11,452.4	11,403.8	11,022.6
PAT	264.8	672.7	959.7	1,195.1	2,230	1,179.3	1,646.4	1,663.4
PBDIT	1,085.8	1,700	2,037.1	3,081.8	5,157.4	4,114	4,924	4,849.1
PBDT	411.3	902.6	1,221.5	2,165.5	4,263.6	3,257.6	3,380.5	3,399.1
PBIT	939.3	1,476.6	1,780.8	2,202.1	3,999.5	2,862.5	4,007	3,903
PBT	264.8	679.2	965.2	1,285.8	3,105.7	2,006.1	2,463.5	2,453
Cash flow from operations	0	0	0	0	4,117.8	3,177	3,989	4,297.3

D.26b

Balance sheet	Mar. '92	Mar. '93	Mar. '94	Mar. '95	Mar. '96	Mar. '97	Mar. '98	Mar. '99
Current liabilities	747.1	1,163.9	1,490	1,691.2	1,529.4	1,602.4	1,896.3	2,463.9
Sundry creditors	546.4	897.7	1,082.1	1,300	995.2	1,075.9	1,283.6	1,715
Creditors for cap. goods	0	0	0	0	0	0	0	0
Accrued interest	86.4	106.4	129.1	140.4	95.2	79.5	105.1	99
Other current liabilities	114.3	159.8	278.8	250.8	439	447	507.6	649.9
Provisions	131.6	208.6	306	504.6	1,508.5	1,608.9	1,675.5	1,668.6
Total liabilities	9,634	12,622.8	16,422.2	21,775.5	23,202.2	24,519	30,228.3	33,075.5
Gross fixed assets	8,657.3	11,167.3	13,300.1	15,958.6	16,365.5	18,331.5	17,470.9	18,948.1
Land and building	383.3	382.4	404.1	472.6	525.7	811	770.2	947.6
Plant and machinery	4,323.6	5,015.4	7,181.7	8,788	9,083.2	10,821.5	12,999.9	13,995
Other fixed assets	98.6	107.3	117	5,683.5	5,696.6	5,438.9	132.5	214.5
Capital work-in-progress	3,851.8	5,662.2	5,597.3	1,014.5	1,060	1,260.1	3,568.3	3,791
Net fixed assets	7,711.9	10,001	11,900.2	13,012.6	12,273.3	12,999.9	13,157.2	13,713.8
Investments	449.7	560.7	1,638.1	4,951.5	5,732.2	6,145.4	10,727.3	12,081.5

(Table D.26b continued)

(Table D.26b continued)

Balance sheet	Mar. '92	Mar. '93	Mar. '94	Mar. '95	Mar. '96	Mar. '97	Mar. '98	Mar. '99
Inventories	511	745.2	844.7	1,038.2	1,158.5	1,209.2	1,121.7	1,338.2
Cash and bank balance	190.9	128.6	314.6	183.2	107.3	430.5	1,665.3	1,306.1
Advances	0	0	0	0	0	0	0	0
Receivables	767.5	1,185.8	1,705.4	2,572.3	3,914.3	3,718.4	3,516.3	4,598.2
Total assets (excl. reval. and dre)	9,572.4	12,536.5	16,285.6	21,521.3	22,651.9	23,598.6	29,228.3	31,965
Current assets	1,869.7	2,485.1	3,863.5	5,379.8	3,469.4	7,500.3	13,628.1	9,416.1
Quick assets	1,117.4	1,341	2,540.2	3,676	1,352.4	5,015.5	11,069.9	6,364.8
Current liabilities and prov. (incl. bank short)	1,151.2	1,397.3	1,796	2,293.8	3,037.2	3,210.7	3,571.8	4,136.3
Working capital	718.5	1,087.8	2,067.5	3,086	432.2	4,289.6	10,056.3	5,279.8
Current ratio	16.2	17.8	21.5	23.5	11.4	23.4	38.2	22.8
Debt–equity ratio	24.3	17.7	12.3	8.8	6.3	5	7.3	7.4
Solvency ratio	13.6	14.8	16.8	19.4	22	25.2	21.1	20.9
Quick ratio	9.7	9.6	14.1	16	4.5	15.6	31	15.4
ROCE	130.5	151.7	132.2	129.2	201.8	138.9	162.4	137.2

D.26c

Profit and loss	Mar. '00	Mar. '01	Mar. '02	Mar. '03	Mar. '04	Mar. '05	Mar. '06
Sales	14,046.4	33,782.5	37,958.5	42,778.6	42,118.9	39,670.8	45,893.5
Other income	879.6	1,625.1	1,114.7	1,194.4	1,436.1	12,31.4	1,623.2
Change in stocks	−9.3	79.3	−98.5	−119.8	−104.9	−80.8	89.5
Net sales	13,824.4	32,907.7	36,519.1	41,429.3	40,640.2	38,611.8	45,403.8
Total income	14,916.7	35,486.9	38,974.7	43,853.2	43,450.1	40,821.4	47,606.2
Raw material purchased	5,949.6	16,874.6	17,677.3	20,625.9	18,673.5	20,565.1	25,487.4
Cost of production	16,458.7	26,162.3	29,041.3	32,407.3	30,863.8	32,795.4	38,601
Selling cost	51	270.9	205.6	44.6	164.7	437.5	638.9
Cost of sales	16,515.7	26,444.6	29,252.6	32,451.9	31,028.5	33,232.9	39,239.9
Admin and other costs	522.9	1,468.5	1,317	938.8	648.4	1,254.7	879.3
Total costs	19,297.3	33,024.8	37,139.8	40,086	38,223.4	38,876.1	43,771
PAT	2,386.4	3,997	5,082.3	5,364.2	5,268.5	5,510	6,106.4
PBDIT	5,435.1	9,781.6	13,364.3	14,720.7	13,667.1	12,642.8	12,003.4
PBDT	4,306	7,316.3	10,087.1	11,452.5	10,871.4	10,807.3	10,430.7
PBIT	4,429.1	7,736.1	10,015.1	10,634	10,327.6	9,046.6	9,220
PBT	3,300	5,270.8	6,737.9	73,65.8	7,531.9	7,211.1	7,647.3
Cash flow from operations	4,144.4	7,748.2	8,768.8	13,219	13.907.7	6,983.6	3,028.5

D.26d

Balance sheet	Mar. '00	Mar. '01	Mar. '02	Mar. '03	Mar. '04	Mar. '05	Mar. '06
Current liabilities	3,876.1	8,910.2	10,564.1	10,672.2	9,072.3	7,068.7	7,318.1
Sundry creditors	3,047.6	7,133.6	8,893	9,070.8	6,996.3	5,341.2	5,488.6
Creditors for cap. goods	0	0	0	0	0	0	0
Accrued interest	124	290.2	509.6	485.1	321.9	341.8	319.3
Other current liabilities	704.5	1,486.4	1,161.5	1,116.3	1,754.1	1,385.7	1,510.2
Provisions	1,885.1	3,234.6	2,732.1	4,544.3	2,724.5	5,807	5,892
Total liabilities	36,806.9	76,804.3	84,848	86,882.3	80,004.9	93,478.7	96,781.8
Gross fixed assets	20,409.5	50,459.7	55,226.4	57,002.1	58,325.4	58,949.4	61,356
Land and building	1,228	3,483.9	4,047	4,427	4,469.4	4,337.1	5,063.8
Plant and machinery	13,102.2	33,908.8	38,631.5	41,689.9	49,743.1	37,689.1	41,336.2
Other fixed assets	2,041.4	9,022.9	8,996.1	8,972	1,498.3	12,546.7	12,837.9
Capital work-in-progress	4,037.9	4,044.1	3,551.8	1,913.2	2,614.6	4,376.5	2,118.1
Net fixed assets	14,190.4	35,996.9	38,002.6	36,692.4	34,735.4	32,445.2	32,148.2
Investments	13,549	15,829.3	22,761.2	24,518.3	27,288.3	35,029.2	34,121.7
Inventories	1,363.7	3,114.8	3,259.6	3,309.8	3,132.2	2,970.3	4,422.6

Cash and bank balance	269.6	10,362.7	3,063.3	1,263.6	519	9,796	9,905.5
Advances	0	0	0	0	0	0	0
Receivables	7,403.7	10,942.7	17,276.3	20,088.3	13,278.9	12,469.9	15,402.3
Total assets (excl. reval. and dre)	35,835.8	74,116.9	82,547.1	83,301.2	77,964.8	90,822.9	95,799.8
Current assets	6,954.5	29,301.3	22,666.3	25,785.8	20,276.7	38,449.4	35,550.4
Quick assets	2,606	21,244.4	13,288.7	13,761.3	12,404.2	28,510.6	25,143.4
Current liabilities and prov. (incl. bank short)	5,761.2	12,144.8	13,296.2	15,280.5	11,924.9	13,106.6	13,382.5
Working capital	1,193.3	17,156.5	8,440.2	9,719.8	7,628.9	25,082.1	21,927.2
Current ratio	12.1	24.1	17	16.9	17	29.3	26.6
Debt–equity ratio	6.7	6.8	6.7	5.1	3.4	5.6	5
Solvency ratio	20.7	20.6	21	23.2	28.7	23.3	24
Quick ratio	4.5	17.5	10	9	10.4	21.8	18.8
ROCE	120.9	139.4	118.1	131.9	151.5	83.8	86.6

Source CMIE Prowess (accessed in 2006).

TABLE D.27 AEC—Chronology

1934	The first thermal power station ("A" Station) with an initial capacity of 7.5 MW consisting of 2 units of 3.75 MW each was installed.
1947–51	"B" Station was installed with a capacity of 60 MW consisting of 4 units of 15 MW each.
1954–58	"C-1" Station was constructed with a capacity of 4 units of 15 MW each, i.e., total 60 MW.
1962	"C-2" Station with capacity of 30 MW.
1963	"C-3" Station with a capacity of 30 MW.
1979	"D" Station with a capacity of 110 MW.
1985	"E" Station with a capacity of 110 MW.
1988	"A" Station was scrapped and disposed off and in its place "F" Station with 110 MW generating capacity was installed and commissioned.
1991	"G" Station Gas based Power plant at Vatva with a capacity of 100 MW was commissioned. 60 MW boiler has been installed at "C-1" station in place of 4 × 15 MW boilers. The company replaced the two existing 30 MW Turbines in "C" Station to match the new boiler.

Source   Author (based on company's information).

AEC distributes power to the twin cities of Ahmedabad and Gandhinagar, spanning an area of 356 sq. km. In 2003–04, AEC distributed over 4 billion units of power to around 1.2 million consumers. AEC has an installed generating capacity of 500 MW, comprising of 400 MW coal based at Sabarmati and 100 MW gas-based dual fuel CCPP at Vatva in Ahmedabad.

AEC adopted a strategy of empowering slum dwellers by providing "legal connections" and reducing AT&C losses. Nearly 1.6 million people, constituting 40 percent in Ahmedabad, lived in slums. Market intelligence revealed the existence of illegal connections and parallel networks resulting in high AT&C losses. In the long term, by March 7, a total of 0.3 million hutments were to be electrified leading to an increase in customer base by 20 percent by tapping this previously ignored segment.

Connections were released under the "Slum Electrification" scheme and AT&C losses were reduced by tapping this energy-intensive segment. Aggressive marketing campaign that deployed distribution of handbills, flyers and booklets, door-to-door canvassing, screening of a specially made film titled *JIVAN NO UJAS*, collaboration with local leaders and NGOs to gain acceptance, providing quick legal power to the applicants, tackling of the power mafia with the help of the police, monitoring of the clusters and regular removal of all illegal cables and connections.

Existing systems were radically simplified. Single window concept at the doorstep of the customer with the help of mobile vans and multiple site offices were introduced. Estimating procedure was abolished and payments were accepted on a "fixed cost" basis. Easy installments were introduced with low down payment.

In 1998, the Torrent Group acquired a 44.49 percent stake in the equity of the company. Financial institutions and nationalized insurance companies hold about 24 percent, the Government of Gujarat holds about 19 percent, and the rest is held by the public.

TABLE D.28 Financials of Ahmedabad Electricity Company (₹ million)

Items	2004	2003	2002	2001	2000
Sales	12,318.2	11,354.2	10,815.6	10,148.4	9,117.1
PBT	819.9	652.2	345.7	271.9	424.5
PAT	465.9	332.9	169.9	235.9	341.9

Source CMIE Prowess (accessed in 2006).

NOVARTIS INDIA

History

On January 5, 1951, the company was incorporated. The company was registered on December 13, 1947, under the name Ciba Pharma Pvt. Ltd., as a wholly owned subsidiary of Ciba Ltd., Basle, Switzerland, to take over the trading business in pharmaceuticals from the parent company's another Indian subsidiary, viz., Ciba (India) Ltd., the name of which was changed later to Ciba Dyes Pvt. Ltd., with effect from March 1, 1948. Ciba Dyes Pvt. Ltd., was registered in India on June 13, 1928, and was dealing in dyestuffs and pharmaceuticals.

The name of the company was again changed to Ciba-Geigy of India Ltd., with effect from October 21, 1970. With effect from January 1, 1983, the name of the company was changed from Ciba-Geigy of India Ltd. to Hindustan Ciba-Geigy Ltd., to reflect the forthcoming change in its status to that of Indian company on eventual reduction of the foreign equity of 40 percent.

From purely trading activities, the company moved to the manufacture of pharmaceutical formulations. Then it undertook the manufacture of a large number of bulk drugs, many involving both high technology and basic manufacture.

On March 7, 1996, an earthshaking announcement was made to the business world: Sandoz and Ciba-Geigy, the two Swiss-based chemical/life sciences giants, had agreed to become one. Novartis, as the new company was called, was at that time the result of the largest corporate merger in history.

Novartis India (NIL), a 51 percent subsidiary of Novartis AG, a Swiss company

In 2002, Novartis was awarded the Prix Galien in France for the second year in succession—this time for Glivec, for first-line treatment of chronic myeloid leukemia.

Pharmaceutical companies are also developing several drug delivery technologies to make therapies easier in terms of treatment and compliance. Novartis led the way with its breakthrough cancer drug Glivec and equally the Glivec International Patient Assistance Program became the most generous and far-reaching access program that has benefited thousands of people, globally, suffering from chronic myeloid leukemia and gastrointestinal stromal tumors. In India, Glivec has provided hope to more than 5,600 people and their families to continue living their lives productively.

In 2003, Novartis united its generics businesses under one single global brand: *Sandoz*.

In 2004, Novartis Medical Nutrition completes the acquisition of the global adult nutrition business of Mead Johnson from Bristol-Myers Squibb. In 2005, Novartis acquires Hexal AG and Eon Labs, creating the world leader in generics.

Novartis is the first European company to receive the Excellence in Corporate Philanthropy Award in recognition of the company's worldwide corporate citizenship activities that benefit millions of patients in need every year.

Operating divisions

The company posted a turnover of ₹4,677 million for FY 2001–02, up 6.7 percent over last year. It attributed this growth to price rise of

2.8 percent and volume growth of 3.9 percent. The turnover breakup in FY 2001–02 is as follows: Pharma contributes 57 percent to the total revenues in FY 2002 followed by Biochemie contributing 26 percent to the total sales. Consumer health and animal health recorded 9 percent and 8 percent sales respectively.

FIGURE D.2 Novartis—Sales Composition (FY 2002)

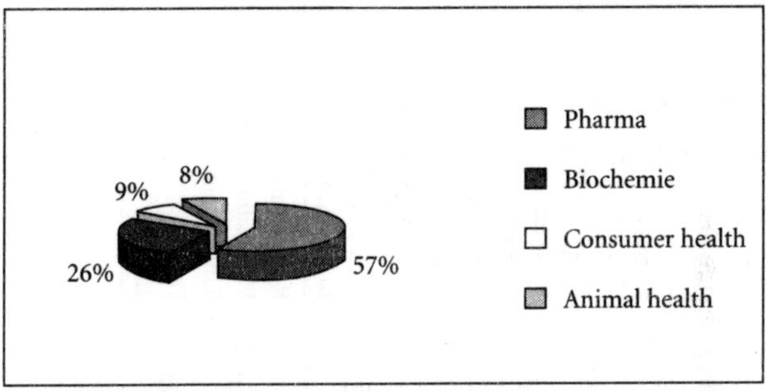

- Pharma: 57%
- Biochemie: 26%
- Consumer health: 9%
- Animal health: 8%

Source Author (based on company's information).

New products well accepted: NIL has introduced eight new products during FY 2002. These products are new generation drugs and are outside the purview of price control and hence offer better margins. The following table indicates the details of new products:

The company introduced nine new products during FY 2001–02. The new products introduced during the last five years contributed around 30 percent to the division turnover while products introduced during the last three years accounted for 15 percent to the division turnover.

The parent company plans to outsource bulk drugs from India but this will be through its 100 percent subsidiary, NPEL (Novartis Pharma Entreprise Ltd).

Corporate citizenship

Novartis financial success over the past 10 years has encouraged it to support several corporate citizenship initiatives on a sustainable basis. The Golden Peacock Award was conferred on it for its innovative services to support elimination of leprosy as well as the Bombay Chamber of Commerce & Industry Award for its work done in tuberculosis.

TABLE D.29 Novartis—Operating Divisions

Division	Products	Brands		
		Brand name	Market share percent	Rank
Pharma division	NIL has a strong presence in the pharma business with strong brands. The company has several major brands occupying significant position in their respective therapeutic segments.	Voveran	12.2	1
		Tegrital	12.5	1
		Methergin	21.2	1
		Macalvit	6.8	6
		Voveran Emulgel	16.4	2
		Brand name	Market share percent	Rank
Biochemie division	The Biochemie division focuses on generic and branded generic products in the area of anti-TB. The company has introduced **Rimactazid Plus** and **4D Plus** new products in the anti-TB segment in FY 2002. Anti-TB drugs constituted 50 percent of the generic sales of Biochemie division in FY 2002. The same is likely to fall to 40 percent due to the introduction of several new products.	Regestrone	12.1	2
		PZA Ciba	38.5	1
		Rimactazid	12.0	2
		Foristal	2.5	4
		4D	4.9	3

		Brand name	Market share percent	Rank
Animal health care division	Eco-friendly fly-control product **Larvadex** has market share of 70 percent and is ranked No. 1 in the segment. The major other brands in the animal health care are: **Carborol, Fasinex, and Protexin**. All these brands occupy the No. 1 rank in their respective segments. This division has registered steady growth for its products.	Calborol/Mifex	30	1
		Larvadex	70	1
		Tiamatin	25	2
		Protexin	40	1
		Fasinex	15	1
		Brand name	Market share percent	Rank
Consumer health care division	The three major products in this division are: **Calcium Sandoz, Sandocal,** and **Otrivin**. Otrivin has 30.3 percent market share and is ranked No.1 in its segment. Calcium Sandoz has market share of 11.1 percent and is ranked second in the category.	Calcium Sandoz	11.1	2
		Otrivin	30.3	6
		Sandocal	5.3	1
		Macalvit	6.8	6
		Voveran Emulgel	16.4	2

Source Author (based on company's information).

TABLE D.30   Novartis—Select Products and Therapeutic Segments

Product name	Therapeutic segment
Miacalcic	Osteoporosis
Visudyne	Muscular degeneration
Zometa	Hypercalcemia
GenTeal	Lubricant for dry eyes
HypoTears plus	Dry eyes
SAS LAR	Acromegaly
Tobrabact	External ocular infection
Glivec	Leukemia

Source   Author (based on company's information).

The Company continues to focus its attention on health and education of the underprivileged. During Community Partnership Week, the employees involved themselves in various social initiatives ranging from field trips for children with special needs and the less privileged, to spending time with the old and the lonely. A mini-NGO mela, organized for employees as a fund-raising effort, drew great appreciation from NGOs and employees alike. The Company's commitment to Health, Safety and Environment (HSE) Protection is also an integral part of its Corporate Citizenship policy.

MICO INDUSTRIES CO. LTD

History

Bosch has grown phenomenally in India, way back since 1922 when the Illies Company established a Bosch agency in the then British India. The founding of Motor Industries Company Limited in 1951 spurred off an accelerated growth in the automotive industry segment which has not stopped till date. Bosch has a strong and voracious presence in the country today at numerous locations in diverse industry segments—both automotive and nonautomotive businesses which include software services, packaging machines, power tools, and security systems.

Incorporated on November 12, 1951, in Chennai and shifted to Bangalore on November 16, 1953, the main objects of the company are

D.31a

TABLE D.31 Financials of Novartis India (₹ million)

	Mar. '92	Mar. '93	Mar. '94	Mar. '95	Mar. '96	Mar. '97	Mar. '98	Mar. '99
Sales	3,358.9	3,937.3	4,407.3	4,693.2	5,160.3	6,132.4	6,733.1	7,575.4
Other income	25.9	35	48.3	102.3	106.5	196.9	180.8	191.1
Change in stocks	249	–152.7	60.2	51.5	213.9	1,97.6	–122.2	238.8
Net sales	3,268.5	3,833.7	4,299.8	4,547.5	4,940.6	5,786	6,390.1	7,141
Total income	3,633.8	3,819.6	4,515.8	4,847	5,480.7	6,526.9	6,791.7	8,005.3
Raw material purchased	993	947.9	939.6	982.3	990.5	1,807.3	1,578	1,841.7
Cost of production	2,743	2,974.6	3,484.4	3,717.2	4,158.7	4,460.7	4,615.8	5,157
Selling cost	260.6	240.1	262.9	286.3	235.8	516.8	518	589.3
Cost of sales	2,750.6	3,349.1	3,692.6	3,948.9	4,178.4	4,874.5	5,131.2	5,513.3
Admin, other costs	146	52.6	80.4	274.9	299.8	600.7	641.5	648.2
Total costs	3,222.6	3,788	4,183.8	4,606.5	4,990.5	6,162	6,512.5	7,066.8
PAT	158.4	142.3	148.4	1,217	237.6	186.1	383.4	746.6
PBDIT	470.2	611.9	556.9	1,577.1	684.1	666.6	925.8	1,358.6
PBDT	386.7	491.7	436.6	1,487.7	600.2	494.4	829	1,313.2
PBIT	399	430	457	1,458.5	541.3	538.3	780.2	1,217
PBT	315.5	309.8	336.7	1,369.1	457.4	366.1	683.4	1,171.6
Cash flow from operations	0	0	0	92.1	14.1	338.6	1,092.4	1,109.3

D.31b

	Mar. '00	Mar. '01	Mar. '02	Mar. '03	Mar. '04	Mar. '05	Mar. '06
Sales	8,312.7	4,463.7	4,739.1	4,837.5	5,202.8	4,887.4	5,382.9
Other income	255.2	227.9	170.9	172.2	172.2	281.3	271.6
Change in stocks	22.2	30.9	12.5	174.9	−231.6	146.2	23.3
Net sales	7,930.9	4,342.7	4,576	4,751.8	5,120.5	4,804.9	5,327.7
Total income	8,590.1	4,722.5	4,922.5	5,184.6	5,143.4	5,314.9	5,677.8
Raw material purchased	1,747.2	34.6	177.5	152.6	196.3	267.1	136.2
Cost of production	5,518.8	3,107.2	3,054.9	3,375.8	3,274.8	3,109.8	3,351.5
Selling cost	634.8	410.2	427.2	451.1	492.8	519	522.5
Cost of sales	6,221.4	3,515.4	3,435.5	3,703.4	3,889.6	3,529	3,855.4
Admin, other costs	469.3	312.8	489.4	590.5	581.9	587.6	612.2
Total costs	7,679.3	4,338.3	4,420.3	4,683.6	4,883.9	4,610.5	4,989.3
PAT	1,034.2	418	653	620	1,137.5	651.2	1,078.9
PBDIT	1,817.5	906.9	1,071	1,092.2	1,599.2	1,114.8	1,629.3
PBDT	1,795.7	785.4	1,038.7	1,083.2	1,564.1	1,061.8	1,569.4
PBIT	1,641	807.1	985.3	924	1,467.6	1,062.6	1,584
PBT	1,619.2	685.6	953	915	1,432.5	1,009.6	1,524.1
Cash flow from operations	1,644.1	814	755.7	816.1	768.2	1,149.1	963.5

D.31c

	Mar. '92	Mar. '93	Mar. '94	Mar. '95	Mar. '96	Mar. '97	Mar. '98	Mar. '99
Current liabilities	420.5	703.9	712.6	737	776.3	1,071.3	1,393.8	1,256.2
Sundry creditors	364.8	345.2	379	357	471.7	713.1	1,094.7	955.1
Creditors for cap. goods	0	0	0	0	0	0	0	0
Accrued interest	1.8	2.5	2.5	1.9	5	7.7	5.3	2.4
Other current liabilities	53.9	356.2	331.1	378.1	299.6	350.5	293.8	298.7
Provisions	44	41.5	41.7	54.4	155.4	367.6	528.8	456
Total liabilities	1,986.2	2,385.6	2,608.9	3,423.1	4,097.1	4,324.5	4,520.2	4,758.8
Gross fixed assets	1,136.1	1,317.9	1,635.2	1,680.3	1,965.2	1,790.3	1,763.8	1,971.7
Land and building	202.4	243.4	263.9	265.2	333.2	429.8	441.2	382.7
Plant and machinery	614.2	898.2	1,021.5	1,233.8	1,322.2	1,097.4	1,073.7	965
Other fixed assets	54.6	58.1	74.8	84.9	105.6	150.4	210.9	348.2
Capital work-in-progress	264.9	118.2	275	96.4	204.2	112.7	38	275.8
Net fixed assets	509.5	547	769.8	753.6	899.5	839.6	810.2	971.9
Investments	56	56	74.5	614.6	473.6	380.5	380.5	380.5

(Table D.31c continued)

(*Table D.31c continued*)

	Mar. '92	Mar. '93	Mar. '94	Mar. '95	Mar. '96	Mar. '97	Mar. '98	Mar. '99
Inventories	777.1	675.9	740.5	808.2	1,055.2	1,429.6	1,235.6	1,432
Cash and bank balance	43.1	29.1	30.5	64.5	11.8	21.3	100.1	109.3
Advances	0	0	0	0	0	0	0	0
Receivables	600.5	737.8	799.7	1,182.2	1,657	1,653.5	1,993.8	1,865.1
Total assets (excl. reval. and dre)	1,970.7	2,042	2,360.3	3,362.7	4,020	4,226.7	4,393.6	4,597.5
Current assets	1,470.7	1,492.8	1,639.3	2,366.5	3,085.8	3,079.2	3,383.6	3,460.5
Quick assets	462.6	561	571.6	1,158.7	1,425.5	874.8	1,223.5	1,171.9
Current liabilities and prov. (incl. bank short)	589.5	1,045.4	1,044.3	1,157	1,456.2	1,918.1	2,134.1	1,942.9
Working capital	881.2	447.4	595	1,209.5	1,629.6	1,161.1	1,249.5	1,517.6
Current ratio	24.9	14.3	15.7	20.5	21.2	16.1	15.9	17.8
Debt–equity ratio	08	12.4	10.7	2.4	4	3.9	1.2	1
Solvency ratio	17.5	14	15.1	27.1	22.9	19.7	21.2	25.2
Quick ratio	7.8	5.4	5.5	10	9.8	4.6	5.7	6
ROCE	355.5	389.6	485.1	234.3	231.9	201.2	333.1	449.9

D.31d

	Mar. '00	Mar. '01	Mar. '02	Mar. '03	Mar. '04	Mar. '05	Mar. '06
Current liabilities	1,972.7	551	550.3	769.4	661.1	724.6	692.7
Sundry creditors	1,115.8	523.4	402.2	432	443.9	518	489.4
Creditors for cap. goods	0	0	0	0	0	0	0
Accrued interest	5.5	20.3	3.5	7.2	1.5	4.8	8.1
Other current liabilities	851.4	7.3	144.6	330.2	215.7	201.8	195.2
Provisions	145.8	472.3	573.3	327.9	496.3	481.2	659.3
Total liabilities	5,542.5	3,832.4	3,526.1	3,803.6	3,776	4,140.8	4,791.1
Gross fixed assets	1,964.1	1,497.6	1,508	1,549.2	896.2	866.5	216.1
Land and building	352.4	446.2	424.5	433.2	171.9	420.1	35.5
Plant and machinery	1,209	921.2	925.7	1,011.9	629.9	1,026.7	123.7
Other fixed assets	357.5	130.1	152	99.6	88.7	70.7	54.8
Capital work-in-progress	45.2	0.1	5.8	4.5	5.7	3.9	2.1
Net fixed assets	925.1	1,180	1,131.7	1,021.1	261.9	220	100.8
Investments	714.4	336.5	387.9	369.9	1,064	475.3	70.8
Inventories	1,401.5	540	547.5	719.7	507.9	658.6	613.1

(Table D.31d continued)

(Table D.31d continued)

	Mar. '00	Mar. '01	Mar. '02	Mar. '03	Mar. '04	Mar. '05	Mar. '06
Cash and bank balance	282	694	181.5	449	86.7	647.5	1,258.5
Advances	0	0	0	0	0	0	0
Receivables	2,209.6	962.6	1,136.8	1,103.1	1,677.5	2,031.1	2,639.8
Total assets (excl. reval. and dre)	5,542.5	3,690.4	3,292.5	3,642.2	3,499.5	3,838.5	4,621.2
Current assets	3,743.4	2,196.8	1,866.1	2,147	2,996	2,817.4	2,876.1
Quick assets	1,447.5	1,152.3	764.4	1,011.4	1,780.5	1,496.8	1,716.2
Current liabilities and prov. (incl. bank short)	2,241.9	1,283.8	1,196.7	1,152.4	1,177.5	1,235.7	1,376.1
Working capital	1,501.5	913	669.4	994.6	1,818.5	1,581.7	1,500
Current ratio	16.7	17.1	15.6	18.6	25.4	22.8	20.9
Debt–equity ratio	0.5	5.7	0.5	0.4	0.2	0.2	0.2
Solvency ratio	24.4	20.2	33.1	35.6	37.2	39.5	37.1
Quick ratio	6.5	9	6.4	8.8	15.1	12.1	12.5
ROCE	489	262.3	366.9	274.7	324.2	353.8	359.4

Source CMIE Prowess (accessed in 2006).

to manufacture spark plugs for petrol engines and fuel injection equipment for diesel engines in technical and financial collaboration with Robert Bosch GmbH, West Germany. Their registered trademark is "MICO."

In 1987, under the modernization program, the company added a number of new machines both at the Bangalore and Nashik factories. Also, a fourth-generation online computer facility was installed at the Bangalore factory.

In 1988, the company was awarded the status of Trading House. The center was appointed as a Bosch Global Development Centre with the global responsibility for design and development of small single cylinder pumps for the entire Bosch Group. The center had already developed a new type of single-cylinder pump for vehicular and stationery applications.

In 1992, the company introduced certain new items such as halogen bulbs, ignition cells, horns, voltage regulators, clutch plates, and clutch cover assemblies for the automobile sector. The company was awarded the ISO 9001 certification by the Technischer Ueberwachungs-Verein, Germany.

In 1993, the company introduced new automotive accessories such as stop-and-tail lamps, fog lamps, and new varieties of horns.

In 1997, the company launched the state-of-the-art Blaupunkt range of car audio systems in June. All the three plants of the company at Bangalore, Nashik, and Naganathapura have been awarded the QS 9000 certificate by TUV, Essen.

In 1998, the company has become a market leader for electrical power tools and accessories.

In 2002, Mico had postponed its investment worth ₹2,500 million because of delay in implementing Euro II emission norms in the country. MICO launched India's first Bosch Car Services Workshop (BCSW) in Delhi and has entered into car servicing business. The company has launched new range of products consisting of in-car multimedia systems, the San Fransisco CD-70; in-car MP3 player; and "velocity" range of amplifiers, speakers, and subwoofers.

In 2005, Bosch moves production of key products to Mico plants in India. Mico also launched the 30 millionth PF pump.

Mico is a market leader in diesel fuel injection equipment and spark plugs.

India operations

Motor Industries Company Limited or Mico is the flagship of Bosch in India. Founded in 1951, the company has emerged to become India's largest auto component manufacturer and a leading exporter. It is the largest manufacturer of diesel fuel injection equipment in the country. It dominates the commercial vehicle and utility vehicle market with these systems.

In addition, Mico also manufactures industrial equipment, auto electricals, and hydraulic gear pumps for tractor applications. It also markets Blaupunkt car multimedia systems and Bosch security systems. The company contributes 0.8 percent to the parent's global revenues.

Diverse business areas include common rail injectors and components, diesel fuel injection equipment, industrial equipment, auto electricals, gear pumps for tractor applications, electric power tools, packaging machines, security technology products, and Blaupunkt car audio systems.

The corporate office is located at Bangalore, India, with state-of-the-art ISO and TS 16949 certified manufacturing plants at Bangalore, Naganathapura (near Bangalore), Nashik, and Jaipur. Of these, the Nashik and Naganathapura plants are export-oriented units.

Operating divisions

The company has four manufacturing facilities—Bangalore, Naganathapura (near Bangalore), Nashik, and Jaipur—and manufactures products as diverse as industrial equipment, auto electricals, hydraulics for industrial and tractor applications, electric power tools, packaging machines, and Blaupunkt car audio systems.

Sales distribution

The nationwide network of Motor Industries spanning across 1,000 towns and with over 4,000 authorized representations ensures widespread availability of both after-sales services and products.

Strategy

Mico derives 45 percent of its revenues supplying to the OEM segment, which includes major players such as Tata Motors, Ashok Leyland, Mahindra and Mahindra, Eicher, and Escorts.

TABLE D.32 Mico—Operating Divisions

Division	Product	Areas of operation
Diesel Systems Division	Diesel Fuel Injection Equipment (FIE) has been the core business of Mico, right from its inception in 1951. Today Mico continues to be a supplier of FIE to a majority of Original Equipment Manufacturers (OEMs) with a market share of over 81 percent.	Mico has also earned a place for itself in the Bosch world, where it has been identified as Center of Competence for Single Cylinder pumps, Multi-Cylinder Inline ("A" type) and Distributor pumps. In addition to the existing range of mechanical pumps, Mico with the support from Bosch is actively working on introducing Electronic Diesel Control (EDC) systems in India.
Gasoline Systems Division	To be the preferred partner in India for gasoline engine management systems. To this end, Mico offers its customers top-class technology, high-quality products and services, with a dedicated team experienced to cater to the requirements and needs of the Indian customer.	Technical Sales Application Manufacture Product service
Car Multimedia Division	The Car Multimedia Division (Blaupunkt) proves that name and brand can be identical. The blue spot, or "blauer Punkt" in German, stands for technical competence in car multimedia on the road.	Blaupunkt GmbH, a Hildesheim-based subsidiary of Bosch, is the European market leader for car radios. The company currently employs approximately 7,500 staff worldwide, of whom some 2,800 work in Hildesheim, Germany. The company makes more than five million car radios per year and 500,000-plus navigation systems.
Automotive Aftermarket Division	The Automotive Aftermarket Division, moreover, is responsible for the Bosch Car Service workshop concept, and the global technical after-sales service for Bosch automotive products and systems.	

Source Author (based on company's information).

Currently, in the passenger vehicle market, Bosch systems are being fitted on vehicles of Mahindra and Mahindra, though Tata Motors—the other major player—has opted for Delphi as its supplier.

Tata is one of the biggest customers for Mico in the commercial vehicle segment.

The company began production for CRDi systems and injectors in 2006 by investing ₹6,000 million. The CRDi technology, being cleaner and more efficient, is expected to rule the market in the coming years.

The positive factors for Mico also include the fact that several leading car manufacturers like Mercedes and Hyundai are driving in their CRDi versions in India. Also, it expects commercial vehicles to run on CRDi diesel in the coming years, forced by higher and stricter emission norms.

The company faces competition from Delphi, Rane Engine Valves Ltd, Banco Products (India) Ltd, Autoline Industries Ltd, and Federal Moghul Goetze Ltd.

KIRLOSKARS BROTHERS LTD

Incorporated on January 15, 1920, Kirloskar Brothers Ltd (KBL) is into the production of industrial pumps, projects and engineered pumps, agriculture and domestic pumps, valves, hydro turbines, and anti-corrosion products.

It is the largest manufacturer and exporter of pumps in India and a leader in providing solutions to fluid handling problems. Its focus on developing precisely engineered solutions to solve complex fluid handling problems has given the company a great reputation across the globe.

It is a leading motor pumps maker, but over the last few years it has transformed itself into an engineering, procurement, and construction contractor for infrastructure projects. The major sectors to which it caters to are (*i*) utilities like power, water supply, and sewerage; (*ii*) irrigation; (*iii*) fire fighting; (*iv*) process industries like refining, petrochemicals, fertilizers, chemicals, sugar, etc.; and (*v*) agriculture.

The company's plants are located at Kirloskarvadi, Kondhapuri, and Shirval in Maharashtra and Dewas in Madhya Pradesh.

It has a strong sales distribution network comprising 16 domestic regional offices and 7 overseas offices located at Cambodia, Egypt, Germany,

D.33a

TABLE D.33 Financials of Mico Industries Co. Ltd (₹ million)

	Mar. '92	Mar. '93	Mar. '94	Mar. '95	Mar. '96	Mar. '97	Mar. '98	Mar. '99
Sales	4,123.8	5,280.8	5,664.6	7,326.2	9,368.1	11,699.3	13,791.1	13,026.8
Other income	84.1	117.7	157	188.5	239.1	200.8	199.2	268.9
Change in stocks	19.4	20.8	21.6	104.2	105.2	87	40.1	45.4
Net sales	3,595.4	4,630.4	5,099.3	6,482.1	8,368.4	10,653.7	12,500.7	11,946
Total income	4,227.3	5,419.3	5,843.2	7,618.9	9,712.4	11,987.1	14,030.4	13,341.1
Raw material purchased	1,024.4	1,202.7	1,192.4	1,856.4	2,359.4	2,990.4	3,290.3	3,038.4
Cost of production	2,942.3	3,801.8	4,280.9	5,237.6	6,637.3	8,706.7	10,216.3	10,194.3
Selling cost	100.9	124.5	209.4	311	320.5	415.8	434.9	297.2
Cost of sales	3,034.6	3,912.6	4,476.7	5,470.9	6,938.5	9,086.1	10,608.4	10,406.3
Admin, other costs	288.5	405.2	407	571.3	696.2	894.9	998.4	1,008.5
Total costs	4,145.2	5,399.2	5,881.5	7,483.8	9,414.9	11,819.2	13,656.6	13,106.1
PAT	154.9	187	246.2	368.9	525.8	609	802.5	698.6
PBDIT	823.3	1,143.8	1,272.8	1,643.6	2,139.3	2,501	2,988.4	2,683
PBDT	749.6	1,017.8	1,125.3	1,516.1	2,008.8	2,313.4	2,829	2,552.5
PBIT	448.6	618	678.7	966.4	1,306.3	1,401.6	1,561.9	1,309.1
PBT	374.9	492	531.2	838.9	1,175.8	1,214	1,402.5	1,178.6

D.33b

	Mar. '00	Mar. '01	Mar. '02	Mar. '03	Mar. '04	Mar. '05	Mar. '06
Sales	15,148.8	16,574.4	16,139.4	17,383.8	21,319.4	26,219.3	33,245.2
Other income	446.2	398	408	366.5	497.6	706.5	941.8
Change in stocks	60.7	932.3	−602.3	−117.3	287.3	165.6	715.5
Net sales	13,651.4	14,738	14,562.2	15,734.3	19,197.6	23,663.4	30,016.2
Total income	15,655.7	17,904.7	15,945.1	17,633	22,104.3	27,091.4	34,902.5
Raw material purchased	3,581.1	4,487.1	3,333.8	3,974.6	5,661	7,948.7	10,287.7
Cost of production	10,874.8	12,067.3	11,639.4	12,084.3	13,978.9	16,675.4	23,930
Selling cost	562.1	603.3	583.5	713.9	596.5	679.5	1,092.6
Cost of sales	11,424.8	12,173.7	12,640.6	12,833.7	14,359.3	17,208.7	24,474.3
Admin, other costs	1,199.8	1,288.9	1,289.4	1,482.7	1,495.2	1,963.3	2,297.4
Total costs	14,853.2	16,054.2	16,156.6	16,793.5	19,674.9	23,954.6	32,297.9
PAT	1,057.8	1,120.8	817.2	1,350.7	2,350.4	3,747.7	3,430.7
PBDIT	3,166.4	3,404.5	2,800.4	3,436.7	5,065	6,963.2	7,708.8
PBDT	3,085.2	3,305	2,766	3,328.1	4,976.4	6,876.5	7,527.1
PBIT	1,789	1,876	1,466.6	2,364.3	4,049	5,974.4	5,727.9
PBT	1,707.8	1,776.5	1,432.2	2,255.7	3,960.4	5,887.7	5,546.2
Cash flow from operations	2,898.6	2,118.8	3,198.5	4,678.8	4,472.5	5,930.2	6,145.2

D.33c

	Mar. '92	Mar. '93	Mar. '94	Mar. '95	Mar. '96	Mar. '97	Mar. '98	Mar. '99
Current liabilities	674.4	821.2	911.3	1,352.1	1,933.6	2,121.1	2,561.6	2,605.2
Sundry creditors	667.1	801.4	894.2	1,338.1	1,921.2	2,097.3	1,698.5	2,009.3
Creditors for cap. goods	0	0	0	0	0	0	0	0
Accrued interest	2.2	4.9	4.5	3.2	2.1	1.4	0.2	0.1
Other current liabilities	5.1	14.9	12.6	10.8	10.3	22.4	862.9	595.8
Provisions	151.7	149	243.2	464.9	541.7	584.1	693.3	539.6
Total liabilities	2,716.5	3,090.9	3,254.7	4,304.1	5,456.9	6,255.2	7,673.7	8,097.1
Gross fixed assets	2,974.5	3,704.2	4,336	5,079.4	6,456.7	8,105.8	10,409.4	11,555.3
Land and building	277.4	335.6	376.2	390.6	446.7	624.8	910.1	1,099.2
Plant and machinery	2,497.1	3,149.4	3,707.8	4,383.2	5,458.6	6,698.7	8,449.2	9,373.1
Other fixed assets	66.5	76.7	92.3	109	133.9	191.5	290.9	302.6
Capital work-in-progress	133.5	142.5	159.7	196.6	417.5	590.8	759.2	780.4
Net fixed assets	1,040.8	1,263.8	1,334.8	1,461.1	2,070.5	2,673.8	3,610.8	3,592.4
Investments	339.6	363.2	484.3	918.6	862.8	516.7	614.9	567.3
Inventories	488.3	498.8	491.4	796.4	1,111	1,194.1	1,210.3	1,060.5

	Mar. '92	Mar. '93	Mar. '94	Mar. '95	Mar. '96	Mar. '97	Mar. '98	Mar. '99
Cash and bank balance	148	107.6	28.8	19.4	52.1	16.2	76.6	561.9
Advances	0	0	0	0	0	0	0	0
Receivables	699.8	857.5	915.4	1,108.6	1,360.5	1,854.4	2,161.1	2,315
Total assets (excl. reval. and dre)	2,716.5	3,090.9	3,254.7	4,304.1	5,456.9	6,255.2	7,673.7	8,097.1
Current assets	1,675.3	1,812.9	1,919.5	2,841.6	3,385.1	3,367.4	3,784.2	4,123.5
Quick assets	1,026.6	1,149.2	1,257.4	1,749.1	1,908	1,632	1,997.6	2,347.4
Current liabilities and prov. (incl. bank short)	1,014.9	1,291.8	1,234.7	2,076.7	2,820.6	2,887	3,430.8	3,422.4
Working capital	660.4	521.1	684.8	764.9	564.5	480.4	353.4	701.1
Current ratio	16.5	14	15.5	13.7	12	11.7	11	12
Debt–equity ratio	5	5.3	3.4	3.4	3	2.7	2.6	2.1
Solvency ratio	18.6	18.1	19.2	17.6	17.3	18.1	18.4	20.3
Quick ratio	10.1	8.9	10.2	8.4	6.8	5.7	5.8	6.9
ROCE	269.7	338.4	313.3	407.1	515	411.8	373.4	245.6

D.33d

	Mar. '00	Mar. '01	Mar. '02	Mar. '03	Mar. '04	Mar. '05	Mar. '06
Current liabilities	2,964.7	2,441.4	2,359.9	3,406.7	3,974	4,648.2	6,759.2
Sundry creditors	2,277.3	1,608.9	1,462	2,076.9	2,146.2	2,872.9	4,345.9
Creditors for cap. goods	0	0	0	0	0	0	0
Accrued interest	00.1	0	0	0	0	0	0
Other current liabilities	687.3	832.5	897.9	1,329.8	1,827.8	1,775.3	2,413.3
Provisions	609.6	1,467.5	1,855.9	2,057	2,352.6	3,096.5	36,369
Total liabilities	9,030.2	9,850.5	11,054.3	13,266.6	16,455.2	21,762.7	27,612.6
Gross fixed assets	12,641.4	13,665.4	13,948.2	14,428.1	14,514.6	15,515.9	19,109.1
Land and building	1,348.4	1,463.1	1,484.9	1,464.4	1,468.5	1,545.6	1,971.2
Plant and machinery	10,317.2	11,271.4	11,746.5	12,309.2	12,362.9	12,718	15,518.4
Other fixed assets	380.1	444.4	468	489.6	539.5	608.7	735
Capital work-in-progress	595.7	486.5	248.8	164.9	143.7	643.6	884.5
Net fixed assets	3,521.7	3,197.6	2,711.9	2,455.1	2,065.6	2,589.1	4,711.4
Investments	1,020.9	687.9	1,017.1	1,666.9	2,914.7	5,541.1	5,208.2
Inventories	1,221	2,478.2	1,660.1	1,520.1	2,213.1	2,841	3,768.5

	Mar. '00	Mar. '01	Mar. '02	Mar. '03	Mar. '04	Mar. '05	Mar. '06
Cash and bank balance	579.9	635.9	1,399.9	3,351.4	4,891.6	4,958.2	5,831
Advances	0	0	0	0	0	0	0
Receivables	2,686.7	2,850.9	2,986.3	2,862.1	2,881.9	4,136	6,519.5
Total assets (excl. reval. and dre)	9,030.2	9,850.5	11,054.3	13,266.6	16,455.2	21,762.7	27,612.6
Current assets	5,107.7	6,075.8	7,012.3	9,149.4	12,847.3	16,842.2	19,968.2
Quick assets	3,031.2	2,635.7	4,527.5	6,710.6	9,749.8	12,591.8	14,658.2
Current liabilities and prov. (incl. bank short)	3,574.3	4,387.1	4,341.3	5,642.6	6,508.6	7,988.8	10,576.1
Working capital	1,533.4	1,688.7	2,671	3,506.8	6,338.7	8,853.4	9,392.1
Current ratio	14.3	13.8	16.2	16.2	19.7	21.1	18.9
Debt–equity ratio	0.8	1.4	0.8	1.1	1.1	1.2	1.1
Solvency ratio	22.7	21.3	23.5	21.4	22.5	23.6	22.8
Quick ratio	8.5	6	10.4	11.9	15	15.8	13.9
ROCE	334.7	36.2	208.8	313.2	446.7	455.7	292.8

Source CMIE Prowess (accessed in 2006).

Kenya, Lao PDR, South Africa, and the UAE. Direct business constitutes 70 percent of its business. The remaining 30 percent comes through its dealers.

The projects pumps business constitutes 59 percent, industrial pumps 18 percent, agriculture and domestic pumps 17 percent, and others 6 percent. Exports constitute 13 percent of the company's sales and the same is expected to increase in future due to increase in demand from Asian, Latin American, and African countries.

The pumps industry in India is more than seven decades old. Though it has a turnover of ₹25,000 million (2005 figures), the size is not even 7 percent of the size of the US market. More than 500 manufacturers of pumps in the country together produce more than 1.2 million pumps every year. The industry meets 95 percent of the domestic demand. The Indian pump industry is characterized by the coexistence of large number of SSI units, some large manufacturers like KBL and KBS pumps, and plenty of foreign manufacturers.

Domestically, multinational companies have attempted for a greater manufacturing and marketing presence, including participation in large tenders floated by the government under infrastructure development plans related to water supply, irrigation, and power. In case of agriculture sector, most of the players in the unorganized sector enjoy the cover of factors such as, the availability of subsidy and cheap or free power, and vulnerability of uninformed farmers. In spite of the above, KBL has been successful in maintaining a leadership position in the market.

TABLE D.34 Pumps Industry in India—Major Players

Company	Sales (₹ million)	PAT (₹ million)	Market cap (₹ million)
Kirloskar Brothers Ltd.	9,201.2	1,723.9	38,609.3
KSB Pumps Ltd.	4,065.7	516.5	8,426.1
Mather & Platt Pumps Ltd.	1,313.7	85.8	2,242.5
Shakti Pumps (India) Ltd.	410.7	21.0	656.6
WPIL Ltd	732.6	5.2	437.0

Source Author (based on business research).

TABLE D.35 Financials of Kirloskar Brothers Ltd (₹ crore)

D.35a

Profit and loss	Mar. '92	Mar. '93	Mar. '94	Mar. '95	Mar. '96	Mar. '97	Mar. '98	Mar. '99
Sales	191.28	222.84	205.86	212.87	269.1	319.25	337.53	340.42
Other income	2.7	4.48	5.59	6.98	6.03	8.09	6.87	10.18
Change in stocks	0.12	2.09	−9.58	6.54	10.29	−0.51	1.48	0.74
Net sales	189.12	220.95	204.72	211.58	267.83	317.83	336.1	337.75
Total income	194.1	229.41	201.87	226.39	285.42	326.83	345.88	351.34
Raw material purchased	71.52	79.21	54.81	78.01	125.94	131.95	130.19	119.51
Cost of production	148.21	175.6	159.29	174.82	220.17	249.84	255.46	245.87
Selling cost	5.26	9.36	9.55	9.97	11.83	16.61	17.15	18.53
Cost of sales	153.47	184.96	175.13	183.62	225.66	266.45	269.86	264.76
Administrative and other costs	18.77	21.28	20.45	21.3	23.91	28.4	42.18	42.77
Total costs	188.08	223.22	209.16	217.82	269.82	317.65	334.78	334
PAT	6.19	18.02	2.7	2.97	6.74	10.85	10.74	16.13
PBDIT	22.53	36.31	18.31	18.29	29.94	37.36	37.77	46.66
PBDT	14.81	24.22	7.85	8.48	14.61	18.52	19.31	27.86
PBIT	19.87	33.11	15.14	14.58	25.72	32.29	32.05	39.93
PBT	12.15	21.02	4.68	4.77	10.39	13.45	13.59	21.13
Cash flow from operations	0	0	0	4.37	10.06	3.6	16.66	37.27

D.35b

Profit and loss	Mar. '00	Mar. '01	Mar. '02	Mar. '03	Mar. '04	Mar. '05	Mar. '06
Sales	371.49	426.31	385.69	492.11	528.95	758.62	956.55
Other income	7.27	9.4	11	8.56	23.27	15.77	21.37
Change in stocks	-3.81	-9.01	14.57	-17.32	4.3	8.31	16.1
Net sales	370.07	414.71	372.86	473.2	505.59	727.21	919.64
Total income	374.95	426.7	411.26	483.35	556.52	782.7	994.02
Raw material purchased	161.66	157.9	149.26	184.1	206.63	261.74	328.83
Cost of production	285.85	322.83	293.04	383.36	412.31	585.37	717.36
Selling cost	13.6	17.3	20.34	28.98	23.74	49.4	46.14
Cost of sales	297.76	343.91	316.24	410.96	434.95	631.36	749.67
Administrative and other costs	45.97	44.56	34.44	37.71	38.87	46.26	53.76
Total costs	361.43	426.65	384.8	486.81	520.26	728.35	869
PAT	12.49	14.04	12.28	14.26	26.49	50.73	172.39
PBDIT	35.98	48.4	41.89	42.93	60.25	80.31	212.96
PBDT	24	26.62	24.11	28.86	47.22	67.03	198.27
PBIT	28.77	40.62	33.56	33.49	49.57	70.31	203.29
PBT	16.79	18.84	15.78	19.42	36.54	57.03	188.6
Cash flow from operations	17.94	38.82	57.34	35.43	35.89	64.57	87.24

D.35c

Balance sheet	Mar. '92	Mar. '93	Mar. '94	Mar. '95	Mar. '96	Mar. '97	Mar. '98	Mar. '99
Current liabilities	54.6	57.66	65.47	71.88	99.71	95.62	75.22	82.06
Sundry creditors	39.34	54.56	50.65	52.91	77.09	68.39	56.67	67.82
Creditors for cap. goods	0	0	0	0	0	0	0	0
Accrued interest	1.34	1.38	1.68	1.59	2.04	2.54	2.8	1.93
Other current liabilities	13.92	1.72	13.14	17.38	20.58	24.69	15.75	12.31
Provisions	13.94	19.86	18.42	21.95	25.63	28.76	31.95	40.08
Total liabilities	137.06	168.71	162.14	214.13	287.28	310.6	327.47	349.6
Gross fixed assets	42.01	49.67	49.1	59.07	70.63	79.08	93.58	103.99
Land and building	6.26	6.91	6.24	9.11	10.06	12.44	16.39	17.52
Plant and machinery	32.86	38.76	37.75	42.98	52.97	61.16	69.67	77.15
Other fixed assets	2.36	2.73	3.89	4.1	4.12	4.24	5.67	6.66
Capital work-in-progress	0.53	1.27	1.22	2.88	3.48	1.24	1.85	2.66
Net fixed assets	20.44	25.03	24.18	30.74	38.21	41.82	50.93	54.99
Investments	4.87	7.16	21.74	50.3	72.5	65.83	65.86	75.14

Inventories	42.63	49.33	34.28	42.95	52.96	50.67	51.57	48.17
Cash and bank balance	1.29	2.38	4.86	2.6	4.74	4.43	13.95	7.42
Advances	0	0	0	0	0	0	0	0
Receivables	67.83	84.81	77.08	87.54	118.87	147.85	145.16	163.88
Total assets (excl. reval. and dre)	123.88	168.03	145.27	195.21	265.94	285.54	298.92	316.62
Current assets	111.75	136.37	116.93	133.97	185.54	204.68	209.53	218.65
Quick assets	38.44	63.93	45.24	52.38	77.97	91.83	82.36	84.62
Current liabilities and prov. (incl. bank short)	88.8	102.85	95.45	115.79	149.55	155.95	139.86	167.92
Working capital	22.95	33.52	21.48	18.18	35.99	48.73	69.67	50.73
Current ratio	1.26	1.33	1.23	1.16	1.24	1.31	1.5	1.3
Debt–equity ratio	1.95	1.27	0.87	0.76	0.77	0.87	1.06	0.9
Solvency ratio	1.23	1.31	1.4	1.54	1.53	1.53	1.56	1.61
Quick ratio	0.43	0.62	0.47	0.45	0.52	0.59	0.59	0.5
Return on capital employed	47.81	34.33	22.81	17.52	21.12	21.9	18.73	22.17

D.35d

Balance sheet	Mar. '00	Mar. '01	Mar. '02	Mar. '03	Mar. '04	Mar. '05	Mar. '06
Current liabilities	99.44	110.52	166.18	193.68	510.33	345.98	504.01
Sundry creditors	85.17	89.1	123.47	145.91	173.43	235.54	330.32
Creditors for cap. goods	0	0	0	0	0	0	0
Accrued interest	0.1	3.34	3.08	2.05	0.85	0.34	2.58
Other current liabilities	14.17	18.08	39.63	45.72	336.05	110.1	171.11
Provisions	41.64	62.31	49.93	53.9	18.87	30.02	36.83
Total liabilities	395.79	428.97	474.32	506.49	801.58	638.21	888.05
Gross fixed assets	116.11	128.5	135.86	142.74	136.4	140.09	184.97
Land and building	21.43	22.98	22.91	24.98	24.86	25.07	25.65
Plant and machinery	83.26	91.89	103.33	106.49	99.53	102.46	131.68
Other fixed assets	7.29	7.43	7.64	9.86	10.57	11.45	11.4
Capital work-in-progress	4.13	6.2	1.98	1.41	1.44	1.11	16.24
Net fixed assets	60.52	66.43	65.72	65.54	55.86	52.98	94.87
Investments	74.65	70.61	70.38	70.44	94.78	82.83	101.44

Inventories	46.78	32.53	41.31	31.67	321.47	82.13	88.3
Cash and bank balance	12.38	32.7	30.22	35.31	8.66	58.27	50.25
Advances	0	0	0	0	0	0	0
Receivables	201.46	224.84	262.97	297.05	313.43	354.15	544.65
Total assets (excl. reval. and dre)	358.44	384.41	428.52	458.58	801.58	638.21	885.29
Current assets	259.88	289.34	330.48	360.3	613.92	493.75	682.95
Quick assets	102.3	136.28	134.69	146	147.74	239.52	294.17
Current liabilities and prov. (incl. bank short)	193.82	213.65	263.75	306.23	583.87	407.93	547.16
Working capital	66.06	75.69	66.73	54.07	30.05	83.48	135.79
Current ratio	1.34	1.35	1.25	1.18	1.05	1.21	1.25
Debt-equity ratio	0.98	0.85	0.76	0.63	0.62	0.35	0.08
Solvency ratio	1.56	1.56	1.54	1.55	1.27	1.45	1.57
Quick ratio	0.53	0.64	0.51	0.48	0.25	0.59	0.54
Return on capital employed	17.7	18.4	16.13	16.99	27.51	30.28	49.46

Source CMIE Prowess (accessed in 2006).
Note 1 crore = 10 million.

Notes and References

CHAPTER 1

1. *Business & Economy*. 2006. "The Rise, Fall and Rise of Indian Business Families," Special Issue, *Business & Economy*, December 1–14.

CHAPTER 2

1. Shergill, G.S. and Revti Raman. 1994. "The Extent and Nature of Diversification in Indian Companies," January–June, *The Decision*, 21 (1 & 2), 97–114.
2. Shah, A.M. 2000. "Critical Success Factors and Effective Strategies in the New Environment," April–June, *Vikalpa*, 25 (2): 31–41.
3. Porter, Michael. 1985. *Competitive Advantage*. New York: Free Press.
4. Karki, Rajnish. 2004. "Corporate Strategy of Indian Organizations: The 'Root-Branch' Framework," July–September, *Vikalpa*, 29 (3): 1–13.

CHAPTER 3

1. *Business Today*. 1998. India's Business Families: The Survival Model," *Business Today*, January 7–February 6, p. 52.
2. *Business World*, April 9, 2007, p. 87.
3. *Business Line*, February 2, 2007, p.
4. www.icicidirect.com and www.bombaydyeing.com (accessed April 2005).
5. www.icicidirect.com and www.mahindra.com (accessed May 2005).
6. www.icicidirect.com and www.excideindustries.com (accessed May 2005).
7. www.icicidirect.com and www.excideindustries.com (accessed May 2005).
8. *The Economic Times*, March 3, 2007.
9. Jaykar, Roshni. 1998. "Can B.K-K.M Birla Survive?," *Business Today*, January 7–February 6, p. 114.
10. *Business Today* (1998, p. 114); *KRChoksey Research Report*, April 4, 2000.

11. A renowned industry analyst firm based in US.
12. Irani, Jamshed J. 2001. "Transforming Organizations—The Tata Steel Experience," July–September, *Vikalpa*, 26 (3): 1–5.
13. INGRES Database and *ICRA Research Report on Petrochemicals*, June 2005.
14. Sridharan, R. 1998. "Can Apollo Survive?" *Business Today*, January 7–February 6, p. 314.
15. *Business World*, April 9, 2007, p. 68.
16. Apollo Tyres Ltd, *Annual Report, 2003–04*.
17. *Business World*. 2003. "Busting Business Cycles," *Business World*, June 23.
18. www.bombaydyeing.com (accessed April 2005).
19. www.mahindra.com (accessed May 2005)
20. www.apollotyres.com
21. www.exideindustries.com (accessed May 2005).

CHAPTER 4

1. Rajpal, Suresh and Ravi-Raj Sagar. 2003. "Business Excellence in the Indian Scenario," October–December, *Vikalpa*, 28 (4): 77–81.
2. Tata Chemicals Ltd. 2004. *Annual Report*, 2003–04, Tata Chemicals Ltd, Mumbai.
3. Chakraborty, Sujata. 2002. "The Taj's Stars Shine Bright." Available online at http://www.tata.com/company/Articles/inside.aspx?artid=PYCTRjzfsuU=
4. Chakravorthy, Gautam. 1998. "Can N. Wadia Survive?,"*Business Today*, January 7–February 6, p. 72.
5. www.mahindra.com.
6. Apollo Tyres Ltd. 2004. *Annual Report, 2002–03*. Gurgaon: Apollo Tyres Ltd.
7. *Business Today*, January 7–February 6, 1998, p. 81.
8. www.sundaram.com.

CHAPTER 5

1. *Business & Economy*. 2006. "The Rise, Fall and Rise of Indian Business Families," Special Issue, December 1–14, pg. 66.
2. *Business and Economy*. 2006. "India's 100 Most Profitable Companies," *Business & Economy*, September 22–October 5.
3. Ahmad, Abad. 2005. *Best of the Best—Insight from Leading International and Indian Organizations*. New Delhi: AIMA.
4. Chakravorthy, Gautam. 1998. "Can N. Wadia Survive?" *Business Today*, January 7–February 6, p. 73.

5. Ibid., p. 71.
6. *Business & Economy*. "Rise, Fall and Rise," 67.
7. Piramal, Gita. 1997. *Business Maharajas*. New Delhi: Penguin Books.
8. *Business & Economy*. "Rise, Fall and Rise," 66.
9. Ibid., p. 67.
10. *Business & Economy*. "Rise, Fall and Rise," 67.
11. Fernand, Larissa. 1998. "Can Mahindra Survive?" *Business Today*, January 7–February 6, p. 287.
12. *Business & Economy*. "Rise, Fall and Rise," 69.
13. *Business & Economy*. "Rise, Fall and Rise," 68.

CHAPTER 7

1. BT 500—India's most valuable companies.
2. Ahmed, Abad. 2004. *Passion to Win*. New Delhi: AIMA Publication.
3. *Business Today*, 7–21 March 1992.
4. *Business Today*, 9 November 2003.
5. *Business and Economy*. 2006. "India's 100 Most Profitable Companies," *Business & Economy*, September 22–October 5.
6. Sheth, Jagdish. 2004. "Making India Globally Competitive," October–December, *Vikalpa*, 29 (4): 1–9.

APPENDIX B

1. Business Today. 2003. "How We Identified India's Best Managed Company," Business Today, June 22, pp. 60–61.
2. Nathan, Narendra. 2003. "The 16 Finalists," *Business Today*, June 22, pp. 62–74.

APPENDIX C

1. Peters, Tom. *In Search for Excellence*.
2. Kennedy, Carol and Duff, Amy. 2003. *Director*, 57 (5): 34, 1/6p.

3. Bogner, William C. 2002. "Tom Peters on Real World of Business," *Academy of Business Executive* 16 (1): 40–44.
4. Fogg, Stephen L. 1985. "Current Reading," October, *Journal of Accountancy*, p. 177.
5. Peters, Tom. *Passion for Excellence.*
6. Collins, Jim and Jerry Porras. 1995. *Built to Last.*
7. Collins, Jim. *Good to Great.*

Index

100 Most Profitable Companies, 175

Abhishek Industries, 38
Aditya Birla Group, 144
   business portfolio, 148–149
   Cash Value Added method, 148
   performance on various parameters, 148
   policy and operational changes, 147–148
   retirement policy, 147–148
agro-based industry, 20, 143, 169, 178
Ahmedabad Electricity, 11, 15, 20, 169, 177, 178
Alcan, 73, 147
ammonia, 88, 91
Analysis of Variance (ANOVA), 109
Andhra Valley Power Supply Company Ltd., 126
Apollo Radial World, 97
Apollo Tyres, 12, 21
   agreement with Continental AG, Germany, 49
   business portfolio, 156
   cost leadership, through economies of scale, 84–87
   cost management, 115
   D/E ratio, 87
   ERP system, implementation of, 115
   exports of LCV and farm tyres, 46
   family dynamics, 155
   global growth, 46–51
   history, 153–154
   leadership skills, 155–156
   as market leader in the replacement tyre market, 46
   openness to change, 154–155
   operational efficiency, 85
   PAT, 50
   PBDIT/total income, 86
   Research & Development, 115
   sales distribution network, 97
   strategic alliance with Michelin, 51
   technology alliances, 88
   total income, 46, 48–49
Apollo Tyre World, 97
Associated Battery Manufacturers (Ceylon) Limited, 52

Bajaj Hindusthan, 11, 20, 24, 169, 172, 177, 178
BCG Matrix, 142
Best of the Best—Insight from Leading International and Indian Organizations (2005), 12
Birla, Aditya Vikram, 144–146
Birla, G.D., 2, 143
Birla, Kumar Mangalam, 145, 146–147
Bombay Burmah Trading Corporation, 142
Bombay Dyeing & Manufacturing Co Ltd., 15, 111–112, 178
   business portfolio, 142–143
   cost leadership, through economies of scale, 79–84
   cotton and animal fiber, 38
   D/E ratio, 83
   dimethyl terephthalate (DMT), 38, 79, 112, 142

Index | 371

export strategy, 79
global growth, 37–40
growth in total income, 39–40
history, 140–141
labor costs, 79
leadership skills and openness to change, 141–142
Malcolm Baldridge Award, 112
PAT, 38, 41
PBDIT/total income, 82
products distribution in foreign countries, 37
purified terepthalic acid (PTA), 79
retail distribution system, 141
sales distribution network, 96–97
SRTEPC and TEXPROCIL Gold Trophies, for outstanding export performance, 37
total income, 38
Total Quality Management (TQM), 112
brand equity, 29, 42, 44, 117, 176
brand names, 94, 96–97, 124, 141, 143
Bridgestone, 46, 49, 84
Britannia Industries, 142
British Safety Council, 109
BSE 500 index, 173
Built to Last (1995), 5
Burmah Oil, 129
business family groups
competition from the MNCs, 4
performance of
data and methodology for studying, 6–10
objectives for studying, 5–6
statistics of, 4
Business Maharajas (1996), 12
business model, themes of, 13–14, 22–26, 179–180
Business Process Reengineering (BPR), 13, 25, 113–115
Business Today (BT), 4, 171, 173

capital market, liberalization of, 2–3
Cash Earnings per share (EPS), 175
Castrol India, 49
Ceat, 49, 51, 84
cellular manufacturing, principle of, 114
channel management, 44, 113
chemical industry, 128–129
Civil Engineering Works, 61, 119–120, 161, 162
CMIE's Prowess database, 6
Cold Rolling Mill (CRM), 130
Collins, Jim, 5–6, 170, 176
companies
critical success factors, 21
with dominant domestic market shares, 20
going global, 16–19, 28–29
Apollo Tyres, 46–51
Bombay Dyeing, 37–40
Exide Industries Limited, 52–59
Gammon India Ltd (GIL), 61–64
Hindalco, 59
Indian Hotel Corporation Ltd (IHCL), 29–31
Larsen & Toubro (L&T), 64–68
Mahindra & Mahindra (M&M), 40–46
Siemens Ltd, 68–70
Sundaram Fasteners (SFL), 51–52
Tata Steel (TISCO), 31–37
Tinplate, 59–61
quest for operational efficiencies, 25
compound annual total returns, 8–9, 168
Construction World, 64
Continental Gummi Werke GmbH, West Germany, 49, 51, 88, 153–154
Coramandel Fertilisers (CFL)
aims and objectives, 91
business portfolio, 149

cost leadership, through economies of scale, 88–94
D/E ratio, 93
divisions and products, 91
fertilizers division, 91–94
PBDIT/total income, 92
total income, 91
twin businesses, 91
cost leadership, 13, 21–22, 24, 27
through economies of scale, 70
Apollo Tyres, 84–88
Bombay Dyeing, 79–84
Coramandel Fertilisers (CFL), 88–95
Hindalco, 73–75
Mahindra and Mahindra (M&M), 88
Tata Steel, 75–79
"cost leadership and differentiation" strategy, 21
critical success factor
of product quality, 22
of strategic alliances, 22
Cummins controversy, 117
currency crisis, Southeast Asian, 35
Customer Relationship Management (CRM), 58
customer satisfaction, 25, 79, 100, 103, 112, 118

Deming Prize Committee, 118
Design of Experiments (DOE), 109
diammonium phosphate (DAP), 94
dimethyl terephthalate (DMT), 38, 79, 142
DMAIC methodology, of Six Sigma, 109
Dunlop Tyres, 85

Eastern Spinning Mills, 145
e-business, 13, 25, 179
economic reforms (1991), 2–3, 8, 15, 118, 169, 178

ECS Limited, 107–108
Electricity Act (2003), 126
electricity demand, household, 127
Electrolytic Tinplate (ETP), 129
employee loyalty program, 110
energy
deficit, 126
demand, 126
Enterprise Process Model, 134, 137, 139
Enterprise Resource Planning (ERP), 13, 25, 114–115, 179
excellence, traits required in an organization to achieve, 100
excellent companies in India
data and methodology for studying, 6–10
findings of companies' performances, 11–12
objectives for studying, 5–6
results of study, 10–11
screening process for selecting, 7
Exide Industries Ltd.
Customer Relationship Management (CRM), 58
export turnover, 53
global growth, 52–59
human resources management, 160–161
leadership, 160
market share in, 57
automotive industry, 55–58
industrial sector, 58–59
milestones in automotives, 57
PAT, 53, 56
sales distribution network, 97–98
total income, 53–55

Failure Mode Effect Analysis (FMEA), 109
Farm Inputs Division (FIND), of EID Parry (India) Limited, 91
fertilizer industry in India, government's subsidy policy for, 94–95

Index | 373

Ford, 58, 96
foreign technology, 4
Foskor, South Africa, 94
free market system, 9
free-trade agreement, 52
fungicides, 91, 95

Gammon India Ltd. (GIL)
   civil engineering works, 120
   global growth, 61–64
   history, 161–163
   ISO 9001 certification, 119, 162
   PAT, 67
   total income, 64–66
Gammon, John C., 161, 162
Gandhi, Rajiv, 9
Ganguly, Satya Brata, 160
GE Capital, USA, 147
General Motors (GM), USA, 17, 22, 51, 118–119
General Tire International Co, USA, 153
German Remedies, 20
GHCL, 128
Ghoshal, Sumantra, 5
Godavari Fertilisers & Chemicals Ltd.
   government policies, 94–95
   pesticides division, 95
"good quality and low price" strategy, 21
Good to Great (2001), 5, 170, 176
Goodyear, 49, 84
Grasim Industries, 143
Green Belts certification, 109
Green's Hotel, 127
Gromor, 94
Groupe Chimique Tunisien, Tunisia, 94
Gujarat Alkalies & Chemicals Ltd., 128
Gujarat Tyres Ltd., 153

Handfan, 38
Hay Management Consultants, 147
herbicides, 91, 95
Hindalco, 12, 21, 143
   Birla, Aditya Vikram, 145–146
   Birla, Kumar Mangalam, 146–147
   business portfolio, 148–149
   Cash Value Added method, 148
   cost leadership, through economies of scale, 73–75
   D/E ratio, 77
   global growth, 59
   history, 144
   leadership skills, 145
   openness to change, 144–145
   PAT, 59, 62
   PBDIT/total income, 76
   policy and operational changes, 147–148
   product offerings and competition, 63
   retirement policy, 147
   total income, 59–61, 76
Hindustan Lever Chemicals Ltd., 129
Hindustan Petroleum, 8, 168, 178
Hinshitsu Hozen concept, for administration and initial flow control pillar, 105
hobby tractors, 42
Holcim, 148
hospitality industry, 40, 96, 110
Hot Dip Plant (HDP), 129
Hot Rolled Coil, 129–130
Hot Strip Mill (HSM), 102, 130
Human Resources Management, 13, 137, 160–161

Indal, 73, 147
Indian companies, diversification of, 21
Indian economy
   challenges during the 1990s, 3–4
   IMF loans, 9
   liberalization of, 9, 75, 176
   reforms (1991), 2–3, 8, 15, 118, 169, 178

Indian Hotel Corporation Ltd (IHCL), 12, 15, 20, 127
   employee loyalty program, 110
   global growth, 29–31
   growth in total income, 30–31
   growth strategy, 29
   PAT, 32
   Special Thanks and Recognition Scheme (STARS), 110
Indian Oil, 8, 168, 178
Indian steel industry, 33, 35
India's most valuable companies, 171, 172
industrial entrepreneurship, 1
industrial investment, 2–3
information and performance management process, 136
Infosys, 8, 168, 177
inorganic chemicals, 128
In Search of Excellence (1982), 170
insecticides, 91, 95
International Harvestor Co., USA, 150
International Tractor Co. of India (ITCI), 150
Irani, Jamshed J., 75
IT companies, 167, 168

Japanese 5-S concept, 109
Japanese Union of Scientists and Engineers (JUSE), 43, 115
J.C. Gammon (Bombay) Pvt. Ltd. *See* Gammon India Ltd. (GIL)
Jiangling Motor Co., 42
Jishu Hozen Pillar (Autonomous Maintenance) concepts, 105
JIT inventory management, 25, 100
JK Tyres, 84
joint ventures
   Apollo Tyres–Michelin, 51
   Mahindra & Mahindra–International Harvestor Co., 150
   Mahindra & Mahindra–Jiangling Motor Co., 42
   Mysore Kirloskar–Snyder General, 117, 157
   Mysore Kirloskar–Toyoda Automatic Loom Works, 117, 157
JRD QV Award, categories of
   customer and market focus, 133–134
   human resource focus, 137
   leadership, 131
   measurement, analysis, and knowledge management, 134–137
   process management, 137
   strategic planning, 132–133

Kaiser Organization, USA, 144
Kanoria Chemicals, 128
Kanwar, Onkar Singh, 88, 154–156
Karki, Rajnish, 22
Khaitan, B.M., 55
Kirloskar Group
   business portfolio, 158–159
   family dynamics, 158
   growth strategy, 117
   history, 156–157
   ISO 9000 certification, 116
   openness to change, 157–158
   quality processes, 116
   Ravi Kirloskar Quality Award initiative, 116
   reverse engineering R&D, 117
   technology alliances, 116–117
Kirloskar Institute of Advanced Management, 159
Kirloskar, Laxmanrao, 116, 156–157
knowledge management, 104, 134–137
Kobestu Kaizen concept, for education and training safety health and environment, 105
Kotak Mahindra Finance, 49
Krishna, Suresh, 159

Lafarge, 148
Larsen, Henning Holk, 163
Larsen & Toubro (L&T)
   global growth, 64–68
   history, 163–164

PAT, 68, 71
  strategic pre-bid tie-ups, 66
  total income, 68, 69–70
leadership skills, 13–14, 25–26, 131
  Apollo Tyres, 155–156
  Bombay Dyeing & Manufacturing Co. Ltd., 141–142
  Exide Industries Ltd., 160
  Hindalco, 145
  Mahindra & Mahindra (M&M), 150–151
  Tata Group companies, 123
lean manufacturing, 44, 112–113
license quota system, 9
Light Commercial Vehicles (LCVs), 150
Lucas Engineering systems, UK, 150

McKinsey & Co, 107, 114, 122, 149
Mahindra, Anand, 150–151
Mahindra, Jagdish Chandra, 150
Mahindra, Kailash Chandra, 150
Mahindra & Mahindra (M&M), 21, 22
  automotive segment, 43–44
  BPR program, 44, 113–115
  business portfolio, 151–153
  cellular manufacturing, principle of, 114
  core business, 151
  cost leadership, through economies of scale, 88
  Deming Prize, 43, 115
  D/E ratio, 90
  engineering research and product development facility, 112
  global growth, 40–46
  history, 149–150
  leadership skills and openness to change, 150–151
  as market leader in farm equipments, 44
  noncore business, 151
  PAT, 44, 47
  PBDIT/total income, 89

  performance on various parameters, 153
  sales distribution network, 97
  technology alliances, 88
  total income, 44–46
  total quality management initiative, 44
  tractor segment, 42–43
  vendor development, 115
  Vishwajeet, Project, 114
Mahindra USA Inc. (MUSA), 16, 40, 42–43, 150
Managing Radical Change (2000), 5
Marattukalam, Mathew T., 153
market and customer segmentation process, 134, 135
market capitalization, 4, 6–8, 167, 171, 173, 175
market development process, 134, 135
Maruti, 57, 58, 88, 96
metal packaging, 130
Michelin, 46, 51, 85, 88, 116, 156
Millenium Steel, 126
Modernization Program, Tata Steel, 101–102
MRF Tyres, 49, 84
Multi Utility Vehicle (MUV), 149

National Institute of Construction Management and Research, 64
Natsteel, 126
"niche marketing" strategy, 21
Novartis, 11, 20, 174, 177
Novelis, 16, 59
nuclear power, 127

Okhamandal Salt Works, 127
operational efficiencies, traits required to achieve, 100
Organization Health Survey (OHS), 137, 138
Original Equipment Manufacturer (OEM), 49, 51, 53, 57, 84, 115

overall equipment efficiency (OEE), 105
Overall Share Price Index (OSPI), 8–11, 168, 176

Paramfos, 94
Parry Super, 94
PAT/Sales ratio, 175
Performance Ethic Program (PEP), Tata Steel, 104
Performance Management System (PMS), 104, 137
pesticides, 91, 95, 128, 149
Peters, Tom, 170
petrochemical industry, 129
Peugeot, 22, 88
Piramal, Gita, 12
polyester staple fiber (PSF), 142
Power Grid Corporation Ltd., 126
Power Storage Solutions Company, 53
Premier Tyres, 49, 154, 156
pricing, government regulation for, 3
process improvement, 25, 100, 113, 115
process management, 137
　overall approach to, 140
product development, 33, 44, 111–114
"product innovation" strategy, 21
product quality, critical success factor of, 22
professional management, 143, 145
Project Top Gear, Tata Steel, 101
P.T. Five Star Industries Ltd., 37, 141
publicly traded companies, 167–168
public sector banks, 8, 168, 178
public sector companies, 129, 167–168
public sector units, 8, 168, 178
purified terepthalic acid (PTA), 79

Quality Council of India, 118

Raman, Revti, 21
Reliance Energy, 126
Reliance Industries Ltd. (RIL), 5, 141, 143
retail distribution system, 141

sales distribution network, 13
　Apollo Tyres, 97
　Bombay Dyeing, 96–97
　Exide Industries, 97–98
　Mahindra & Mahindra (M&M), 97
　Siemens Ltd., 98
　Tata Steel, 95–96
Satyam, 8
Shah, A.M., 21
Shergill, G.S., 21
Sheth, Jagdish, 175
Siemens Ltd., 12, 20–21
　business segments, 99
　Centre of Excellence, 98
　exports, 68
　Four Point Program, 165
　global growth, 68–70
　as global supply center, 68
　history, 164
　India operations, 165
　PAT, 74
　people strengths, 165–166
　sales distribution network, 98
　social responsibility, 166
　total income, 70, 72–73
Siemens, Werner von, 164
Singh, Raunaq, 153, 154
Six Sigma, 13, 25, 107–109
　DMAIC methodology of, 109
SKF India, 20, 172
Snyder General, 117, 157
Special Thanks and Recognition Scheme (STARS), 110–111
SPRINGTEX, 141
Sree Rayalaseema Alkalies, 128
Srinivasan, Venu, 159
Standard Batteries Ltd., 55
Standard Furukawa, 55, 58
Steel Authority of India Limited (SAIL), 33
steel industry, 31, 33, 35, 102, 124
steelmakers, world-class, 78
steel production, private sector contribution to, 33

stock prices, 8
storage battery industry in India, 53
   turnover of the different segments of, 57
strategic and global sourcing, 44
strategic planning, 131, 132–134, 155
Sundaram Clayton, 159
Sundaram Fasteners Ltd (SFL), 22, 159–160
   global growth, 51–52
   ISO 9000 certification, 117
   Total Quality Management (TQM), 118
"superior quality and premium price" strategy, 21
supplier up-gradation, 44
supply chain management, 44, 112

Taj Intercontinental Hotel, 127
Taj Mahal Hotel, 29, 127
   "compliment a colleague" forums, 111
   Hermes Award, 110
   Taj People Philosophy (TPP), 110
Tariff Commission, 95
Tata Business Excellence Model (TBEM), 12, 121, 130–131, 140
   core values, 131
Tata Chemicals (TCL), 12, 20–21, 127–129
   environmental protection, 109
   ISO 9001 certification, 109
   Japanese 5-S concept, 109
   safety and occupational health programs, 109
   Total Productive Maintenance (TPM) initiative, 109
Tata Chemicals Society for Rural Development, 109
Tata Code of Conduct, 131, 133
Tata Consultancy Services (TCS), 125
Tata Engineering, 125
Tata Group companies, 12, 20, 121–123
   business portfolio, 123–124
   history of, 124–125
   leadership skills and openness to change, 123
   performance on various parameters, 123
   restructuring of, 122
Tata Hydro-Electric Power Supply Company Ltd., 124, 126
Tata, Jamsetji Nusserwanji, 2, 124, 127
Tata Motors, 96, 108–109, 122, 124
Tata Power, 12, 15, 20–21, 124, 126–127, 169, 178
   human resources processes, 140
Tata Quality Management services, 125
Tata, Ratan, 121–123, 125, 141
Tata Shaktee GC sheet, 95
Tata Steel (TISCO), 12, 20–21, 125–126
   branded products, 96
   branding and marketing initiatives, 96
   Business to Business (B2B) segment, 96
   Business to Customers (B2C) segment, 96
   Corus Steel acquisition, 31–37
   cost leadership, through economies of scale, 75–79
   Customer Value Management program, 96
   de-integrated production, philosophy of, 31
   D/E ratio, 81
   global growth, 31–37
   greenfield projects, 33
   growth in total income, 34–35
   JRD QV Award, 131
   lowest-cost producer of steel, 75
   modernization program, 33, 101–102
   operating cost, 35
   operational efficiencies, 101
   PAT, 36
   PBDIT/total income, 80
   Performance Ethic Program (PEP), 104

Project Top Gear, 101
range of products, 37
sales distribution network, 95–96
Tata Management Training center, 101
Total Operational Performance (TOP)
  implementation of, 75, 78, 101
  improvement initiatives, 103
Tata Steelium, 96
Tata Tea, 123–125
Tata Tiscon Rebars, 96
technology leadership, 13, 24, 27–28, 117, 179
Test of Hypothesis, 109
Tetley Group, UK, 125
TEXSPRING, 141
textile production, 38, 79
  value chain of, 42
thermal power, 127
Thomas, Jacob, 153
Tin Free Steel (TFS), 18, 59, 129
Tinplate Company of India Ltd. (TCIL), 12, 20, 104–105, 129–130
  global growth, 59–61
  Hinshitsu Hozen concept, for administration and initial flow control pillar, 105
  Jishu Hozen concept, for planned maintenance, 105
  Kobestu Kaizen concept, for education and training safety health and environment, 105
  Six-Sigma initiative, 107–109
  Total Operational Performance (TOP), 106–107

Total Productive Maintenance (TPM) initiative, 105
TMBP Coils, 130
Torrent Power, 11, 15, 20, 169, 177–178
Total Operational Performance (TOP), 75, 78, 106–107
  phases of, 107
Total Productive Maintenance (TPM), 105, 109, 119
Total Quality Management (TQM), 13, 25, 44, 100, 112, 118–119
Toubro, Soren Kristian, 163
Toyoda Automatic Loom Works, 117, 157
Travel & Leisure, 29
TVS Group, 159–160
  performance on various parameters, 160

Ultra Mega Power Projects, 127
Unilever Group Company, 129

Vakil, Kapil Ram, 127
vendor development, 115
Vishwajeet, Project, 114

Wadia Group, 141, 143
Wadia, Nowrosjee, 140–141
Welspun, 38
Williamson Magor Group, 55
Willys-Overland Corporation, 150
Wipro, 8, 168, 177
World Class in India (2001), 5
World Steel Dynamics (WSD), 75

Zydus Cadila, 20

About the Author

B. Karunakar is the Director of the Narsee Monjee Institute of Management Studies (NMIMS), Hyderabad, India, where he is engaged in institution building, teaching, and consulting. He is a management thinker and practitioner having 26 years of experience with a diverse background in strategic planning, business development, finance and general management. He has held responsible positions in financial services, manufacturing, IT and pharmaceutical industries, with a focus on education and training in the last 10 years.

As a professor of Business Strategy and Leadership Development, he has designed and delivered several management development programs for various companies. He has also conducted faculty development programs for premier educational institutions. Further, he has authored articles on various management issues and authored/edited three books in the areas of strategy, leadership, and change management. His previous publications include *Balanced Scorecards: Concepts and Experiences* (ICFAI 2003), *Leadership Perspectives and Profiles* (ICFAI 2003), and *Business Strategies: Concepts and Cases* (ICFAI 2003).

Earlier in his career, he has worked with organizations such as ILFS and Canbank Financial Services in the area of Investment Banking; UB Group in Corporate Finance; and subsequently with the Pennar Group in a leadership role, with experiences that involved start-ups and turnaround success stories. Prior to his current role, he worked with Dr Reddy's, where initially he led their Learning and Development efforts. In that role, he was responsible for strategizing, developing, and supporting the learning needs of the organization. Later he headed Dr Reddy's Foundation for Health Education where the mission and work involved capacity building and training interventions for the health care community, creating professional health care educators for the future, and leading patient-support initiatives with the objective of strengthening the health care delivery system for better patient care.

Dr Karunakar is a B. Tech (Mechanical Engineering) from IIT Mumbai, India, Post Graduate in Management from IIM Calcutta, and PhD in Business Management from Osmania University, Hyderabad, India.